How Parliament Works

We work with leading authors to develop the strongest
educational materials in politics, bringing cutting-edge
thinking and best learning practice to a global market.

Under a range of well-known imprints, including
Longman, we craft high-quality print and
electronic publications which help readers to understand
and apply their content, whether studying or at work.

To find out more about the complete range of our
publishing, please visit us on the World Wide Web at:
www.pearsoned.co.uk

How Parliament Works

Fifth edition

ROBERT ROGERS

RHODRI WALTERS

Harlow, England • London • New York • Boston • San Francisco • Toronto
Sydney • Tokyo • Singapore • Hong Kong • Seoul • Taipei • New Delhi
Cape Town • Madrid • Mexico City • Amsterdam • Munich • Paris • Milan

Pearson Education Limited
Edinburgh Gate
Harlow
Essex CM20 2JE
England

and Associated Companies throughout the world

Visit us on the World Wide Web at:
www.pearsoned.co.uk

First published 1987
Second edition 1989
Third edition 1995
Fourth edition 1998
Fifth edition 2004

ISBN 0 582 43744 X

British Library Cataloguing-in-Publication Data
A catalogue record for this book is available from the British Library

Library of Congress Cataloging-in-Publication Data
Walters, R. H. (Rhodri Havard)
    How Parliament works / Rhodri Walters and Robert Rogers. — 5th ed.
    p. cm.
    Includes bibliographical references and index.
    ISBN 0–582–43744–X (pbk.)
    1. Great Britain. Parliament. I. Rogers, Robert, 1950– II. Title.

JN550.W35 2004
328.41—dc22   2003069515

10 9 8 7 6 5 4 3 2
08 07 06 05 04

Typeset in 10/12.5pt Sabon by 35
Printed in Great Britain by Henry Ling Limited, at the Dorset Press, Dorchester, DT1 1HD

The publisher's policy is to use paper manufactured from sustainable forests.

To those who believe that
Parliament matters

Contents

Foreword

How Parliament Works first appeared in 1987. Three more editions by Paul Silk and Rhodri Walters followed, the last one in 1998. It rapidly became a standard work on Parliament.

Two changes preceded the appearance of the present volume. The first was the departure of Paul Silk from Westminster, after twenty-five years' distinguished service as one of the Clerks of the Commons, upon his appointment as Clerk to the National Assembly for Wales. With admirable conscientiousness, he decided that his distance from the day-to-day business of the Westminster Parliament meant that he could not participate in the new *How Parliament Works*, and he invited Robert Rogers to take his place.

The second change resulted from the first. After four editions – but also after a period of change in both Houses unparalleled for half a century or more – the time had come for a complete recasting of the work. We have kept the broad scheme, but almost all of the text is entirely new. Rhodri Walters contributed the material on the House of Lords, and Chapter 4 on parliamentary sovereignty, legislative supremacy and devolution; Robert Rogers was responsible for the rest. As with the previous Silk/Walters partnership, our origins within a few miles and months of each other in South Wales may have helped to make the process of joint authorship both happy and enjoyable.

In writing this new *How Parliament Works*, we were conscious that even a combined sixty years' experience of Parliament was unequal to the task. We are extremely grateful to the many people inside and outside the two Houses who have given us advice. So many have been so generous with their time and expertise that it would be invidious to name individuals, but that does not lessen our gratitude.

How Parliament Works is aimed at a wide audience: civil servants, lobbyists, journalists, witnesses before select committees, and all whose work brings them into contact with Parliament; constituents who want to know how they are represented and how their problems can be addressed; those in the UK or overseas who want to know more about the workings of the institution; and those who study Parliament at school, college and university. We also hope that members of both Houses, especially new members, will find the volume useful.

The book seeks to explain Parliament in a more accessible way: as well as describing the institution, to give the reader a feel for the pressures and the tensions, and why things happen.

At a time of significant change, but also when the effectiveness and relevance of Parliament is the subject of criticism (even if not always well-informed), this approach is more important than ever. The institution has great strengths as well as weaknesses. It is not just an organisation; it is an organism, with all the unpredictability – and adaptability – that that implies. If Parliament is to be effective, much of the responsibility for making it so rests upon its members; but the people Parliament represents – the real owners of the institution – have a part to play as well. This book is dedicated to those who believe that Parliament matters. We hope that a greater understanding of Parliament will help to swell their numbers.

Robert Rogers
Rhodri Walters
Westminster, January 2004

Acknowledgements

We are grateful to the following for permission to reproduce copyright material:

The Chamber of the House of Lords on p. 7, Parliamentary Copyright House of Lords 2003; The House of Lords in session on p. 8, Parliamentary Copyright House of Lords 2003, Terry Moore; The Chamber of the House of Commons on p. 10, Deryc R. Sands, Parliamentary Copyright House of Commons 2001; The House of Commons in session, June 2001 on p. 11, Deryc R. Sands, Parliamentary Copyright House of Commons 2001; Part of the Order of Business for a typical day in the Chamber of the House of Commons on p. 136, Parliamentary Copyright House of Commons 2003; Notices and Orders of the day: The House of Lords Order Paper on p. 152, Parliamentary Copyright House of Lords 2003; The stages in the passing of a public bill on p. 184, Parliamentary Copyright House of Lords 2002; The European Union (Accessions) Bill on p. 185, Parliamentary Copyright House of Commons 2003; A typical selection list for the first day of a Commons standing committee's consideration of a bill under a programme order on p. 198, Parliamentary Copyright House of 2003; The selection list for part of the report stage of a bill in the House of Commons, under a programme order on p. 199, Parliamentary Copyright House of Commons 2003; House of Commons Oral Questions Rota on pp. 286–7, Parliamentary Copyright House of Commons 2003; Oral Questions on the Commons Order of Business on p. 291, Parliamentary Copyright House of Commons 2003; Hansard report of Question Time on 9th July 2003 on pp. 292–5, Parliamentary Copyright House of Commons 2003; The Work and Pensions Committee taking evidence in one of the modern Portcullis House committee rooms on p. 331, Deryc R. Sands, Parliamentary Copyright House of Commons 2003; European Union Committe, sub-committee D on p. 343, Parliamentary Copyright House of Lords 2003, Terry Moore; Members of the House of Lords Science and Technology Committee launching their report, 'Fighting Infection' in 2003 on p. 346, Parliamentary Copyright House of Lords 2003, Terry Moore; Parliamentary copyright material is reproduced with the permission of the Controller of Her Majesty's Stationery Office on behalf of Parliament; Parliamentary Environs on p. 17, Give Way Ltd; Table 8.1 The annual parliamentary cycles on pp. 255–6, adapted from

Evans, P. (2002) House of Commons Procedure, 3rd edition, p. 108, Vacher Dod Publishing Ltd; Crown copyright material is reproduced with the permission of the Controller of Her Majesty's Stationery Office and the Queen's Printer for Scotland.

1   Parliament: its home and origins

Mid-Victorian masterpiece: Parliament in its setting

The Palace of Westminster, that magnificent range of Gothic buildings along the banks of the Thames, is probably the United Kingdom's most famous landmark. The Clock Tower at the north end of the palace and the striking of Big Ben, the hour bell of the Great Clock, are known throughout the world. The palace is one of the greatest achievements of nineteenth-century architecture and art, and even those who work there every day remain awed by its power and confidence.

If the Palace of Westminster were empty, it would still be one of the great tourist attractions of Europe. But this Grade I listed building, part of the World Heritage site that includes Westminster Abbey as well as the palace, contains a parliament that is one of the biggest and busiest in the world. This is a source of many tensions. Whatever its working methods, and however effective it may be, it is very difficult for a parliament housed in a heritage icon to *look* modern and efficient. And the constraints of conserving and caring for such a building mean that any structural change for parliamentary purposes – from new door locks to the possibility of constructing a visitor centre – must run the gauntlet of English Heritage, the planners of Westminster City Council, and countless others who love the building for its art and history. The building is expensive to maintain precisely because everything must be done to the highest standards for the benefit of future generations. Finally, the palace is a perfect example of how buildings shape the activity within them. As we shall see, the nature of the buildings of Parliament has a powerful influence on how business is conducted and the way that members of both Houses work.

The King's palace

It may seem odd that a parliament should meet in a palace; but the Palace of Westminster has been a royal palace for well over a thousand years. Before the Norman Conquest it was the residence of Edward the Confessor, and it continued to be used by the monarch until the reign of Henry VIII, who bought Whitehall from Cardinal Wolsey in 1529 and then built St James's Palace in 1532. Although Westminster was thereafter no longer a royal residence, it continued to be a royal palace. Property in what is now London SW1 was clearly as much in demand in the sixteenth century, and the buildings huddled around the great bulk of Westminster Hall were rapidly taken up for use by the two Houses, the law courts (which remained at Westminster until they moved to the Strand in 1882), courtiers, placemen and shopkeepers – and others plying less reputable trades.

The King's summons

Although parliaments have met at Westminster for some 750 years, there is no requirement to do so. Parliament has met, and could meet elsewhere, and still conduct its business with constitutional and legal propriety. Second World War bomb damage forced the two Houses from their own Chambers; and were the modern spectre of global terrorism to make it necessary, Parliament could meet elsewhere with the minimum of infrastructure.

The word 'parliament', from the French *parler*, to speak or talk, was first used in England in the thirteenth century, when it meant an enlarged meeting of the King's council, attended by barons, bishops and courtiers, to advise the King on law making, administration and judicial decisions. The germ of the modern institution can be traced back to the parliament summoned on Henry III's behalf by Simon de Montfort in 1265, when representatives from the towns were present for the first time. Parliaments still meet in response to a royal summons; the parliament that met after the 2001 general election was summoned by a proclamation from the Queen, which in part said:

> And We being desirous and resolved, as soon as may be, to meet Our people and have their advice in Parliament, do hereby make known unto all Our loving Subjects Our Royal Will and Pleasure to call a new Parliament.

Those words may fall strangely upon a modern ear, and at a time when the role of the monarch in the governance of the nation is increasingly questioned; but the purport of Elizabeth II's proclamation was the same as those issued during the reigns of thirty-four of her predecessors.

The development of the two Houses

By the middle of the fourteenth century, the King's Parliaments were attended by knights of the shire and burgesses from the cities and boroughs (the Commons), the magnates (the Lords Temporal) and the bishops and abbots (the Lords Spiritual). At this time, the reign of Edward III, the Commons began to claim that their agreement was required for any taxation by the monarch, in particular the tax on wool. By now the Commons and Lords had emerged as two distinct houses. The Commons met in the Painted Chamber or in the refectory or the chapter house of Westminster Abbey, and they moved to St Stephen's Chapel in 1547. The Lords settled in the White Chamber of the old palace, moving to the larger White or Lesser Hall in 1801 when the Union with Ireland introduced extra members into the House. After the fire of 1834, they moved to the re-roofed Painted Chamber until they were able to move into their present accommodation in 1847.

This book seeks to explain the workings of the modern House of Lords, the 'Upper Chamber', and of the House of Commons, the 'Lower Chamber', but not their historical development. Let us therefore see how the New Palace, and not the jumble of mediaeval buildings next to Edward the Confessor's Abbey, came to be the home of the modern United Kingdom Parliament.

The fire

The night of 16 October 1834 was fine, with some high cloud. By seven o'clock that evening the London sky was lit by flames. Two workmen had been told to dispose of large quantities of Exchequer tallies – notched hazel sticks used from early mediaeval times to show what each taxpayer owed; the stick could be split to provide both a record and a receipt. The workmen burned the tallies in the furnaces that heated the flues under the floor of the House of Lords, and their enthusiasm, or possibly their impatience, led to the destruction of the mediaeval palace and the meeting places of both Houses. Thousands watched.

> An immense multitude of spectators assembled at Westminster to witness the ravages of the fire, the lurid glare of which was visible for many miles around the metropolis. Even the river Thames . . . was covered with boats and barges . . . and the reflections of the wavering flames upon the water, on the neighbouring shores and on the many thousands thus congregated, composed a spectacle most strikingly picturesque and impressive.

wrote one contemporary observer.

The winning design

The destruction of a large part of the old palace and of much of its contents, including irreplaceable manuscripts, paintings and tapestries, was a great loss. Westminster Hall survived, as did other parts of the building that today would undoubtedly have been preserved or restored. But the authorities of the day saw the fire as an opportunity to start afresh. A competition was held for the design of a completely new parliamentary building, which resulted in an extraordinary architectural and artistic partnership. The scheme produced by the architect Sir Charles Barry and the interior designer Augustus Welby Pugin was chosen from among ninety-seven designs submitted, and the foundation stone was laid on 27 April 1840.

A Victorian Parliament

The Barry and Pugin palace had, apart from its visual merits, one great advantage: it was a purpose-built parliamentary building. As well as the two Chambers, it provided residences for the principal officers and officials, dining rooms, smoking rooms, writing rooms, committee rooms, libraries and all the paraphernalia of a grand country house and London club combined.

This was all a mid-Victorian Parliament needed. There were 658 members of the Commons, and some 500 members of the Lords, no more than 350 of whom turned up to speak in any session; but an MP or peer wrote his correspondence in longhand, and if he wanted to find something out, he went and looked it up, just as he would have done in his library or study at home. Members of the Commons were careful to keep on the right side of local political magnates, but modern constituency pressures were unknown. Indeed, illuminated addresses survive that were presented to the local MP 'on his visit (sometimes *annual* visit!) to the Constituency'.

The New Palace today

Sadly, the ever-present threat of terrorism has meant that public access to the Palace of Westminster has to be closely controlled. During term time, the parties of constituents and other visitors who tour the principal parts of the palace must be sponsored by an MP or peer (although visitors may pay to see the palace during the commercial summer opening (see page 419)).

Those who come to see the Palace of Westminster begin by following the Queen's route at the State Opening of Parliament, and in the part of the palace still devoted to the monarch. With the exception of the Commons Chamber, much of what they see has changed little and would have been familiar to Gladstone or Disraeli. A plan of the palace is shown opposite.

The Robing Room and Royal Gallery

When the Queen opens Parliament, her state coach drives under the great archway of the Victoria Tower, the 323-foot tower at the south end of the palace that houses the parliamentary archives. She then ascends the Royal Staircase and passes through the Norman Porch (so called because it was intended to place statues of the Norman kings there, but somehow Victorian prime ministers supplanted them) to the Robing Room, where she puts on the state robes and Imperial State Crown before walking in procession through the 110-foot long Royal Gallery, into the Prince's Chamber and then into the Chamber of the House of Lords.

This southern end of the palace is magnificent and ornate – deliberately conceived as a backdrop to state ceremonial. The perfect proportions of Barry's

The Houses of Parliament: plan of the principal floor

The Palace of Westminster

rooms are complemented by the sumptuousness of Pugin's decoration. His themes of portcullis, rose, lily and lion, together with Queen Victoria's VR cipher, run throughout the palace's decoration, with its Gothic features and linenfold panelling, but his 'graceful fancy' is nowhere more evident than at the south end of the building – the Robing Room and the Royal Gallery.

The Robing Room has not been in use, except for the day of the State Opening, since the Lords sat there after the Commons Chamber was destroyed by enemy bombing during the Second World War. The Royal Gallery is occasionally used when a visiting head of state addresses both Houses of Parliament; the King of Spain and the presidents of France, Russia and the USA have done so in recent years. As there is no concept of joint sittings of the two Houses (unlike the practice of the US Congress, for example), the Royal Gallery is a convenient place for such events.

The Chamber of the House of Lords

The visitor then moves to the Chamber of the House of Lords, which is fitted out in the same rich style. At one end, the throne faces north under a gilded canopy and Cloth of Estate. In front of it is the Woolsack, on which the Lord Chancellor sits, as Speaker, or presiding officer, of the House of Lords. The Woolsack is a seat stuffed with wool from the different countries of the Commonwealth. Edward III decided that a sack of wool would be a useful reminder to their lordships of the pastoral basis of the country's economy – and the chief source of his revenue – and the tradition has persisted. In front of the Lord Chancellor are the two judges' woolsacks. These remind us that the Appeal and High Court judges still receive Writs of Assistance to attend the House. Nowadays they attend only in a representative capacity on the day of the State Opening. To the Lord Chancellor's left and right are four rows of red benches for peers, divided into three sections. In the centre of the floor is the Table of the House, and on the opposite side of the table to the Lord Chancellor there are three further benches.

Looking from the throne, the right of the House is known as the spiritual side, because the bishops sit there in the front rows of the section nearest the throne. The left is called the temporal side, while the benches beyond the table are called the cross-benches. As well as the bishops, government supporters sit on the spiritual side, with ministers who are peers in the front row of the central section. Other parties sit on the temporal side. Peers who do not belong to a party sit on the cross-benches. A labelled view of the Chamber and a photograph of the House in session taken in October 2003 are on pages 7 and 8.

Beyond the Lords Chamber, the visitor passes through the Peers' Lobby to the Central Lobby, a large octagonal room at the very centre of the palace, beneath the third-largest of the palace's towers. Almost all visitors on business

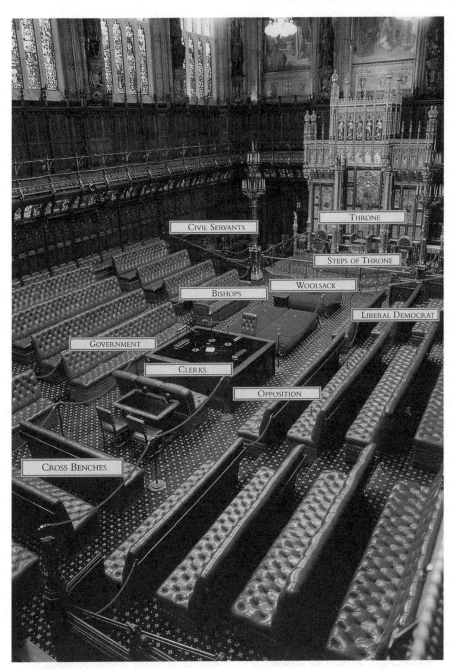

The Chamber of the House of Lords
Source: The House of Lords 2003

The House of Lords in session, October 2003
Source: The House of Lords 2003, Terry Moore

come to the Central Lobby; it is the place where constituents who wish to lobby an MP come to fill in a green card requesting an interview. It lies directly between the two Chambers; and when on State Opening day all the doors are thrown open, the Queen sitting on the throne in the Lords can see the Speaker presiding over the House of Commons more than a hundred metres away.

Members' Lobby and the Chamber of the House of Commons

Moving towards the Commons Chamber, the visitor passes into the Members' Lobby. This is a much larger space than the Peers' Lobby. When the House is busy, especially before and after votes, it is thronged with MPs and is the haunt of 'lobby' journalists; and it is then a clearing-house of opinion, news and rumour. It contains a message board with a slot for each member's messages, pigeonholes for members' select committee papers, a counter where members can get a wide range of parliamentary and government papers, and a post office, which deals with some 35,000 items every sitting day. The whips' offices of the major parties (see page 87) adjoin the Members' Lobby.

The Commons Chamber was destroyed in an air raid on the night of 10 May 1941. Even Barry's original Chamber was less ornate than that of the Lords; the rebuilt Commons Chamber, designed by Sir Giles Gilbert Scott, is austere by comparison with that of the Lords. A labelled view of the Chamber and one of the House in session are shown on pages 10 and 11. Looking down from the public gallery one sees the Speaker's canopied Chair as the focal point. During Question Time and ministerial statements the Speaker's secretary stands to the right of the Chair (as seen from the gallery) helping the Speaker to identify members and keeping a record of whom he has called. To the left of the Chair, against the far wall, is the officials' box for civil servants advising ministers. In front of the Chair is the Table of the House, at which sit the bewigged Clerks at the Table, who advise the Speaker and his deputies, and any other member, on the conduct of proceedings, and who also compile the legal record of the House's decisions.

On each side of the Chamber are five rows of green benches, divided by a gangway into two sections. On the left as seen from the gallery are the benches occupied by the government party, and on the right those of the opposition parties. Ministers sit on the front bench by the Table, and the main opposition party's spokesmen and women (or 'shadow ministers') opposite them. Ministers and their shadows are thus known as 'front-benchers'; all other MPs are 'back-benchers'.

On each side of the table are the despatch boxes at which ministers and their counterparts from the main opposition party speak; and at the near end of the table is the Mace, which symbolises the authority of the House.

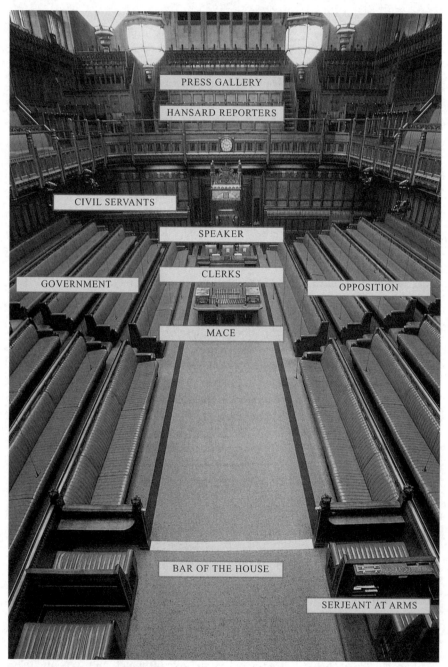

PRESS GALLERY

HANSARD REPORTERS

CIVIL SERVANTS

SPEAKER

CLERKS

GOVERNMENT

OPPOSITION

MACE

BAR OF THE HOUSE

SERJEANT AT ARMS

The Chamber of the House of Commons
Source: Deryc R. Sands; The House of Commons 2001

The House of Commons in session, June 2001: the first Prime Minister's Question Time of the new Parliament

Source: Deryc R. Sands, The House of Commons 2001

At our observer's eye level, above the Speaker's Chair, is the Press Gallery, with seats in the centre for the *Hansard* reporters who compile the verbatim record of proceedings. Other galleries are for members of the House of Lords, personal guests of the Speaker and distinguished visitors, as well as for the general public. Two galleries are reserved for MPs and are technically part of the floor of the House, although Speakers have indicated that they will not usually call members sitting there to speak. Down below, but not visible except from the front of the gallery, sits the Serjeant at Arms, responsible for order around the House and in the galleries. There too are the cross-benches; but as the 1997 and 2001 parliaments each contained only one member (apart from the occupants of the Chair) who owed no party allegiance, these are in practice extensions of the seating for government and opposition members.

Westminster Hall

This brief description of the Palace of Westminster would be incomplete without reference to what must be one of the finest rooms in Europe – Westminster Hall, the great hall of the mediaeval palace and, along with the crypt Chapel of St Mary Undercroft, the only part of the original building to remain. The hall has been much restored over the years, but at its core it remains an eleventh-century building with a late fourteenth-century hammerbeam roof. It is used today for ceremonial occasions. The Lying in State of the Queen Mother took place in Westminster Hall in April 2002; and a few weeks later the Queen received the Humble Addresses of the two Houses of Parliament there on the occasion of her Golden Jubilee.

The palace and parliamentary vocabulary

The layout of the Chambers, derived from earlier meeting rooms of the two Houses, is reflected in the vocabulary of Parliament, which in many cases has passed into general everyday use, as well as around the world with the Westminster model of parliamentary government.

The *opposition* parties sit physically opposite the government party (as well as opposing it). A meeting of the House is a *sitting*, at the end of which the House *rises*. Matters considered by either House are debated *on the floor*. If a member changes parties he or she is said to have *crossed the floor*. When MPs and peers hand in questions, amendments to bills or notices of motions, or when ministers place documents formally before either House, they are said to have *tabled* them, even if they do not place them on the massive Table of either House. If a bill has its committee stage in a Commons standing committee, it is said to be taken *upstairs* because the palace's committee rooms are on the first floor. When either House votes, it is said to *divide*, because those voting divide physically into two groups ('ayes' and 'noes' in the Commons, 'contents' and 'not contents' in the Lords) and walk through separate lobbies on either side of both Chambers to be counted. Securing something *on the nod* – that is, without debate or division – may derive from a member's brief bow of respect to the Chair when moving a motion formally.

Some supposed parliamentary derivations are bogus. *In the bag* stems not from the petition bag on the back of the Speaker's Chair but from the much older idea of a game bag. It is just as fanciful as the myth that the red lines on the floor of the Commons Chamber are two sword lengths apart. There is indeed a rule that a member speaking from the front row of benches (above or below the gangway) should not step over the lines; but there is no record of a time when members were permitted to bring swords into the Chamber.

We shape our buildings and afterwards our buildings shape us

From the start the clublike rooms and common spaces of Barry's palace have encouraged members of both Houses to congregate and meet informally. In the Commons, the Smoking Room, the Tea Room and the Members' Lobby after a big vote (as well as the division lobbies themselves during it) are places where opinions are formed and exchanged, support is canvassed and tactics planned. This pattern of informality and personal contact also produces a certain volatility: rumours travel quickly, even through so large a membership; views – and perhaps back-bench rebellions – can gather momentum with surprising speed.

A first-time visitor almost always finds the Commons Chamber smaller than expected; and, for an assembly of 659 members, it is surprisingly intimate. Its seating capacity (together with the galleries reserved for members) is usually said to be 427; but as there are no individual seats and members inevitably take up varying amounts of the green leather, this is in practice an approximation.

As there are no individual places, so also there are no desks, telephones or computer terminals; and members speak from their places, not from a podium. When the House is full, perhaps towards the end of a major debate or during Prime Minister's Questions, the atmosphere is made tense by the crush of MPs, and one can appreciate the way in which the House can become great political theatre. The small size of the Chamber also means that, even when only a few MPs are present for some abstruse debate, the feeling of speaking to empty space, which is a problem in many foreign parliaments, is minimised.

It is likely that the rows of benches facing each other derive from the use by the Commons of St Stephen's Chapel in the old palace. The clergy faced each other in choir stalls on each side of the altar, and the arrangement was unchanged when the Tudor House of Commons took over the chapel. Some feel that this encourages adversarial politics (and even, perhaps fancifully, a two-party system). The Commons, unlike the Lords, have no cross-benches spanning the width of the Chamber. It may be significant that standing committee rooms, where legislation is debated in the same way as in the House, are laid out like the Chamber; but for select committees, where there is a more consensual approach, members sit around horseshoe tables, and MPs and peers do not necessarily sit on party lines.

Certainly the idea of replacing the Chamber with a hemicycle, of the sort found in many continental parliaments and also in the European Parliament, has its supporters, especially among those who shun confrontational politics. A hemicycle would almost certainly bring with it individual desks and seats, and accommodating a Chamber of that size in Barry's palace would be next to impossible. It may be that architectural constraints prevent such a change, although the House of Commons had an opportunity to break this particular mould after Barry's and Pugin's Chamber was destroyed in 1941. However, neither a hemicycle nor a larger traditional Chamber found favour. Churchill represented the majority view in the House when he said in the debate on the rebuilding:

> if the House is big enough to contain all its Members, nine-tenths of the debates will be conducted in the depressing atmosphere of an almost empty or half-empty chamber . . . We wish to see our Parliament as a strong, easy, flexible instrument of free debate. For this purpose a small chamber and a sense of intimacy are indispensable . . . The conversational style requires a fairly small space, and there should be on great occasions a sense of crowd and urgency . . . We shape our buildings, and afterwards our buildings shape us.

Time and space

In an echo of metaphysics, the way any parliament operates is dictated by time and space. Time: to allow full scrutiny of government, examination of draft legislation, airing of concerns affecting constituencies and constituents, and the political causes espoused by political parties and individual members. Space is almost as important: space to provide meeting rooms for committees, political parties and lobby groups; space for library and research facilities; adequate office accommodation for MPs and their staff to provide the service that their constituents expect, and for members of both Houses to support their parliamentary duties.

Add to that the space that is needed for the infrastructure of Parliament: support for the work of the two Chambers and of legislative and investigative committees; provision of IT, security, catering, housekeeping, maintenance, and administration of pay, allowances and personnel. Then there are those who are in Parliament but not of it: TV, radio and print journalists, civil servants supporting ministers, and lawyers appearing before the House of Lords Appellate Committee. Last, but emphatically not least, are the owners of Parliament: constituents and taxpayers and their families, who may want to bring problems to their local MP, or have a cause taken up by a member of either House, or who may simply want to see how Parliament works.

Nor are these demands constant. Parliament must react to expectations of it as well as to events. The creation of a new government department will need a new select committee to shadow it in the Commons; a concern for constitutional issues may lead to the establishment of a new select committee in the Lords. More draft bills will need more select committee consideration, and in turn space for the staff to support the process. We consider below the ways in which the two modern Houses have tried to cope with the constant pressure on their accommodation.

The shoe pinches

The new Palace of Westminster was largely completed by 1852, although it was not finally finished until 1860. The Lords occupied their Chamber on 15 April 1847; the Commons first sat in theirs on 30 May 1850 but did not move in permanently until 3 February 1852. In 1854, Sir Charles Barry produced plans to build additional offices surrounding New Palace Yard, but these were never pursued. By 1867, a select committee was examining how the size of the Commons Chamber could be increased, and in 1894 another Commons select committee was looking at the adequacy of accommodation more generally.

The pressures

The shortage of accommodation was a recurring theme over the next hundred years. In the Commons, it became particularly acute during the last twenty or thirty years of the last century with the increasing burdens of constituency work, the need to house larger numbers of MPs' own staff, and the growth in select committee work and in research facilities. The administration and support of the House became more professional and better resourced, needing more staff and office accommodation. Every new facility, however desirable in itself, has imposed new strains, from the introduction of broadcasting (with its need for control rooms and archive space) to the establishment of information offices for the public.

A visitor following the route from the Victoria Tower to the Commons Chamber has an impression of lofty ceilings and spacious rooms, but on the floors above and below (except along the Committee Corridor on the river front) the story is rather different and includes subdivided rooms, mezzanine floors and even temporary huts on flat roofs.

For many years in the Commons, members were prepared, however reluctantly, to share offices – even with nine or ten of their colleagues – or to do much of their constituency work around the House, writing letters in the library or dictating to their secretaries in the Committee Corridor while waiting to vote. That this did not lead to changes may have been partly the 'never did me any harm' principle, but also the scope for change was limited. As early as 1953, the Select Committee on House of Commons Accommodation concluded that no real progress would be possible except through extensive new building.

New building

The only realistic possibilities lay to the north of the palace, across Bridge Street towards Whitehall. Various schemes blossomed, were rejected and withered. Between 1984 and 1991, however, the buildings in Parliament Street, at the end of Whitehall, were converted to provide some ninety offices for MPs, together with library, catering and meeting facilities. Nearby, the old Scotland Yard police headquarters (the Norman Shaw buildings) have been taken over and refurbished; and the adjacent Canon Row buildings will also be modernised for office accommodation. (And at the other end of the palace, Westminster House at 7 Millbank contains most of the staff of Commons select committees, together with the Department of Finance and Administration of that House.)

Portcullis House

However, if MPs and their staff were to have proper modern office accommodation that would allow them to give a proper service to their constituents, the key site was that overlooking the river. Here between 1998 and 2000 Portcullis House was constructed to provide offices for 210 MPs and 400 of their staff, together with a variety of meeting rooms. Designed by Michael Hopkins and Partners, from the outside the building appears austere, even forbidding, but inside, from the airy atrium to state-of-the art committee rooms and offices, it shows a confident and innovative style that has won a string of awards.

The £234 million price tag was controversial even for a building designed to complement a world-famous site and to outlast any conventional office accommodation – even though the project came in under budget and almost exactly on schedule. However, the House of Commons Commission, responsible for the House's administration and for the construction of the building, said of it:

> The building is often described as one purely for Members of Parliament and their staff. This is indeed an important function, and good working conditions play their part in the service which Members give their constituents. But more important are the outstanding facilities for public hearings of select committees, and for meetings of groups of all kinds. This access of the people to the political process is an essential part of the working of a modern Parliament.

THE PALACE OF WESTMINSTER AND THE PARLIAMENTARY ESTATE

Public Transport

By Rail
Nearest stations are Charing Cross, Victoria and Waterloo.

Underground
Westminster (Circle, District & Jubilee)

By Bus
Buses: 3, 11, 12, 24, 53, 77A, 88, 109, 159 & 211 all stop nearby.

P Use of public transport is advised as the NCP car park is often full and meter parking is expensive and scarce.

KEY

(A)	NORMAN SHAW NORTH	(1)	CANON ROW PASS OFFICE
(B)	1 DERBY GATE	(2)	PARLIAMENTARY BOOK SHOP
(C)	1 CANON ROW	(3)	CARRIAGE GATES
(D)	NORMAN SHAW SOUTH	(4)	MEMBERS' ENTRANCE
(E)	PORTCULLIS HOUSE	(5)	ST STEPHEN'S ENTRANCE
(F)	1 PARLIAMENT STREET	(6)	PEERS' ENTRANCE
(G)	10 GT. GEORGE STREET	(7)	CHANCELLOR'S GATE
(H)	PALACE OF WESTMINSTER	(8)	SOVEREIGN'S ENTRANCE
(J)	7 OLD PALACE YARD	(9)	BLACK ROD'S GARDEN PASS OFFICE
(K)	3 DEANS YARD		
(L)	1 & 2 THE ABBEY GARDEN		
(M)	7 MILLBANK		

Parliamentary Estate and Environs
Source: Give Way Ltd (for left-hand map)

It is safe to say that those who commissioned the new palace after the fire of 1834 would not have recognised any part of this description of the uses of a parliamentary building.

Lords accommodation

Like the Commons, the House of Lords has outgrown the 40 percent of the original palace that it occupies and, rather late in the day compared with the House of Commons, has started to acquire office space for staff and members in nearby streets. In 1994, 7 Old Palace Yard – an elegant Georgian house opposite the west front of the palace – was returned by the Commons to Lords use; in 2001, Millbank House was leased from the Church Commissioners for mixed office and member use; and in 2002 Fielden House, an office building in Little College Street, was bought for £13 million and is currently being renovated. This expansion reflects both the increased activity of the Lords as a chamber of Parliament and the increased expectations of its membership in regard to desk space, IT facilities and so on. Unsurprisingly, as in the Commons, this scattering of staff and members' offices has made the Lords seem less of a homogeneous organisation.

The parliamentary estate

Today's parliamentary estate is like a small town. It covers 185,400 square metres in sixteen buildings, and its normal daily population is well over 6,000 people. A plan of the parliamentary estate appears on page 17.

We now move on to consider the institution housed in those buildings.

2   Who is in Parliament?

The Commons

The size of the Commons

Even in the early fifteenth century there were more than 250 members of the Commons – two knights from each of thirty-seven counties, two citizens or burgesses from each of the eighty or so cities and boroughs, and fourteen members from the Cinque Ports. More were steadily added by statue and royal charter, and by 1673 the membership of the House – at that time only from England and Wales – stood at 513. Union with Scotland in 1707 added forty-five members, and a further 100 came from Ireland with the Union of 1801, making 658.

The House grew to 670 members in 1885, and to 707 – the most at any stage – in 1918. Irish independence reduced the numbers to 615 by 1922. Subsequent changes (only one of them downwards) have resulted in a total since 1997 of 659 members, one for each of 529 constituencies in England, seventy-two in Scotland, forty in Wales and eighteen in Northern Ireland. There is thus one MP for every 89,200 people (or for every 67,358 people entitled to vote).

Too big?

Even for a population of nearly 59 million, this is a very large House. By comparison, the Italian Camera dei Deputati has 630 members, or one for every 91,300 people, the French Assemblée nationale has 577 members (one for every 103,200 people) and the Spanish Congreso de los Diputados has 350 members (one for every 114,400 people). A comparison with the US House of Representatives is even more striking (435 members, one for every 647,000 people) but of course in the USA representation at state level also has to be taken into account.

A big House of Parliament has some disadvantages – at least from the point of view of the individual member. Parliamentary time is at a premium. The back-bencher must compete with colleagues to ask questions or to be called in debate (it is sometimes said that more speeches are prepared for the House of

Commons than are ever delivered). The individual's share of both influence and parliamentary resources is less than in a smaller House.

On the other side of the equation, the historically large numbers of MPs have led to a large number of ministers; in 2003, ninety-one (the maximum allowed by law is ninety-five) sat in the Commons out of a total of 114 in both Houses. This means that many individual members get ministerial experience (although the proportion – 14 percent – might well be the same in a smaller House). A large House provides more back-benchers to under-take the scrutiny of government through select committee work; in session 2002–03, some 300 MPs were members of investigative or scrutiny select committees.

However, from the point of view of the electorate, the main feature of a large House is that an individual MP represents a relatively small number of people. An MP's focus on the constituency is very sharp, not only because it is a power base, and he or she must woo the electors to maximise the chances of being re-elected, but also because most constituencies are small enough to be fairly homogeneous in terms of character, population and economic activity. Your chances of engaging an MP's attention on an issue are very much greater if it is something that directly affects his or her constituency. And it is certainly the case that the close and valued relationship between a single MP and a single constituency has been a factor in opposition to some forms of propor-tional representation.

The constituencies

Four Boundary Commissions, one for each part of the UK, keep under review the size, boundaries and numbers of parliamentary constituencies, especially to take account of population changes. The commissions are guided by the 'electoral quota': the total number of electors divided by the number of con-stituencies. The latest (2002) quotas are: England, 70,135; Northern Ireland, 67,596; Wales, 55,955; and Scotland, 55,570, which shows a considerable disparity in size – or, as some would have it, the over-representation of Wales and Scotland. There are plans to reduce the number of Scottish MPs at Westminster, probably to fifty-nine, by 2007; this would produce a quota of about 68,000 electors.

Drawing constituency boundaries is not mechanistic. The process must take account of geography, and of existing county and London borough boundaries, so constituencies vary considerably in size. The largest is the Isle of Wight at 103,654 electors (where there would be little to be gained in dividing the island into two constituencies), and the smallest is the Western Isles at 21,706 (where the identity of the islands is so distinct that combination with a mainland constituency is not an option).

The candidates

Anyone may stand for election to the Commons if he or she is a British subject or citizen of the Republic of Ireland, is aged 21 or over, and is not disqualified. Those disqualified include undischarged bankrupts, people sentenced to more than one year's imprisonment, members of the House of Lords (but hereditary peers not sitting in the Lords are eligible; one, Viscount Thurso, was elected to the Commons in 2001, and another, Douglas Hogg, succeeded his father as Viscount Hailsham in 2001) and holders of offices listed in the House of Commons Disqualification Act 1975. These last, often described as those holding an office of profit under the Crown, include civil servants, judges, members of the regular armed forces and police, some local government officers and some members of public bodies. They amount to about one in twenty-five of the electorate.

Independent candidates are occasionally elected. The first for many years was Martin Bell as the anti-sleaze candidate in Tatton in 1997, followed by Richard Taylor in Wyre Forest in 2001 on a platform of saving Kidderminster Hospital (beating a sitting member, who was also a minister, by the large majority of 17,630). However, it is necessary to be the formally adopted candidate of a political party to have any realistic chance of success. In the 2001 general election there were 3,319 candidates altogether; 1,922 of these were from the three major UK-wide parties.

Candidates are chosen by the party organisations in the constituency concerned, although there has been increasing involvement of the central party organisation in the process, especially at high-profile by-elections. In the Labour and Conservative parties, a committee of the local party will draw up a short-list of five or six candidates from as many as a hundred names, who will usually also be on the party's 'approved' list, although it is possible for the central organisation to impose its own short-list. The Labour Party has recently reintroduced all-women short-lists for some seats in an attempt to increase the number of women in the Commons. Candidates are interviewed at a meeting of local party members and then elected by eliminating ballot to be the 'prospective parliamentary candidate' (PPC).

The Liberal Democrats draw up panels of suitable candidates in England, Wales and Scotland, and the local party must advertise a vacancy to the people on the relevant list. The local party then prepares a short-list (which must include men and women and pay due regard to the representation of ethnic minorities), and all party members in the relevant constituency may vote to select their PPC.

The selection of candidates is thus subject to local control, although no procedure as elaborate as the primary system in the United States of America has evolved. However, unlike the USA, it is not necessary for a would-be MP to have considerable personal means. The deposit required is £500 and is forfeited only if the candidate receives less than 5 percent of the votes cast. In any case, it is found by the party, as are most of the candidate's expenses (see below). In June 2003, the Electoral Commission suggested that the system of deposits might be abolished.

Once elected to the Commons, an MP can usually expect to remain the party's candidate at the next election. The Labour Party has a system of mandatory reselection; that is, the sitting member must undergo the selection process before being adopted by the constituency party. For the 1997 general election, nine sitting Labour MPs were not reselected (and three more were expelled from the party); but none failed to secure reselection for the 2001 general election. In the other parties an initiative has to be taken to force a reselection process (as happened with John Browne, the former Conservative MP for Winchester, in 1992).

Elections: when?

General elections are held after Parliament has been dissolved, either by royal proclamation on the advice of the Prime Minister or because the maximum life of a parliament – five years – has expired. Since 1945, no parliament has run its full term, although the 1992–97 parliament came within a fortnight of doing so. The average length of parliaments since 1945 has been a little over three years and seven months. This contrasts with the fixed terms of the US Congress or the practice in countries like Belgium or Germany, where parliaments are dissolved early only in exceptional circumstances. The ending of a parliament by royal proclamation – in effect, by decision of the Prime Minister, gives him or her a tactical advantage in the timing of the election, although this did not profit the party in government in June 1970 or February 1974.

Although elections are held only for the Commons (elections for any part of the Lords seem unlikely), a dissolution covers both Houses: the Queen's proclamation says that she dissolves 'the said Parliament accordingly; And the Lords Spiritual and Temporal, and the Members of the House of Commons, are discharged from further attendance thereat'.

A by-election takes place when a seat becomes vacant because the MP dies or is otherwise no longer eligible to sit (see *The candidates* above). A by-election is not required if an MP changes party. An MP cannot in terms resign from the House but in effect does so by accepting one of the 'offices of profit' of steward or bailiff of Her Majesty's three Chiltern Hundreds of Stoke, Desborough and Burnham, or of the manor of Northstead. These are not real jobs but purely symbolic offices used to allow an MP to stand down. By convention, a by-election takes place within three months of the vacancy occurring. Until a new MP is elected, constituency matters are normally handled by a neighbouring MP of the same party.

Elections: who can vote?

The United Kingdom is more generous than many countries in those whom it allows to vote in parliamentary elections. There is no property qualification, since 1928 no sex discrimination, and there are voting rights for Britons who live abroad and choose to register. Commonwealth and Irish citizens resident in Britain are entitled to vote, and the only main categories excluded are those under 18, convicted offenders still in prison, people detained under mental health legislation for criminal activity, and anyone with a seat in the House of Lords. You do not have to have an address in order to vote; homeless people may make a 'declaration of local connection'. However, you must be on the register of parliamentary electors in a constituency. The register is updated every year on the basis of who was resident in the constituency on 15 October, but under the rolling register introduced in 2000 you can have your name added at any time during the year.

Elections: the timetable

This is set out in the Representation of the People Act 1983, as amended in 1985. The whole process, from the last sitting of the old parliament to the State Opening of the new, can take as little as six weeks, although in 1992 it took just over seven. The basic rule is that a general election takes place on the seventeenth day (excluding Sundays and holidays) after the royal proclamation summoning the new parliament (which nowadays accompanies the dissolution of the old). The 2001 timetable ran as follows:

Friday 12 May:	Parliament met for the last time.
Monday 14 May:	Parliament was dissolved by royal proclamation.
Thursday 7 June:	Polling day.
Wednesday 13 June:	Parliament met on the day specified in the proclamation to swear in Members and, in the Commons, to elect a Speaker.
Wednesday 20 June:	State Opening of Parliament.

The timing of the dissolution ensures that the general election itself will be held on a Thursday; not since 1931 (when it took place on a Tuesday) has a general election been held on a different day of the week. The last day on which the general election following that in 2001 can be held is 6 July 2006.

Election expenses

We have seen that personal wealth is not a prerequisite for standing for Parliament. Indeed, however well-off a candidate or party may be, the Representation of the People Act 1983 limits what may be spent in each constituency during an election. At a general election, the limits are £4,965 plus 5.6p per elector in a county constituency and £4,965 plus 4.2p per elector in a borough constituency. Limits are higher for by-elections. The total of a party's campaign expenditure over the 365 days before a general election is £30,000 times the number of constituencies that party is contesting: a maximum of £19.77 million if all 659 constituencies are contested.

Does the Commons represent the balance of opinion in the electorate?

Electoral law on the timing of campaigns is clear, the franchise is wide and elections are frequent. But whether an election result is representative and properly reflects the views of the voters, depends on the voting system. The British system is based on the relative majority method, sometimes called 'first past the post'. The voter marks a ballot paper with one X against the name of his or her favoured candidate – hedging bets with two X's will mean that the ballot paper is spoiled and will not be counted – and the candidate with the most votes wins. In this system there are no prizes for coming second; and it also means that the proportions of MPs of each party are not the same as the parties' shares of the votes cast across the nation as a whole.

In the 2001 general election, 25,691,239 votes were cast for parties that won seats in the House of Commons (leaving out votes cast for the Speaker and the one other independent MP); 23,896,237 of these, or 93 percent, were for one of the three main UK-wide parties. Shares of that total, and the number of seats that each party won in the House of Commons, are shown in Table 2.1.

But if the share of the vote were to be reflected in seats won in the Commons, the story would be very different. Labour's seats would fall to 267, the Conservatives would have 208, and the Liberal Democrats would have 120. The smaller parties would be little affected (although the SNP would have twelve seats instead of five). Tony Blair's huge overall majority of 161 seats would be wiped out, and no party would have control of the Commons. And on this basis the UK Independence Party, which failed to win any seats, would have ten MPs.

The other side of the story is what is sometimes known as the 'wasted vote'. For example, all three major parties must have seen the constituency of Bristol West as winnable. The result was:

Labour	20,505
Liberal Democrat	16,079
Conservative	16,040
Green	1,961
Socialist Labour Party	590
UK Independence Party	490

Table 2.1 Voting patterns in the 2001 general election

Party	Votes received	Percentage of total votes	Seats won	Percentage of total seats
Labour	10,724,623	40.68	412	62.6
Conservative	8,357,586	31.70	166	25.2
Liberal Democrat	4,814,027	18.26	52	7.9
Scottish National Party	464,314	1.76	5	0.8
Plaid Cymru	195,893	0.74	4	0.6
Ulster Unionist	216,839	0.82	6	0.9
Democratic Unionist	181,999	0.69	5	0.8
Sinn Fein	175,933	0.67	4	0.6
SDLP	169,865	0.64	3	0.5

Valerie Davey won the seat for Labour with only 36.8 percent of the votes cast; 35,160 people voted for other parties, but their votes were not reflected in the result locally or nationally. However, the *potential* power of each voter in Bristol West (by switching parties as a 'floating voter') was much greater than that of a voter in Bootle who did not wish to vote for the Labour candidate. There Joe Benton won the safest Labour seat in the country with 77.6 percent of the vote, 21,400 votes compared with his closest rival, the Liberal Democrat, with 2,357 votes.

Proponents of the first-past-the-post system usually make three main points in its favour. It is a simple system – no preferences, or second and third choices – and it is easily understood by voters. It usually produces clear results, with one party having a strong mandate to govern. And it avoids 'smoke-filled rooms', shorthand for the situation where political choices are made by negotiation between parties after an election, where deals are made and policies agreed that have not been put before the electorate.

The riposte of critics of the system is that voters are more canny and sophisticated than many pundits might think; that strong governments may be overbearing and insensitive, and actually the last thing that the voters want; that, once in office, governments produce policies that have never been put before the electorate anyway; and that most voters would prefer consensus to adversarial politics.

Despite the Labour Party's traditional opposition to electoral reform, its 1997 manifesto pledged an inquiry into voting systems, to be followed by a referendum. The incoming Labour government set up the Independent Commission on the Voting System, chaired by Lord Jenkins of Hillhead, which reported in October 1998. Its main recommendation was for a two-vote 'mixed system'. The majority of MPs (80 to 85 percent) would continue to be elected on an individual constituency basis by the alternative vote (AV) method, in which voters indicate their preferences for all the candidates. If a candidate wins more than half the votes cast on the first count of first preference votes, he or she is elected. If not, the candidate with the fewest first preference votes is eliminated and his or her second preferences allocated to the other candidates. This process continues until one candidate has achieved an overall majority. The AV method might have produced a different result in Bristol West in 2001, but it would not have produced a different result in Bootle.

However, in an attempt to correct disproportionality, Lord Jenkins recommended that to elect the remainder of MPs ('top-up members') voters should have a second vote, which could be cast for a party or for an individual candidate on a party list.

No action has been taken on the Jenkins recommendations, and indeed in January 2003 Charles Kennedy, the leader of the Liberal Democrats – the party in the vanguard of campaigning for electoral reform – stated that 'as things stand, proportional representation for Westminster is unachievable'.

Ironically, forms of proportional representation are already in widespread use in the UK. The Scottish Parliament has seventy-three constituency members (elected using the first-past-the-post system) and fifty-six additional regional members drawn from party lists. Similar systems are used for the National Assembly for Wales (forty and twenty) and for the Greater London Assembly (fourteen and eleven). The 108 members of the Northern Ireland Assembly are elected using the single transferable vote (STV) system, and the eighty-seven UK MEPs are elected using a 'closed-list' system in large multi-member regional constituencies.

Are the members of the Commons representative?

Despite a local democratic element in the choice of candidates, the MPs who sit in the Commons are not a microcosm of the electorate as whole.

Age

The House of Commons is overwhelmingly middle-aged. The average age of MPs in the last three parliaments has been almost exactly 50. In the House elected in 2001, 481 MPs were aged between 40 and 60 (73 percent of the total compared with 26 percent of the population of the UK as a whole);

and only four were younger than 30 when they were elected, compared with eleven in the previous parliament. The average age of the House is perhaps not surprising. Few young aspiring politicians are lucky enough to be selected for a winnable seat; constituency parties often prefer candidates with some experience outside politics. Nevertheless, although the average age of the population as a whole is rising, the age profile of the Commons may be a factor in distancing younger voters from the political process.

Occupation and education

In the parliaments elected in the four general elections from 1987 to 2001, the number of MPs in the three main parties with professional backgrounds remained constant at just over 40 percent. Within that category, the number of barristers fell from 9.1 to 5.2 percent, while school teachers increased from 7.6 to 10.2 percent. Those with a business background fell from 25.6 to 17.0 percent, largely because of the sharp fall in Conservative numbers in 1997. Those who were previously involved in politics full-time almost doubled from 5.4 to 10.5 percent. Educational attainments among MPs are higher than in the electorate generally. About a third of the adult population has been to university, but three-quarters of MPs had a university education.

There are many reasons why certain occupations produce a disproportionate number of MPs while others, for example manual work (8.4 percent in the House compared with 32.4 percent in the country as a whole), nursing and engineering, are less well represented. MPs do not have secure jobs in Parliament and often want to retain part-time work in their old professions – something criticised by those who believe that election as an MP with a salary of just over £55,000 demands full-time attention. Some jobs are communicative and more likely to appeal to those who want to enter politics. In some jobs it is impossible to devote large amounts of time to politics – normally an essential precondition if one intends to stand for Parliament. And despite a salary more than twice the national average of £24,498, some who might consider standing would have to take a substantial pay cut.

Women in Parliament

After decades of campaigning, culminating in the suffragette movement, the bill to allow women to stand for Parliament was passed on the day that Parliament was dissolved for the 1918 general election. Paradoxically, it allowed women to be candidates at the age of 21, although women did not then have the right to vote until the age of 30 (reduced to the same age as men, then 21, in 1928).

The first woman elected to the Commons, Countess Markievicz, was elected in 1918 for the St Patrick's division of Dublin as a Sinn Fein member but, in protest against British policy on Ireland, never took her seat. It was ironic that the first woman to do so, Viscountess Astor, who was elected at a by-election on 15 November 1919, had never campaigned for women's rights. Since 1918, a total of 4,534 MPs have served in the House of Commons. Of these, 253, or 6 percent, have been women.

The numbers of women MPs remained very low for seventy years, only passing 5 percent at the 1987 general election and rising to 9.2 percent in 1992. In 1997, the 120 women elected (18.2 percent) was the largest number ever; the 2001 parliament saw a reduction of two to 17.9 percent – although women make up more than 51 percent of the population.

The average representation of women in national parliaments worldwide is 15 percent. Sweden comes closest to representing the population with 45 percent women members of the Riksdag (although the National Assembly for Wales hit 50 percent at the 2003 elections). In the league table published by the Inter-Parliamentary Union the UK comes 50th, sandwiched between the former Yugoslav republic of Macedonia and the Philippines and some way ahead of France (65th), Italy (70th) and India (88th), but behind Germany (11th), Australia (24th) and Pakistan (32nd).

Ethnic minorities

There have been non-white members of the House of Commons in the past (a Liberal, a Conservative and a Communist, who each sat for brief periods between 1892 and 1929) but, since the substantial immigration into the United Kingdom from its former colonies in the West Indies and from the former Indian Empire in the 1950s and later, no representative of these communities was elected to Parliament until 1987 (although several had been created life peers). There is still no representative of the substantial ethnic Chinese community. Efforts have been made in all parties to nominate ethnic minority candidates, but not with great success. In the 1992 parliament there were six MPs who described themselves as being from an ethnic minority. This increased to nine in the 1997 parliament and to twelve, or 1.8 percent of the membership of the House, in the 2001 parliament. That figure compares with 7.1 percent of the population in the country as a whole.

Does it matter?

In one sense, it matters very little that the make-up of the membership of the House of Commons does not reflect the population as a whole. Every MP is there to represent all the people in a constituency, whether they voted for the MP, or one of the other candidates, or did not vote at all. A man, or a woman, or someone from an ethnic minority, or a single parent, may perhaps be thought to have a better understanding of the outlook of men, of women, of ethnic minorities, or of single parents. Nevertheless, the MP's job is to represent the diversity of the people in the constituency in a conscientious and professional way. Understanding your constituents is part of doing the job well, whether or not you have a particular affinity with one group or another.

The reputation of Parliament

Another factor is how the House of Commons is seen by the people it represents. There are many factors that affect the standing of Parliament. A powerful executive and a large parliamentary majority for one party condition the perception of Parliament's powers and what it can do for the citizen. Cynicism about spin and soundbites does not help. The behaviour, and thus the standing, of individual MPs is another factor.

Despite increasing direct access to Parliament and its work, through the BBC Parliament channel, webcasting on www.parliamentlive.tv and the Parliament website www.parliament.uk, most people hear about Parliament through the media. *Political* reporting in the UK is of a generally high standard, but *parliamentary* reporting, requiring a knowledge of the institution and the way it works, is less so. Trivial and ignorant coverage, especially in some of the print media, may sell newspapers, but it does not do justice to the institution.

It is an open question whether, if the House of Commons were seen by all sectors of the population as containing 'people like us', the institution would be held in higher esteem; and, if it were, whether that would increase public interest and participation. In this respect, the 2001 general election gave considerable cause for concern.

Turnout: reconnecting Parliament with the people

In the general election of 1992, nearly 78 percent of those registered to vote did so. The turnout fell to 71.5 percent in 1997, perhaps because so many people assumed that Labour would win. Even though the result of the 2001 election might also have been easily predicted, the fall in the turnout – to just over 59 percent – was dramatic. It was lower than at any election since the introduction of the universal franchise, and it was of concern for two reasons. First, a government with an overwhelming Commons majority, and apparent *carte blanche* to do as it wished, had been elected with the support of only one in four people entitled to vote. Perhaps more seriously, the low turnout seemed to signal a loss of interest in the country's central democratic institution.

Many factors have been blamed. Was an adversarial style of politics putting the voters off? Or, equally, did people see the less polarised relationship of the two major parties as offering less choice than before? Was it that the result seemed a foregone conclusion to many? Did the electorate see Parliament as less able to control an over-mighty executive – the 'it won't make any difference' syndrome?

If there was no agreement on the cause, there was certainly no agreement on the cure. A change in the electoral system? More access to the political process, through on-line consultations, draft bills and the work of select committees? Fostering a wider understanding of what Parliament does and how it works? We will have a closer look at the possibilities in Chapter 13.

The Lords

Unlike the House of Commons, the House of Lords has never been representative. From its earliest times it was a chamber of individuals. Originally members of the House were mainly the rich and powerful landed magnates on whom the King relied for his support and whose retainers would turn out to assist him (or when things went wrong, oppose him!) on the battlefield. From the late seventeenth century, the House came to include members whose influence lay elsewhere, in money, commerce and political patronage. During the twentieth century, this changed as new members were increasingly drawn from the ranks of former MPs and others without landed or moneyed connection – such as trade unionists, academics, former public servants, local politicians and so forth. But members continued to have one thing in common throughout the ages: they represented no one but themselves.

Current membership

Membership of the House in January 2003 was 693, twelve of whom were on leave of absence – that is to say, they had been granted leave of the House not to attend in response to their writs of summons to Parliament. The categories of membership are as follows:

Archbishops and bishops	24
Life peers under the Appellate Jurisdiction Act 1876	28
Life peers under the Life Peerages Act 1958	538
Hereditary peers under the House of Lords Act 1999	91
Total	**681**

Let us now take a closer look at these different categories. Who are they and how are they selected?

Archbishops and bishops

The Anglican Archbishops of Canterbury and York, the Bishops of Durham, London and Winchester and the twenty-one senior diocesan bishops from other dioceses of the Church of England sit in the House as 'Lords Spiritual'. All the other Lords are known as 'Lords Temporal'. In the mediaeval Parliament, the Lords Spiritual (bishops and mitred abbots) made up about half the membership. Currently they represent about one in twenty-eight. Only the Church of England is represented. The other established church, the Church of Scotland, has no nominees; nor do other religious denominations, non-Christian religions or the Anglican churches outside England. When the then Chief Rabbi, Lord Jakobovits, was made a peer in January 1988, it was personal to him. When a bishop retires, he loses his seat in the Lords.

Life peers under the Appellate Jurisdiction Act 1876

Besides exercising its purely parliamentary functions, the House of Lords also acts as the supreme court of appeal for the whole of the United Kingdom in civil cases and for England, Wales and Northern Ireland in criminal cases. About seventy cases a year are heard, and the business is done in the Appellate Committee, although judgements are delivered in the Chamber at specially convened sittings. When Parliament is not in session – usually in early October – the appeals themselves are also heard in the Chamber. The Lord Chancellor and lords who hold or have held high judicial office may sit on the Appellate Committee, provided that they are under 75 years of age, but the backbone is provided by up to twelve Lords of Appeal in Ordinary, salaried life peers appointed under the Appellate Jurisdiction Act 1876 specifically to hear appeals. Currently twenty-eight serving and former law lords sit in the House, having become members by this route.

Life peers under the Life Peerages Act 1958

Until the passage of the House of Lords Act in 1999, the Life Peerages Act 1958 was the most significant influence in determining the House as we know it today. Under this legislation, men and women can be created peers for life. The title ceases on death. In January 2003 there were 550 life peers, twelve of whom were on leave of absence. Many of them are politicians, often those who have worked for their party outside Parliament, who have retired from the Commons, or who have been defeated in elections. Other life peers have been drawn from different aspects of national life and have brought considerable and very valuable expertise to the House of Lords – former senior officers in the armed forces, civil servants, heads of large private sector industries, trade union leaders, doctors and academics and even the occasional actor or teacher.

The power to create peerages belongs formally to the Crown but in effect new peerages are a gift of the Prime Minister of the day – and a considerable source of patronage. By convention, other party leaders are also asked to make nominations for new peerages. This is often the only way open to opposition parties to strengthen their teams of front-bench spokesmen. The creation of most new peerages (other than Lords Spiritual and Lords of Appeal in Ordinary) is announced in the regular Honours Lists – the New Year and Queen's Birthday lists, which appear annually, and the Dissolution and Resignation lists, which occur when Parliament is dissolved or a Prime Minister resigns, respectively. But from time to time lists of so-called working peers – exclusively political appointees of the major parties – are presented. And occasionally individual peerages will be announced *ad hoc*.

Following the 1997 general election, the House witnessed a large influx of new members – twenty-one from the Dissolution list (19 April), three from the Birthday list (14 June), ten from the Resignation list (2 August) and forty-eight from a working peers list (2 August). Adding a further four peerage creations made outside these lists to enable people without seats in either Chamber to be offered ministerial posts, the House was required to absorb eighty-six new members within a very short period.

Since May 2000, a non-statutory Appointments Commission sits to make recommendations to the Queen for non-political peers and to vet for propriety all nominations for peerages, including those from the political parties. One of the first acts of the commission was to conduct a public nomination scheme for the selection of fifteen eminent men and women from non-political backgrounds who might be granted peerages. In the event, the fifteen so-called people's peers that resulted were very similar in background and qualities to the independent members nominated by more conventional means. It will be interesting to see whether the commission is invited to repeat this exercise. It is the government's intention to develop the role of the Appointments Commission as part of its proposals for further reform (see page 392).

Hereditary peers

Until the passing of the Life Peerages Act, all members of the House of Lords, except for the bishops and Lords of Appeal in Ordinary, were hereditary. The principle of a hereditary peerage is that, at some historical point, an individual is created a peer or lord (in one of the different ranks of dukes, marquesses, earls, viscounts or barons), and the legal document conferring that peerage (the 'letters patent') stipulates that his heirs (normally only the males) may inherit his title and with it the right to sit in the House of Lords. Some peerages descend through the female as well as the male line, and after 1963 women holders of hereditary peerages were also able to take their seats in the Lords.

Current membership of the House of Lords includes ninety-two hereditary peers who have seats as a result of the House of Lords Act 1999. This Act reformed the House's membership by excluding hereditary peers from sitting, but following an agreement between the government and the then Leader of the Opposition in the Lords, Lord Cranborne, the bill was amended so that seventy-five hereditary members were excepted from the general provisions of the Act by election from among their own party or group, a further fifteen by election by the whole House to serve as Deputy Speakers and committee chairs, and two (the Earl Marshal and Lord Great Chamberlain) *ex officio*.

These arrangements were expected to be transitional pending further reform of membership (see Chapter 13), but their effect meanwhile is to make the hereditary principle a continuing feature of British political life. From the passing of the House of Lords Act until the end of the 2001–02 session, vacancies arising out of the death of one of the ninety elected members were filled by the runners-up in the relevant category with the most votes. Two cross-bench vacancies were filled in this way. Thereafter a system of by-elections came into force. Anyone in receipt of a writ before the passage of the Act, or anyone who has subsequently established a right to be included, may ask to be on the register of eligible candidates. The electors are the whole House in the case of the fifteen excepted as Deputy Speakers or chairs but only the hereditary peers in a party or group in respect of the seventy-five elected by party or group. The first such election was held in March 2003.

Before the 1999 Act, the House of Lords was on paper at least a predominantly hereditary body, although in terms of regular attendance the hereditary element was just under 50 percent. Now the ninety-one hereditary members represent just over 13 percent of membership. The government intends to remove the remaining hereditary element as part of its further reform proposals (see page 392).

Attendance

We have already noted that members of the House are not representative. They are also part time and do not always attend. In the long post-general election session 2001–02, average daily attendance was 370. It is worth noting that the proportion of members attending is much higher since the exclusion of all but ninety-two of the hereditary peerage in 1999. In the 1996–97 session, average daily attendance was 381 out of a total potential membership of no fewer than 1,272! But the fact remains that, although many members of the House attend regularly, some life peers attend relatively infrequently.

Of the total current membership of 693, 113 are women, four of whom hold hereditary peerages. The percentage of women members is 16.3 percent, close to that in the Commons.

Table 2.2 Composition of the House of Lords, 1 January 2003

	Life	Hereditary	Bishops	Total
Conservative	167	50	–	217
Labour	184	4	–	188
Liberal Democrat	61	5	–	66
Cross-bench	145	32	–	177
Bishops	–	–	24	24
Other	9	–	–	9
Total	566	91	24	681

Note: 12 members were on leave of absence.

Politics

Although members of the House are not representative and are unelected they are nearly all political animals. Most members of the House take a party whip, and of course many of the life peers owe their membership of the House to political patronage. The non-aligned cross-bench members have political opinions on issues, although none of them supports a political party. Party political allegiance on 1 January 2003 is shown in Table 2.2.

Although the passage of the House of Lords Act 1999 and the creation of more Labour life peers since 1997 has done much to promote greater parity between the two main parties, the Conservative Party is still the biggest single group in the House. In consequence, the government often relies on Liberal Democrat and cross-bench support to get its way in the face of Conservative opposition. On those occasions when such support might not be forthcoming, the government is more prone to compromise. We look more closely at this in Chapter 7.

The Queen

It is easy to think of Parliament as consisting simply of the two Houses; but the sovereign is also part of the institution. Indeed, the words that precede every Act of Parliament remind us that, to become law, a bill must be must be approved by the Queen as well as by both Houses:

Be it enacted by the Queen's most Excellent Majesty, by and with the advice and consent of the Lords Spiritual and Temporal, and Commons, in this present Parliament assembled, and by the authority of the same, as follows:–

The Queen's name appears again and again in the proceedings of Parliament. Bills go for Royal Assent; if a bill affects the Royal Prerogative or the Queen's personal interests, then the Queen's consent must be signified before it is passed; the spending of taxpayers' money in connection with a bill must have the Queen's recommendation; the government's legislative programme is set out at the beginning of a session in the Queen's Speech; many papers presented formally to the two Houses are presented 'by Command of Her Majesty'; Orders in Council – a category of delegated legislation – are made in her name; the government is 'Her Majesty's Government'; and ministers are 'Ministers of the Crown'.

This terminology may seem more appropriate to the mediaeval relationship between the monarch and his fledgling parliament, but in the early twenty-first century the language is entirely symbolic. The Queen does indeed give her consent to bills – by signing a list of bills passed rather than each one – but she has no practical power of refusal. The last sovereign to refuse Royal Assent (to a bill for settling the militia in Scotland) was Queen Anne in 1707–08, and in subsequent centuries sovereigns have progressively distanced themselves from the business of politics.

Above politics: political neutrality

The conventional phrase is that the Queen is 'above politics' or, as Walter Bagehot said of royalty and Queen Victoria, 'Its mystery is its life. We must not let in daylight upon magic. We must not bring the Queen into the combat of politics, or she will cease to be reverenced by all combatants; she will become one combatant among many'. Most would agree that events of the last fifteen years, aided and abetted by the tabloid press, have dispelled much of Bagehot's 'magic'; but the Queen's political neutrality is still of constitutional importance. On the one hand, most people would regard it as unacceptable for the monarch to be identified with a particular political party (even a political party that they themselves supported); on the other hand, the Queen may have to perform a crucial constitutional task: deciding who should form a government after a general election.

Choosing a Prime Minister

Normally this is straightforward. The day after polling day the leader of the party with the most seats in the House of Commons – and so able to command the House and get the business of government through – is summoned to

Buckingham Palace and asked as Prime Minister to form a government, which in practice means appointing the members of the Cabinet and other ministers and taking responsibility for the administration of the country.

Similarly, when a sitting Prime Minister resigns, as Harold Wilson did in 1976, or Margaret Thatcher did in 1990 having lost the confidence of her party, the sovereign's task is an easy one. The government party will choose a new leader under the procedure required by its party rules, and – assuming that that party still has a majority in the House – the Queen will invite the winner to form a government.

A hung parliament

However, in a hung parliament after a general election, where no one party has a majority, the Queen's task may be more difficult. When the final tally of seats is clear, there will probably be intense negotiation between the parties to see how much common ground there might be for the formation of a coalition (where ministers would be drawn from two or more parties) or for one party to govern with the formal support of another. When the Conservative Party lost its majority in the general election of February 1974, Edward Heath negotiated with the Liberal Party in an attempt to continue in government with Liberal support. When it was clear that he would be unsuccessful, the Queen asked Harold Wilson to form a minority government, which struggled on until a general election in October that year, at which Wilson won a narrow overall majority of three seats.

More difficult for the sovereign would be a situation where a general election produced a three-way split in seats in the Commons but very little common ground between any of the three parties. If it was quickly clear that the party leader first asked to form a government could not sustain it – for example by losing the vote on the proposed legislative programme in the Queen's Speech – she would probably invite another party leader to attempt to form a government.

It would be a matter of judgement as to how long this process could be allowed to go on. On the one hand, the argument goes, the people have spoken (as former President Clinton famously said of the 2000 US presidential election, 'but we're not sure yet what they've said') and it is for politicians to agree a constructive way forward. To force another poll so soon after the first would inflict another general election on a weary electorate, with no guarantee that it would produce any different result. On the other hand, the business of government needs to be carried on, and a second general election might be preferable to months of inter-party squabbling and horse trading.

In these circumstances, the sovereign's political neutrality is crucial. While others may be concerned about party advantage, she must consider only the national interest. The process is not risk-free: when in Australia in 1975 the

Governor-General dismissed the Prime Minister on the grounds that the two Houses of Parliament could not reach agreement on the budget and the business of government could not be carried on, that undoubtedly fuelled the flames of republicanism. By contrast, in Belgium, where coalition governments are the norm, there was little criticism of the King in 1985 when he refused the Prime Minister a dissolution because the coalition government had broken down.

Another method?

It is sometimes suggested that the Queen's powers to dissolve Parliament and invite a party leader to form a government should be delegated to the Speaker of the House of Commons (as has been the case in unicameral Sweden since 1974, where the King's functions are purely ceremonial). But even if it were acceptable to give the presiding officer of one House powers over the other – for a dissolution affects the Lords as well – the same problems would remain to be solved.

The sovereign as statesman

To quote Bagehot again: 'the sovereign has, under a constitutional monarchy such as ours, three rights – the right to be consulted, the right to encourage, the right to warn'. He was speaking of Queen Victoria, who perhaps exercised more influence than does her great-great-grand-daughter, but those principles still hold good today. It is worth remembering that the present Queen has more experience of the nation's affairs than anyone in politics. She sees a wide range of state papers and is briefed frankly by the government on the issues of the day. British ambassadors ('Her Majesty's' Ambassadors) and high commissioners call upon her when they leave to take up their posts and when they return, and she sees their most important despatches.

She has known ten Prime Ministers, from Churchill to Blair, and at weekly audiences has discussed with them the crises and dilemmas that they have faced. Almost all have had an excellent relationship with her, and some have described the weekly audiences in terms almost of therapy: being able to talk about major problems in total confidence with someone of immense political experience who is neither a political opponent nor a rival. The role of the present Queen demonstrates that Bagehot's rights of the sovereign are still of great value.

The Crown prerogative

We saw how frequently the Queen's name is used in the business of Parliament, mostly in relation to matters that require the approval of Parliament or are subject to the authority of Parliament. However, the ability of a mediaeval monarch to wage wars, appoint ambassadors and conclude treaties without the approval of Parliament survives in a modern form through the government's use of the Crown prerogative. Ministers make a large number of public appointments every year (3,506 in 2001–02, including reappointments), many to posts of power and importance. The Prime Minister can reorganise government departments and their responsibilities overnight, and negotiate and sign treaties with few constraints. The government can even take the country to war without parliamentary approval; putting the matter to the House of Commons, as was done on 18 March 2003 before the invasion of Iraq, was a remarkable precedent.

All these things are done in the Queen's name through the use of the Crown prerogative, usually bypassing the two Houses of Parliament. We examine the implications of this in Chapter 4.

3 Running Parliament

The House of Commons

The Speaker

The Speaker of the House of Commons is the most visible player on the parliamentary stage. His 'Order, order' opens every parliamentary day in the Chamber; he is usually in the Chair for the stormiest parliamentary events, and he is the representative of the House on occasions of state ceremony, sorrow and rejoicing.

Not only does the Speaker have the task of chairing the House; he is also an enormously influential figure in almost every aspect of the way that the House and its administration are run. As the presiding officer of the Commons he may seem the exact counterpart of the Lord Chancellor as the presiding officer of the Lords; but, as we shall see, their functions are very different.

The office of Speaker

The first member known as Speaker was Sir Thomas Hungerford in 1376, although it seems clear that individual members presided over the early mediaeval House before then, perhaps as early as Peter de Montfort in Henry III's 'Mad Parliament' at Oxford in 1258. The title of Speaker (Mr Speaker or Madam Speaker, as he or she is always referred to in the House) comes from the ancient position of official spokesman of the Commons to the monarch. In the days when sovereign and Commons were frequently at odds, this aspect of the job was rather more arduous than today, and more hazardous: between 1471 and 1535, six Speakers were executed.

Some of the ancient functions of the Speaker survive in more symbolic form. Once elected by the Commons, he makes claim to the Crown of the House's

ancient and undoubted Rights and Privileges, particularly to freedom of speech in debate, freedom from arrest, freedom of access to Her Majesty whenever occasion may require, and that the most favourable construction should be placed on all its proceedings.

although this may perhaps appear a little at odds with the modern relationship between the monarch and a House elected by universal suffrage.

The Speaker still occasionally acts as the House's spokesman. After the terrorist atrocities on 11 September 2001 he expressed the House's condolences to the US Congress; and on the occasion of the Golden Jubilee in 2002 he presented an Address of the House to the Queen in Westminster Hall.

The independence of the Speaker

In many foreign parliaments, the presiding officer is a party politician. In the US House of Representatives, for example, the Speaker is a leading party politician and frequently takes part in controversial debate. In Germany, the president of the Bundestag is normally a senior member of the government party who continues to play an active part in his party's affairs, and the same is true of the president of the French Assemblée nationale.

However, in the House of Commons there is a long tradition of impartiality, which began with Arthur Onslow (Speaker for thirty-three years from 1728) and which is so strong that all Speakers are seen as genuinely independent of party. There was a welter of press comment when the current Speaker, in the Chair, thanked a government minister for the *content* of a statement the minister had just made to the House. Speaker Martin's words were not unduly controversial, and he made it clear that he was voicing a constituency concern that he felt was shared by all members, but the incident demonstrated how the real independence of the Speaker is valued not only in the House but also more widely. The Speaker could not do his job, or exercise the considerable powers that the House has given him, were he not seen as in every way above the party battle.

In practice, this means that the Speaker resigns from his party – perhaps after having been a party member for thirty years or more – and has nothing more to do with its internal affairs. When he stands at a general election, it is not under a party banner but as 'the Speaker seeking re-election'; and he is usually unopposed by the major parties. He draws the salary of a cabinet minister and can look forward on retirement to a generous pension and a peerage. He wears formal dress, a court coat and barrister's bands, and when in the Chair a gown – but as Speaker Boothroyd abandoned the full-bottomed wig and Speaker Martin has followed suit, that particular tradition has probably ended for good. When the Speaker goes to and from the Chamber he is preceded by a trainbearer. Warned by cries of 'Speaker!' from the doorkeepers, even the most senior MPs stop what they are doing and bow as he goes by.

In the Palace of Westminster the Speaker has a personal staff to support him and splendid state apartments, which are his official residence, with a comfortable and less formal flat above. He no longer eats with other MPs in the dining rooms or takes part in the political gossip of the Tea Room. Members now come to him. Every Speaker must keep a finger on the pulse of the House and the concerns of its members, and much of his time is taken up with meetings not only with, for example, the Leader of the House or the Chief Whips, but also with a wide variety of MPs with concerns, problems – or bright ideas.

The Speaker is also the embodiment of the House as far as the outside world is concerned. He receives ambassadors, Speakers and ministers from other parliaments, delegations of all sorts, and he presides over a number of parliamentary associations and other bodies.

The Speaker still carries out constituency work and duties like any other MP. It is sometimes suggested that the Speaker should sit for a notional constituency – perhaps called St Stephen's – but this idea has never found much favour. Speakers want to understand and share at first hand the constituency pressures and problems faced by other MPs; and their own constituents are fortunate in having the Speaker for their Member of Parliament as ministers understandably give special attention to constituency cases raised by the Speaker.

The election of the Speaker

Since 1945, some Speakers have been former ministers (Morrison, Selwyn-Lloyd and Thomas had all been cabinet ministers, while Hylton-Foster had been Solicitor-General and Weatherill had been government Deputy Chief Whip); the careers of others had been mainly on the back benches (King and Martin; Boothroyd had been a government assistant whip for two years). However, since 1965 five out of the six Speakers have been former Deputy Speakers (King, Thomas, Weatherill, Boothroyd and Martin); not only did they come to the Speakership with experience in the Chair, but also the House had been able to make some assessment of them in that role.

Perhaps surprisingly in view of the rigid political independence of the office, all postwar Speakers except Betty Boothroyd have come from the government side of the House, whichever party has been in power. Given that one of the roles of the Speaker is to protect the House's interests when they conflict with those of the executive, this may have required a rapid reorientation; but it is often said that, particularly at the outset, Speakers tend to be harder on their former party than on the other side of the House.

Since 1945, there has normally been only one candidate for the Speakership. In 1992 there was rather more of a contest: the former cabinet minister, Peter Brooke, was defeated by 372 votes to 238, and Betty Boothroyd was elected. She was re-elected unopposed at the start of the 1997 parliament.

On her retirement in 2000 there was an unprecedented election for the Speakership, with no fewer than twelve candidates standing. Propositions are normally put to the House in the form of a motion to which amendments may be moved, and this had always been the procedure for the election of the Speaker, where the motion 'That X do take the Chair of this House as Speaker' could be amended by leaving out 'X' and inserting 'Y'. Thus in 2000 the motion named Michael Martin, and the other candidates were put to the House one by one in a series of amendments. Speeches proposing and seconding the candidates, and by the candidates themselves, together with the votes on each amendment and the final decision, took nine hours. As of course there was no Speaker, the member with the longest continuous service (the 'Father of the House'), Sir Edward Heath, presided.

In one sense, a day's sitting to fill a post of such importance to every single MP and to the House as a whole was not excessive; but there was understandable pressure to see whether matters could be handled differently. Following a report from the Procedure Committee, in 2001 the House agreed new arrangements. These favour a Speaker who returns to the House after a general election; only if a motion that he or she should take the Chair is defeated does the new procedure for a contested election come into play.

In a contested election, nominations (supported by twelve to fifteen MPs, at least three of whom cannot be from the candidate's own party) are submitted to the Clerk of the House on the morning of the election. When the House meets later that day, the candidates address the House in turn, in an order chosen by lot, and MPs then vote by secret ballot. If one candidate gets more than half the votes, his or her name is put to the House straight away; but if not, the lowest-scoring candidate and any candidate with less than 5 percent of the votes are eliminated, a second ballot is held, and so on until one candidate gets more than half the votes. The system is designed to be as fair as possible and not to give an advantage to the candidate who is proposed first (as did the previous system). It is unlike any voting system used in any of the House's other decisions; but it has not yet been used.

The roles of the Speaker

Maintaining order

Perhaps the most obvious function of the Speaker and his deputies is to maintain order when the House is sitting. All speeches made in the Chamber are addressed to the Chair, and the Speaker 'calls to order' any MP who offends against the rules of the House. Some of these are conventions, and others are laid down in standing orders or in past resolutions of the House. The definitive guide to them is *Erskine May's Treatise on the Law, Privileges, Proceedings and Usage of Parliament*, usually known as *Erskine May*. Sir Thomas Erskine

May, Clerk of the House from 1871 to 1886, edited the first nine editions, and thirteen more have been edited by his successors.

The House's rules range from the relatively trivial, such as requiring members to refer to each other by constituency rather than name, to the more serious, such as the *sub judice* rule (see page 274), which is designed to prevent criminal trials or civil actions in the courts being prejudiced by comment in the House. Other rules require speeches to be relevant to the matter before the House (and supplementary questions to be relevant to the subject of the question on the Order Paper), forbid the use of insulting words or 'unparliamentary expressions' (see page 274), specify when an MP may speak a second time in a debate, regulate the proper conduct of votes, and so on. The Speaker has both to make sure that these rules are observed and to give his rulings when MPs raise points of order about the application or interpretation of these rules.

In a democratic assembly, passions can run high and tempers flare. It is then that the Speaker and his deputies need to be most sensitive in gauging the mood of the House. Will a humorous intervention from the Chair defuse the situation, or is there serious trouble that must be dealt with firmly from the outset? At need, they have powers to discipline individual MPs, either by ordering them to resume their seats, to leave the Chamber for the day or, for more serious offences (usually involving a disregard for the authority of the Chair), naming them. After a member has been named, a motion is moved by the senior minister present, which the House invariably agrees to, and which has the effect of suspending the MP, so barring him or her from the building for five sitting days on the first occasion, twenty sitting days on the second and indefinitely on the third (and stopping payment of the member's salary for those periods). If there is general disorder in the Chamber, the Speaker can suspend the sitting.

These are powers used with great reluctance by the Speaker. He does not want to create martyrs or give an individual MP's political protest added force by expulsion from the Chamber; but he has also to protect the reputation of the House and the business before it. In February 2003, the way in which Speaker Martin dealt with the protest by the Father of the House, Tam Dalyell, that Parliament was not being properly consulted on impending war with Iraq, was a good example of the merits of restraint. A whole column of *Hansard* was taken up with an exchange between the Speaker and the Father of the House, which was courteous rather than angry, and the incident ended with Mr Dalyell leaving the Chamber of his own accord. Precipitate disciplinary action can rebound upon the Chair, as with the Victorian Speaker who was foolish enough to have the police called to deal with disorder in the Chamber. Thereafter, whenever the House was rowdy, his authority was routinely undermined by shouts of 'send for the police'.

Holding the ring

The Speaker and his deputies have absolute discretion over which members they call to speak. There may be some fixed points in a major debate: perhaps a cabinet minister will open the debate, responded to by his or her opposition shadow, with a Liberal Democrat representative speaking shortly afterwards, and the winding-up speeches at the end might be made by another member of the shadow cabinet and by another cabinet minister.

In between, the character of the debate is shaped by which MPs the Chair calls to speak. Balancing their claims is no easy task. Let us suppose that there is a full day's debate on policy towards asylum seekers: in practice, five or six hours' debating time. The five front-bench speeches might leave no more than three or four hours for everyone else who wishes to take part. Let us also suppose that pressure on existing reception centres for asylum seekers has led the government to propose a number of additional sites. Unrest in two or three centres has been followed by violence and extensive damage. There will be MPs with asylum centres in their constituencies; those who represent people who are up in arms that a new centre might be located near them; those who represent Channel ports; those who are close to the unions representing asylum centre staff; perhaps the chairman and members of the Home Affairs Select Committee, who have just produced a critical report on asylum policy. And, as well as juggling these urgent claims to speak, the Speaker and his deputies have to ensure that the party balance is maintained.

During Question Time (see Chapter 10), the Speaker's ability to shape events is even more marked. He can cut short over-long supplementary questions (and ministerial answers), but he can also decide how long to go on calling MPs to ask supplementaries on a particular question. If the subject is one on which the government is vulnerable, eight supplementary questions – perhaps including some hostile ones from the minister's own side – instead of two or three may give a minister a torrid time at the despatch box. And it is the occupant of the Chair alone who decides how long questioning on a ministerial statement or an urgent question (see page 300) should continue. Again, if political and media pressure has forced a ministerial statement on some high-profile problem, the government's exposure will be much greater if questions run for an hour instead of half an hour.

The Speaker's powers in the Chamber

In sharp contrast to the House of Lords, the Commons has given its presiding officer extensive powers. The House of Lords may largely regulate itself, but in the much more contentious and politically polarised Commons the Chair has a considerable armoury.

First, as we have seen, there is *the power to call MPs to speak in a debate or to ask a question*, described by Speaker Thomas as his most potent weapon. Although Speakers strive to be fair to every MP, the member who is disruptive or abusive, or disregards the authority of the Chair, may find it difficult to catch the Speaker's eye at Prime Minister's Questions for some little while thereafter. Allied with this is the power to decide *how long questioning on a particular topic may continue.*

In most debates, the Speaker also has the *power to limit the length of back-bench speeches*, down to a minimum of eight minutes. He can also intervene to *prevent deliberate time wasting* by MPs either speaking repetitiously or calling for unnecessary votes. The decision on whether to accept the closure – in other words, to *allow the House to decide whether a debate should end and a vote be taken on the subject under discussion* – is entirely in the hands of the Chair.

The Speaker also has absolute discretion on *whether amendments to bills or to motions before the House should be debated and voted upon.* This can be of great significance. For example, when in February 2003 options on the future composition of the House of Lords were put before the Commons by the government, the choices were in the form of seven free-standing motions, on each of which the House would take a decision (in fact, every one was defeated). There was no option that would have allowed a decision on whether there should be a House of Lords at all. However, a Labour back-bencher put down identical amendments to each of the options, declining approval as 'it does not accord with the principle of a unicameral parliament'. The Speaker selected the amendment (in other words, allowed it to be debated and voted upon) and it was defeated by 390 votes to 172. But it was only because of the Speaker's decision that a substantial minority in favour of abolition were able to record their view.

The debates on Iraq in February and March 2003 provide even more vivid examples. When on 26 February 2003 the Commons debated a government motion calling upon Iraq to recognise this as its final opportunity to comply with its 'disarmament obligations', the Speaker selected a Labour back-bench amendment to the effect that the case for military action against Iraq was 'as yet unproven'. The amendment was defeated by 393 votes to 199, but the 199 included 122 Labour MPs voting against the government's policy – a rebellion of huge political significance.

Less than a month later, the government put before the House of Commons a motion authorising the use of all means necessary to ensure the disarmament of Iraq's weapons of mass destruction – in effect authorising war. Again, the Speaker selected a Labour back-bench amendment asserting that 'the case for war against Iraq has not yet been established, especially given the absence of specific United Nations authorisation'. This time the amendment was defeated by 396 votes to 217; the 217 included 139 Labour MPs (twenty-nine of whom had not rebelled on the previous occasion), again a seismic political event.

The Speaker can also set part of the political agenda, and allow the House to call the government to account, through *urgent questions* (formerly called 'private notice questions' because they are applied for to the Speaker privately rather than being printed on the Order Paper). If the Speaker thinks a matter is sufficiently urgent or important, and there is unlikely to be another way of raising it in the House in the next day or so, he allows a question to be put to a minister (often by the Opposition spokesman on the subject) at the end of Question Time. Although ministerial statements are made voluntarily by the government, urgent questions are granted when in the Speaker's view the House needs to be informed but no ministerial statement is forthcoming. Urgent questions are described in more detail in Chapter 10 (page 300).

The Speaker also has the power to decide whether *a complaint of privilege* – in other words, an allegation that an MP, or a servant of the House, or perhaps a select committee, has been obstructed or threatened. Such an allegation must be made privately to the Speaker – a procedure designed to prevent frivolous complaints. If the Speaker believes that there may be grounds for action, he allows the matter to take precedence over other business and a motion to be moved referring the complaint to the Committee on Standards and Privileges for investigation. Such complaints are increasingly rare. Privilege is described in more detail in Chapter 6 (page 164).

The casting vote

Once put to the vote in the House, a matter must be decided; it cannot be left as a draw. If the numbers of 'ayes' and 'noes' are equal, then the occupant of the Chair must decide the question by casting a vote; and it is only on these occasions that the Speaker or his deputies do vote. However, the Chair is protected from controversy by clearly established historical principles. These are, broadly, that a decision should be taken by a majority of the House, not just on the basis of a casting vote; and that there should be opportunity for further discussion. Thus the Chair will vote 'aye' on a casting vote on the second reading of a bill, because the bill can continue its progress and be amended if the House wishes. But the Chair will vote 'no' if the vote on the third reading is tied, because that is the moment at which the Commons approves the bill, and the law should not be changed except by a majority of the House. If the vote is on a motion for the adjournment, the Chair votes 'no' in order to allow the House to proceed with other business.

In the Thatcher and the Blair years, big government majorities made the need for casting votes much less (although on issues of conscience, or unwhipped votes on private members' bills the possibility was always there;

and it is worth remembering that the 80 percent elected/20 percent appointed House of Lords option was defeated only by 284 votes to 281 on 4 February 2003). However, when the government has a small majority the more likely is the need for a casting vote; it was used seven times between 1974 and 1979. It was almost needed when the Callaghan government fell as a result of losing a vote of confidence on the night of 28 March 1979; 311 MPs voted against the government, and 310 for.

Had the casting vote been needed then, it would have been 'no' on the principle that the decision had to be taken by a majority and not on a casting vote. But so clear is the principle that, even in the greatest political controversy, there is no question of political bias. The most recent casting vote is a good example. On 22 July 1993 the House was voting on the Leader of the Opposition's amendment to a motion on the Social Protocol of the Maastricht Treaty. The votes were 317 ayes and 317 noes. Speaker Boothroyd voted 'no' on the basis that the decision should be taken only by a majority. The government lost the vote on the motion itself and put a motion of confidence before the House the next day, which it won comfortably, without the need for a casting vote.

Recalling the House

It occasionally happens that because of some grave event the House is recalled during a recess (as it was on three occasions in 2001 following the 11 September attacks in the USA, on 3 April 2002 following the death of the Queen Mother, and again on 24 September 2002 to debate possible action against Iraq), the media normally report that it is the Prime Minister who has recalled Parliament. In fact, the standing orders provide that ministers may represent to the Speaker that the public interest requires an earlier meeting of the House; and, if the Speaker agrees, he appoints a time for the House to sit. This may be a distinction that is not much of a difference because, following precedent, the Speaker always agrees to the government's request. However, the Iraq crisis has given rise to concern in some quarters about the role of Parliament at a time of international tension, and to pressure for the Speaker to have the power to recall the House regardless of the views of the government. The Procedure Committee has now recommended that the decision should be one for the Speaker alone.

Statutory and other functions

The Speaker is *ex officio* chairman of each of the Boundary Commissions mentioned in Chapter 2, although the work falls to the other members, led by a High Court judge (or Scottish equivalent). This function will end if the responsibilities of the Boundary Commissions are transferred to the new Electoral Commission set up under the Political Parties, Elections and

Referendums Act 2000. The Speaker also chairs the Speaker's Committee, which oversees the funding of the Electoral Commission.

The most important and time-consuming of the Speaker's statutory responsibilities is as chairman of the House of Commons Commission, which is the financial and employing authority for the House administration, and whose work we describe on page 54.

The voice of the House

The Speaker's role as official spokesman of the Commons to the monarch may survive only in ceremonial form, but the core of his job is still protecting and expressing the interests of the House. He protects the interests of the House through securing orderly proceedings, the courtesies of debate, and consistent and fair rulings on points of order and matters of contention. Expressing the interests of the House is more complex and potentially more politically exposed, as it centres upon the House's relationship with the government of the day. The Speaker can grant urgent questions, select unwelcome amendments, allow questions to run on, and ensure that a wide spectrum of opinion is called in debate if this helps Parliament better to air issues and hold the government to account.

One key area on which both Speaker Boothroyd and Speaker Martin have expressed strong views is what Speaker Martin has described as 'the fundamental importance for the proper functioning of Parliament that this House is the first to hear of important developments in government policy'. This is a sensitive area; governments of both political parties have wanted to set the media agenda outside the House, to brief selected journalists, perhaps to prepare public opinion for unwelcome news. But if Parliament is to be the focus of national attention, then, whether the news is momentous or not, the principle that the nation's representatives in Parliament are told first is an important one; and the Speaker must be its main advocate.

Precedent and change

Precedent provides the framework within which any Speaker operates. It is a powerful ally in making rulings robust against challenge and – as with casting votes – emphasising the impartiality of the Chair. But no Speaker can simply rest on precedent. Parliament is constantly changing, not only internally in terms of its membership and political complexion but also in terms of the influences and pressures upon it. There are always new problems and situations with which a Speaker must grapple, and set new precedents in the process. These may be as far-reaching as the procedures adopted by Speaker Brand in the 1870s and 1880s to deal with the Irish Home Rule MPs who were obstructing the House's business; before his unilateral action to limit MPs' rights to speak with the introduction of the closure, members could speak for as long as they liked on any question before the House. More often, changes come about almost imperceptibly as a result of a series of Speaker's rulings.

The Speaker works closely with the Clerk of the House and the Clerk's senior colleagues; he draws on their professional knowledge and long experience and has the political and professional advice of often highly experienced deputies. But the decisions are for him alone. Members may criticise the Speaker only by putting down a substantive motion for debate; if such a motion is not withdrawn, the government quickly finds time for a debate in order to resolve the matter. The fact that only three such motions have actually been debated since the Second World War suggests that, despite the fact that they exercise a great deal of power in a politically highly contentious House, Speakers do a pretty good job.

The Deputy Speakers

The Speaker is assisted by three deputies – the Chairman of Ways and Means and two Deputy Chairmen. They are senior back-benchers who are appointed by the House for the duration of the parliament, normally all at the same time on the first business day of a new parliament, and in a far less elaborate way than the Speaker is chosen; after informal soundings have been taken, a motion to appoint them appears in the name of the Prime Minister or the Leader of the House. This rather informal procedure has answered well enough for many years, although in April 2002 the Procedure Committee recommended a more formal approach with wider consultation.

The Chairman of Ways and Means is so called because from the late seventeenth century he presided over the Committee of Ways and Means (dealing with taxation) as well as the Committee of Supply (dealing with government expenditure), at that time the only two permanent committees of the House. It was not until 1853 that the Chairman began formally to deputise for the Speaker.

Today the Chairman of Ways and Means exercises most of the powers of the Speaker in the Chamber (and has the power to select amendments in Committee of the whole House, when the Speaker never presides). The Chairman also has three other distinct roles. He oversees the consideration of private bills (as distinct from private members' bills) (see page 224); he supervises arrangements for sittings in Westminster Hall (see page 268); and through his chairmanship of the Chairmen's Panel (see page 193) he has general responsibility for the work of legislative standing committees. From 1902, a Deputy Chairman of Ways and Means was appointed, and a Second

Deputy Chairman from 1971. They exercise the same powers in the Chamber as the Chairman of Ways and Means. No decision of any of the three may be appealed to the Speaker.

The three Deputy Speakers come from both sides of the House and, together with the Speaker, cancel out the loss of numbers from government and opposition sides of the House. Thus Speaker Martin came from the government (Labour) side; Sir Alan Haselhurst, the Chairman of Ways and Means, from the opposition (Conservative) side; Sylvia Heal, the First Deputy Chairman, from the government side; and Sir Michael Lord, the Second Deputy Chairman, from the opposition side. The deputies are rigidly impartial in the Chair and other House duties, and they do not vote (except to resolve a tied vote). However, unlike the Speaker they remain members of their parties, and they fight general elections on a party basis.

The Speaker and the deputies have a rota of duty in the Chair; normally the Speaker takes the first two hours, disposing of Question Time, one or more ministerial statements thereafter, and any points of order before the main business of the day begins. The deputies do stints of two hours or so, although the Speaker may return to preside over the end of the main business and any votes that take place.

In 2002, the Procedure Committee attempted a job description for the deputies:

> an ability swiftly to command the respect of the whole House . . . a demonstrable knowledge of procedure and its application, as well as wider experience of the House and the way it works, together with an ability to chair the most challenging debates with demonstrable fairness and authority . . . a good team player. An appetite for hard work, unremitting punctuality and a sense of humour and proportion are also highly desirable.

The Leader of the House

The Leader of the House of Commons is a key figure in both government and Parliament. He or she is a cabinet minister as well as an MP; but although the Leader has collective Cabinet responsibility for defending the government's policies in the House, he or she also has the wider task of upholding the rights and interests of the House. With the Chief Whip, the Leader is responsible for the arrangement of government business in the Commons, and for planning and supervising the government's legislative programme as a whole by chairing the Cabinet Committee on the Legislative Programme (known as LP).

He or she has an extensive power base in government through membership of some of the most important Cabinet committees and sub-committees, including those on domestic affairs, economic affairs, environment, local government, public services, international terrorism and European issues. The Leader of the House has normally also been President of the Council and ministerial head of the Privy Council Office, which supports the Privy Council in advising the Queen on various prerogative functions and which deals with the affairs of some 400 bodies incorporated by Royal Charter, and with regulatory bodies for many of the professions. When Peter Hain was appointed Leader of the House in 2003, he also kept his previous job as Secretary of State for Wales; Lord Williams of Mostyn, the Leader of the House of Lords, became President of the Council, as did his successor Baroness Amos.

Following the Labour victory in the 1997 general election, a Select Committee on the Modernisation of the House of Commons was appointed (see page 320) and has been chaired by successive Leaders of the House: Ann Taylor and Margaret Beckett, and then by Robin Cook, who has been particularly closely associated with the process of parliamentary and constitutional change. When Robin Cook resigned in March 2003 over the government's policy towards Iraq, his place was taken briefly by Dr John Reid, and then by Peter Hain.

The Leader reports weekly to Cabinet on forthcoming parliamentary business. He announces that business – firm for the following week, provisional for the week after – to the House every Thursday, an event that emphasises the control that the government of the day has over the time of the House of Commons. He also answers oral questions once a month on his wider responsibilities as Leader.

The Leader usually moves (and defends) motions to determine how Commons business is to be dealt with, or to introduce procedural change, and often winds up at the end of major debates on behalf of the government. He also plays a role in House administration as an *ex officio* member of the House of Commons Commission and as the minister responsible for the Members Estimate (see page 68).

The Clerk of the House

The Clerk of the House of Commons – from January 2003 Roger Sands – is the House's senior official and combines a variety of roles. He is the House's adviser on all aspects of parliamentary procedure, practice and privilege, the editor of *Erskine May* and a frequent witness before Procedure Committees. He is the Speaker's right hand on a wide range of issues but is also available to advise any Member of the House. He is Chief Executive of the House Service, chairs the Board of Management, which is responsible for providing the services that support the work of the House, its committees and its members, and is the principal adviser to the House of Commons Commission. He is accounting officer for the House of Commons Administration Estimate and the Members Estimate and so is personally responsible for the propriety and economy of expenditure. He is the House's corporate officer and so formally holds property and enters into contracts on the House's behalf, and is legally responsible for the actions of the House Administration. He is also the professional head of the Clerk's Department, which is the part of the House Service most closely concerned with the work of the House and its committees.

It may seem strange that the Clerk combines the somewhat academic precision of procedural matters with overall responsibility for the management of the House's services. In fact it would be strange if he were not to do so. He is the authority on all aspects of the House's core business – not just the drier matters of procedure – and no one is in a better position to understand from long experience how the main functions of the House need to be supported and how they can be made more effective.

The first known Clerk of the House – formally styled 'Under-Clerk of the Parliaments, to wait upon the Commons' – was appointed in 1363, and there has been an unbroken line since then. The title 'Clerk' probably derives from the fact that in early mediaeval times literacy was by no means universal and was most widely found among priests, or clerks in holy orders. The Clerk of the House is appointed by the Queen by letters patent (as is the Clerk Assistant), which emphasises his independence.

The House Service

The permanent staff of the House (some 1,500 people[1]) are not civil servants but employees of the House of Commons Commission. This distinction may not be of great importance for those staff who are responsible for the upkeep of the buildings or for catering services, but for many it is of constitutional importance. The clerk of a departmental select committee who manages a committee's inquiry into something that has gone wrong within government and then has to draft a report strongly critical of ministers and civil servants would face an intolerable conflict of loyalties if he or she owed allegiance to the Civil Service. To take another example, analysis prepared by the subject experts in the library's research services is expected to be rigorous regardless of the possibility that their findings may not be palatable to the government of the day.

The House Service must also be politically impartial. Again, this is more important in some areas of work than in others. Staff in the Clerk's Department may find themselves in quick succession advising both government and opposition on procedural tactics for highly contentious business in the House, or within the space of a few minutes advising both the member in charge of a private member's bill and those MPs who want to scupper its chances of proceeding any further. If they are to retain the confidence of MPs, it is essential for their credibility that clerks giving that advice are seen to be absolutely impartial as to both parties and issues.

The House administration

The administration of the House of Commons is fairly complex. This is not surprising; on the one hand, it has to deliver a wide range of disparate services, from regilding Pugin decoration in a Grade I listed building to supporting select committee work, which covers every aspect of public life, to producing overnight a record of all the proceedings in the House and in Westminster Hall. On the other hand, professional management and planning must take into account the changing, and not always consistent, wishes of MPs as well as the unpredictable pressures on Parliament itself.

A 1999 review of the way the House services were run summed up the problem.

> The effective operation of the House is of enormous constitutional and public importance. The elector (and taxpayer) expects Governments to be held to account; constituents to be represented and their grievances pursued; and historic Parliamentary functions to be extended and adapted to changes in the wider world.
>
> These things do not come cheap, and no-one should expect them to. Seeking to hold to account a complex, sophisticated and powerful Executive; dealing with an unremitting burden of legislation; and meeting ever-increasing expectations on the part of constituents; all this requires substantial, high-quality support. . . .
>
> There is no shortage of complicating factors. Each Member of Parliament is an expert on what he or she wants from the system, and what the system should provide. With their staffs, Members are in effect 659 small businesses operating independently within one institutional framework. Managers in both the public and private sectors have to meet the needs of demanding customers; but they do not have customers every one of whom can take a complaint to the Floor of the House of Commons – perhaps televised nation-wide.
>
> At the same time the House and its Members are funded by the taxpayer. This spending is inevitably high-profile, exposed to media interest which is not always friendly and which may not pause to assess the wider value of Parliamentary expenditure. The House must be able to demonstrate proper stewardship of public money, and to show that expenditure is efficient, effective and economical.

That is the task facing the House administration.

The House of Commons Commission

The Commission is the supervisory body of the administration, responsible for the House's finances and the employer of almost all its staff. Set up under the House of Commons (Administration) Act 1978, it is chaired by the Speaker; its other members are the Leader of the House, a member nominated by the Leader of the Opposition (in practice, always the Shadow Leader of the House), and three senior back-benchers, one from each of the main parties. The Commission operates in a wholly non-party way; in any event, it has never had a majority of government members.

The Commission meets monthly. Its meetings are private, usually with senior staff who are responsible for the subject under discussion; but it posts its minutes on the Internet and also publishes an annual report that is a mine of information about the activities of the House administration, its plans and performance. The Commission deals with a wide variety of subjects. At its January 2003 meeting, for example, it considered among other things its response to the report of the Wicks Committee on MPs' standards of conduct, the House's retailing and merchandising activities, and priorities for information technology investment. One member of the Commission acts as its spokesman and answers written parliamentary questions on its behalf, as well as oral questions in the Chamber once a month.

Strategic planning

The House of Commons may not have a mission statement, but the House administration is subject to normal public sector disciplines. Each year the Commission approves a five-year corporate business plan for the administration. There are four core tasks: supporting the House and its committees; supporting individual MPs and their staff; providing information and access to the public; and maintaining the heritage of buildings, objects and documents. These core tasks are supplemented by objectives covering governance, value for money, flexibility, good working environments, the use of information and communications technologies (ICT), and so on. The tasks and objectives are the framework for a wide range of projects and plans, with specific objectives and milestones, in the more detailed corporate business plan.

The Board of Management

Responsibility for running the House services, and for employing staff, is delegated by the Commission to the Board of Management. This consists of the heads of all the House departments, plus the Clerk of Committees as a representative of the Clerk's Department so that the Clerk of the House himself can take an overall view as Chairman of the Board and Chief Executive.

The Board is supported by the Office of the Clerk, which acts as a corporate office as well as the Board's secretariat. Four groups of senior officials work under the Board's direction on business planning, human resources, information technology and information for the public.

The Finance and Services Committee

On most matters involving significant expenditure, the Commission is advised by the Finance and Services Committee (F&S), which is a select committee of Members chaired by a member of the Commission. F&S also considers the House's three-year expenditure plans and the six-year corporate business plan before these go to the Commission for approval.

The domestic committees

Four 'domestic committees', also select committees of MPs, on accommodation and works, administration, catering and information, together with the Broadcasting Committee, have the task of reflecting the views of MPs generally in the planning and provision of services. Their role is not executive, but to advise the Commission and the Speaker.

The Audit Committee

This consists of two members of the Commission (one as chairman) and two external members. Its has general oversight of internal audit and review, with emphasis on achieving value for money; it advises the Clerk of the House in the exercise of his responsibilities as accounting officer, and on the programme of internal audit; and it has the task of encouraging best financial practice, use of resources and governance in the House administration. It reports annually to the Commission, and its report is published with the Commission's own annual report. The National Audit Office are the House's external auditors.

The House departments

For reasons of good governance and economy, the House administration must seek to operate as a corporate whole. There are also issues such as financial planning, the use of accommodation, ICT, health and safety, data protection, human resources and so on that can be dealt with effectively only across the board. However, both their historical origins and the specialised nature of the services they provide mean that the individual House departments have distinct characters and roles.

The Clerk's Department

The Clerk of the House and some senior members of his department are perhaps the most visible of all the House staff; in television coverage of the Chamber they are seen sitting at the Table of the House in front of the Speaker, dressed as a QC would be in court: court coat, wing collar (but with a white tie rather than barrister's bands), wig and gown. Their task there is to advise the Chair, ministers, whips and any other MP on the business the House is transacting; to record the decisions the House has taken (but not what has been said, which is taken down by the *Hansard* reporters in the gallery above them) and to help to conduct votes. The Clerks at the Table have other roles as well, usually as head of one of the offices of the department.

The *Committee Office* provides the secretariat of each investigative select committee and contains more than half of the 280 staff in the department. The *Legislation Service* deals with primary and secondary legislation on its passage through the House and provides the secretariat for legislative scrutiny committees. The *Overseas Office* represents the House overseas and provides secretariats for delegations to international assemblies. The *Journal Office* advises on parliamentary privilege and procedure generally and compiles the daily permanent legal record of proceedings. The *Table Office* prepares the Order Paper and processes parliamentary questions; and the *Vote Office* is responsible for the provision of official papers to MPs. The department also contains the *Legal Services Office*, the *Broadcasting Unit*, concerned with televising and archiving proceedings, and the *Parliamentary Office of Science and Technology*, which provides advice on scientific and technological issues to members of both Houses.

The Serjeant at Arms's Department

The first recorded Serjeant at Arms was given office by King Henry V in 1415, the year of the Battle of Agincourt. In previous centuries he was responsible for carrying out orders of the House, including making arrests; the splendid silver gilt Mace that the present Serjeant carries in the Speaker's Procession every day, and which then lies upon the Table while the House is sitting, was in times past a necessary symbol of the House's authority outside the precincts.

Today the Serjeant at Arms heads the largest Commons Department, of some 400 staff, together with a substantial security force. He is responsible for order inside the precincts, in the galleries of the Chamber and committee rooms, and for the security of the Commons part of the parliamentary estate. His *Operations Directorate* is also concerned with housekeeping, mail, car parking, visitor tours and other services. The *Parliamentary Estates Directorate* serves both Houses and is responsible for the preservation and strategic management of the parliamentary estate. The *Parliamentary Works Services Directorate* also serves both Houses and provides maintenance, engineering, furnishing and horticultural services. The *Parliamentary Communications Directorate* provides ICT services to both the Lords and the Commons and is responsible for the Parliamentary data and video network, which runs throughout the estate but can also be accessed from MPs' constituencies, and which provides a wide variety of on-line services. We look in greater detail at the use of ICT in Parliament in Chapter 13 (page 380).

The Library

Although the grand rooms running along the river front of the palace may seem reminiscent of the sort of Victorian library we mentioned in Chapter 1, the modern House of Commons Library, with more than 200 staff, is a very different institution. As well as offering the reference facilities one might expect, it also provides MPs with high-quality, impartial, research and information services.

The researchers are highly qualified, and their work is respected both inside and outside the House. When a member says in the Chamber 'the Library have told me', what they have said is unlikely to be challenged. Library staff undertake research in response to specific requests from MPs, as well as producing research papers on bills and other current issues. This research back-up is highly valued by MPs, and especially by opposition spokespeople in shadowing ministers, when the latter can call upon the extensive resources of government departments.

The Library is also a source of information for the public through the House of Commons Information Office, which answers queries by telephone and e-mail, and the Parliamentary Education Unit, which provides educational material and school tours on behalf of both Houses (see page 419).

Other departments

More commonly known as *Hansard*, the *Department of the Official Report* (110 staff) records what is said in the Chamber, in Westminster Hall and in standing committees, together with the answers to written parliamentary questions (some 20,000 pages a year) (see page 301). *Hansard* is substantially a verbatim report; repetitions and obvious mistakes are corrected, but the editor strongly resists any attempt by an MP, no matter how senior, to make any change of substance. The *Department of Finance and Administration* (140 staff) is responsible for the pay and allowances of MPs and provides financial, payroll, personnel, health and safety, and internal review services for the House administration as a whole. Finally, the *Refreshment Department*

(300 staff) supplies more than 1,300,000 meals each year across the Commons part of the Parliamentary Estate.

Services shared between the Lords and the Commons

The House administrations of the Commons and Lords are constitutionally separate, but they work jointly, or share services, when it makes sense to do so, for example on estates and works, communications, information systems, records, ceremonial, security, visitors and educational work. Costs are apportioned between the Houses, usually on a 60:40 Commons: Lords basis. In areas where each House has distinct needs, there is nevertheless informal consultation and cooperation.

MPs' pay, allowances and staff

MPs' pay

Members of Parliament were first paid in 1911. Ever since, their pay levels have been controversial, not least because MPs are one of the few groups of people who can in effect set their own salaries. However, in order to provide an objective assessment, pay and allowances have, since 1970, been referred to an outside organisation, now the Senior Salaries Review Body. The SSRB bases its recommendations on general principles: that pay should not be so low as to deter or so high as to make it the main attraction; that, although some MPs take on work outside Parliament, pay should be at a level reflecting the full-time job that it is for most MPs; that there should be no compensation for job insecurity or reflection of length of service; and that there should be a clear distinction between pay and expenses.

Starting in 2000, the SSRB now reviews MPs' pay every three years. Upratings between these reviews are linked to changes in the pay of senior civil servants. In recommending pay levels, the SSRB takes into account the pay of people with a similar 'job weight'; it equates the job of an MP with, for example, a director in a district general hospital, the head teacher of a large secondary school, a chief superintendent of police, or a lieutenant-colonel commanding a battalion. In its 2000 review, the SSRB found that, at the 2000 figure of £48,371, the pay of MPs had fallen behind their comparators' average of £54,000, and it recommended an increase of £2,000 a year as well as the annual upratings. An MP's salary now (2003) stands at £55,118. Ministers are paid on top of their parliamentary salaries: the Prime Minister gets an additional £116,436, a cabinet minister £69,861, a minister of state £36,240 and a junior minister £27,506.

MPs' allowances

These are also based on SSRB reviews, but again it is the House that effectively decides their levels. Following the House's approval in July 2001 of SSRB recommendations, the old all-in-one office costs allowance was phased out and specific allowances introduced. These are a significantly increased *staffing allowance* of between £61,980 and £72,310 a year (depending on the extent to which staff work in London), allowing MPs to employ up to three staff; an *incidental expenses provision* of £18,234 a year, mainly to cover the costs of constituency offices; and an *additional costs allowance* of £19,722 a year to cover the costs of staying away from home while at Westminster. In addition, MPs have free travel throughout the UK while on parliamentary business, a generous motor mileage allowance (54.4p per mile for the first 20,000 miles a year and 25.1p per mile thereafter). Three visits a year to EU institutions or the national parliaments of EU member states or candidate countries are also paid for. IT equipment (three PCs, a laptop and two printers/scanners) is provided by the House for parliamentary business.

These allowances (the staff and office elements total some £90,000 a year) are in real terms eighteen times the level of the first allowance of £500 a year introduced in 1969. They are nevertheless lower than those for the European Parliament or the German parliament but significantly higher than those for the devolved assemblies. Members of the Scottish Parliament may claim up to £49,300 for staff and office costs; members of the National Assembly for Wales £52,200, and members of the Northern Ireland Assembly £36,578. The SSRB based its recommendations for Westminster on evidence of greatly increased constituency caseloads needing more staff time, and the fact that many more MPs had constituency offices to deal more effectively with constituency matters, maintaining a local presence close to local issues and often providing direct access to the public.

The driver for these allowances is thus to allow MPs to provide a better service to their constituents, but it is no surprise that the level of allowances and salary comes in for routine criticism in the media. Particular prominence was given to the additional costs allowance in February 2003, when a member was found by the Standards and Privileges Committee to have been 'muddled and naive' in wrongly claiming a total of some £90,000 on this allowance, and it recommended his suspension from the House for two weeks. The member concerned had paid back the money and announced that he would not stand at the next election, but the Parliamentary Commissioner for Standards also recommended tightening up on the checks and auditing of allowances. In October 2003, allegations by an investigative journalist that the Leader of the Opposition had improperly paid his wife from the staffing allowance resulted in an inquiry by the Parliamentary Commissioner for Standards.

MPs' staff

MPs are the employers of their staff, although staff are paid centrally by the House administration and are hired on standard contracts. There is no one pattern of the way an MP uses staff, and there are many permutations.

Some MPs, particularly those with a heavy constituency caseload, base all their staff in the constituency. This makes practical sense; as the March 2001 SSRB report pointed out, staff in constituency offices can network more easily with local agencies and make arrangements for surgeries, visits and so on more conveniently, and staff costs are lower outside London. Others, especially London members, whose constituencies are not far away have all their staff at Westminster (where they also have the advantage of free accommodation and other services). In the country as a whole, staff are split about one-third at Westminster and two-thirds in constituencies.

The types of people that MPs employ, and what they expect from them, vary from member to member, reflecting the fact that there is no standard way of doing the job of an MP. Some need caseworkers; some need a PA to organise a diary and act as their right hand; others need researchers to support work on their specialist subjects; yet others need a 'deputy MP' in the constituency, someone they can trust to handle their local profile and press relations, combined with a sure touch on constituency cases.

Opposition front-benchers have a particular need for specialist support because they are taking on ministers who can draw on the non-party-political but nevertheless substantial resources of government departments. Sometimes MPs pool their staff; for example, in opposition the Conservative Party established its own parliamentary research unit of a dozen or so graduates who researched topics in depth on request from subscribing MPs. Opposition front-benchers are also heavy users of the independent researchers in the House of Commons Library.

An appreciable number of MPs have worked at Westminster before winning a seat of their own, and a post as a researcher is a recognised apprenticeship in a political career. But it is also not unusual to find staff who do not identify fully with their MP's political views and see themselves as servants of the constituency as much as of a party politician.

Some, especially the traditional secretary or PA, spend much of their working lives in the job. For others, such as the 'interns' on the US model, working for an MP may be more for the experience than the pay, as a prelude to a career in a different field. A few universities now have a sandwich year as a formal part of a politics degree.

Just as the use made of staff varies, so too does its effectiveness. Having personal staff is a new experience for many newly elected MPs. Some take to it readily and use staff to add real value to their work. A few allow researchers to operate with a good deal of independence, which sometimes gives rise to criticisms that these are surrogate members pursuing their own agendas and encouraging MPs to commission Library research or table questions that are more for the benefit of researcher than member.

Finance for opposition parties

'Short money': parties in the House of Commons

Since 1975, there has been financial support for opposition parties in the Commons (often called 'Short money', after Edward Short, Leader of the House at the time) to go some way towards redressing the imbalance between the support available to opposition parties and that available to the government through the Civil Service. In order to qualify, a party must have at least two MPs – or one MP provided that the party also polled 150,000 votes nationwide. In either case, the MPs must have been elected for their party at the previous general election, which disqualifies new party groupings formed in the current parliament from claiming financial support.

There are three categories of support: the basic funding established in 1975; travel and associated expenses, introduced in 1993; and support for the Leader of the Opposition's office, which began in 1999. All are uprated annually in line with the retail price index. The current amounts for basic funding are £11,411.45 per MP and £22.79 for every 200 votes cast for the party in the last general election. On this basis, in 2002–03 the Conservative Party was entitled to £2,846,649 (166 MPs and 41,788 times 200 votes). Basic funding for the Liberal Democrats (52 MPs and 24,064 times 200 votes) was £1,141,814).

For travel and associated expenses, in 2002–03 the sum of £125,352 was divided between all the parties claiming, in the same proportions as their amounts of basic funding. Support for the Leader of the Opposition's office was £531,621 for the year.

For each party in 2002–03, the grand totals were: Conservatives (including the Leader of the Opposition's office), £3,459,536; Liberal Democrats, £1,174,410; Scottish National Party, £113,092; Plaid Cymru £69,897; Ulster Unionist Party £95,832; Democratic Unionist Party £80,017; and Social Democratic and Labour Party £55,112.

The basic funding may be used only for parliamentary business, which includes research to support shadow ministers and their work, and developing and communicating alternative policies. The money may not be used for political campaigning, fund raising or membership drives. Each party has to produce an auditor's certificate every year that the money has been spent only on parliamentary business.

Opposition salaries

Six opposition members in the two Houses receive a salary by virtue of the posts they hold. In the Commons, the Leader of the Opposition gets £65,482 a year, and his Lords counterpart receives £65,936. In the Commons, the Opposition Chief Whip gets £37,055 and his deputy £23,847. In the Lords, the Leader of the Opposition receives £65,936 and the Opposition Chief Whip £60,972 a year.

Why subsidise the opposition?

It may seem reasonable for a taxpayer to say: 'I'm prepared to fund hospitals, or the education system; but why should I pay for party politicians?' Fair enough; but there is a powerful counter-argument. Ministers are not allowed to use their civil servants for overtly party political purposes, although they can still use the huge resources of their departments to research, develop and present new policies. But no government has a monopoly of truth and right. It must surely be to the advantage of the country as a whole when opposition parties have the resources to test and challenge those policies in a reasoned, well-researched way, and to put forward credible alternative proposals.

This was recognised in the Political Parties, Elections and Referendums Act 2000, which made provision for 'policy development grants'. The Electoral Commission is now developing a scheme for distributing those grants, which will initially be worth a total of £2 million a year.

State funding for political parties?

More generally, the extent to which the non-parliamentary activities of political parties should be publicly funded remains contentious. The present combined membership of the Labour and Conservative parties is about 600,000, or about 3 percent of those who actually voted for those parties in the low turnout of the 2001 election (and down from a total of about 800,000 at the time of the 1997 election). So the ability of major parties to fund themselves from their membership is declining. This inevitably makes them readier to look to major donations by wealthy individuals; but these in turn give rise to suspicions of peddling influence and politicians in hock to vested interests (despite the degree of disclosure required by the Political Parties, Elections and Referendums Act 2000).

On the other hand, there is considerable opposition in some quarters to the state funding of *all* the activities of political parties (in contrast to the parliamentary functions of challenge referred to above). And there are also the arguments that state funding tends to make recipient parties complacent and – because the obvious way of setting levels is to base them on the previous election results – that it over-rewards those who do well. So, despite the 1998 recommendation of the Committee on Standards in Public Life that donations to parties should be tax-deductible and the Labour Party's 2002 consultative document, there is no immediate prospect of an agreed way forward.

The House of Lords

The Lord Chancellor

The Speaker of the House of Lords is the Lord Chancellor but, important figure though he is, his role as presiding officer of the House of Lords is much more circumscribed than that of the Speaker of the House of Commons. Most of his duties lie elsewhere, for in him are combined functions relating not only to the legislature but also to the judiciary and executive – functions normally kept separate in other jurisdictions and in classical political theory.

The Lord Chancellor is first and foremost an appointee of the Prime Minister and a member of the Cabinet, heading a department responsible among other matters for the administration of the courts and tribunals, judicial appointments, constitutional and electoral matters, and justice. Only distinguished lawyers are appointed to the Lord Chancellorship because of the Lord Chancellor's second role as head of the judiciary and his function of presiding over the House of Lords when it sits in its special judicial capacity (a function he is able to perform only occasionally). His tasks as Speaker of the House of Lords are, on the whole, subsidiary to his work as a member of the government.

The Lord Chancellor's powers as Speaker are very limited indeed. The Lord Chancellor does not arbitrate on rules of order. The preservation of order in the House is the responsibility of all the Lords who are present, and any Lord may call the attention of the House to any breaches of order or laxity in observing its customs. If the House is in need of advice on matters of procedure and order, it is to the Leader of the House (also a government minister), rather than the Lord Chancellor, that they look. And the Leader – or in his absence, the government Chief Whip – will often intervene to interpret and give voice to what he considers to be the wish of the House when procedural difficulties occur.

The Lord Chancellor and Deputy Speakers do not call lords to speak. As we shall see on page 278, the order of speaking in debates is prearranged. Each item of the day's business set out on the Order Paper is called on by the Clerk at the Table. The Lord Chancellor or his deputies will call members to speak to their amendments when the House is considering legislation, but no one calls the subsequent speakers in a debate on an amendment. The Lord Chancellor cannot curtail debate, and when debate is concluded, his function is limited to putting the question – announcing what it is on which the Lords are about to vote – and then declaring the result of the vote. He votes just like any other Lord, and, if the vote is tied, he has no function – the standing orders of the House then govern the result.

The Lord Chancellor is empowered to recall the House of Lords whenever it stands adjourned if public interest requires it – for example, for the debate on the outbreak of the Falklands War in 1982 and following the terrorist attack on the World Trade Center in September 2001. But because of his position as a cabinet minister, there is no suggestion that the Lord Chancellor should be impartial. He speaks in debate in defence of government policy, and votes accordingly. With the agreement of the House, from time to time he represents it at conferences overseas. He also represents it on ceremonial occasions at home – for example when visiting heads of state address members of both Houses, on the opening of inter-parliamentary conferences meeting in the United Kingdom, or the presentation of Humble Addresses to the Queen. But unlike the Speaker in the Commons, the Lord Chancellor plays no part in the day-to-day administration of the House. That role is undertaken by the Chairman of Committees.

In June 2003, following the resignation of Lord Irvine of Lairg, who had been Lord Chancellor since the 1997 general election, the government announced its intention to reform the office so that the Lord Chancellor's roles of Speaker of the Lords, as a judge and head of the judiciary, and as a minister of the Crown, would become separate. The House of Lords would be asked to decide on a means of appointing its own Speaker; the Lord Chancellor would no longer sit judicially in the Lords; a Judicial Appointments Commission would undertake the function of making judicial appointments; and the Lord Chancellor's Department was renamed the Department for Constitutional Affairs, also acquiring overall responsibility for the Scotland and Wales Offices. The office of Lord Chancellor, it was envisaged, would eventually be abolished. (At the same time, the government announced its intention to establish a supreme court to replace the appellate function exercised by the law lords sitting in the House of Lords.)

In July 2003, the House set up a select committee to consider the question of the Speakership. Meanwhile, Lord Falconer of Thoroton, the new Lord

Chancellor, continues to sit as Speaker but has announced that he will not sit judicially.

The Chairman of Committees, Deputy Speakers and deputy chairmen

The Lord Chancellor normally presides at the beginning of business each day, and he returns to the Chamber to preside over the House when it votes. But for the rest of the time a panel of Deputy Speakers sit on the Woolsack.

The principal Deputy Speaker is the Chairman of Committees, a member of the House who is appointed by the House at the beginning of every session to take the chair in all Committees of the Whole House. The Chairman of Committees is a very influential figure in the Lords and is paid the salary of a minister of state in consequence. He organises the panel of deputy speakers and deputy chairmen and assigns them their duties week by week. He has considerable powers in the field of private legislation (see page 224) by selecting opposed private bill committees and himself presiding over unopposed bill committees. During the nineteenth century – the heyday of private legislation – this gave the holder of the post immense power and influence over many of the greatest public works projects of the day. This aspect of his work takes up far less of the Chairman of Committees' time today.

Indeed, most of his work is now concerned with the administration of the House. It is he who chairs the House Committee – broadly the Lords equivalent of the House of Commons Commission – and the Select Committee on Administration and Works, which is described below. The Chairman of Committees also chairs the Liaison Committee, which meets from time to time to review and allocate resources to the policy select committees of the House, and also the Procedure Committee. Such is his prominence in the life of the House that he often acts as its representative at international conferences in place of the Lord Chancellor.

The Leader of the House of Lords

Like the Leader of the Commons, the Leader of the House of Lords is a cabinet minister, usually holding a non-departmental office like that of Lord Privy Seal. Her allegiance is to the government and its policies, but she too has a wider task of upholding the rights and interests of the House as a whole. It is the Leader of the House, for example, who assists the House in keeping its own order during proceedings; who determines whether or not a private notice question is of sufficient urgency to be taken; and who makes representations on behalf of the House on such matters as members' allowances.

She works closely with the Leader of the House of Commons in planning and supervising the government's legislative programme; she is a member of the Legislative Programme Committee of the Cabinet; and she reports to the Cabinet itself on business in the Lords. She is responsible for delivering the government's business in the House, although most of the planning of this is done on her behalf by the Government Chief Whip and in particular by the Chief Whip's private secretaries. These private secretaries, who are clerks on secondment to the Cabinet Office, also assist the Leader of the House in her parliamentary work.

Much of the Leader's influence is exerted behind the scenes, for example through meetings of the business managers (as the Leaders and government Chief Whips of the two Houses are known). Within the Lords, she secures agreement on matters relating to the business of the House and other matters by discussions with other party leaders. Similar negotiations are held by the Chief Whip with other party whips. As in the Commons, these contacts are known as the usual channels. They are entirely informal and by their very nature devoid of any ground rules save perhaps one – that a deal struck through 'the usual channels' will normally stick. The Leader of the House, together with other party leaders, sits on all key decision making bodies within the House – like the House Committee, the Liaison Committee and the Procedure Committee.

The former Leader of the House, Lord Williams of Mostyn, also took an interest in the modernisation of working methods. In the 2001–02 session, he chaired a working group on the working of the House, many of whose recommendations on sitting hours, question time, legislative procedure, committee work and other matters have already been implemented.

The Clerk of the Parliaments and the staff of the House

The most senior official of the House of Lords is the Clerk of the Parliaments. Like the Clerk of the House of Commons he combines a variety of roles. He is the principal adviser to the House on all aspects of parliamentary practice and procedure, and the daily business of the House proceeds on the basis of briefs prepared by the clerks in the procedural offices. But he also has wide administrative responsibilities as Chief Executive of the service of the House – a pre-eminence derived from his position as accounting officer for money spent under the two Lords Requests for Resources (formerly Votes), and as the employer of all House of Lords staff under the Clerk of the Parliaments Act 1824 and the Parliamentary Corporate Bodies Act 1992. The 1992 Act makes the Clerk of the Parliaments corporate officer of the House of Lords, and in this capacity he gives the House legal personality and enters into contracts on its behalf. He is also Registrar of the Court when the House sits judicially, and signs its Orders. The Clerk of the Parliaments is appointed by the Crown under letters patent, usually from among the longer-serving clerks of the House, following advertisement and interview by the party leaders. His immediate deputies, the Clerk Assistant and the Reading Clerk, are appointed by the Lord Chancellor in a similar way.

Different offices of the House's administration deal with accounts, committees, legislation, human resources, the Journal of the House and public information, overseas business, the official report or *Hansard*, records, catering services, and the library. The Department of the Gentleman Usher of the Black Rod, to give him his full title, deals with accommodation, services and security, reflecting Black Rod's appointment as agent of the Administration and Works Committee. (Although principally a servant of the House like any other, Black Rod also has ceremonial duties within the palace – it fell to him to make the arrangements for the Lying in State of Queen Elizabeth the Queen Mother in April 2002 – and in connection with the Order of the Garter. In the past the post used to be offered to a retired senior member of the armed forces, but the present holder was appointed following public advertisement and interview.)

The total number of staff employed in these offices is about 400. This figure excludes staff in services shared with the Commons – in the Parliamentary Works Services Directorate, the Parliamentary Estates Directorate and the Parliamentary Communications Directorate (all of which are part of the Serjeant at Arms's Department) and the security staff contracted to both Houses from the Metropolitan Police.

House of Lords administration

The chief decision-making body in the administration of the Lords is the House Committee, a select committee of twelve members, including the Leader of the House and other party leaders and the Convenor of the Cross Bench Peers. The Clerk of the Parliaments and Black Rod also attend. Other senior officers attend as required. The committee's role is to determine strategy, to take major policy decisions, especially financial decisions not previously authorised, and to agree the annual estimates of expenditure. Its work is assisted by a management board of senior officers of the house. Both the House Committee and the management board meet monthly when the House is sitting, and their decisions are published on the Internet.

Four further domestic select committees – on administration and works, refreshments, information, and works of art – have responsibility for determining policy in those areas. But any decision requiring major expenditure requires the agreement of the House Committee. To the extent that the House of Lords has an equivalent to the House of Commons Commission, it is the House Committee.

These arrangements were introduced at the beginning of the 2002–03 session following a review by a working group chaired by the Chairman of Committees. They supplanted the former Select Committee on House of Lords Offices and its sub-committees. The House has also established an Audit Committee as part of the modernisation of its administrative arrangements.

Expenses

Members of the House of Lords are unpaid, in the sense that with the exception of certain office holders they do not receive a salary. But they do receive expenses and allowances of various kinds, the most significant of which are free travel to and from Westminster, an overnight and day subsistence allowance and a modest secretarial and office expenses allowance. The levels of these allowances are kept under review by the SSRB. The allowances are free of tax; if all are claimed they amount to £234 for every day of attendance, excluding the value of any travel expenses. This is not meant to amount to a full-time salary, so many members, particularly those below normal retirement age, have other jobs elsewhere. Having said that, if a member were to claim all his or her expenses having attended every sitting day of, say, a calendar year like 2000 he or she would now be eligible to receive £39,546.

Finance for political parties in the Lords: Cranborne money

For many years, the chief opposition parties in the Lords received funding from money made available from public funds to opposition parties in the Commons (see page 61). Since October 1996, the Official Opposition (currently the Conservative Party) and the second-largest party (the Liberal Democrat Party) have been provided with a separate allocation, funded by the House. Since 1999, the Convenor of the Cross Bench Peers has received similar funding to provide secretarial support. These sums are determined by resolution of the House and are uprated annually in line with inflation. With effect from 1 April 2003, the amounts available were £402,662 to the Official Opposition, £201,045 to the Liberal Democrats and £36,085 to the Convenor.

Paying for Parliament

The House of Commons

Perhaps rather surprisingly, the House of Commons is funded from two separate Estimates, or budgets of public expenditure (also called Accounts). The

House of Commons Administration Estimate pays for the staff of the House, the services supplied by all the House departments, and buildings, works, rates and energy costs. Unlike the rest of public spending, the government does not determine what the House's expenditure should be; the House of Commons Commission proposes an Estimate – after a lengthy planning process – and puts it directly to the House for approval.

However, the *Members Estimate*, which covers MPs' pay and allowances, is a government Estimate for which the Leader of the House is the responsible minister. Levels of pay and allowances are recommended by the SSRB, are put to the House by the government, and are then set following a free vote. MPs voting for increases above the SSRB recommendations (which has happened on occasion) inevitably comes in for criticism.

The House of Lords

The House of Lords is funded directly from the Treasury on the same lines as a government department, but for constitutional reasons – and unlike a department – the House is not cash-limited. That does not mean that it can spend what it wants. Great self-restraint is, in fact, exercised on the demands made upon the public purse. The House has two Requests for Resources (RfRs) or Estimates, one for administration (including members' expenses) and one for works. In 2002–03 the RfR for House of Lords administration was £42.2 million (actual expenditure £40.4 million) and for works £18.1 million (actual expenditure £17.1 million).

Overall financial control rests with the House Committee, and as we have seen the Clerk of the Parliaments, who is head of the Lords' administration, is the accounting officer and is responsible for all its expenditure, including its propriety and effectiveness. The House of Lords accounts are examined and certified each year by the National Audit Office.

How much does Parliament cost?

In 2002–03, the House of Commons cost £280 million, almost exactly half of which went on MPs' pay and allowances. The whole of the House administration cost £140.8 million. To put these figures in context, public expenditure as a whole was £466 billion, of which the Commons – responsible for calling government to account for the effectiveness of its spending – cost 0.06 percent. Expenditure on the House of Lords on administration and works was £57.5 million. As a whole, Parliament thus costs about 0.07 percent of what the government spends.

4 Parliamentary sovereignty, legislative supremacy and devolution

Sovereignty and supremacy

In this chapter we consider the nature of Parliament's powers: what many writers on the constitution would have described in the past as the 'sovereignty of Parliament' but for which a better term might be 'legislative supremacy'.

Let us look briefly at the ways in which Parliament is not sovereign. First, Parliament is clearly not sovereign in the sense that it embodies any concept of national sovereignty, although it may contribute to the sentiment. Second, it is not sovereign in the sense that it vies with the Queen to be head of state. Third, it is not the centre of the day-to-day decision making of government. It is the government (or executive as it is often called in this context) that conducts the business of the state, often acting within the powers and resources that have been granted by Parliament, and claiming its authority to govern by virtue of its ability to command a majority in the House of Commons. Although Parliament may try to influence the government's actions by a variety of means, it does not and cannot micro-manage the affairs of state. Parliament does not govern.

Fourth, Parliament is not the sole source of the government's powers, many of which are derived from the government's exercise of the prerogative powers of the Crown with little or no recourse to Parliament at all. Prerogative powers and the concept of prerogative range widely. Thus international treaties are entered into without reference to Parliament. Although they are laid before Parliament, usually as Command Papers, Parliament plays no formal role in respect of them. Treaties involving the European Union are the exception, because they require amendment of the European Communities Act 1972. Parliament does not have to be consulted before the armed forces are used – whether as peacekeepers or in military conflict. Although the House of Commons was given the opportunity to vote on a substantive motion before the commitment of troops in Iraq in 2003, no such opportunity preceded the involvement of British troops in Kosovo in 1999 or previous deployments or conflicts. Parliament has no say in matters relating to honours or patronage. The Civil

Service answers to the Crown, that is to say the government, and not to Parliament; and there is no concept of parliamentary oversight of appointments to public office, or of control of the actual machinery of government. Finally, it is the government that, by royal proclamation, summons, prorogues and dissolves Parliament. There is increasing support for the view that Parliament should have a greater role in the exercise of the government's exercise of these prerogative powers.

Legislative supremacy

So when people use the phrase 'the sovereignty of Parliament', what they really mean is the legislative supremacy of Parliament, that is to say its unique ability, in the words of the nineteenth-century constitutional writer A.V. Dicey, to 'make or unmake any law whatever'.

The principle was set out elegantly in 1844, when Thomas Erskine May published the first edition of his *Treatise on the Law, Privileges, Proceedings and Usage of Parliament* – a work that was to become the authoritative text on the procedures of Parliament. He began his second chapter with this paragraph:

> The legislative authority of Parliament extends over the United Kingdom, and all its colonies and foreign possessions; and there are no other limits to its power of making laws for the whole empire than those which are incident to all sovereign authority – the willingness of the people to obey, or their power to resist. Unlike the legislatures of many other countries, it is bound by no fundamental charter or constitution; but has itself the sole constitutional right of establishing and altering the laws and government of the empire.

Parliament no longer legislates for an overseas empire, but Erskine May's words are in all other respects still applicable. Clearly this legislative supremacy is the source of enormous power.

Characteristics of legislative supremacy

Legislative supremacy is essentially a legal concept, and it manifests itself in a number of different ways. For example, the courts of law are under a duty to apply legislation, even if that legislation might appear to be morally or politically wrong. This is a powerful reason why legislation must always be got right so as to avoid the possibility of unexpected consequences. Moreover, unlike other countries with written constitutions – the United States for example – it would not be possible to challenge an Act of the United Kingdom Parliament in the courts on the grounds that it was unconstitutional. In any event, even the constitution can be subject to statute. New constitutional principles can be established, like reform of the membership or powers of the House of Lords or devolved government in Scotland, Wales and Northern

Ireland. And existing principles can be modified or changed, like the succession to the throne or the parliamentary privileges set out in the Bill of Rights of 1688–89.

One of the consequences of Parliament's legislative supremacy is that it is commonly held that one parliament cannot bind its successor parliaments, which, after all, have an equal claim to legislative sovereignty. In some cases, things that Parliament does by legislation are in practical terms so difficult to reverse that successor parliaments are, in effect, bound by those Acts – like the Acts that gave self-government or confederation to the former dominions, or independence to the former colonies, or votes to women, or even devolution to Scotland and Wales. (Devolution in Northern Ireland has been revoked and then restored by Parliament, as is considered more fully below.)

But in other areas the principle of legislative supremacy remains strong – even in the field of human rights. It was for many years held that a bill of rights – in modern language, a bill to incorporate the European Convention on Human Rights into UK law – could never be entrenched into law so as to protect such fundamental rights from the possibility of subsequent infringement by a future parliament. Indeed, when the government brought forward its Human Rights Bill in 1997–98, it made no attempt to do so.

Limitations upon legislative supremacy

Parliament's legislative supremacy is a powerful concept, but it has its limitations. Erskine May put his finger on the chief limitation – 'the willingness of the people to obey, or their power to resist'. Most of the time, in these days of universal suffrage, this manifests itself through the ballot box rather than in mass civil disobedience, but the repeal of the disliked community charge or poll tax legislation in 1992 was undoubtedly hastened by the mass demonstrations of 1990.

Other limitations derive from the radical changes in society since Erskine May first wrote. On the one hand, more and more areas of life have been subjected to statutory regulation since the mid-nineteenth century as public policy has made provision in areas that formerly went unregulated or were considered private matters not deserving the intervention of the state – like education, working conditions, social security, health, and so on. But on the other hand, modern technology, and in recent years especially information technology, has placed some activities almost beyond the reach of statutory provision – electronic international transfer of funds, for example, or intellectual property rights in material placed on the Internet.

Apart from the ultimate limitations of public consent and of practical constraint, the legislative supremacy of Parliament can be said to have been circumscribed in a number of quite specific and practical ways in recent years:

▲ in consequence of the passing of the Human Rights Act;
▲ as a result of accession to the European Union (at that time the European Economic Community); and
▲ by devolution to Scotland and Wales, and, with some qualifications, to Northern Ireland.

Each of these represents a major constitutional development worthy of separate consideration.

Human Rights Act 1998

Background

The incorporation of the European Convention on Human Rights (ECHR) into UK law in 1998 potentially had a major impact on the legislative supremacy of Parliament. The background is as follows. The ECHR was originally drawn up by the Council of Europe both as an affirmation of principles in a postwar Europe and as a test that potential new members of that body would be required to pass. The United Kingdom took a leading role in drafting it and duly ratified it in 1951. However, the British government – unlike other signatories – did not subsequently incorporate it into domestic law; nor, until 1966, did the United Kingdom accept the optional provisions allowing individuals to petition the European Court of Human Rights (set up under the ECHR to adjudicate on infringements) and the compulsory jurisdiction of the European Court of Human Rights.

The rights covered by the ECHR are for the most part unremarkable and would be taken for granted by most British people. They include the right to life, liberty and security of person; the prohibition of torture; the freedom of expression; and the right to a fair trial. One might well wonder why successive administrations, both Conservative and Labour, declined to incorporate the ECHR into British law. After all, they had modified the law in a number of areas where the European Court had found the United Kingdom to be in breach of the ECHR – for example on homosexuality in Northern Ireland, the right of appeal against life sentences and corporal punishment in schools, to name but a few.

One of the chief reasons revolved around legislative supremacy. Previous schemes for incorporation had raised the possibility that, by invoking a bill of rights or the European Convention, UK courts would have been able to strike down provisions in Acts of Parliament and thus undermine Parliament's supremacy in legislative matters. This was the line taken by the Conservative government during debates in the House of Lords on Lord Lester of Herne Hill's Human Rights Bill (a private member's bill that sought to incorporate the

ECHR into UK law) during the 1996–97 session. Another reason was the impossibility of entrenchment of the provisions of any such Act into UK law in a manner that would render its provisions unamendable at some future date.

The Human Rights Act 1998

Following the 1997 general election, the new Labour government carried through a commitment to incorporate the ECHR, and the Human Rights Act was passed in 1998. It enables the rights of an individual under the ECHR to be tested in UK courts without recourse to the European Court of Human Rights. Central and local government must act in a way that is compatible with the convention. If in any case the courts decide that an Act of Parliament is itself incompatible with the convention, a declaration of incompatibility may be made. Although that will not in itself change the law, it will certainly prompt the government and Parliament to take action, by means of primary legislation or a remedial Order – a statutory instrument subject to affirmative resolution of both Houses of Parliament. Since the passage of the Act, one such Order has been made (relating to the Mental Health Act 1983).

So far as the Westminster Parliament is concerned, the concept of legislative supremacy has been preserved more or less intact. But the powers of the courts are different in respect of legislation by the Scottish Parliament and of Orders issued by the Welsh Assembly. The courts are able to hold Scottish legislation to be unlawful if it is incompatible with the ECHR; and Welsh Assembly Orders may be quashed. Secondary legislation passed at Westminster may also be quashed by the courts.

So the legislative supremacy of Parliament is preserved under these arrangements – or is it? The government has said that there may be circumstances in which it may be unwilling to act upon a declaration of incompatibility. But in most cases it will almost certainly feel morally bound to take steps. In any event, without remedial action the legislation in question would be fatally weakened and liable to further challenge. Parliament often legislates, or amends existing legislation, because the courts have found the statutes wanting, or have exposed loopholes. But the Human Rights Act is novel in that it forges a direct link between a declaration in a court of law and an expectation of remedial action by Parliament.

European Union

In 1973, following the passage of the European Communities Act 1972, the United Kingdom joined what is now called the European Union. Parliament's relationship with the European Union is fully set out in Chapter 12, but some discussion of this in the context of legislative supremacy is inevitable. Parliament's legislative supremacy is compromised by EU membership in a number of different ways.

First, Parliament plays no part in the European legislative process. As we demonstrate in Chapter 12, it may try to influence the stand taken by the government at meetings of the EU Council of Ministers where EU legislation is agreed, but national parliaments play no formal part in European decision making. Once agreed, regulations become directly applicable throughout all member states without the involvement of Parliament, while directives have to be incorporated into United Kingdom law, usually by means of secondary legislation in the form of statutory instruments. As we will see in Chapter 7, secondary legislation is not amendable and is poorly scrutinised at Westminster. And of course this legislation comes before Westminster parliamentarians very late in the day, after the contents have been agreed in Brussels.

Second, the 1972 Act provides that any existing or future legislation passed at Westminster shall be subject to any directly applicable obligations under EU law. Where Acts of Parliament are inconsistent with EU law, it is expected that the latter will prevail. This is the line adopted by the UK courts, which will not apply national legislation, whether enacted before or after 1972, if to do so would conflict with EU law. Thus, in areas of EU competence, any conflict of laws will always be resolved in the EU's favour.

The fact remains that Parliament acquiesced in these arrangements in passing the 1972 Act (and the subsequent amending Acts to take account of successive treaties). In theory these Acts could be repealed. But meanwhile Parliament has chosen that in certain areas of EU competence, EU legislation will prevail – legislation, what is more, that it had little or no part in formulating.

Devolution of government

The new Labour government of 1997 was committed to establishing devolved government in Scotland and Wales and to attempting to resurrect devolved arrangements in Northern Ireland. The Referendums (Scotland and Wales) Bill was passed by the summer recess of 1997, and referendums were held in Scotland and Wales in September 1997. These endorsed (ringingly in Scotland, more equivocally in Wales) the government's proposals for a Scottish Parliament with tax-varying powers, and for a Welsh Assembly. The referendums were held before the details of the bills to implement the proposals were published. In 1998, three Acts were passed – the Scotland Act, the Government of Wales Act and the Northern Ireland Act – to give effect to these devolution proposals. Each Act is very different from the others, both in the detailed arrangements relating to the assemblies they established and – more particularly – in the extent to which legislative powers were transferred.

The Scotland and Northern Ireland Acts – but not the Government of Wales Act – transferred primary legislative powers to a Scottish Parliament and Northern Ireland Assembly. Under both Acts, the Westminster Parliament reserved the power to legislate for both Scotland and Northern Ireland. And of course both Acts could in theory be repealed – and the Northern Ireland Assembly was in fact suspended and then restored. But in effect the Westminster Parliament has chosen to forgo its powers to legislate in the wide areas of policy that are specified as devolved matters in both Acts. We shall now look at each region in turn.

Scotland

Since 1999, Scotland has had its own unicameral Parliament consisting of 129 members (MSPs), seventy-three of whom are elected directly on the basis of the current Westminster constituencies (although Orkney and Shetland have been split into two constituencies), with fifty-six additional MSPs (seven from each of the eight European Parliament constituencies) elected under a form of the additional member system of proportional representation. MSPs are elected for four-year terms; the second election was held on 1 May 2003. Early dissolution of the Parliament may occur if more than two-thirds of the members vote for it or if the Parliament fails to agree on the appointment of a First Minister. The First Minister is appointed by the Queen on the advice of the Parliament's Presiding Officer and is normally the leader of the party able to command the support of a majority in the Parliament. The First Minister appoints the other Scottish ministers, and this executive has, in all essentials, the same relationship to the Scottish Parliament as UK ministers have to the Westminster Parliament.

The Scottish Parliament has powers to legislate for Scotland in certain areas, but other areas are reserved to Westminster – like foreign affairs, defence, the armed forces, finance and the economy. A schedule to the Scotland Act also lists more specific reserved matters within policy areas that are otherwise devolved. These tend to be areas where it would make no sense for different parts of the UK to have different laws – for example, import and export control, misuse of drugs, immigration and nationality, and broadcasting. The Act also provides that matters may, by Order in Council (a particular type of secondary legislation), be transferred from and to the list of reserved matters.

The Westminster Parliament retains power to legislate for Scotland on any matters, and it could override decisions taken by the Scottish Parliament on devolved matters. But a convention has arisen that Westminster will not legislate on a devolved matter without the prior agreement of the Scottish

Parliament, demonstrated by its passing of a so-called 'Sewel motion' (Lord Sewel was a minister in the then Scottish Office when the Scotland Act was passed).

In addition to these legislative powers, the Scottish Parliament has powers of scrutiny over the activities of the executive, power to determine spending priorities within devolved areas, and a power, not yet exercised, to vary basic rate income tax by up to 3 percent.

The effect of these developments at Westminster has been considerable. There is no longer specific Scottish legislation, and ministers may not be asked questions about matters that are now the responsibility of the Scottish Executive. The Scottish Affairs Select Committee in the Commons has continued in existence, but with narrower formal terms of reference (although they now include 'relations with the Scottish Parliament'). So, too, has the Scottish Grand Committee as a debating forum, but it has met less frequently: nine times in the first three full sessions after devolution.

As we saw in Chapter 2, the government has recognised that the present seventy-three Scottish MPs will need to be reduced in number – probably to fifty-nine – to reflect the changes. A continuing issue is the West Lothian question, named after Tam Dalyell, then MP for West Lothian (now MP for Linlithgow and Father of the House), who frequently raised the issue during the devolution debates of the late 1970s – why should Scottish MPs at Westminster be able to speak, question and vote on matters affecting the rest of the United Kingdom when in Scotland the same matters are devolved?

Wales

Unlike the Scottish Parliament, the National Assembly for Wales does not have the power to pass primary legislation, which remains with the Westminster Parliament, but it does have the power to make secondary legislation. The Assembly consists of forty constituency members and twenty proportionately elected additional members (four from each European Parliament constituency). The Assembly has a fixed four-year term with no possibility of early dissolution, and the second elections were held on 1 May 2003. It is fully bilingual, conducting its business in both Welsh and English.

The Assembly has been established on an executive model with a cabinet-style system. The Scottish Parliament has a staff independent of the executive, but the Welsh Assembly is staffed by government officials. In theory they are like the staff of a county council, who provide services to the council in its deliberative role but more importantly execute and administer the decisions it takes. In practice, the staff who provide the chamber and support services to the Assembly itself have developed some sense of separate identity. The

Assembly took over the Welsh Office's function for the distribution of almost all the block grant allocated by the Treasury to Wales, and it acquired the Welsh Office's functions in relation to local authorities in Wales and other public bodies like the Welsh Development Agency.

At the apex of the Assembly structure is the equivalent of the Cabinet – the Executive Committee, chaired by the Assembly First Secretary, who is elected by the Assembly as a whole. The other members of the Executive Committee ('Assembly Secretaries') are appointed by the First Secretary, and one serves on each of the subject committees of the Assembly. The Executive Committee is able to meet in private, and it consists of members of one party only. The number and size of the subject committees, currently six, is determined by the Assembly, and their political balance will reflect the membership of the Assembly as a whole. Each committee has a chairperson, and the chairs are allocated proportionately between parties. However, the key figure on each committee is the Assembly Secretary. The standing orders of the Assembly designate the functions that can be discharged by the hierarchy ranging from the Assembly as a whole to the Executive Committee, subject committees, leaders of subject committees and unelected officials.

The Assembly's legislative role is currently restricted to making secondary legislation that formerly would have been made by the Secretary of State for Wales or for which, since 1998, powers have been delegated to the Assembly by subsequent Acts of Parliament. Pre-1998 secondary legislation within the Assembly's area of competence can be replaced, revoked or amended. Assembly Orders are prepared by subject committees and the Executive Committee; and, before being laid before the Assembly as a whole, Orders go before a committee known as the Subordinate Legislation Scrutiny Committee in order to ensure that the Assembly has the powers to make the Order proposed. Any dispute about the Assembly's use of its powers can be referred by the Attorney General to the Judicial Committee of the Privy Council for decision.

In addition to these executive and limited legislative functions, the Welsh Assembly also has some parliamentary functions. The Assembly First Secretary is subject to questioning by the Assembly as a whole; Assembly Orders are approved by the Assembly before they can pass; and the Assembly acts, in accordance with the government's July 1997 White Paper, as the forum for the nation, able to debate all matters of concern in Wales, not only those that it directly controls. The Assembly has committees representing the regions of Wales, but without executive functions, and an Audit Committee. However, the Public Accounts Committee of the House of Commons and the Parliamentary Commissioner for Administration continue to be able to investigate matters within the competence of the Welsh Assembly, although in such cases the latter reports to the Assembly.

The Secretary of State for Wales retains all his functions so far as primary legislation affecting Wales is concerned, and he negotiates the block grant with the Treasury. His role is thus much stronger than that of the Secretary of State for Scotland.

As all primary legislation for Wales remains the prerogative of the Westminster Parliament, there has been no proposal to reduce the number of Welsh MPs – at present forty. If Wales were represented *pro rata* with England, it would have thirty-three MPs. However, the creation of the National Assembly for Wales has considerably reduced the number of matters on which the Secretary of State for Wales is answerable and on which secondary legislation comes before the Westminster Parliament. There has thus been some diminution in Westminster MPs' role in Welsh affairs. But the Welsh Affairs Select Committee in the Commons continues (like the Scottish Affairs Select Committee, with a narrower formal remit, but which now includes 'relations with the National Assembly for Wales'), and the Welsh Grand Committee holds debates, but less frequently: ten times in the first three full sessions after devolution.

The legislative supremacy of the Westminster Parliament has been compromised far less by the establishment of the National Assembly for Wales than by the setting up of the Scottish Parliament. If at some future date a Welsh Assembly Executive Committee promoted secondary legislation not in tune with the policies of the United Kingdom government, the government could introduce primary legislation at Westminster to override anything the Assembly did. This lack of primary legislative power is one aspect of the Assembly's functions that was reviewed by an independent commission under the chairmanship of Lord Richard, which will report in spring 2004, but it is difficult to imagine how any such power could be acquired by the Assembly – even if this was thought desirable – without a much more extensive devolution of policy responsibilities.

Northern Ireland

Unlike Scotland and Wales, Northern Ireland government was first devolved long ago – under the Government of Ireland Act 1920, which gave Northern Ireland its own executive (Prime Minister and Cabinet) and two-chamber legislature. A reduced number of MPs continued to sit at Westminster. Foreign affairs and defence, customs and excise and certain other matters were reserved, and the ultimate legislative supremacy of Westminster was preserved. These arrangements continued until 1972, when, due to civil unrest, direct rule was resumed and in 1973 the former arrangements were brought to an end. This is an example of how, ultimately, the legislative supremacy of the Westminster Parliament can be reasserted under devolved arrangements, albeit in extreme circumstances.

Despite attempts in 1973 and 1982 to revive some kind of devolved arrangements, not until 1998, in the wake of the Belfast (Good Friday) Agreement between the Northern Ireland political parties, were new devolved arrangements attempted and the Northern Ireland Act 1998 passed. The new Northern Ireland Assembly consists of 108 members, six for each of the eighteen Westminster constituencies, under the single transferable vote system. A complicated system of power sharing between the major parties governs all major decision making, so that power is effectively shared between the Unionist and Nationalist communities. The First Minister, Deputy First Minister and other ministers are appointed under power-sharing arrangements and constitute the Executive Committee of the Assembly.

Devolved arrangements do not apply to defence, immigration, elections and political parties, and other issues such as aviation, criminal law and emergency powers are reserved. Westminster still reserves the right to make laws for Northern Ireland on transferred matters. The Assembly has no power to vary rates of tax.

At Westminster, the Northern Ireland Affairs Select Committee considers matters within the responsibilities of the Northern Ireland Office, but, by contrast with the Scottish and Welsh select committees, it does not have relations with the Northern Ireland Assembly in its terms of reference. The Northern Ireland Grand Committee meets for occasional debates (ten times in the first three full sessions after devolution). Both the select committee and the grand committee operate against the background of some political uncertainty in Northern Ireland.

Continuing political difficulties caused the Assembly to be suspended from February to May 2000 and again in October 2002, and it was dissolved in April 2003. The elections due to take place in May 2003 were deferred until 26 November 2003, but the results showed an increased polarisation of the Unionist and Nationalist communities, making a return to devolved government more difficult. During these periods of suspension and direct rule Northern Ireland legislation is passed by the Westminster Parliament in the form of Orders in Council – in other words, as secondary legislation requiring only the affirmative resolution of the two Houses.

5 Influences on Parliament

The House of Commons

The job is what you make it

Almost everyone in employment in the United Kingdom has a job description. And those who are self-employed – perhaps running a shop or other small business – have pretty clear indications of what constitutes success or failure. Members of Parliament have neither, unless it is to be re-elected at the next election. As we shall see, there is no shortage of people who will tell the newly elected MP what he or she should be doing; but there is no formal statement of what the job involves.

In 1996, consultants working for the Senior Salaries Review Body (SSRB) had a go at writing a job description, and in their 2001 report on parliamentary pay and allowances said that they thought it remained 'broadly valid'. The 1996 version had three main elements:

- ▲ contributing, whether in the Chamber, Committees, or to the party, to developing policy on general or specific issues, and communicating this outside Westminster, especially within the constituency. This encompasses the fundamental responsibility to scrutinise and monitor the Executive.
- ▲ representing the interests of the constituency as a whole, for example on planning and development matters; and staying closely in touch with local business and significant public services within the constituency (e.g. education and the health service) to understand and feed back experience.
- ▲ representing, especially to public authorities, individual constituents who may need what they perceive to be high level support to understand their rights, obtain what they need, or explain why their wishes cannnot be satisfied.

This was a very good description of 'what MPs do', but it was strictly a *description*, drawn from observing the many, and not a *definition*. And the truth is that no definition exists. As a newly elected MP, it is entirely up to you to decide how you do the job. Will you devote yourself entirely to your constituents and their problems? (Unless you are both selective and realistic, you will rapidly discover that you could easily spend twenty-four hours in every day on this.) Will you become a standard bearer for some product of your constituency – apples, computer software, shellfish, sports cars? Will you pursue an abiding political interest, which you had before you came into the House: perhaps Third World debt, or renewable sources of energy? Possibly you are attracted by select committee work, the business of calling the government to account, and making yourself an expert on a particular area of policy. Perhaps you might set yourself to contribute to better understanding between the United Kingdom and the Arab world, or to ensuring that the UK makes the most of commercial opportunities on the Pacific Rim. If you are in the party of government, might your ambitions be focused on ministerial office and getting a foot on the first rung of the ladder as a parliamentary private secretary (PPS; see page 83)?

In practice, most MPs will do some or all of these various aspects of the job. But few will do exactly what they expected when first they came into the House. And the main reason for that is the complex web of influences on the House and its members.

The government's control of the House of Commons

We saw in Chapter 2 how, in order to be invited to form a government, a prospective Prime Minister must have control of the House of Commons – that is, for his or her party to have enough of a parliamentary majority to be certain of getting approval for the legislative programme (announced in the Queen's Speech) and for government taxation and spending (through the Finance Bill and the Estimates). But the government's day-to-day control of the Commons is much more extensive.

Control of time

Perhaps the most evident symptom of that control is the fact that, every Thursday, the Leader of the House announces what the business will be – that is, what items will be taken on each day – for the next fortnight. In many parliaments, particularly those on the continental model, there is a business committee or *bureau*, involving not only the business managers and other party representatives but also the president of the assembly and his deputies, who decide what business to propose. And even then, that draft agenda is subject to approval by the assembly as a whole.

However, in the House of Commons, it is primarily for the government of the day to propose and to dispose. Ever since the Balfour reforms at the turn of the nineteenth/twentieth centuries, all House of Commons time that is not ring-fenced is at the disposal of the government of the day. In 150 or 160 sitting days in a parliamentary session, only twenty 'opposition days', thirteen days for private members' bills, some time for private bills, three 'Estimates days', the daily half-hour adjournment debate, urgent questions and the daily Question Time are not in the gift of the government. Even then, it is for the government to decide *when* the opposition days, private members' bill days and Estimates days shall be taken. In terms of time in the Chamber, nearly three-fifths of business is initiated by the government, about a tenth by the opposition and about a quarter by back-benchers. Even though business initiated by the government provides debating opportunities for the opposition and for back-benchers generally, the extent of that power of initiative is considerable. In addition, the standing orders provide that only ministers may move certain key motions for the arrangement and organisation of business. The vast majority of legislation passed by Parliament is government legislation, and even private members' bills stand little chance of enactment unless they have government support.

The 'elective dictatorship'?

The former Conservative Lord Chancellor, Lord Hailsham, described the Westminster system of parliamentary government as an 'elective dictatorship': that is, one in which a government, once elected, is free to do very much what it wants. To an extent, Lord Hailsham was and is right. The Westminster system is not government by Parliament but government through Parliament, and (perhaps especially obvious when the government has a large parliamentary majority) one of the roles of Parliament is to legitimise what the government does.

Government patronage and collective responsibility

The government's position is further entrenched by the Prime Minister's ability to choose the members of the government. In late 2003 there were 114 paid ministerial posts in both Houses, ninety-two in the Commons and twenty-two in the Lords. In addition, in the Commons there were fifty-three PPSs, who are not ministers but who act as unpaid aides to secretaries of state or ministers of state.

Not only is the power of ministerial appointment a key prime ministerial weapon, but it is also allied to the constitutional doctrine of 'collective responsibility', under which all the members of a government support any public statement of the government's policies. Ministers may (and often do) disagree privately and seek to change or modify their colleagues' minds and policies, but if they disagree publicly they are expected to resign (as did the Leader of the House, Robin Cook, in March 2003 over the government's proposed military action against Iraq) or face the sack from the PM of the day. This doctrine also applies to PPSs and means that in any vote the government can always rely on the support of ministers and PPSs (often called collectively 'the payroll vote').

Theory and practice

It might appear that little stands in the way of the government doing precisely what it wants (or, perhaps more precisely, what the Prime Minister with the backing of the Cabinet wants). But the picture is a little more subtle than that. There is indeed an expectation that a government having won a mandate at a general election, with a majority in the House of Commons, will be able to 'get its business through'. However, in practice this depends on a number of factors. A government must retain the support of its back-benchers; and, as we shall see, it is not enough to issue orders; persuasion is often needed. Public and media opinion also needs to be benign – or, at least, not so critical as to give government back-benchers cold feet.

In addition, all governments are aware of the fact that, perhaps not too long distant, they may be on the opposition benches. In the heady days after a big election victory, or with the insulation of a large parliamentary majority, this recollection may be sometimes less vivid, but it underpins any government's need to maintain a working relationship with the opposition, and especially with the largest opposition party ('the official Opposition'). New MPs who have known only the government benches may want to press on regardless, but their enthusiasm tends to be tempered by longer-serving MPs who can remember all too many occasions when in opposition they won the arguments but lost the votes.

This working relationship with the opposition means, in House terms, general agreement on the arrangement and timing of business and accord on less contentious matters such as the dates of parliamentary recesses, normally through 'the usual channels' (see page 88). An effective working relationship may also colour the relationships between the parties on much more significant matters, such as a measure of agreement on how to approach the firefighters' strike, or the possible imposition of sanctions against a foreign country.

The opposition, too, has a considerable interest in maintaining this working relationship. The traditional statement that the opposition's power is one of delay is now largely out of date given the routine programming of government bills (see page 179). However, cooperation with the government in the arrangement of business will give the opposition the chance to express (and sometimes secure) priorities for debate, and to trade time and tactics, perhaps along the lines of no division on second reading of bill X and only half a day on its report stage, but in return an extra day on the report stage of bill Y. The opposition gets the extra day on bill Y, which it sees as more important; the government

saves some time on bill X and also knows that it can slacken the voting requirements for its MPs on the second reading of that bill.

Explanation and accountability

A.J. Balfour described democracy as 'government by explanation'. Even if it
is inevitable that the government will in the end get its way, Parliament is
the forum in which it must explain itself and be held to account. Explanation may take various forms: responding to criticisms of proposed legislation
at the second reading of a bill, or on detailed amendments put forward at
report stage; explaining and defending a broader policy, perhaps on asylum
seekers or NHS funding, as part of a full day's debate initiated by the opposition; or giving a detailed account of its actions to a major select committee
inquiry. The requirement on governments to explain and justify can in itself
be a brake on executive power; but it is up to Parliament to make this process
effective.

Ministerial accountability is a concept that it is easier to recognise than to
define. There is extensive case law over a number of years, beginning with the
Crichel Down affair in 1954, when the Minister of Agriculture, Sir Thomas
Dugdale, resigned apparently because he was taking responsibility for errors
made by his civil servants (but more likely because he was left high and dry by
a change in government policy), to the Westland affair in 1986 and Jo Moore
'burying bad news' in 2001, which led eventually to the resignation of Stephen
Byers as Secretary of State for Transport, Local Government and the Regions.
On Westland, Leon Brittan resigned as Secretary of State for Trade and
Industry, taking responsibility for errors by officials but refusing to explain
exactly what had happened. The Defence Select Committee, which investigated
the saga, remarked drily: 'A Minister does not discharge his accountability
to Parliament merely by acknowledging a general responsibility and, if the
circumstances warrant it, by resigning. Accountability involves accounting
in detail for actions as a Minister'.

The principle of accountability to Parliament is now underpinned by resolutions of both Houses in March 1997 on how ministers should behave towards
Parliament:

> Ministers of the Crown are expected to behave according to the highest standards
> of constitutional and personal conduct in the performance of their duties. In
> particular, they must observe the following principles of Ministerial conduct:
>
> i. Ministers must uphold the principles of collective responsibility;
>
> ii. Ministers have a duty to Parliament to account, and be held to account, for
> the policies, decisions and actions of their Departments and Next Steps
> Agencies;

iii. It is of paramount importance that Ministers give accurate and truthful information to Parliament, correcting any inadvertent error at the earliest opportunity. Ministers who knowingly mislead Parliament will be expected to offer their resignation to the Prime Minister;

iv. Ministers should be as open as possible with Parliament and the public, refusing to provide information only when disclosure would not be in the public interest, which should be decided in accordance with relevant statute and the Government's Code of Practice on Access to Government Information;

v. Similarly, Ministers should require civil servants who give evidence before Parliamentary Committees on their behalf and under their directions to be as helpful as possible in providing accurate, truthful and full information in accordance with the duties and responsibilities of civil servants as set out in the Civil Service Code.

In Chapters 10 and 11 we will look more closely at the ways in which the government is called to account.

The party

However close an MP's relationship with the constituency, the party to which he or she belongs is the key element in an MP's parliamentary life. This is not surprising; as we saw in Chapter 2, the only realistic prospect an aspiring politician has of being elected to the House of Commons is to join a political party and then have the backing of that party to fight an election. But for most MPs, their relationship with their party has an element of compromise about it. No party is ever in the happy position that every one of its MPs would sign up to every last detail of every one of its policies. Some would like to see greater emphasis in this or that direction; others are uneasy about the party committing itself on something else. However, just as the collective responsibility of ministers has its strength in public unity, so MPs are content to exchange occasional disagreements or private doubts for the shelter and support of the party that best represents their political outlook.

Given the enormous importance of political parties in Westminster politics, it is perhaps surprising that they are not more explicitly recognised in the rules of the two Houses. In the Commons, the standing orders notice parties only so far as 'committee memberships reflect the composition of the House', that smaller opposition parties have a share of opposition day debates, and that one MP speaking for the Liberal Democrats is exempted from any limit that may be imposed on speaking time for back-benchers in a particular debate.

In a formal sense, party structures and disciplines exist in parallel with the regulation of the House and its proceedings, although in practice they interlock at every level.

By contrast, in some parliaments – for example the Canadian House of Commons – the role of parties is explicitly recognised in the allocation of oral questions and speaking time, which means that the Speaker plays a smaller role in allocation than at Westminster.

The whips

The whips are key players in party organisation and discipline, and in the arrangement and timing of business, on both sides of the House. The title derives from 'whippers-in' or 'whips' in the hunting field – a light irony at a time when hunting has become so politically contentious. Whips act as a two-way channel of communication between the party leadership and the back benches, on the one hand feeding back MPs' views and warning of areas of possible difficulty or dissent, and on the other, making clear to back-benchers what the leadership wants from them.

An effective whip needs to be a strong character and a shrewd operator but also has to balance personal authority with an understanding of the pressures on the MPs for whom she or he is responsible. Much is written and more speculated about the black arts of the whips – their techniques for bringing recalcitrant MPs into line – and of their intelligence gathering. There is no doubt that whips can on occasion be fearsomely effective, whether by use of stick or carrot, in persuading potential rebels to live with their doubts rather than express them; and there is no doubt, either, that a good whips' office knows more about the views and foibles of its back-benchers than it would ever wish to see made public.

However, whips also need to be good personnel managers. New (and some more experienced) MPs may find life at Westminster difficult and frustrating; and spending much of the working week perhaps hundreds of miles from home and family, combined perhaps with constituency casework that is especially tragic or emotionally draining, can impose real strains. In such circumstances, a good whip is a source of advice and support.

Whips are ever-present in proceedings in the House, Westminster Hall and standing committees. In the House there is always a government and an official opposition whip sitting on the front benches keeping an eye on proceedings, jotting down notes on speeches (and speakers) in the debate and alert for any procedural or political difficulty that may arise. Whips have a talent-spotting role, and their good opinion (and especially that of the Chief Whip) may lead to ministerial office, a shadow post, or perhaps a coveted place on a popular select committee.

The government Chief Whip is known formally as the Parliamentary Secretary to the Treasury (and sometimes as the Patronage Secretary – a reminder of the carrot rather than the stick of parliamentary discipline). It is her responsibility to get the government's business through the Commons with the greatest efficiency and the least dissent from government back-benchers. She normally attends Cabinet meetings and advises the Prime Minister and his senior colleagues on opinion within the parliamentary party, and how proposed policies are likely to play with back-benchers. On the government side, the next three senior whips carry formal titles of posts in the Royal Household: the Deputy Chief Whip is the Treasurer of HM Household, followed by the Comptroller and the Vice-Chamberlain. There are five other whips (known as Lords Commissioners of the Treasury) and five to seven assistant whips.

The Conservative official Opposition has a Chief Whip and a deputy (who receive salaries even though they are in opposition) and ten or eleven other whips. The Liberal Democrats have a Chief Whip, a deputy and four other whips. The smaller parties each have someone who acts as a Chief Whip, although with relatively few MPs their role is more as their parties' voice in the arrangement of business than as organisers and disciplinarians. In the major parties, the whips have regional and subject responsibilities: for example, the north-east and defence, and they attend the relevant party committees and groups.

The usual channels

This is deliberately vague shorthand for the informal discussions that take place between the business managers on both sides of the House. It embraces the Leader of the House and shadow Leader, and the government and opposition Chief Whips (and of other parties as circumstances require), but it also includes day-to-day and minute-to-minute conversations and arrangements between whips on both sides. A key player is the private secretary to the government Chief Whip, who, although a civil servant and so under the Chief Whip's instructions, plays a highly political role as a go-between.

The usual channels deal with a wide range of business, from issues such as the amount of time to be spent on a government bill in committee and which party should get which select committee chair, to extempore arrangements in which a whip will go round the Chamber asking his side's last two or three speakers to limit their speeches so that the 'winding-up' speeches from the front benches can start at the time agreed. Off-the-cuff arrangements are sometimes referred to as being done 'behind the Chair', which is indeed where they happen when whips from both sides have whispered conversations behind the Speaker's Chair.

Discussions through the usual channels are private – were they to be made public it is unlikely that they would take the same form or be so effective. But this secrecy, and the feeling on the part of some that deals cooked up behind the scenes may be more for the convenience of the participants than of back-benchers on one side or another, has led to criticism: the former Labour cabinet minister Tony Benn, for example, described the usual channels as 'the most polluted waterway in Europe'.

There is no doubt that, on occasion, the whips on both sides are closer to each other than to some elements of their own parties. It was widely thought, for example, that an alliance of the whips on both the government and opposition sides was responsible in October 2002 for defeating a proposal by Robin Cook as Leader of the House that would have greatly reduced the power of the whips over which MPs should serve on which select committees.

The Whip

A vital document for every MP is *The Whip*. This is circulated weekly by the whips of each party to their own members and lists the business for the following week, together with the party's expectations as to when its MPs will vote. The importance of the business is reflected by the number of times it is underlined, hence the phrase 'a three-line whip' for something seen as an unbreakable commitment. An example is shown overleaf.

By arrangement with the whips, an MP may miss even an important vote if he or she is paired – that is, if an MP from the other side makes a formal arrangement not to vote, so that the effect is neutral. This is of less importance when the government of the day has a very large majority, but it may be of considerable importance when the numbers are close; for example, it allows the Foreign Secretary to be at the UN, or other ministers to take part in crucial negotiations in Brussels, rather than being called back to vote. When the government party can rely on a large majority, it will normally excuse some of its MPs from voting, on a rota basis, so that they can spend time in their constituencies.

Occasionally it happens that the usual channels break down, and the opposition withdraws pairing arrangements. This can be a considerable inconvenience to the government, which must keep many more of its MPs in the precincts or nearby in case of a snap vote.

Party discipline

The whips are responsible for delivering the votes to give effect to their parties' policies and intentions. On matters that are likely to be contentious within the party, the leadership normally takes care to trail proposals in advance and to assess whether there is likely to be dissent. It follows that, for the whips, a

MONDAY, 27th OCTOBER

House meets at **2.30pm** for:

Home Office Questions

Last day for tabling, at **12.30pm,** for:

Education and Skills Questions

Solicitor General Questions (also answers on behalf of the Attorney General)

Main Business

Opposition Day (20th Allotted Day)

Debate on **"NATO and EU Defence Policy".**

Followed by Debate entitled **"Effect of Government targets on the provision of healthcare".**

Important divisions will take place and your attendance at 6.30pm for 7.00pm and

9.30pm for 10.00pm is essential

TUESDAY, 28th OCTOBER

House meets at **11.30am** for:

Scotland Office Questions

Advocate General's Questions

Constitutional Affairs Questions (includes Questions for the Lord Chancellor and the President of the Council)

Leader of the House and House of Commons Commission Questions

Last day for tabling, at **12.30pm,** for:

Defence Questions

Wales Office Questions

Main Business

1. Ten Minute Rule Bill: **Non-Prescription Contact Lenses** (John Robertson)

2. **Waste and Emissions Trading Bill [Lords]: Remaining stages.**

Important divisions will take place and your attendance from 12.30pm is essential

unless you have received authorised absence from the Assistant Chief Whip.

WEDNESDAY, 29th OCTOBER

House meets at **11.30am** for:

Northern Ireland Questions

Prime Minister's Questions

Last day for tabling, at **12.30pm,** for:

Health Questions

Deferred Divisions (voting between 12.30pm and 2.00pm): Colleagues should be prepared to

respond to a 2-Line Whip for any Deferred Divisions.

A political party's 'Whip', which tells its MPs when they should be present for votes in the Commons

lic pressure for MPs to be more independent, but at the same time, a feel-
at a party that cannot keep its own members on side has somehow failed.

nt and rebellion

IP will think very carefully before voting against the party, or even
ning in an important vote. Unless it is unassailably on a matter of
nal conscience, the action will be seen as disloyal and will often have an
on the prospects for preferment; whips have long memories.

e reasons for rebellion are varied: the issue may be one of general prin-
as on the Criminal Justice (Mode of Trial) (No. 2) Bill in 2000 and the
nal Justice Bill in 2003 over limitations on the right to jury trial, or on the
ect of military action against Iraq. It may be on an issue that is seen by
of its members as contrary to a party's traditions and best interests, for
ple for the Conservatives on the Maastricht Treaty in the 1992 parliament,
or the Labour Party on university tuition fees in the 2001 parliament.

e size of a government's majority is obviously an important factor. In
, the Conservatives under John Major were returned with an overall
rity of twenty-one. By the end of the parliament, by-election defeats and
tions to other parties had reduced this to a minority of three. Rebellions
ig Conservative MPs resulted in a total of nine defeats for the government
g that parliament. By contrast, in 1997 Tony Blair had an extraordin-
high majority of 179 over all other parties. Actual defeat on the floor of
louse was therefore much less likely; but rebellions were still of no less
ern to the leadership.

ent since 1997

e 1997 parliament, the level of dissent on the government back benches
less than in previous parliaments, perhaps because of a feeling of being on
after eighteen years in opposition, perhaps because of memories of dam-
g divisions in the party during the last Labour government in 1974–79.
ertheless, there were 104 occasions on which Labour members voted
nst the government on the floor of the House. A significant rebellion took
e in December 1997 on a proposal in the Social Security Bill to cut lone
nt benefits for new claimants. Forty-seven Labour MPs voted against the
rnment, and many abstained. On the Welfare Reform and Pensions Bill
999, sixty-seven rebelled on a proposal to means test disability benefit. The
ects of other rebellions have included the imposition of a settlement in the
ghters' strike (twenty-seven), the limitation of the right to jury trial in
2003 Criminal Justice Bill (thirty-four) and the introduction of foundation
oitals (sixty-seven). By contrast, in session 1998–99 on the Asylum and
igration Bill, the conciliatory and consultative approach of the govern-
t and the then Home Secretary, Jack Straw, was probably instrumental in

Main Business
1. No Ten Minute Rule Bill
2. Motion to approve **The Misuse of Drugs Act 1971 (Modifica**

Important divisions will take place and your attendance from 12.3

Order is concluded is essential unless you have received authoris

Assistant Chief Whip.

3. At 4pm, **Opposed Private Business: Mersey Tunnels Bill:** Fur

Your attendance is requested.

THURSDAY, 30th OCTOBER
House meets at 11.30am for:

Education and Skills
Solicitor General's Q
answers on behalf of
General)

At about 12.30pm:

Business Questions

Last day for tabling, at **12.30pm**, for:

Prime Minister's Ques

Main Business
Motion relating to **Pay for Select Committee Chairmen.**

Your attendance is requested.

FRIDAY, 31st OCTOBER
The House will not be sitting.

back-bencher's cardinal sin is to abstain, or worse, v
party, without giving any warning. An MP who express
able to support the party will normally be asked to disc
his or her own whip, and probably also with the Chief W
the party leader may want to try to change minds. In
policy towards Iraq in February and March 2003, for
Minister sought to persuade waverers personally.

Party discipline is normally not a problem for most M
membership of a party, with all the advantages that its str
tion bring, involves some degree of compromise; and the
to vote as the party wishes, especially in subject areas of
close knowledge. They are also well aware that a divided
ary, and certainly an electoral, liability. It is ironic that, o

reducing what might have been a major revolt on financial support for asylum seekers to only seven Labour members voting against the bill on third reading.

The biggest rebellions since Labour came to power in 1997, and in fact the biggest for more than a quarter of a century, took place over the government's policy on military action against Iraq. On 26 February 2003, 122 Labour MPs voted against the government on an amendment asserting that the case for military action was 'as yet unproven'; and on 18 March, 139 Labour MPs voted for an amendment to the effect that the case for war had not been established.

The dynamics of dissent

Voting against one's party, however good the reasons, is not a decision lightly taken. The aims vary. Quite apart from their views on matters of principle, MPs may want to make a point about being consulted by the party leadership. They may want to establish their credentials, both within the party as a whole and with their constituents, on a major issue (many Labour MPs came under a great deal of pressure in their constituencies on the impending war with Iraq).

Especially if the government's majority is small, a threatened revolt may secure substantial changes in policy. But small majorities work both ways; when the boat is low in the water, people are less inclined to rock it, and, however strongly they feel, government MPs will be reluctant to risk the 'nuclear option' of defeating their party on a major issue and perhaps triggering a vote of confidence (as happened when in July 1992 the Conservative government was defeated by 324 votes to 316 over the Social Protocol to the Maastricht Treaty – even though it won the confidence motion the next day by the luxurious margin of 110 votes).

Dissent and rebellion can become a habit for some MPs. More than 80 percent of the Labour rebels on the second Iraq vote had voted against their party at least once since 1997. Repeated rebellion sometimes indicates a growing disenchantment with the mainstream views of the party – for a few, this may be the first step towards defection to another party (see *Crossing the floor* below). It is also the case that rebellion becomes easier; an MP may think that, having damaged his prospects by voting against the government several times, full membership of the 'awkward squad' will not make things much worse. The presence of a major figure, perhaps a former cabinet minister who is on the back benches because he or she resigned over a major policy difference, may also be a potential focus of dissent.

Because of their wish to present a united front to the electorate and the media, political parties tend to undervalue dissent – or at least, dissent in public. In most organisations and businesses, challenge is seen as a healthy process, leading to better decision making. Had Margaret Thatcher's government taken more account of its dissenters over the Local Government Finance Bill in 1988 (which introduced the community charge or 'poll tax'), and particularly the proposal of one back-bencher, Michael Mates, that there should be banding of the charge according to income, the political history of the next two or three years might have been rather different.

Punishment

Voting against the party is not normally a good career move; most parties are unwilling to reward rebels with promotion. There are more formal sanctions. The Parliamentary Labour Party (PLP) has a code of conduct that requires its MPs to behave in a way that is consistent with the policies of the party, to have a good voting record and not to bring the party into disrepute. However, it does contain a 'conscience clause', which recognises a right of dissent on 'matters of deeply held personal conviction'. The Chief Whip may reprimand an MP in writing (which may also be reported to the member's constituency party). The PLP as a whole may 'withdraw the whip' from one of its MPs – in effect expelling them from the party. In a case of alleged serious misconduct, an MP may be suspended from the party pending an investigation, as happened with the Labour MP George Galloway in May 2003.

The Conservative Party has similar rules, also with 'conscience' provisions. But in the 1992 parliament eight Eurosceptic Conservative MPs had the whip withdrawn from them for six months because of their repeated voting against the party on European issues, and crucially on the Maastricht Social Protocol, which became an issue of confidence for the government.

Whether to make an example of rebels is a matter of judgement. There is a balance between doing so *pour encourager les autres* and the risk of creating martyrs. And if dissent is on a large enough scale, the whips may have little practical power; the solution then is for the party to re-examine its policy.

Crossing the floor

In an extreme case, an MP who falls out with his or her party may leave altogether and join another party. This is relatively rare; there were four in the 1992–97 parliament; and since 1997 the Conservative MP Peter Temple-Morris joined the Labour Party in October 1998 after a short spell as an independent; the Conservative Shaun Woodward joined the Labour Party in December 1999; the Labour MP Paul Marsden joined the Liberal Democrats in 2001; and the Conservative Andrew Hunter sits as an Independent Conservative following disagreement with his party's policy on Northern Ireland. An MP changing parties does not trigger a by-election, as he continues to represent constituents whether or not they voted for him;[2] but there is usually some local pressure for the defector to resign so that a new candidate can be chosen.

Large-scale defections may rewrite part of the political map, as in 1981 when twenty-seven Labour MPs and one Conservative joined the newly formed

Social Democratic Party founded by the 'Gang of Four' former Labour ministers Roy Jenkins, David Owen, Shirley Williams and William Rodgers. The importance of established party backing was demonstrated by the fact that only four of the twenty-eight survived the 1983 election (and one of those lost in 1987).

Party organisation in Parliament

The whips do not spring political surprises on MPs, for MPs are themselves part of the decision-making processes in their party, and their influence is felt in the committees and groups that each party organises. This organisation is obviously more complex in larger parties, but each party has a formal structure, supported by its own secretariat.

The Labour Party

The PLP

All Labour MPs, back-bench and front-bench, and Labour peers, are members of the Parliamentary Labour Party. The PLP meets at 5.30 p.m. every Monday for between 45 and 90 minutes. The main agenda item is normally forthcoming business in the House, and the Chief Whip tells MPs what the whipping will be. When the party is in government, secretaries of state may report on the work of their departments, foreshadowing policy initiatives; when in opposition, there will be reports from the shadow Cabinet. There will be reports from the PLP's regional groups and subject committees (see below). A major agenda item is usually topical issues raised under 'any other business'. Individual MPs may move motions to make a point or to test opinion; notice of these must be given to the Chief Whip at least a week before the meeting. Attendance at the weekly PLP meetings is usually between 100 and 150. The chair of the PLP (since July 2001 Jean Corston, the first woman to hold the position) is elected by a ballot of all Labour MPs (not just back-benchers) and is a key party figure.

The Parliamentary Committee

When the Labour Party is in government, the Parliamentary Committee of the PLP, in effect its executive committee, consists of the Prime Minister and Deputy Prime Minister, four ministers including the Leader of the House and the Chief Whip in the Commons, the chairman of the PLP and six back-bench MPs elected by other back-benchers, and one peer elected by back-bench Labour peers. In opposition, the Parliamentary Committee is elected by the PLP as a whole and forms the shadow Cabinet.

Subject committees

Each of these monitors the work of a government department from a party point of view; there is also a Women's Group, which only women members may join. Labour MPs may belong to a maximum of three subject committees (not counting the Women's Group) but may attend any other committee in a non-voting capacity. The committees meet approximately fortnightly, often with the participation of ministers; attendance varies greatly according to the interest of the agenda, down to half a dozen or so. On its own subject each committee has a range of tasks, including ensuring adequate attendance and participation in the Chamber for debates and Question Time, suggesting suitable members for appointment to relevant select committees and keeping in touch with the work of those committees. The profile and effectiveness of these committees often depends on the energy of their officers, but also on political circumstances. During the war in Iraq, the defence, foreign affairs and international development party committees met jointly, with attendances of sixty to seventy, for briefings from the Foreign Secretary, and Secretaries of State for Defence and for International Development.

When the party is in government, the chairman and officers of a subject committee keep in close touch with the ministers of the relevant department. Committees are consulted about forthcoming policy initiatives and legislation, and ministers must report three times each year to the relevant committee on the work and plans of their departments. In government, the committees act as pressure groups, but in opposition their importance increases as they then have a direct role in formulating party policy.

Regional groups

Every Labour MP belongs to the appropriate regional group: for example, Greater London, the North-East or Wales. These usually meet fortnightly and focus on issues of particular local concern or interest. They can play an important part in setting the broader agenda within the party, and they are also a target for local government, agencies and institutions that want to shape opinion among the MPs for their area.

The Conservative Party

The 1922 Committee

The Conservatives' equivalent of the PLP is the 1922 Committee, which was founded in 1923 by MPs who came into the House for the first time at the 1922 general election. Despite its former formal title of 'the Conservative Private

Members' Committee', it has always been known as 'the 1922 Committee' or 'the 22'. In opposition, every Conservative MP is a member of this committee; when the party is in government, it is usual for ministers not to attend unless invited. Conservative MEPs and peers attend but do not vote. The 1922 Committee meets on Wednesdays at 5.30 p.m.; the business taken is similar to that in the PLP. The chairman of the 1922 Committee (since June 2001 Sir Michael Spicer) plays an important role in the party as the representative of the interests of back-benchers, with direct access to the leader of the party, and he also sits as the representative of the parliamentary party on the Conservative Board, the governing body of the party.

The Executive Committee of the 1922 Committee

This consists of the chairman of the 1922 Committee, two vice-chairmen, a treasurer, two secretaries and twelve other back-benchers, elected each year. The Executive Committee meets for an hour on Wednesday afternoons at 4.30 p.m., immediately before the meeting of the 1922 Committee itself. The Executive Committee has always had a significant influence on party policy and direction.

Policy groups

These play very much the same role as the Labour Party's subject committees, engaging in dialogue with shadow ministers and feeding back-bench views into the formation of policy. The structure has been greatly simplified with the establishment of four policy groups open to all members of the party, on home, foreign, economic and environmental affairs. They meet on successive Tuesdays at 5 p.m.

The Liberal Democrats

Liberal Democrat MPs meet on Wednesdays at 5.30 p.m. for an hour or more. Forthcoming business is likely to be discussed first, followed by items submitted by individual MPs, and a lengthier 'any other business' slot. Occasional longer meetings take place, including 'awaydays' outside Parliament during recesses. Partly attributable to the size of the party (fifty-three MPs in the 2001 parliament), there is no formal committee structure.

Other parties

The five Scottish National Party and four Plaid Cymru MPs meet jointly on Wednesday evenings, with the chair alternating between the leaders of the parties. An important purpose of these weekly meetings is to arrange for the coverage of debates and to develop coherent tactics. This is a problem for small parties – business is arranged principally between the two major parties, and the Nationalists might find that they have to decide between support for the government and support for the opposition when they may not wholly support either. The option of abstention is not recorded officially and so is not distinguishable from absence.

The Ulster Unionists, with six MPs, hold weekly meetings, usually on Wednesday mornings at Westminster, and in Belfast when the House is not sitting. When the Northern Ireland Assembly has been in operation, these meetings have been complemented by monthly meetings with Ulster Unionist Assembly members. The Democratic Unionists, with five MPs, and the Social Democratic Labour Party, with three, have similar arrangements. The four Sinn Fein MPs elected in 2001 have not taken their seats; and although they have access to Westminster facilities in order to serve their constituents, they take no part in the business of the House.

Political groups

We said earlier that membership of a party involved a degree of compromise, that some MPs would like to see greater stress placed on some areas of policy or might be uneasy about other areas. For many years, in all political parties, these differences of emphasis have led to the formation of political groups within parties that more closely represent particular currents of opinion. However, the Labour Party in government probably has less formal activity of this sort than for many years. Membership of the left-wing Campaign Group has fallen to about thirty members, and the Tribune Group, closer to the centre of the party, became largely defunct (although a relaunch took place in May 2002). The Conservative Party has the centre-left Nick's Diner and One Nation groups, and the 92, which is to the right of the party.

Party leadership

No assessment of influences on MPs within their own parties (and the influence that they in turn can exercise) would be complete without a mention of the way in which party leaders are elected. Dissatisfaction with a party leader, or the perception that there is a leader-in-waiting, can produce blocs of opinion within a party (as witness the press's enthusiastic labelling of Labour ministers as 'Blairite' or 'Brownite', and identification in the Conservative party of MPs as 'Portillistas', or potential supporters of Michael Portillo for the leadership).

It can also give rise to an extreme form of dissent, as when in 1990 Margaret Thatcher was deposed as party leader (and so as Prime Minister) following a leadership challenge by Michael Heseltine, who had resigned from the Cabinet over the Westland affair almost five years before. Thatcher won the ballot by 204 votes to 152, but the scale of support for Heseltine led her to withdraw from the contest.

In the Conservative Party, a challenge to the leadership may be triggered only if 15 percent or more of Conservative MPs (in the present Parliament, at least twenty-four) ask the chairman of the 1922 Committee for a vote of confidence in the leader. If the leader then receives a majority of the votes cast, there can be no further challenge for a year. If the leader loses, votes of all Conservative MPs then reduce the number of candidates for the leadership to two, and the contest is decided by a ballot of all party members in the country at large. In 2003, Iain Duncan Smith lost the party leadership following a vote of confidence amongst Conservative MPs (90 votes to 75); Michael Howard was the only candidate to succeed him, and became leader with no further vote by MPs, nor a ballot of party members.

In the Labour Party, the leader and deputy leader are elected by three elements of the party: Labour MPs and MEPs, party members, and affiliated organisations (mainly trade unions), each element disposing of one-third of the vote. A candidate with more than half of the votes is elected (after elimination ballots if necessary). A nomination must be supported by 12.5 percent of the PLP (in the present Parliament, fifty-one MPs) if there is a vacancy, and by 20 percent (eighty-two MPs) if there is a challenge. In government, a Labour leader is more secure than a Conservative leader: a challenge may take place only if requested by a majority of the party conference on a card vote – something virtually impossible to achieve.

The Liberal Democrat leader is elected by a ballot of the party in the country as a whole under the alternative vote system. Candidates must be Liberal Democrat MPs, and they have to be proposed and seconded by other Liberal Democrat MPs, with the support in each case of 200 party members in at least twenty local parties.

The party – conclusion

Political parties consist of much more than Members of Parliament, but MPs are at the forefront of political activity, and they have an important role in the determination and presentation of their parties' policies. The multi-faceted organisation of parties in Parliament is a constant influence on the individual MP, in terms of voting expectations, exposure to the views of other MPs and changing currents of opinion, and, in the major parties, interaction with ministers when the party is in government and with shadow ministers when it is not.

In turn, MPs have the opportunity to take part in the development of party policies through formal committee and group structures, and also through informal personal contacts and relationships – the newest MP may spark off an important new idea with the leadership in a three-minute conversation in the Tea Room or the division lobby.

Personal influences

People are shaped by their experiences, and MPs are no exception. They bring with them into the House what they have acquired in previous careers, whether as teachers, lawyers, social workers, as craftspeople (in the case of Speaker Martin, as a sheet-metal worker) or in more recondite fields, as in the case of the Labour MP who was a microbiologist, the Liberal Democrat with a doctorate in logic or the Conservative who was a fighter pilot and flying instructor. MPs are also influenced by more personal experiences. In the present parliament, members' contributions have reflected, for example, being on the receiving end of racial discrimination, acting as a carer for a terminally ill partner, and being gay. Many of these experiences will condition how an MP reacts to some of the myriad issues of parliamentary life.

The constituency: the MP's relationship

The constituency is a vital part of the life of every MP. As we noted in Chapter 2, it is a power base, and its voters must be wooed to maximise the chances of being elected. An MP's identification with the interests and concerns of a constituency is also sharpened by the fact that UK constituencies are small enough to be fairly homogeneous in terms of character, population and economic activity.

An MP represents all the people in a constituency, whether or not they voted for him or her, or indeed whether they were old enough to vote; an average constituency in England may have 70,000 electors but a total population of 90,000 if you count those under 18. This non-party representation of a constituency is emphasised by the fact that in most cases (and especially in the low turnout in the 2001 general election) the majority of people entitled to vote will not have voted for the person elected as an MP. In the super-safe Labour seat of Bootle, for example, the elected MP won 77.6 percent of the vote, but this represented only 38.2 percent of those entitled to vote.

The closeness of an MP's relationship with the constituency, and the extent of its influence on the MP's actions in Parliament, has steadily increased. The classic statement of the relationship of member and constituency is that contained in Edmund Burke's speech to the electors of Bristol in 1774:

It ought to be the happiness and glory of a representative to live in the strictest union, the closest correspondence, and the most unreserved communication with his constituents. Their wishes ought to have great weight with him; their opinion, high respect; their business, unremitted attention. It is his duty to sacrifice his repose, his pleasures, his satisfactions to theirs – and above all, ever, and in all cases to prefer their interest to his own. But his unbiased opinion, his mature judgement, his enlightened conscience, he ought not to sacrifice to you, to any man, or to any set of men living. . . . Your representative owes you, not his industry only, but his judgement; and he betrays, instead of serving you, if he sacrifices it to your opinion.

The first part of this antithesis – the close relationship with and unremitting attention to the constituency – may be seen as years before its time, even though Burke was speaking to electors a century and a half before universal suffrage. For the whole of the nineteenth century and in many cases into the twentieth, constituencies were platforms on which MPs stood to take part in public life and which they visited rarely. Such absenteeism would not wash today, and below we describe some of the constituency pressures on the modern MP.

The second part – the assertion that an MP is the representative of a constituency who votes according to his judgement and conscience, and not a delegate who votes according to constituents' instructions – has undergone a transformation. An MP may still exercise judgement and conscience, and in doing so may represent a minority of opinion in the constituency – for example for additional rights for gay couples, or for additional powers for the European Union – but, as we saw earlier in this chapter, the main constraint on the way an MP votes is now the party to which he or she belongs.

Listening to constituents

The 2001 SSRB report on MPs' allowances noted that it is now the norm to have a constituency office to deal more effectively with constituency matters and to have a presence close to local issues. It also noted the trend towards basing the majority of support staff in constituencies rather than at Westminster.

In recent years, the core of an MP's work on behalf of constituents has been the 'surgery', when the MP's availability to discuss problems is advertised in the local press and elsewhere. In a small constituency, this may be at a central constituency office; in a larger one, it may be in a succession of town and village halls during the day, or even in a caravan that the MP tows around. Surgery work is on the increase; in 2001, the SSRB found that many MPs had moved to twice-weekly surgeries, and the change in the sitting patterns of the Commons in 2002 included many more non-sitting 'constituency' Fridays.

Constituents also raise issues and problems with their MP by letter – most MPs receive thirty to fifty letters a day, rising into the hundreds when there is a matter of great local or national contention. E-mail is increasingly used; in June 2003, 556 out of 659 MPs were contactable by e-mail or through their own websites (see also page 381). E-mail brings its own problems, however; the speed of communication leads many constituents to expect an equal speed of reply on what may be a hideously complicated problem, and some very conscientious members prefer not to use e-mail for this reason.

Constituents' problems

People will raise literally any subject with their MP. They do so for a variety of reasons: they think the MP will be able to get action; they have exhausted all other possibilities; they do not know whom to approach and so start with the MP; or they go to the MP as a personification of an establishment that they see as being the problem itself. This last category inevitably includes the desperate and the disturbed, and at surgeries security is often an issue; it is not long since an MP's researcher was killed and the MP himself badly injured, and other MPs have been attacked.

When a constituent seeks help, the MP must first establish exactly what the problem is. This is often much more difficult than it might seem. The constituent may be coming to the MP only after months or years of struggle with some organisation or agency, and his or her opening gambit may be to present a box file overflowing with documents of all sorts, some more legible than others. Unravelling the tangled skein to find out exactly what has happened, whose fault it was and what can be done about it can be enormously time-consuming. On the other hand, the problem – perhaps 'neighbours from Hell' – may be very straightforward, but what can be done without legal action, which the constituent cannot afford, may be much more difficult.

People often assume that an MP can do something about anything but, strictly speaking, an MP's role is limited to matters for which ministers are answerable to Parliament – in general, the responsibilities of government departments or executive agencies. This nevertheless covers a huge range of things that give rise to constituents' problems: immigration and asylum, pensions and social security, income tax, the Child Support Agency, the National Health Service, and animal health and farming subsidies being just a few.

The MP does not have a direct role in matters that are the responsibility of a local authority – the running of local schools, rubbish collection and recycling, council housing, council tax, and so on, as 'constituency cases' here are the responsibility of local councillors. But although an MP will be careful not to step on the toes of councillors (whether of the same party or not), he or she may on the basis of local difficulties pursue a broader issue of principle for which central government *is* responsible: for example, in the extent of central government funding for local authorities and what is taken into account in setting the level of that funding.

A constituent may bring to the MP a 'private sector' problem: perhaps the mis-selling of pensions, rogue builders, or rocketing insurance premiums in an area prone to flooding. A letter from an MP may or may not have any influence directly with the company concerned, but in cases such as these the MP's best bet is to engage the responsibilities of ministers for regulating these sectors of industry in the public interest, or perhaps to seek the assistance of an industry's own watchdog body, which has an interest in the reputation of the industry as a whole. If the problem is a failing company and job losses, the MP may be looking for government support for European Union grants, or money for retraining redundant workers.

Even if the MP really has no direct role, and the possibility of doing something constructive is very limited, there is always the risk that an honest answer to this effect may be misrepresented by the constituent, the press or a political opponent as 'Ms X doesn't care' or 'Mr Z isn't prepared to put himself out'. There is thus a good deal of pressure on the MP to make some sort of positive or helpful response, even if it is only to suggest some other person or agency to approach.

MPs are extremely careful to check that the person raising a problem is indeed their constituent and not that of a neighbouring member (you can find out who your MP is by putting your postcode into the *Locata* system on the parliamentary website: www.locata.co.uk/commons/). Occasionally an MP faced with a case in which he or she might be thought to have a personal interest may ask another MP to take it on. This also happens from time to time when an MP has taken a strong public stand on an issue, in order to avoid a constituent with a contrary view feeling that there might be a conflict of interest. However, if an MP dies or resigns, it is usual for constituents' problems to be dealt with by one or more neighbouring MPs.

A new MP is always warned by colleagues not to take up planning cases; planning has its own machinery at both local and national level, and the applicants and the objectors are usually all constituents; to favour one is to disadvantage another. Similarly, although the 'neighbours from Hell' referred to above may be a public nuisance for a whole local area, MPs are generally reluctant to take up neighbour or family disputes; all concerned are likely to be constituents.

What can the MP do?

An MP does not have executive power but is an analyst and advocate. In taking up a constituent's case, he or she must identify what the problem is and who is responsible (or direct a constituent elsewhere if someone else is more likely to be able to take effective action). Then it is a matter of exposure and persuasion. A letter on House of Commons writing paper may be enough to break a bureaucratic log jam or to persuade a company that it has indeed treated someone unfairly.

On most things for which central government is responsible, the most usual first step is the letter to the minister. This may ask for a case to be reviewed, for the minister's observations on the problem or simply for a clear statement of the department's policy on the point at issue. We return to MPs' letters to ministers in Chapter 10.

If the minister's response does not solve the matter, and the constituent has a good case that the MP is determined to take forward, the possibilities are limited only by energy and ingenuity. The MP may seek a meeting with the minister. If the problem is a wider one within the constituency, perhaps involving mass redundancies, or a manufacturing or farming sector in crisis, this may take the form of leading a deputation to a formal meeting in the department, with the minister and civil servants present. The MP may make an informal approach – the classic way is to corner a minister in the division lobby during a vote in the House. Perhaps there are other members who have had similar problems in their constituencies, who can make common cause. Maybe the issue can be given a higher profile through parliamentary questions or an early day motion (see page 271); or the MP may apply for one of the daily half-hour adjournment debates in the House, when there will be an opportunity to set out the case in detail and the responsible minister will have to reply. A case of maladministration may be referred to the Ombudsman (see page 317). At any of these stages, the support of the local or possibly the national media may be enlisted.

However good the constituent's case, success is not guaranteed. But, as with so many issues in parliamentary and political life, a good argument, persuasively and energetically deployed, the support of sympathisers, and above all, persistence and determination, offer the best chance of success.

Constituents' views

Constituents also write to MPs on the issues of the day. These naturally vary with the political agenda, but over the last two or three years the Middle East, embryo research, the European Union, hunting, the National Health Service, immigration, and asylum seekers have been at or near the top of the list. In most cases, an MP's response will reflect party policy or personal views. However, the strength of popular opinion shown by the size of the postbag – provided that it consists of individually written letters and not duplicated campaign mailings – may influence both individual MPs and their parties.

Constituency profile

A new Labour MP for a Welsh valley constituency had previously been an energetic local councillor. Within weeks of being elected to Westminster, he was stopped in the street by a constituent he had known for a long time. 'We don't see much of you now', she said. He replied that he had been elected as an MP. 'Yes', she said. 'I voted for you. But we still don't see much of you'. He explained that he was very busy in the House for most of the week. 'So you're not going to be here as much as you were?' 'No', he said. 'I'm sorry, but I'm not'. 'Oh', she said. 'If I'd known that, I'd never have voted for you'.

This anecdote (not apocryphal) illustrates a tension in the life of the constituency MP. The centre of parliamentary life is Westminster, and to satisfy the requirements of the parliamentary party and the whips, to promote constituency interests and to take part in select committee work, as well as to pursue personal political priorities, that is where the MP needs to spend a good deal of time. But there is a strong gravitational pull from the constituency as well. The local MP is expected to be on the spot: to open bazaars and fairs; to speak to working mens' clubs and the WI; to put in an appearance at school prize givings or road safety days; to comment knowledgeably on livestock at an agricultural show or present quality awards at the diesel engine works; to read the lesson at the civic service; to attend the Remembrance Day parade; or to draw the fund-raising raffle.

Those activities are public duty rather than party duty; but an MP must also spend time cultivating local party links and support (especially, perhaps, in the Labour Party with its mandatory reselection process; see page 22). This may involve party social events, from wine and cheese to beer and crisps, and a round of dinners and lunches (the so-called 'rubber chicken circuit') as well as reporting back on the MP's work at Westminster.

For many MPs, constituency activity fills up the rest of the week not occupied by work at Westminster. Some constituencies are within easy distance of Westminster and the distinction is less sharp, but, for most members, the Westminster week finishes on Thursdays; they travel to their constituencies that afternoon, and Friday, the weekend and Monday mornings are given over largely or even entirely to activity in the constituency; they then travel back to Westminster on Monday in time for votes in the evening.

Fighting the corner

The SSRB's 2001 report covered the work of MPs in representing the constituency as a whole:

> Our interviewees [a sample of MPs] were nearly unanimous that expectations in this area had grown substantially from business, public institutions such as

schools, and indeed the public generally. The Press have become much more insistent on the local MP contributing to local debate (for example through regular columns) and everyone expects them to 'fight the local corner' with Ministers and other influential players at national or European level.

Dealing effectively with constituents' problems is only half of being a 'good constituency MP'. The local member is also expected to be an advocate and ambassador for the constituency as a whole. This may involve seeing that his or her patch is not left out when EU grants or subsidies are bid for, or ensuring that ministers do not forget how the crisis in farming is hitting the constituency, or perhaps (for some Scottish MPs with distilleries) making the case against a Budget tax rise on spirits. As well as direct approaches to ministers and the media, subject debates and particularly Question Time are good opportunities for this; there is a convention that members should not use select committee work to make the constituency case.

In the last analysis, constituents expect important constituency matters to be paramount for the MP, even if that means rebellion against the party line. For example, during the last Conservative administration the otherwise loyal Tory MPs in the south-west consistently expressed their willingness to vote against the government if they thought that their fishermen were getting a raw deal in EU Common Fisheries Policy negotiations.

The constituency comes to Westminster

The closer a constituency is to London, the more likely an MP is to see his or her electors at Westminster. This may be an individual visit to put a problem to the MP; it may be an organised party to see around the Palace of Westminster and perhaps listen to a debate; it may be a school visit as part of the Education Unit programme; or it may be tea on the Terrace for senior members of the party in the constituency and their spouses. MPs value these connections; they give constituents a chance of seeing the other side of an MP's life and understanding more about Parliament – and of course they may be a special day out that demonstrates the MP's regard for his or her constituents.

Dual mandates

Few MPs are members of other legislative bodies. In the 2001 parliament, none was a member of either the Scottish Parliament or the National Assembly for Wales. In Northern Ireland, twelve MPs also represented their Westminster constituencies in the Northern Ireland Assembly; and two Northern Ireland MPs were also members of the European Parliament.

All-party groups

Some 280 'all-party groups' bring together MPs and peers to discuss issues of common interest. These groups must consist of at least ten members of the government party and at least ten from other parties. About forty associate parliamentary groups also include people who are not members of one or other House; the most significant is the Parliamentary and Scientific Committee, which brings together MPs, peers, scientific organisations, science-based companies and universities.

In addition to these are over a hundred country groups, which are formed of MPs and peers who are interested in the affairs of particular countries. States such as Kazakhstan and Yemen, as well as many more familiar countries, have their own group. Most country groups receive briefing from the embassies of the countries in which they are interested, and their members are sometimes invited to visit or to receive overseas delegations to the UK. Country group members do not normally see themselves as defenders of the governments of the countries concerned but as people who know something of the politics, culture, economics and history and so are able to make some contribution to the UK's relationship with that country. Most country groups are under the auspices of the Inter-Parliamentary Union or the Commonwealth Parliamentary Association.

All three types of group meet as often as enthusiasm sustains them; they elect their own officers and (because they are often seen as potential lobbying targets and in some cases receive outside funding) they are officially – and publicly – registered. The principal groups are Westminster fixtures; others are established or disappear as the mood takes. Some have formal secretariats and planned programmes; others may simply have a social event from time to time, perhaps with a guest speaker.

The extent and variety of activity is well shown by the meetings advertised in the *All-Party Whip* (this is not about party voting requirements but is a sort of Westminster noticeboard) for 29 and 30 April 2003. The Group for Parents and Families held its AGM and was addressed by a government minister. The Inter-Parliamentary Union had a report-back session for a parliamentary delegation that had visited the Slovak Republic. The Saudi Arabian Group's AGM was addressed by the Saudi ambassador, while the Group on Heavily Indebted Poor Countries heard from a senior US diplomat about US debt relief policy. The managing director of Shell UK Exploration spoke to the Offshore Oil and Gas Industry Group, and there were meetings of the Rugby League Group, the Obesity Group, the World Heritage Site Group, the British–German Group and the AIDS Awareness Group. There was a visit from a delegation from the parliament of the Ukraine, a director of the International Labour Office addressed the UN Group, a solicitor specialising in class actions spoke to the Deep Vein Thrombosis Awareness Group, and the Maritime Group heard about the operation to salvage HMS *Nottingham*.

All-party and associate groups give MPs and peers the opportunity to discuss a wide range of issues, often with major players. Their work influences members, but it also provides an opportunity to focus opinion and in turn to influence ministers. The groups are also invaluable to lobby groups and lobbyists in assessing parliamentary and political opinion.

Lobby groups and lobbyists

The word 'lobby' used in the sense of a House of Commons ante-room first appears in 1640. It later crossed the Atlantic to be applied to the geography of the US Congress. But 'to lobby', meaning to seek to exert influence on parliamentarians, and 'lobbyist', one who does so, are American coinages first appearing in 1850 and 1863 respectively. By the end of the nineteenth century, both had crossed the Atlantic the other way and became commonly used in the Westminster Parliament.

The term 'lobby group' is usually used of political pressure groups that might, for example, be campaigning for more resources to provide clean water in the Third World, or for healthier children's diets, or homeopathy – or for the ordering of new aircraft carriers or lower taxes on electric cars. 'Lobbyist' is usually used of the professional advocate whose skills in presentation, making contacts and persuasion are for hire.

Modern lobbying is mainly directed at governments, whose executive power and power of initiative make them obvious targets, and covers the whole field of government activity. Political pressure groups, charities or commercial interests may try to have particular provisions included in (or, just as often, excluded from) forthcoming legislation, or seek favourable tax treatment in a forthcoming Budget. The government is a huge contractor and purchaser (for example of defence equipment), and selling to government is a major area of lobby activity.

Single-issue politics, embracing campaigns such as those on such subjects as animal rights and anti-globalisation, often with an international dimension, have become more prominent in recent years. They tend not to use traditional lobbying methods but use the Internet both to bring their supporters together and to target politicians who are seen as opponents, often running campaigns against those with slim majorities. Some organisations that have used more traditional techniques in the past are either switching to this approach or are running both methods in tandem.

Lobby groups and lobbyists are interested in MPs for two main reasons. First, if they espouse a cause they can give it a high profile through writing to ministers, parliamentary questions, early day motions or tabling of helpful amendments to legislation. Second, they can influence opinion, both outside the House through the media and, more important, with their colleagues, both back-bench and front-bench. This influence will usually be greater if their party is in government.

Effective lobbying means effective targeting, either through knowledge of an MP's interests and experience, or by exploiting the vital constituency link. Too many would-be lobbyists have an entirely unrealistic idea of how interested most MPs will be in what they have to say. The Conservative MP for North Wiltshire, who had been a director of one of the larger lobbying consultants, wrote in April 2003:

> Bombarding decision-makers with excess and useless information will often be counter-productive. Those people who believe that they are achieving something useful by sending their annual accounts out to 659 MPs with a stereotyped covering letter with 'Dear James Gray' at the top (only worse is 'Dear James Gray, Esq., MP', which happens all too often) are mistaken – 659 waste paper baskets round Westminster will be the only beneficiaries.
>
> By contrast, a simple letter along the following lines will hit the mark every time: *Dear Mr Gray [preferably handwritten], the widget-makers of North Wiltshire are very concerned about the effects of a forthcoming government Statutory Instrument about widget specifications, which may put 25 jobs in your constituency at risk. I know that Mr Blodgett, the managing director of Widgets to the Gentry, Bumpers Farm, Chippenham, would very much welcome the opportunity of meeting you to explain the matter and to introduce you to his workforce if you could spare an hour or so, perhaps one Friday, in the near future. [Handwritten:] Yours sincerely, Fred Plunket, National Association of Widget-Makers.*

This description of an MP's reactions is reinforced by Paul Tyler, the Liberal Democrat Shadow Leader of the House, who formerly ran a public affairs consultancy:

> Anything that looked like a real message from a real constituent – preferably a local postmark – got priority attention . . . Targeting from a constituency viewpoint, and timing to coincide with the parliamentary agenda, has always seemed to me to be much more likely to achieve impact than the most elaborate hospitality or printed material.

Although lobby groups and lobbyists influence MPs, they are also extremely useful to MPs – and to others – as well. James Gray again:

> . . . those of us in Parliament, and no doubt in government, find truly professional lobbying very useful indeed. A shadow minister handling an obscure statutory instrument debate; a back-bencher searching for an original line in a select

committee or during oral questions; a journalist looking for a new perspective on legislation; a civil servant seeking to summarise an industry or public response to a ministerial initiative – all of these and others will value a truly professional, concise and targeted exposition of a particular argument.

Good lobbying (objective, factual, well argued) provides some of the research resource that many MPs feel they lack, despite the support of their own staff and the work of the researchers in the House of Commons Library. And if it obeys the golden rules of being on an MP's particular political interest, or relating to the constituency, it is likely to be used.

Lobbyists, or parliamentary or public affairs consultancies, are used by many organisations and interests. Some simply want to have parliamentary and government activity monitored in order to have early warning of what is coming forward. Others feel they need help in making their case. A typical assignment might be to attempt to head off a policy proposal that the client believes might damage his business. The lobbyist will need to understand the proposal and its context and master the arguments against it.

Contacts between ministers, MPs, civil servants, journalists and others must then be used, or new ones developed, to get the message over. The EU dimension is increasingly important, both at the stage when a proposal is only a gleam in the eye of the European Commission and as it advances through the European Parliament. Above all, the earlier the problem is tackled, before political capital is invested and it quickly becomes much harder to get a proposal modified or dropped, the better.

One fundamental difference between lobbying in the USA and in the UK is that lobbyists in Washington are advocates for their clients; US politicians seem to prefer dealing with a 'hired gun' than directly with the client. In the UK, however, parliamentarians prefer to hear the message direct, and lobbyists prepare their clients for meetings rather than being the principal actors.

In the late 1980s and 1990s, some types of lobbying acquired a doubtful reputation, becoming associated with the parliamentary sleaze described below and appearing to be based more on lavish entertainment than strength of argument. In 1994, the Association of Professional Political Consultants was set up by a group of lobbyists who wanted to brighten the industry's rather tarnished image by promoting high ethical standards. The APPC operates a code of conduct that bans any financial relationship with politicians or advisers, and the association also publishes a register of members, including the names of clients and consultants. Other trade bodies have followed suit.

However, no survey of the influences on MPs would be complete without an examination of the ways in which possible financial influence is regulated and policed.

Members' interests and parliamentary standards

Although individual MPs may not have executive power, they do have influence through the ability to bring subjects to public notice; to raise the profile of particular issues through parliamentary questions (see chapter 10) or early day motions (see page 271); or to press their cause in debate. All these processes can move matters up the political agenda or persuade the government of the day to take action.

It is clearly of the first importance for public confidence in Parliament that MPs act in the national and constituency interest rather than with the expectation of private gain. This has not always been so; the seventeenth- and eighteenth-century approach seems to have been rather more relaxed, although when Sir John Trevor as Speaker received the then colossal bribe of £1,100 from the Common Council of London for helping to get a bill passed, the House expelled him in short order. The fact that he remained Master of the Rolls for the next twenty-two years may say something about the judicial standards of the day.

The Victorian House of Commons recognised the importance of MPs' advocacy in the House being divorced from private gain and in 1858 resolved that: 'It is contrary to the usage and derogatory to the dignity of this House that any of its Members should bring forward, promote or advocate in this House any proceeding or measure in which he may have acted or been concerned for or in consideration of any pecuniary fee or reward'. This was aimed especially at MPs who were practising barristers, but it was reinforced in 1947 by a further resolution forbidding contractual arrangements under which, for any benefit, a member promoted any point of view on behalf of an outside interest. In 1974, the House agreed that MPs should be required to declare any financial interest that they might have in matters being debated or otherwise before the House or its committees, and that they should register their financial interests. A Select Committee on Members' Interests was established to supervise this process.

Parliamentary sleaze

In the late 1980s and early 1990s there was a steady growth in professional lobbying firms on the US model, many with multi-million- or multi-billion-pound businesses as clients. They saw parliamentary influence as a valuable commodity, and by 1995 more than a quarter of MPs had paid consultancies with lobbyists (twenty-six) or with other bodies outside the House (142).

Whether or not this was against the public interest, public unease was greatly increased by some high-profile incidents: the 'cash for questions' affair, in which *Sunday Times* journalists approached twenty MPs offering £1,000 for simply tabling parliamentary questions (which was accepted by two of them); and the allegations by the businessman and owner of Harrods, Mohamed al-Fayed, that he had rewarded MPs for lobbying on his behalf.

The Committee on Standards in Public Life

At the same time there was a growing public suspicion – both reflected in and to an extent fuelled by a high media profile – of the uses that certain individuals made of their position or wealth. Donations to political parties to buy influence, newly retired or resigned ministers and senior civil servants obtaining lucrative directorships, important public appointments being made of the basis of personal connections rather than merit – however widespread (or not) this might have been, the important thing was that it was widely believed. Finding his government dogged by such allegations, Prime Minister John Major set up the Committee on Standards in Public Life in October 1994.

The committee has ten members; it has no parliamentary character (although two peers and one MP are members) but is appointed by the Prime Minister and reports to him. It has taken on the title of each of its chairmen: first, 'the Nolan Committee' (Lord Nolan, a Lord of Appeal), then 'the Neill Committee' (Lord Neill of Bladen, a QC and academic), and most recently 'the Wicks Committee' (Sir Nigel Wicks, a retired civil servant).

Following the first report of the Nolan Committee in 1995, the House of Commons set up a Select Committee on Standards in Public Life to consider the Nolan findings and to recommend how they should be reflected in the rules of the House. The main changes made in 1995 were:

▲ the appointment of a Parliamentary Commissioner for Standards;
▲ the setting up of a new Committee on Standards and Privileges to replace the separate Committees on Privileges and on Members' Interests; and
▲ the drawing up of a code of conduct for MPs (the current version appears on page 421).

Members' interests: the current arrangements

Registration of interests

The purpose of the Register of Members' Interests is 'to provide information of any pecuniary interest which a Member receives which might reasonably be *thought by others* to influence his or her actions, speeches or votes in Parliament, or actions taken in his or her capacity as a Member of Parliament'. New MPs must submit a registration form to the Parliamentary Commissioner for Standards within three months of their election; thereafter, they are responsible for reporting any change in their circumstances within four weeks of it occurring.

The main categories of interests that have to be registered are paid directorships; paid employment, including practising in a profession or being a member of Lloyd's; clients and consultancies, including those arising out of being an MP (and any agreement to provide services must also be deposited with the Parliamentary Commissioner for Standards); sponsorships for fighting an election or supporting an MP's work once elected; gifts and hospitality; overseas visits as an MP that are not paid for wholly out of public funds; land and property; and shareholdings.

Various thresholds are used, mostly by reference to the level of the current parliamentary salary. Generally, an interest worth less than 1 percent of the current salary (so, at present, less than £550) does not have to be registered. (This comes in for some criticism at county and parish council level, where the threshold is £25.) A shareholding must be registered if it is more than 15 percent of issued share capital, or if it is worth more than the current parliamentary salary). For land and property, the threshold for registration of income is 10 percent of salary, and for value, 100 percent of salary. Sponsorships must be registered if they amount to £1,000 or more from a single source.

The Register of Members' Interests is published soon after the beginning of each parliament, and annually thereafter; in between, a version is kept up to date as changes occur. Both are available at www.parliament.uk.

There are also registers of the interests of MPs' staff (to make transparent a situation where an individual may be working part-time for an MP and part-time for a pressure group or commercial organisation); for parliamentary journalists; and for all-party groups. These too are available on the parliamentary website.

Declaration of interests

An MP must disclose a financial interest when speaking in a debate, in a way sufficiently informative to allow a listener to understand the nature of the interest, although it is up to the member whether he or she draws attention to a registered interest or explains it in more detail. Interests must also be declared when tabling parliamentary questions, when tabling early day motions or amendments to bills (or adding names to them), and when introducing private members' bills. When an interest is declared, the symbol [R] appears on the Order Paper beside the name of the member concerned.

An MP must also declare if he or she has a reasonable *expectation* of future financial advantage – for example, an MP whose family business made industrial cleaning equipment would be expected to declare an interest when speaking on a bill that would set up an inspectorate to monitor standards of cleanliness in schools and hospitals.

In select committees, all the members declare their registrable interests before electing a chairman, on the grounds that this aspect of an MP's independence is a factor in his or her suitability for the chair. Thereafter, members of a select committee must declare any relevant interest, or even withdraw from an inquiry completely if there is a conflict of interest.

Voting

The classic rule was stated from the Chair almost two centuries ago, when Speaker Abbott ruled that 'no Member who has a pecuniary interest in a question shall be allowed to vote upon it'. In modern times this is interpreted as a *direct* financial interest, and in the context that an MP's interests have been declared. To take two examples: in 1983 the Speaker ruled that MPs who were solicitors might vote on a bill that removed their exclusive rights on conveyancing, as the bill was a matter of public policy; however, in 1981 MPs who were also members of Lloyd's were advised not to vote on a bill to regulate the Lloyd's insurance market.

Lobbying for reward

This rule, based on the 1858 and 1947 resolutions referred to above and borrowing some of their language, takes the declaration of interests several steps further. It outlaws paid advocacy – that is, doing anything in the House (speaking, voting, tabling amendments or urging other MPs to do so, or approaching ministers or civil servants) directly for payment. In practice, this means that an MP who is a director of a company, or a paid adviser for an organisation, may not try to get any preferential treatment for that company or organisation (for example in tax relief, subsidies or some special treatment or opportunity) in any use of his or her functions as an MP.

The Ministerial Code

MPs (and peers) who are ministers are also covered by the Ministerial Code laid down by successive Prime Ministers to ensure that there is no actual or apparent conflict between their private interests and their public duties as ministers.

The Parliamentary Commissioner for Standards

The Commissioner's main responsibilities are maintaining the Registers of Interests; advising MPs (especially new MPs) about the rules; monitoring the operation of the code of conduct; and investigating complaints against members.

When a complaint is made that an MP has broken the rules, the Commissioner decides whether there is enough evidence to justify a preliminary inquiry; if so, he investigates further and decides whether a full investigation is warranted. If he judges that it is, he interviews those involved and reports to the Committee on Standards and Privileges. The committee may make further inquiries and report to the House with its recommendations, which may include suspension from the House (with loss of pay) or loss of pay without suspension. It is for the House itself to decide what penalty should be imposed.

The first Commissioner, appointed in 1995, was Sir Gordon Downey, formerly the Comptroller and Auditor-General (see page 253). In 1998 he was succeeded by Elizabeth Filkin, formerly an Inland Revenue independent adjudicator, who was followed in 2002 by Sir Philip Mawer, formerly Secretary-General of the General Synod of the Church of England.

Concerns about parliamentary sleaze in the early 1990s should not be underestimated; but, as so often when urgent political solutions are sought in the glare of publicity, what resulted was a set of complex legalistic rules (the Guide on the Internet runs to thirty-five pages), some of which had unexpected results. For example, in its original form the advocacy rule meant that, if an MP had been invited to visit, say, Brazil at the expense of the Brazilian government (as the British government has for years invited foreign politicians on study visits so that they may better understand the UK and its concerns) he or she could not have initiated a debate on UK relations with Brazil for a year thereafter, despite the fact that the MP concerned might have been much better informed than other speakers in the debate. That rule has now been relaxed, but the rules on interests remain detailed and more complex – and more restrictive – than in many parliaments.

Parliamentary standards shot back into the headlines when in 2001 the then Commissioner, Elizabeth Filkin, was not reappointed. The media assumed that this was a resurgence of the sleaze of ten years before, and the Wicks Committee swung into action with a further inquiry into parliamentary standards of conduct. In fact, at the end of an exhaustive inquiry, Sir Nigel Wicks in reporting to the Prime Minister acknowledged that 'real progress has been made in establishing and enforcing high standards of conduct'. No inquiry is ever recommendation-free, however, and the Wicks Committee put forward further changes designed to make the process more evidently independent. The thrust of these recommendations was accepted by the Committee of Standards and Privileges, and in June 2003 the House agreed to changes that entrenched the Commissioner's independence and provided an additional inquiry mechanism to assist the Commissioner in serious contested cases.

Standards now

There has been a sea-change since the assumptions of 'MPs for hire' of ten years ago, when the offenders were in any event in a small minority. This is probably as much to do with changed attitudes two parliaments on as with tough rules properly enforced. Some have taken the higher numbers of cases investigated by Filkin than by Mawer as significant. However, the previously frequent tit-for-tat complaints, party against party, have virtually disappeared, and the emphasis is now on 'education and prevention'. In addition, the 'rectification procedure' has introduced a much simpler way of disposing of cases of admitted failure to register or declare interests where the interest involved is minor, or the failure to register or declare is inadvertent.

No system will satisfy everyone. There are those who believe that all MPs should be full-time; others believe equally strongly that current outside experience makes an MP more knowledgeable and effective. But if outside interests are to be allowed, then public disclosure of those interests, allied to rigorous investigation of complaints and effective sanctions when the rules are broken, is the right way to build public confidence.

Influences on the House of Lords

Lords and Commons

Members of the House of Lords are subject to much the same influences as MPs, except that they do not have constituencies. Perhaps the chief influence – constraint even – on the House of Lords is its unequal position in Parliament *vis-à-vis* the House of Commons. The limitations on Lords' powers to reject or amend bills are fully described in Chapter 7, but it is important to grasp at this stage that the Lords, by not being elected and therefore being unrepresentative, are put at considerable disadvantage in terms of power compared with the Commons. If the Lords always attempted to insist on its will against that of the elected House, especially if the Commons were giving effect to policies endorsed by the electorate as part of the election manifesto of the governing party, there would be a constitutional showdown between the two Houses that would almost certainly result in further diminution of the Lords' powers. Because of this, the Lords tacitly recognises the right of the government to govern and of the House of Commons to see its will prevail most of the time. They willingly sacrifice their power in the same sort of compromise as that involved in the supremacy of the government in the House of Commons.

The introduction of an elected element into the House under any proposal for further reform of composition of the House (see page 390) would be bound to lead to a readjustment of these assumptions – assumptions that have held good since the House of Commons became a truly representative chamber following the extension of the franchise in the nineteenth and early twentieth centuries. That said, the House of Lords is also subject to government, party, personal and external pressures just like the House of Commons, although these influences are perhaps less obtrusive in the Lords.

Government

The position of the government in the Lords is not as well entrenched as in the Commons. Following a general election the party with the majority of seats in the House of Commons forms the government, and it is this party that occupies the government benches in the Lords too. The government front bench in the Lords currently consists of two cabinet ministers and twenty other ministers, from junior whips to ministers of state. Thus the government presence is, relatively speaking, much smaller in the Lords than in the Commons, and promise of ministerial office is accordingly much less influential. The government's influence over its own back-benchers and over other members of the House is, in the absence of a large 'payroll' membership, that much weaker. And party discipline – including that of the government party – is weaker because peers do not have to submit themselves to the rigours of selection by the constituency parties.

However, there is an understanding that the government can expect to get its business through. As we will see on page 222, under the 'Salisbury convention' the Lords will not reject at second reading legislation relating to commitments contained in an election manifesto. But a more general understanding on business is indispensable for the proper functioning of the House, as there are no procedural devices for curtailing debate on legislation; nor do the Lords' standing orders give government business precedence over other business. In the House of Commons, we have seen that a high proportion of sitting time is reserved for government business. In the Lords, anything up to 60 percent of sitting time can be occupied with government business, but none of it is formally reserved for government use. In the last resort, a government might try to suspend standing orders in order to give its own business precedence, but fortunately this is rarely necessary. Provided that the government business managers respect the conventions of the House, consult the opposition through the usual channels and do their best to accommodate the demands of the private member, the other parties and private members alike are content to leave the arrangement of business to the government Chief Whip. Governments are able to get their business through because they make sure that they are seen to deal fairly with the other parties and interests in the House.

The political parties

Although the members of the House are not elected, many of them – but by no means all – belong to political parties. A breakdown appears on page 34. Because lords are not elected, it is important to remember that the political composition does not change after a general election.

Officially, the House scarcely recognises the existence of the political parties. They are nowhere referred to in standing orders, and they are barely mentioned in the *Companion to Standing Orders*, the House's own procedural handbook. But the reality is very different. Each party has its leader and its whips and a small secretariat. We have already seen how opposition parties and the Convenor of the Cross Bench Peers receive public funding (the so-called 'Cranborne money') to assist them in their activities. The government party has the advantage of an office manned by civil servants to organise its affairs. Committees of the House tend to reflect the composition of the House, as in the House of Commons, and the government party negotiates through the whips' offices of the other parties (the usual channels) and, where appropriate, with the Convenor nominated by the cross-benches in the arrangement of business.

As in the Commons, the party whips send their members statements of forthcoming business in the House, with items underlined to indicate their importance to the party leadership. But discipline is not as strong as in the House of Commons, and there is no pairing system. There are weekly party meetings – every Thursday afternoon – at which future business is discussed and there is, even in the Lords, a general predisposition to toe the party line. However, for many members of the House, their political careers are not their principal interest, and the allure of office carries less weight. So there is often some cross-voting. And the cross-benchers – who profess no party line – are all, theoretically, floating voters.

The leader of the government party in the Lords is the Leader of the House, who, together with the government Chief Whip, advises ministerial colleagues on any problems that might be encountered in getting their business through the House.

Personal interests

The composition of the House guarantees great diversity of interest. The non-political element provides a lay presence. Then there are the politicians – either those elected hereditary peers who have taken up political careers based in the Lords or those created peers who have formerly been MPs or prominent in local government. Finally there are those, mainly but not exclusively life peers, who are experts in their field. Very often they are retired or approaching retirement, but their expertise still places them at an advantage where detailed scrutiny of policy is required – in debates on funding of scientific research or in scrutiny in committee of some abstruse piece of EU agricultural legislation, for example. The diversity of the members of the House ensures that personal interest and influences are very strong in the Lords.

And, of course, many have business interests. In a survey conducted in 1996 (before the passage of the House of Lords Act 1999) by Pensions Investment Research Consultants found that 134 peers were directors of eighty-eight companies. Some were directors of companies formed to manage family assets, but many were successful business people who had been ennobled in recognition of their achievements or had been appointed for the useful contacts they brought or the status they gave. Two sectors, banking and transport, had a particularly high proportion of 'lords on the board'.

Registration of interests

It is a long-standing custom of the House that lords speak always on their personal honour but, unlike the Commons, there was for many years no registration of members' interests in the Lords. In November 1995, however, following a study by a sub-committee of the Procedure Committee chaired by Lord Griffiths, a former Lord of Appeal in Ordinary, the House clarified its rules governing members' interests and resolved that lords should never accept any financial inducement as an incentive or reward for exercising parliamentary influence.

A simple but rigorous set of rules was put in place with voluntary registration of interests. Failure to register consultancies or interests in lobbying firms could be investigated by the Committtee for Privileges. Following a review of these arrangements by the Committee on Standards in Public Life, a system of compulsory registration of interests and a code of conduct came into force on 1 April 2002.

The code reminds members of their public duty under their oath or affirmation of allegiance and that they should observe the seven general principles identified by the Committee on Standards in Public Life (the 'Nolan Principles': selflessness, integrity, objectivity, accountability, openness, honesty and leadership). Members must comply with the code, must act on their personal honour, must never accept financial inducement for exercising parliamentary influence and must not vote or ask questions or promote any matter in return for money or other benefit (the 'no paid advocacy' rule). And they must register all relevant interests, that is to say interests that might reasonably be thought by the public to affect the way in which a member discharges his or her parliamentary duties. When they speak or otherwise act in a parliamentary capacity they must declare any interest relevant to the subject matter in hand. Those interests may be financial, such as paid consultancies, or involvement in the lobbying business, or regular employment, or shareholdings, or receipt of any payment or service: or they can be non-financial, like membership of or the holding of office in organisations or institutions, trusteeships and the like.

Allegations of non-compliance may ultimately be determined by the Sub-committee on Lords' Interests of the Committee for Privileges. If an allegation is proved, the member complained against can appeal to the Privileges Committee itself. The reports of both committees are made to the House. Under these arrangements, the House of Lords, unlike the House of Commons, has no power to suspend its members. The whole process of investigation and the publicity that surrounds it are thought to be sufficient sanction.

In a House which is essentially unpaid and to that extent is sometimes described as 'amateur', the personal connections and outside activities of individual members provide the House with a valuable source of talent and expertise. On the whole, this was not diminished by the 1995 registration scheme and only slightly diminished by the more demanding 2002 code in that at least one prominent member has sought leave of absence from the House rather than declare his very considerable private interests.

Territorial

Members of the House of Lords have no constituencies: they are not representatives. As Lord Birkenhead once remarked of a member of the House who had incurred his ire, 'The noble Lord represents no one but himself and I don't think much of his constituency'. It follows therefore that they do not have 'surgeries' or make representations to government or other authorities in respect of individuals' problems or grievances. Nor are they answerable to local party organisations or selection committees.

However, sometimes members of the House will be approached by interests in the locality in which they live or whose title they bear by reason of some long – and sometimes extinct – association, asking them to take up a particular stance on a public matter. Members are undoubtedly responsive to such approaches.

Lobby groups

As we examine in detail later on, all legislation has to be considered in the Lords as well as in the Commons, and some legislation begins its passage through Parliament in the House of Lords. Members of the House therefore find themselves courted in much the same way as members of the House of Commons by lobby groups either directly or through parliamentary consultants. The dramatic increase in lobbying since the end of the 1970s has been a conspicuous feature of the revival in the House of Lords' influence in recent years – part cause and part effect. Some lobbyists are skilful and selective in their targets. Others resort to an indiscriminate 'mail-drop'. These organisations will prepare evidence for committees, draft amendments to be moved to bills and provide briefing notes, offer to take peers on visits, or arrange lectures at which their policies are expounded. Thus over forty groups, for example, lobbied peers during the passage of the Criminal Justice and Public Order Bill in 1994, from the National Gypsy Council to the Prison Reform Trust and Save the Children. More recently, over thirty organisations lobbied members on the Communications Bill in 2003. Of these, one organisation was a consortium of twelve well-known charities, and another represented over a thousand businesses active in IT, telecommunications and electronics.

As a result of these contacts, some peers form potentially close associations with, for example, local authority organisations, industry groups, bankers, major exporters or libertarian groups. These contacts not only influence members of the House but also help to provide briefing and a wide range of assistance to what is essentially still a part-time – even amateur – Chamber of the legislature.

Like MPs, peers also belong to the all-party and registered special interest and country groups.

The independence of the Lords

Despite party and other influences, members of the House of Lords are rather more unpredictable in their allegiances and voting than MPs. This manifested itself strongly under the successive Conservative administrations between 1979 and 1997 and continues to do so under the subsequent Labour administration, with marked consequences for legislation, as we shall see in Chapter 7.

6 The parliamentary day and the organisation of business

The parliamentary calendar

Before we look at the various items of business that make up a typical day in Parliament, and how members of both Houses are likely to spend their time, it is worth looking more broadly at the parliamentary calendar and the cycle of business in each House.

A parliament

In Chapter 2, we encountered the main division of parliamentary time: *a parliament*. This is the period between one general election and the next. Under the Septennial Act of 1715, the maximum life of a parliament was set at seven years. This was reduced to five years by the Parliament Act of 1911, although during the First and Second World Wars, to avoid a wartime general election, the life of the 1911 parliament was extended to eight years; that of the 1935 parliament was extended to ten years. Although the maximum life of a parliament – that is, the period between the day of first meeting and dissolution – is five years, few parliaments run their course, because the Prime Minister of the day seeks a dissolution at a time that he or she sees as giving the best electoral advantage. The average length of parliaments since 1945 has been a little over three years seven months, and four years or so is the modern norm. Parliaments are numbered; the 2001 parliament is the fifty-third parliament of the United Kingdom since the Union with Ireland in 1801.

The beginning of a parliament

Some events always happen at the start of a parliament. Both Houses assemble on the day specified in the sovereign's proclamation dissolving the previous parliament. The Commons go to the House of Lords, where they are directed to elect a Speaker (see page 41). Having gone back to their own House and done so, the Commons return to the Lords the next day, where the Queen's approbation of the Speaker-Elect is signified. (These ancient usages reflect a mediaeval relationship with the sovereign; but should it ever happen that the Commons were unwilling to go to the Lords on either occasion, it would be difficult to imagine that their choice of a Speaker could be challenged as being somehow illegal or ineffective.)

The Commons then return to their own Chamber, and the new Speaker takes the oath of allegiance, standing on the upper step of the Speaker's Chair and holding a New Testament: 'I swear by Almighty God that I will be faithful and bear true allegiance to Her Majesty Queen Elizabeth, her heirs and successors, according to law. So help me God'. Other MPs then take the oath, starting with the Prime Minister and the Cabinet, and the shadow Cabinet, then Privy Counsellors (usually former cabinet and other senior ministers), then other back-benchers. The order of taking the oath is of significance only when the longest-serving MPs were elected in the same year; if their seniority is equal, the Father of the House (there has not yet been a Mother of the House) is the member who takes the oath first.

MPs queue up before the Table; the oath is administered by the Principal Clerk of the Table Office; under the supervision of the Clerk Assistant each MP then signs the 'test roll', a bound parchment book, and is then formally introduced to the Speaker by the Clerk of the House. The swearing in of members goes on for three or four hours that day and then continues on the next three or four days.

Jews may swear on the Old Testament, and Muslims on the Qur'an; and an MP who does not wish to take the oath may instead make a solemn affirmation. The oath or affirmation must be taken in English, but the Speaker has allowed it to be said additionally in Welsh or Gaelic. An MP must take the oath or affirm before sitting, speaking or voting in the House (except for the election of a Speaker); and if by chance he or she does not, the penalty is severe: the seat is vacated and there must be a by-election. The four Sinn Fein MPs elected in 2001 refused as a matter of principle to swear or affirm allegiance to the Crown and would thus not have received any parliamentary allowances (see page 59) or had access to the facilities of the House. However, in January 2002, against Ulster Unionist and Conservative opposition, the government secured a resolution of the House to give those MPs access to House facilities and to pay their allowances, arguing that not to do so would deprive their constituents of the services of their Members of Parliament, and would not assist the Northern Ireland peace process. However, the Sinn Fein MPs do not receive their salaries.

Most MPs take the oath or affirm in these first days of a new parliament, but those remaining may do so in the days following the first Queen's Speech of the new parliament (and occasionally much later if prevented by illness). When the 'swearing days' are completed, the House adjourns to the day of the State

Opening, which takes place at the start of a new parliament and also at the start of each of the sessions of that parliament.

Similarly, the Lords sit for oaths and affirmations and like the Commons then adjourn until the State Opening.

A session

This is the period that begins with the State Opening of Parliament and the Queen's Speech outlining the government's plans for legislation during the remainder of the session. It ends with prorogation (see below), or with a dissolution (see page 22) if it is the last session of a parliament. The timing of general elections often means that the final session of a parliament is a short one.

A session normally lasts from a State Opening in the first or second week in November until prorogation a year or so later, and it is denoted by both years (thus the '2002–03 session'). When a general election takes place in the spring or summer (as has been the case since 1979), the first session of a parliament is usually a long session lasting until the November of the following year. This is convenient for a new government as it provides a long first legislative period.

The State Opening

A session begins with colourful ceremony as the Queen drives in procession to Westminster with an escort of Household Cavalry, normally arriving at about 11.30 a.m. The processional route is lined with troops and thronged with tourists; bands play; the police even wear white gloves. The Queen arrives under the Victoria Tower at the south end of the Palace of Westminster and proceeds to the Robing Room, where she puts on the Imperial State Crown and then moves in procession to the House of Lords, which is a bright theatre of peers' scarlet and ermine, judges' robes and wigs, and ambassadors and high commissioners in evening dress and decorations.

Black Rod ('the Gentleman Usher of the Black Rod') is directed to summon the Commons. In a symbolic reminder of the right of the Commons to exclude any royal messenger, the doors leading to the Chamber are closed in his face; he knocks, is admitted and delivers the summons. Led by the Speaker and Black Rod, and followed by the Clerk of the House, Prime Minister and Leader of the Opposition, and members of the Cabinet and shadow Cabinet, MPs walk the hundred metres or so to the House of Lords, where they crowd behind the Bar of the House (the formal boundary of the Chamber) to hear the Queen's Speech.

The Queen's Speech

The Queen's Speech is the parliamentary core of this state ceremony. The speech is drafted by the government and will have been approved by the Cabinet. It normally refers to any recent or forthcoming royal events or state visits, and it contains some very broad policy intentions; the 2003 speech began: 'My Government will maintain its key commitment to economic stability and growth'. A sentence in the speech tells the Commons (because they, rather than the Lords, have financial authority) that estimates for financing the public services will be laid before them.

The meat of the speech is the legislative agenda for the coming session: the 2003 speech foreshadowed eighteen bills and seven draft bills. Bills are usually described in very broad terms; in 2003, for example, Parliament was told that 'A Bill will be introduced to improve the services designed to protect children'. Bills do not have to be in the Queen's Speech to be introduced, but the speech outlines the main legislative activity for the year ahead.

When the Commons return to their Chamber the sitting is suspended until 2.30 p.m., when the House passes the 'sessional orders', providing for good order around the House, the protection of witnesses and the now unknown circumstance of an MP elected for two seats deciding for which he or she will sit.[3] These are historical survivals of the days when the Commons had a greater need to assert their rights; but the sessional direction to the Commissioner of the Metropolitan Police to allow free access to the House has a modern relevance in the context of mass lobbies and demonstrations. The House also gives a formal first reading to the Outlawries Bill 'for the more effectual preventing of clandestine outlawries', whose purpose belongs to the distant past but which is a symbol of the right of the House to proceed with its own business before considering what the Sovereign has just told Parliament.

The Lords sit at 3.30 p.m., when certain sessional orders, including that to prevent 'stoppages in the streets', are passed; certain office-holders like the Chairman of Committees are elected; and a *pro forma* bill (in the Lords it is the Select Vestries Bill) is read a first time.

Debate on the Queen's Speech

This is the first debate of the session, normally lasting four or five days. The debate is formally on a motion to present 'an Humble Address' to the Queen thanking her for the 'most Gracious Speech' addressed to both Houses, but it is in practice a review of the government's policies and intentions. The debate is opened by a mover and a seconder from the government back benches (the only occasion on which a motion in the House of Commons is seconded). It is something of an honour to be selected (by the whips) to make these first two speeches. The MPs concerned (usually one new and one long-serving) are expected not to be contentious but to be reminiscent and witty and to extol the virtues of their constituencies.

Then the business gets more seriously under way. The Leader of the Opposition speaks next, with the disadvantage that he gets no advance text of the Queen's Speech and has only a couple of hours to decide on much of what he will say. Then the Prime Minister makes what is in effect the keynote speech, outlining the government's plans and programme and going into much more detail than in the Queen's Speech itself. The leader of the Liberal Democrats follows, and then the debate is open to MPs generally. The first day is a general debate, when any aspect may be raised; the subsequent debates are themed as agreed through the usual channels, perhaps on home affairs, or foreign affairs and defence, or the economy, and are opened and closed by the relevant ministers or shadow ministers. On the last two days amendments in the name of the Leader of the Opposition are moved and voted upon, usually regretting the fact that the Gracious Speech contains no plans to legislate to do this or that. When the government has a comfortable majority the outcome is not in doubt; but were there to be a minority government or a shaky coalition, these votes, and that on the substantive motion at the very end of proceedings, would be the first test of whether the Prime Minister of the day could command a majority in the House. On the last day, a further amendment may be voted upon; this is usually in the name of the Liberal Democrats, and it provides an opportunity to have a formal vote on the key policy priorities of that party.

In the Lords, the motion for 'an Humble Address' in reply to the Queen's Speech is moved and seconded from the government back benches, but the debate proper is then adjourned and takes place over the subsequent five days. Like the Commons debate, each day has a theme, but unlike the Commons no vote is taken at the end.

The pattern of the session

The reference points in any parliamentary session are a combination of the sacred and the secular: the State Opening, Christmas, Easter, Whitsun, the summer adjournment, the September sitting, the spillover and prorogation.[4]

Early business in a session usually includes a government motion to fix the thirteen Fridays on which private members' bills will be taken (seven for second readings and six for 'remaining stages'; see page 208) and the non-sitting or 'constituency' Fridays for the rest of that session. In the first few days of a new session the first two or three of the major government bills foreshadowed in the Queen's Speech will be introduced (at that stage they will be given a purely formal first reading, with second reading debates on the principle of each bill following ten or so days later).

Second readings of government bills starting in the Commons (others will be beginning their parliamentary journey at the other end of the building in the House of Lords) are a feature of business in the Chamber up to Christmas and again after the House returns in January, usually almost to Easter. (In the 2002–03 session, partly because of parliamentary time taken up by the Iraq crisis, major bills were still receiving second readings in May.) Also before Christmas, the Commons will approve the *Vote on Account* for the current financial year and the *Winter Supplementary Estimates* on the first *Estimates day* (see page 248).

After their second reading in the Chamber, the *government bills will go into standing committees* (see page 191), and in the period from Christmas to Easter standing committee activity builds up. At its peak, six or seven standing committees may be sitting for much of Tuesdays and Thursdays, occupying 100 to 150 MPs altogether, with each bill taking several weeks to pass its committee stage, and each being the main focus of activity for the ministers responsible for each bill and for the shadow ministers opposing them. As the bills complete their committee stages they return to the House for *report stages*, and in the period up to Easter and beyond this starts to take up time on the floor of the House. Government legislation will usually be contentious between the parties and so will require the presence of MPs to vote even if they are not directly involved in the business.

Most *second readings of private members' bills* will normally be taken between Christmas and Easter, but many will fall by the wayside. Around Easter the successful (up to then!) private members' bills will be coming through their standing committee stages and queuing up for the *six remaining stages days* in the summer. An MP's presence on a private members' bill Friday is less likely to be required by the whips (with the exception of the payroll vote of ministers and PPSs), so unless the MP has agreed to support a colleague's bill (or wants to obstruct or kill a bill) these may be days when the MP can work in the constituency.

Before Easter, the House approves the remaining *Supplementary Estimates* for the current financial year and any *Excess Votes* for the previous financial year (see page 250). A key event before Easter (it took place in the autumn from 1993 to 1997) is the *Budget*, usually in March or early April, followed by four days' debate on the Chancellor of the Exchequer's proposals.

From early spring onwards, *bills that started in the Lords begin coming down to the Commons* and going through all the same stages as those bills that originated in the Commons. The Commons rises in mid-July and in past years has had an unbroken summer recess until the first or second week in October. In 2003, however, the House had its first routine September sitting (as opposed to a recall), in the weeks beginning 8 and 15 September and then rose for the party conferences, returning as in previous years in October.

At a fairly late stage in the session, the two Houses consider the amendments each has made to bills that started in the other House: *Commons amendments* and *Lords amendments*. If amendments made by one House are not accepted by the other (most often, this arises because the government wishes to reverse a defeat it has suffered in the Lords) a passage of 'ping-pong' between the two Houses may ensue, with alternative amendments being offered in an effort to get agreement before the bill is killed by the end of the session.

The *spillover* of two or three weeks in the second half of October and early November is usually a hectic and often unpredictable period of tidying up the to and fro of bills between the two Houses, often with other business being inserted as a makeweight while waiting for one House or the other to complete proceedings on this or that bill.

We have described the pattern of the session largely in terms of legislation and financial business, but a great deal else is going on. Time must be found for the twenty *opposition days*, each of which is a full day's debate on a subject on which the opposition feels the government may be vulnerable; the second and third *Estimates days*, on which select committee reports linked to particular Estimates are debated; time may need to be found for private bills; and there will also be a number of debates on general subjects, from the hardy perennial of the Welsh affairs debate on or near St David's Day to general debates, often 'on the adjournment' (in other words, not with a substantive motion before the House) on subjects in which there is general parliamentary interest: perhaps NATO, the introduction of broadband technology, manufacturing industry, or European Union affairs. And every day except Friday there is the framework of Question Time, ministerial statements and the half-hour adjournment debate at the end of each day's proceedings, as well as debates in Westminster Hall on Tuesdays, Wednesdays and Thursdays (see page 268).

Business in the Lords follows a slightly different cycle. Although the business managers make every effort to introduce a certain number of bills in that House to occupy it in the early part of the session, most bills start in the Commons and arrive in the Lords after Easter. This makes for longer sitting hours and more sitting days in the latter part of the session. Thus the Lords often sit later into July than the Commons (although both Houses rose in the third week of July in 2003) and start their spillover one or two weeks earlier. Unlike the Commons, the Lords have no fixed points in the calendar for consideration of financial matters, except for their formal consideration of the Finance Bill in July.

Prorogation

This is the formal end of a session. It is a 'prerogative act' of the Crown, another survival of the early relationship between sovereign and Parliament (and used on occasion by monarchs to curb an inconvenient House of Commons). In modern times such royal powers are exercised by the government of the day, so it is the government that decides the length of the parliamentary session. There is no formal requirement for an annual October–November session (and the first session of a parliament in recent years has been one of eighteen months or so), but the constitutional convention of an annual session is a strong one.

The timing of prorogation is often settled in the last few days of the session; the government business managers want to be sure that they have left enough time to get the last bills through, which may involve a degree of brinkmanship in achieving agreement between the two Houses.

At prorogation, the House of Commons goes up to the House of Lords just as at the State Opening, although in rather fewer numbers; but on this occasion the Queen will not be there. The Queen's Speech – a retrospective of the session – and the proclamation proroguing Parliament and setting the date for the State Opening will be read out by one of the five peers who form the Royal Commission to do this on the Queen's behalf. Parliament may also be prorogued by proclamation when both Houses are adjourned. During the period of prorogation neither House, nor any committee, may meet.

Clearing the decks

A prorogation brings to an end almost all parliamentary business (which is why the business managers are so keen to secure the passage of government bills before the end of the session). There are a few exceptions: private bills (see page 224) and hybrid bills (see page 227) may be carried over from one session to the next; and recently the House has agreed to a procedure whereby public bills may also be carried over. This has been used only three times, for the Financial Services and Markets Bill from the 1998–99 to the 1999–2000 session, and for the Planning and Compulsory Purchase Bill and the European Parliamentary and Local Elections (Pilots) Bill from the 2002–03 to the 2003–04 session. In some ways it is surprising that the procedure has not been used more often for government bills. Although in some ways it is convenient for the business managers, it can also allow longer scrutiny of legislation – the pressure of time is both a bone of contention between government and opposition and a source of criticism of the quality of legislation. It could also smooth the legislative programme by allowing major bills to be introduced later in the session.

This 'sudden death' at the end of the session is practised by relatively few parliaments and may have disadvantages in the case of legislation; but it also acts as a clear-out of the parliamentary agenda and imposes some discipline on the legislative process. Early day motions (of which there may be well over a thousand by the end of the session) lapse, and private members' bills die – both those that are clearly going to make no progress however much time might be available and those that their backers feel might have had a chance 'if only'.

Adjournments

The standing orders prescribe when the House of Commons sits, both in terms of time and days of the week, so when the House finishes its sitting ('adjourns') on any day, it will automatically meet on the next sitting day. Longer times of adjournment, commonly called recesses – although strictly speaking this word applies only to the time during prorogation – are discussed through the usual channels and decided by the House on the basis of a motion normally in the name of the Leader of the House.

The normal pattern of recesses and sitting periods (sometimes called 'terms') is:

November   State Opening

December

               Christmas adjournment: about two weeks

January

February   A 'constituency week' coinciding with school half-term

March

               Easter adjournment: one or two weeks

April

May

               Whitsun adjournment: one or two weeks

June

July   House rises in the second half of July until September (summer adjournment)

August

September   A two-week sitting, after which the House adjourns for the party conferences

October   House returns in the first or second week for the 'spillover'
            Prorogation in late October or early November

November

The September sitting was an innovation in 2003, recommended by the Modernisation Committee on the grounds that there were otherwise no opportunities for parliamentary scrutiny and debate, and the tabling of parliamentary questions, for some twelve weeks during the Summer adjournment. It should be clear from the earlier account of constituency pressures that recesses are not MPs' holidays. Constituents do not stop writing because the House of Commons is not sitting, and many MPs will do more surgery work, and certainly more constituency engagements, than during a sitting week. But every year when the House rises in July, the media remorselessly report that 'MPs are off on x weeks summer holiday'.

Sittings of the Lords follow the same pattern but with some small variations; for example, the Lords do not always have a February break. Although in 2003 they rose in July at the same time as the Commons, in previous years congestion of business has often resulted in their continuing to sit a week or two longer. And in October the Lords invariably start their spillover a week or two before the Commons.

The annual calendar

Although the pattern of sitting times has always been broadly predictable to within a week or two, exact dates used not to be announced until a short time before each recess. In October 2002, again following a recommendation of the Modernisation Committee, the calendar for the next twelve months was announced. This has proved extremely useful, allowing those who deal with Parliament as well as those in it to make long-term plans. There is a tension between announcing sitting times a long way ahead and the wish of business managers to retain flexibility; and any change (as for example when the Easter 2003 recess was changed to allow for the Budget debate) may lead to criticism. In October 2003, the Leader of the House again announced the sitting dates for the next twelve months.

The annual calendar is a prediction of *likely* sitting and recess dates. Some suggestions for reform have gone further, with proposals for a fixed parliamentary year (so that, for example, the summer adjournment would always begin on the third Thursday in July), and the other non-sitting periods would be fixed in the same way. This, it is argued, would mean that the government would have to make concessions to get its business through without running out of time and could not use the threat of sitting into late July or even August. However, if such a fixed calendar were to be introduced (and it is hard to see government business managers being enthusiastic about such a change), the result might be a greater proportion of parliamentary time given over to legislation, and stricter programming of bills to ensure that time did *not* run out.

As long as the pressure of government legislation remains at the levels of the last few years, the same might be the result of the more radical suggestion that the Commons should meet in alternate weeks, with the rest of the time being allotted to constituency or committee work. Given the size of the House, a net reduction in parliamentary time would limit the debate and question opportunities for back-bench MPs.

Recalls of Parliament

In Chapter 3 we noted the Speaker's role in recalling the House if, as Standing Order No. 13 says, 'it is represented . . . by Her Majesty's Ministers that the public interest requires' that the House should meet during an adjournment. The Speaker always grants such a request; and in the last twenty years there have been fourteen days on which the House has been recalled to debate events, including the invasion of Kuwait (1990), the UK's withdrawal from the European exchange rate system (1992), the Omagh bombing and subsequent emergency legislation (1998), the terrorist attacks in New York and Washington (2001), possible military action against Iraq (2002), and to mark the death of the Queen Mother (2002). On 3 April 1982, the House met on a Saturday to debate the invasion of the Falklands; this was not strictly speaking a recall, as the House would have been adjourned only over the weekend, as the standing orders provide; on the Friday a motion to meet additionally on the Saturday was agreed to. The only Sunday sitting in the last century was on 3 September 1939, on the outbreak of the Second World War.

The sitting week in the Commons

From April 1946, the House sat at 2.30 p.m. each day, with the 'moment of interruption' (see page 143) normally ending the main business at 10.00 p.m., and on Fridays at 11.00 a.m., with the moment of interruption at 4.00 p.m. In each case, after the disposal of the business before the House (including business that was 'exempted' and so could proceed after the moment of interruption) there would be the daily adjournment debate (see page 267) for a further half-hour. In 1980, Friday sittings were moved to 9.30 a.m., with the moment of interruption at 2.30 p.m.

In 1994, following the recommendations of a select committee chaired by the former Conservative Chief Whip Michael Jopling, attempts were made to rein back the amount of business and the impact it had on the hours the House sat, particularly late at night. One of the changes was the introduction of Wednesday morning sittings starting at 9.30 a.m. As with the brief experiment under the 'Crossman reforms' in the 1960s (from the then Leader of the House, Richard Crossman), these were used primarily for non-contentious business and debates initiated by back-benchers. From 1999, Thursday sittings began at 11.30 a.m.; and at the end of 1999, with the additional back-bench opportunities afforded by the establishment of Westminster Hall as a second debating forum, the House went back to sitting on Wednesdays at 2.30 p.m.

When the House sat at 2.30 p.m. Mondays to Fridays, select committee meeting times tended to be 10.00 a.m. or 10.30 a.m. on Tuesdays, Wednesdays or Thursdays, or 4.00 p.m. or 4.30 p.m. on Mondays, Tuesdays or Wednesdays (most select committees meet once or twice a week). Standing committees on legislation would meet at 10.30 a.m. and 4.30 p.m. on Tuesdays, Wednesdays and Thursdays.

The new timetable

As a result of changes recommended by the Modernisation Committee chaired by Robin Cook as Leader of the House, 2003 saw a radical rearrangement of sitting hours. The original hours are kept for Monday (or for a Tuesday or Wednesday if this follows a recess), but the House now sits at 11.30 a.m. Tuesday to Thursday, with an earlier finish on Thursday. The few remaining Friday sittings stay at 9.30 a.m.

The programme for a normal sitting week is shown in Table 6.1.

In recommending these changes, the Modernisation Committee pointed out that over history the House's hours had changed in response to changes in social custom and business practice. Later hours were convenient when MPs were unpaid and could do much of a day's work in the City or the courts and still be at Westminster for the main business of the House. The committee felt that this was no longer appropriate when most members were full-time MPs.

It also observed that major events such as statements and PM's Questions came relatively late in the day; and the House responded to an agenda of public debate – in effect media coverage of events – which had already been set by then. Major votes usually came at 10.00 p.m., often too late for adequate coverage in the next day's papers.

In making its proposals, the Modernisation Committee warned that there was no consensus on sitting hours, and so it proved. Earlier sittings on Wednesdays were approved by 288 votes to 265, and those on Tuesdays by a narrower margin: 274 to 267. Opinion among MPs is still sharply divided: on the one hand, some believe that more conventional working hours make Parliament seem less alien, and that a more family-friendly approach will encourage more people with family responsibilities to become MPs. Others dislike earlier starting times for committees and the House sitting during a morning that could be used for constituency and other parliamentary work.

Table 6.1 Programme for a normal sitting week in the House of Commons

	Monday	Tuesday	Wednesday	Thursday	Friday
House sits	2.30 p.m.	11.30 a.m.	11.30 a.m.	11.30 a.m.	9.30 a.m.
	Prayers (every day, for about three minutes)				
	private business after Prayers (not on Fridays)				
	Question Time (not on Fridays)				
urgent questions, statements by ministers	3.30 p.m.	12.30 p.m.	12.30 p.m.	12.30 p.m.	11.00 a.m.
(On Fridays, the main business will begin after Prayers and will be interrupted if there is a statement or urgent question at 11.00 a.m.)					
	main business (perhaps legislation, an opposition day or a debate on a topic in government time)				
main business interrupted	10.00 p.m.	7.00 p.m.	7.00 p.m.	6.00 p.m.	2.30 p.m.
	after the end of any votes (or of proceedings on 'exempted business'): daily adjournment debate (up to half an hour)				
Sittings in Westminster Hall:					
begin		9.30 a.m.	9.30 a.m.	2.30 p.m.	
suspended		11.30 a.m.	11.30 a.m.		
resume		2.00 p.m.	2.00 p.m.		
end		4.30 p.m.	4.30 p.m.	5.30 p.m.	
select committees (typically)		9.30 a.m.	9.30 a.m.	9.30 a.m.	
	4.00 p.m.	2.45 p.m.	2.45 p.m.		
standing committees (typically)		8.55 a.m.	8.55 a.m.	8.55 a.m.	
		2.30 p.m.	2.30 p.m.	2.30 p.m.	
	(sittings in Westminster Hall, and in select and standing committees, are suspended for divisions in the House)				

Those with constituencies (and families) in or near London tend to prefer the new hours; those hundreds of miles from Westminster are less enthusiastic.

The new sitting hours were introduced only for the current parliament, and unless the House approves their continuation, it will revert to the old timetable. There is pressure in some quarters for a vote well before the end of the parliament, perhaps on the grounds that the longer there is to adapt to the new arrangements, the more likely they are to continue.

The sitting day in the Commons

This is often complicated and, although the business is taken in a prescribed order and subject to the House's rules, is never entirely predictable. Here we describe both the unchanging parts of the day and events that may happen only occasionally. Some of the more important proceedings are described in more detail later in this book. The Order of Business for a typical day appears on pages 136 and 137.

Before the sitting, the *Speaker's Conference* will have taken place. Here the Speaker goes over the business for the day with the Deputy Speakers and the Clerk of the House and his senior colleagues, assessing possible problems or procedural complexities, deciding, for example, what will be a reasonable scope of debate on a particular item, or what response he will give to a likely point of order. The Speaker will also take a view on applications for urgent questions or urgent debates that may have been submitted. The Serjeant at Arms is also present and may know of a planned demonstration or mass lobby, which may affect access to the palace or may delay MPs getting to the House to vote.

The start of a sitting

Every sitting begins with the *Speaker's Procession* from Speaker's House. The Speaker, preceded by a doorkeeper and the Mace carried by the Serjeant at Arms, and followed by his trainbearer, secretary and chaplain, walks to the Chamber by way of the Central Lobby (where the police inspector shouts 'Hats off, Strangers!', even though these days it is very unlikely that any male visitor will be wearing a hat). The Speaker and his chaplain (who is usually also Rector of St Margaret's, Westminster (the parliamentary church), and a canon of Westminster Abbey) and the Serjeant at Arms then enter the Chamber. The Serjeant places the Mace on the Table to show that the House is sitting, and the Speaker and chaplain kneel at the Table for *Prayers*. These Anglican prayers for the Parliament take about three minutes and are in private. (A member who wants to reserve a seat in the House for the whole of a sitting may leave a prayer card on a place to show that he or she will be there for prayers.)

As the Speaker rises, the doorkeepers shout 'Prayers are over'; the galleries are opened to guests and visitors; the Clerks' chairs are set at the Table; and, as the Speaker rises to begin proceedings with 'Order, order', television coverage starts.

Up to the end of Question Time

Although infrequent, any *report of the Queen's answer to an Address* (for example the 'Humble Address', which was formally before the House during

House of Commons

Tuesday 14th October 2003

Order of Business

At 2.30 p.m. Prayers

Afterwards

Private Business

Note: Private business is not debated at this time, and may not be proceeded with if opposed.

FURTHER CONSIDERATION OF BILL, AS AMENDED

Mersey Tunnels Bill. (*By Order*).

Mr Ben Chapman
Stephen Hesford
Mr Andrew Miller

On further Consideration of the Mersey Tunnels Bill, as amended, to move, That the Bill be further considered upon this day six months.

[*For Amendments, see pp. 127 to 132 of the Notice Paper relating to Private Business*]

Afterwards

Oral Questions to the Secretary of State for Foreign and Commonwealth Affairs

★1 **Mr Wayne David** (Caerphilly): If he will make a statement about the EU's political relationship with countries which will border the expanded European Union.

(131998)

★2 **Mike Gapes** (Ilford South): If he will make a statement on prospects for a comprehensive peace settlement in the Middle East. (131999)

★3 **Mr George Osborne** (Tatton): When he last discussed the situation in Iraq with the US Secretary of State. (132000)

★4 **Ross Cranston** (Dudley North): If he will make a statement on the UN's role in Iraq. (132001)

★5 **Mr Michael Connarty** (Falkirk East): If he will make a statement on the bilateral India-United Kingdom relationship. (132002)

Notes: ★ *indicates a question for oral answer.*
[R] indicates that the Member has declared a relevant interest.

Questions for oral answer not reached receive a written answer.
Supplementary questions will also be asked. Other Ministers may also answer.

Part of the Order of Business for a typical day in the Chamber of the House of Commons (oral questions 6 to 25 have been omitted). The House sat at 2.30 p.m. rather than 11.30 a.m. on a Tuesday because this was the first day back after the 'conference recess'
Source: The House of Commons 2003

| At 3.30 p.m. | Urgent Questions (if any) |
| | Ministerial Statements (if any) |

Preliminary Business

Ten minute rule Motion

1 MINISTRY OF PEACE *[Up to 20 minutes]*
John McDonnell

That leave be given to bring in a Bill to establish a Ministry of Peace with the function of promoting conflict resolution and the avoidance of military conflict.

The Member moving and a Member opposing this Motion may each speak for up to ten minutes (Standing Order No. 23).

Main Business

† **2 CRIME (INTERNATIONAL CO-OPERATION) BILL [*LORDS*]:** As amended in the Standing Committee, to be considered. *[Until 10.00 p.m.]*

For Amendments, see separate Paper.

Third Reading will also be taken.

Proceedings on Consideration shall, so far as not previously concluded, be brought to a conclusion at 9.00 p.m. and proceedings on Third Reading shall, so far as not previously concluded, be brought to a conclusion at 10.00 p.m. (Order of 1st April).

† **3 CONTRACTING OUT** *[No debate]*
Mr Secretary Clarke

That the draft Contracting Out (Local Education Authority Functions) (England) (Amendment) Order 2003, which was laid before this House on 11th July, be approved.

To be decided without debate (Standing Order No. 118(6)).

† **4 INTERNATIONAL IMMUNITIES AND PRIVILEGES** *[No debate]*
Mr Secretary Straw

That the draft Vienna Document 1999 (Privileges and Immunities) Order 2003, which was laid before this House on 3rd July, be approved.

To be decided without debate (Standing Order No. 118(6)).

At the end of the sitting:
5 ADJOURNMENT

*Proposed subject: **Inner city poverty in Leeds** (Mr George Mudie).*

Debate may continue until 10.30 p.m. or for half an hour, whichever is later (Standing Order No. 9 and Order of 29th October 2002).

†*indicates Government Business.*

the Queen's Speech debate) will come at the start of business. The sovereign's response is normally read out by one of the government whips who holds a post in the royal household (see page 88), and is generally very brief, as 'I have received with great satisfaction the dutiful and loyal expression of your thanks for the speech with which I opened the present session of Parliament'.

There may be a *formal communication by the Speaker*. When this happens, it is most often the announcement of the death of a member and is in brief, formal terms. There is normally no opportunity for a eulogy, although the House adjourns on the death of the Prime Minister or a former Prime Minister, or the Leader of the Opposition, after tributes have been given. The Speaker may also announce that he has sent or received messages of condolence or congratulation (for example to the Royal Family or to foreign parliaments or heads of state). He may announce the outcome of an 'election court' set up to resolve a dispute about the conduct of an election, which can declare a particular candidate to have been elected or can order a rerun of the election. He may even report the imprisonment of an MP (of which the courts must inform the House).

A *motion for a new writ* may be moved. This triggers a by-election in a seat made vacant by the death, resignation or disqualification of the sitting MP. It is normally moved by the Chief Whip of the party to which that member belonged but has occasionally been moved by a back-bencher wishing to make a point about a delay in holding a by-election, or to frustrate later business. By convention, new writs are moved within three months of the vacancy occurring, but there is no formal limit. If a motion for a new writ is opposed at this time, it is taken later in the sitting, after statements but before the main business.

After these uncommon proceedings comes *private business* – that is, private bills and related motions (including motions relating to the Committee of Selection (see page 321). At this time in the sitting day, only private business to which a blocking motion has not been tabled, or that is not opposed by even a single MP shouting 'object' can pass. Much private business is uncontroversial, and it is not unusual for private bills to go through all their stages on different days at this time.

A *motion for an unopposed return* may be moved. It may be that an official inquiry has criticised individuals who might sue if the report were published in the conventional way (for example, Sir Richard Scott's 'arms for Iraq' inquiry in 1996 and Sir Thomas Legg's Sierra Leone inquiry in 1998). This device gives the report the protection of parliamentary privilege.

Even if all the items of business listed above were to take place, they would probably delay the House for only four or five minutes. *Question Time* then follows and continues for an hour (although it may be extended by another twenty minutes or so if an *urgent question* has been granted, or if a minister has decided to answer a *question at the end of Question Time*). This is described in greater detail in Chapter 10.

After Question Time and up to 'the commencement of public business'

The main events at this time are *statements by ministers*. These may announce a new policy initiative, progress on a major industrial dispute, or perhaps the government's reaction to the outcome of a court case or an official inquiry. A statement may report on an international meeting, perhaps of the UN or European Council, or the outcome of significant EU negotiations. Statements are also used to inform the House about serious accidents or terrorist crimes and to set out the government's response. A series of statements over several weeks kept the House informed about the political, diplomatic, military and humanitarian aspects of action against Iraq in early 2003. In cases of great urgency, a statement may be made at another time; on 6 May 2003, after the decision had become known in Dublin earlier in the day, the Secretary of State for Northern Ireland reported the government's decision to postpone elections to the Northern Ireland Assembly at 10.45 p.m., after the main business and before the half-hour adjournment debate.

Significant statements are made by the responsible cabinet minister (or by the Prime Minister); less important statements are made by more junior ministers directly responsible for the subject. Ministers notify the Speaker in advance of their intention to make a statement, but (although they conventionally begin a statement with the words 'with permission, Mr Speaker') they do not need his permission, or that of the House, to do so. Notice that a statement is to be made appears on the television annunciators around the House two and a half hours beforehand, and a minister will as a courtesy give his or her opposition 'shadow' an advance copy of the text an hour or so before it is delivered. However, unless the subject is one that has been simmering on the political agenda, much of the political initiative rests with the government (especially so if the statement announces a surprise policy development), and the opposition will have to be quick on its feet to react effectively.

As we saw in Chapter 3, it is up to the Chair to decide how long questioning goes on. This will depend on the significance of the statement, but the Speaker will also have in mind the need to protect any important business that follows, at the same time as exposing the minister fully to questioning.

On Thursdays, the Leader of the House's *weekly statement of forthcoming business* is normally in reply to an urgent question from the shadow Leader (and so follows immediately after Question Time) rather than a conventional ministerial statement. However, if there is another statement on a Thursday, the Leader's announcement usually follows it and is technically a statement in its own right.

After statements, *any new Member of the House elected at a by-election* is formally introduced to the House and *takes the oath or makes affirmation* (see page 123) – normally on the Tuesday following the by-election. He or she waits below the Bar of the House (in other words, within the Chamber but just outside what is formally the floor of the House; the Bar itself does exist, but as it consists of two heavy metal rods that slide back into the woodwork of the benches on each side it is seldom seen). If there is a statement – or, worse, two statements – this can be a long and nervous wait for the new member.

When the Speaker recites the old formula 'members desirous of taking their seats will be pleased to come to the Table', the new MP, flanked by two members who act as sponsors (perhaps old friends or constituency neighbours), comes forward, clutching the certificate from the Clerk of the Crown that is proof of election. He or she bows and then takes the oath, signs the test roll and is announced to the Speaker and the House by the Clerk of the House. There will have been a lot of political interest in the by-election campaign and its outcome – particularly if the seat has been captured by a different party – and the introduction of the new MP is in some ways the culmination of the campaign, hailed with cheers from MPs of the victorious party and good-natured heckling from other parts of the House.

Also after statements, MPs have the opportunity of *requesting an urgent debate*, sometimes known as 'an S.O. No. 24 application', on what the standing order calls 'a specific and important matter that should have urgent consideration'. The MP must give notice to the Speaker beforehand and has three minutes in which to make the case for an urgent debate. The Speaker then gives his decision (and is forbidden by the standing order from giving any reasons). If he allows the application and the House agrees, a three-hour debate will take place the next day (or the same day if there is sufficient urgency).

Urgent debates are very rare; the most recent was in March 2002 following the deployment of British troops to Afghanistan, but the one before that was in 1993. Applications are less frequent than in previous years, no doubt because Speakers do not encourage hopeless applications; but they are used as a means of raising a constituency crisis as well as events on a bigger scale: in April 2003, one MP sought a debate on steel redundancies that were going to hit her constituency very badly; and in May 2003, an MP applied for a debate on the heavy financial deficit of her constituency's main hospital.

There is then a slot for (rare) *ceremonial speeches* – perhaps on the death of a former Speaker or some other distinguished figure, *motions to give the Speaker leave of absence* for some specific reason, and *personal statements*. These may be of apology, perhaps for failing to register an interest or for using 'unparliamentary language', or a minister may apologise for giving the House wrong information; or they may be of explanation after resignation. This second category can be dramatic. Sir Geoffrey Howe's statement after resigning as Deputy Prime Minister in 1990, delivered in an electric atmosphere in the House, was a defining moment just before the end of Margaret Thatcher's Prime Ministership. Equally memorable were Norman Lamont's statement in June 1993 after he had been sacked as Chancellor of the Exchequer; Robin Cook's in March 2003 after he resigned from the Cabinet on the eve of war against Iraq (his personal statement was unusually made at 9.45 p.m., but that was just after the equally unusual timing of a statement by the Foreign Secretary that talks in the UN had broken down); and Clare Short's attack on the Prime Minister's style of government following her resignation in May 2003.

Personal statements may be made only with the permission of the Speaker, and because the practice of the House is to hear statements in (near) silence, and not to allow interventions, the Speaker sees the text beforehand.

Matters relating to privilege (see page 167) may be taken at this time. Alleged breaches of privilege have to be raised privately with the Speaker, so matters of privilege are raised on the floor of the House only if he is prepared to give them precedence over other business. An opposed motion for the issue of a new writ in a by-election would also be taken at this stage of the day.

Usually at about this time, MPs will raise *points of order* with the Speaker (although points of order on the business actually before the House may be raised at any time). The test of a 'genuine' point of order is whether the Chair can actually rule upon it because it relates to the rules and practice of the House – for example, whether a phrase is acceptable parliamentary language, or perhaps in some complex business, the order in which the House would take decisions, or whether something was amiss in one of the House's working papers. The Speaker will either give his decision on the spot (particularly if the MP has given him notice of the point to be raised) or undertake to give a decision later. These rulings are part of the case law that is an important element in the practice and procedure of the House.

Even if a point of order is genuine, Speakers will normally not rule on something that is hypothetical, or on something that has happened in committee; that is the responsibility of the chairman concerned. Nor will the Chair give detailed procedural counsel, normally suggesting that the MP seeks the advice of the Clerks.

Genuine points of order sometimes relate to the administrative responsibilities of the Speaker, such as access to the precincts or the use of facilities. But the majority of points raised at this stage in the parliamentary day are to a greater or lesser degree bogus in that they make political or debating points. One of the most frequent from the opposition benches is an inquiry as to whether the Speaker has received a request from a minister to make a statement on some contentious subject (usually implying undue reticence on the part of the government). Assertions by ministers, or the content of their replies to parliamentary questions, are often raised. There is a Catch-22 in that the Chair has to allow the MP to go some way towards making the point, as it is only then that it becomes clear that this is not a real point of order. However, because of the limited opportunities that MPs have to raise current issues other than in relevant Question Times or debates (some parliaments have a period each day in which the members may speak briefly on any subject of current concern) these points of order can act as something of a safety valve. (A point of order specifically on the business before the House at that moment may be raised with the Chair at any time during a sitting.)

'At the commencement of public business'

It may seem strange that this title occurs only at this stage of the sitting day; but for almost all the preceding business most of the very few decisions that arise have to be taken by unanimity, and for much of the time there is no question before the House – that is, a matter put forward for decision by the House. Confusingly, there is no 'question' in this technical sense before the House during Question Time.

Four main types of business are taken at this time. The first is the *presentation and first reading of public bills* – a formality, which is explained in Chapter 7. Then come government motions to regulate the business of the House for that day – perhaps to allow several items to be debated jointly, or to allot time to a particular item of business, or to allow an urgent bill to be taken through all its stages at one sitting. Such motions can be debated and may be voted upon. To avoid the (perhaps unpredictable) loss of time for the main business, these are often taken on a previous day. The third category is of motions to give particular tasks to standing committees (for example, to refer a subject or a bill to the Welsh Grand Committee for consideration, or to take an EU proposal on the floor of the House rather than in a European standing committee).

The best-known category of business 'at the commencement' is the *ten-minute rule bill* (strictly a motion, because the member seeks permission to bring in the bill rather than a decision by the House on the bill itself). Every Tuesday and Wednesday, a back-bencher has the chance to propose new legislation in a speech lasting not more than ten minutes; if there is opposition, one MP may put the contrary case, again for no more than ten minutes, and if necessary there is a vote. These are very popular opportunities for back-bench MPs, not least because a back-bencher's opportunities to initiate business on the floor of the House are very limited, but also because they take place in 'prime time', which may be immediately before a major debate. Ten-minute rule bills are discussed further in Chapter 7.

The main business

It is unusual for the events described so far to go on longer than 1.45 p.m. on a Tuesday, Wednesday or Thursday (or 4.45 p.m. on a Monday). The House then embarks on the main business of the day, which consists of *orders of the day* (typically, a stage of a bill) and *notices of motions* (typically, a debate either on a substantive motion, as on an opposition day, or a motion for the adjournment, which allows a subject to be discussed on the 'technical' motion 'that this House do now adjourn').

It often happens that the usual channels have agreed that the main business should be in two halves, or that the Liaison Committee has recommended two estimates for debate on an estimates day. In that case, the halfway point is at about 7.00 p.m. on a Monday or 4.00 p.m. on the other days ('half days' do not happen on Fridays).

The moment of interruption

At 10.00 p.m. on Mondays, 7.00 p.m. on Tuesdays and Wednesdays, 6.00 p.m. on Thursday and 2.30 p.m. on Fridays comes the 'moment of interruption'. This is normally the end of the main business and is the time when most major votes are taken. Unless there has been a previous decision of the House to the contrary, business still under way when that moment comes will lapse. Thus an MP can 'talk something out' by continuing to speak as the Speaker says 'Order, order' to signify that the business is being interrupted. To prevent this the closure (see page 45) must be moved, which will be granted by the Chair after a full day's debate and is normally agreed without a vote, the House passing straight on to a vote on the main business itself.

'Talking out' is a traditional weapon used against private members' bills; 100 MPs must vote for the closure for it to be effective, and the sponsor of a private member's bill may find it difficult to round up enough supporters at the end of business on a Friday. In addition, if the bill is second or third on the order paper, the Chair may think that there has been insufficient debate to allow the closure to be put to the House. Strictly speaking, 'talking out' happens only when there is opposition to further proceedings. Theoretically, if the Chair detected no objection from any member, debate on 'non-exempted' business could survive the moment of interruption, and the House could then take a decision at the end of that debate; but such cases are extremely rare.

Non-exempted business, which is not expected to be debated, is sometimes described as 'nod or nothing after seven o'clock' (or ten o'clock); in other words, either it is agreed 'on the nod' without any objection, or there is objection and the matter cannot be put to the House.

Exempted business

Not all business has to end at the moment of interruption. A motion moved (only by a minister, and only if notice has been given on the order paper) may allow an item to be proceeded with 'until any hour' or for a specific time.

Some other business is automatically exempted: finance bills (unlimited time); Statutory Instruments and European Union documents (an hour and a half – although any that have already been considered in standing committee cannot be debated again); changes to the membership of select committees (an hour); and some thirty other types of business, although not debatable, may nevertheless be decided.

On the first four days of the week, after decisions and votes taken immediately after the moment of interruption have been disposed of, *public petitions* may be presented (on Fridays, this happens at the start of business). Petitions are described in more detail in Chapter 10. There is then the *half-hour adjournment debate*, which is covered in Chapter 9.

The last words spoken in the Chamber are the same as the first: 'Order, order'. The occupant of the Chair (by this time, usually one of the Deputy Speakers) leaves the Chair, and the Serjeant at Arms takes the Mace from the Table and joins the Deputy Speaker behind the Chair. The Deputy Speaker says '11.30 [or 9.30] tomorrow' or '2.30 on Monday', which is repeated by the Serjeant. The doorkeepers shout 'Who goes home?' – usually abbreviated to a long drawn-out 'ho-o-o-me', a relic of days when MPs homeward bound in the same direction would band together as a defence against footpads and highwaymen – the division bells ring for the last time, and the parliamentary day is over.

Late sittings

Late sittings were a regular feature of the House of Commons in the 1970s and 1980s. The average time the House rose in the decade to 1990–91 was well after midnight (so – taking Fridays into account – an average sitting of some nine hours), with some sittings lasting much longer. More than a fifth of sitting time was after the moment of interruption. Sometimes proceedings were greatly prolonged by back-benchers or by opposition parties to emphasise criticism of the government or its proposals. This occasionally went as far as sitting beyond the House's scheduled time of meeting the next day, thus 'breaking the sitting' and losing the government's planned business for the following day.

By contrast, the average sitting day in the 2001–02 session was seven hours and forty minutes, and the sitting time after the moment of interruption was only a tenth of total sitting time. There have been various reasons for this change – although all have their critics. They include the *routine programming of bills* (see page 179), whereby time limits are imposed on bills at an early stage in their passage through the House; *the move of a substantial amount of debating time to Westminster Hall* (and indeed a net increase in debating time thereby; in the long seventeen-month 2001–02 session the House sat for 1,540 hours in total, and sittings in Westminster Hall totalled 470 hours, or $2\frac{3}{4}$ hours for each day that the House sat); the taking of *more business in standing committee rather than on the floor of the House*; and *money and ways and means motions* (authorising expenditure or taxation in relation to bills) normally *being taken without debate*.

Time in the House

The Modernisation Committee pointed out that the House of Commons (and, by extension, the House of Lords, which has similar sitting patterns)

> spends far less time in recess than most other democratic parliaments. The House of Commons meets for more days than any of the parliaments of the larger Commonwealth countries and indeed for twice as many days as all of them except Canada. The typical pattern among European parliaments is for the legislature to sit around 100 days in the year, compared with 150 days for the UK Parliament.

Comparisons with continental legislatures, where the work of the plenary is fuelled to a much greater degree by committees, are not exact; but there is no doubt that the Westminster Parliament is one of the longest-sitting parliaments in the world. There are a number of reasons for this: the unremitting legislative programme of successive governments; the number of members and so the pressure for parliamentary time to raise a wide range of issues; even a degree of habit.

Use of time

In the 2001–02 session, the sitting time of the House of Commons broke down as shown in Table 6.2.

This fairly typical breakdown of a session shows that some three-fifths of the House's business is initiated by the government (although a small proportion of this – for example in 2003 in the debates on Iraq – may also be a response to opposition requests) and that more than two-fifths of time on the floor of the House is spent on legislation – not counting the hundreds of hours that are spent on legislation in standing committees.

Although questions, debates and statements provide opportunities for back-benchers, proceedings initiated by them took up only one-tenth of the time, whereas debates on select committee reports represented less than 1 percent. This picture was redressed to some extent by 470 hours of debates in

Table 6.2 Breakdown of sitting time in the House of Commons, session 2001–02

Business	Percentage of time
Daily prayers	1.0
Questions	10.4
Statements	6.7
Business statements	2.1
Ten-minute rule motions	0.9
Points of order	0.5
Government bills	33.0
Private members' bills	4.1
Private bills	0.8
Estimates	0.9
Affirmative instruments	1.3
Negative instruments	0.3
Government motions	16.0
Opposition motions	9.0
Petitions	0.2
Back-bench adjournment motions	6.0
Miscellaneous	6.8

Westminster Hall, where, as percentages of total *House* sitting time, debates initiated by back-benchers would have represented 23 percent and those on select committee reports would have represented 4 percent.

An MP's day

There are as many ways of doing an MP's job as there are MPs. The influences upon them, which we surveyed in Chapter 5, and the variety of priorities that they have, mean that there is no standard working week or day, although there are some common ingredients. An MP will normally come to Westminster from midday onwards on a Monday, depending on how far away the constituency is, and go back to the constituency on a Thursday or Friday, subject to the business in the House.

Some of the parliamentary agenda is set by the media, and devouring a variety of newspapers, together with breakfast news or the *Today* programme (or sometimes appearing), is a usual start to the day. Some time in the office at the House, talking over the in-tray with researcher and assistant, may be followed by attendance at a standing or select committee, and then to the House for Question Time (especially on a Wednesday, when Prime Minister's Questions are at noon). Or the morning may be given over to constituency work, perhaps also seeing a delegation representing an important local industry and then taking them to meet a minister in Whitehall. Lunch – these days for many MPs more likely to be a sandwich and a yogurt than anything more elaborate – may be in the office, or chatting with other members in the Tea Room, or hearing the case a pressure group wants to put. The afternoon might include writing the MP's weekly column for the local newspaper, signing letters, an interview with local or national media, telephone calls following up constituency cases, or back to standing committee or select committee business – perhaps interrupted by votes in the House. If the MP retains business or professional interests outside the House, he or she may find time for these. Later in the day there may be a meeting of a party committee and an all-party group on a subject in which the MP is heavily involved.

Perhaps the MP wants to speak in the Chamber; in that case, most of the afternoon may be taken up waiting on the green benches, leaping up to catch the eye of the Chair at the conclusion of each speech, and then being in the Chamber again for the wind-up speeches by the front benches at the end. Or possibly he or she has been able to secure the half-hour adjournment debate; in that case, much of the time that day will have been spent looking over notes for the speech, and perhaps discussing the issues with the constituent whose case has been raised, or a group interested in the subject to be debated; and, as the parliamentary day nears its end, narrowly watching the progress of business so as to be in the Chamber in time. Thereafter, a telephone call home to a distant family to exchange news about the day.

Ministers

If the MP is one of the ninety or so ministers in the Commons, the day will be very different. Whitehall, not Westminster, is their focus; their departments' concerns rule their day, and their officials feel that they own a minister's time. As well as work at the desk, there will be a range of meetings – with civil servants, ministerial colleagues (for the more senior, in Cabinet and Cabinet committees), official visitors and delegations (perhaps led by one of their back-bench colleagues). There will be opening ceremonies, keynote speeches at conferences, ministerial visits, EU negotiations in Brussels, press conferences. Their relationship with the House will change; now they are concerned only with one subject area, and their time in the House will centre on when their department is top for Questions (see page 288), when they open or reply to a debate, take 'their' bill through its stages or appear as a witness before a select committee. Their weekends are dominated by red despatch boxes with papers they need to read or approve by Monday morning – in effect, the homework set by their department. And they still have to keep up with their constituency work.

Most ministers' workloads are very heavy; just how heavy often comes as a surprise to newly appointed ministers. A senior member of the former Conservative Cabinet said (sympathetically rather than critically) after the first few months of the Blair government: 'Labour ministers have one thing in common; they're all knackered'. The pressure is considerable; for example, in June 2003 Alan Milburn, the Secretary of State for Health and seen by many as a strong candidate for higher office, concluded that he could not combine official and family responsibilities and resigned from the Cabinet.

To a lesser extent, the same is true of opposition shadow ministers, who have fewer resources to support them. Although they do not have the burden of departmental work, much of their day is spent in keeping up with developments in their subject brief, or perhaps leading for the opposition on a bill in committee or a debate on the floor of the House.

Attendance in the Chamber

Most visitors to the galleries, or viewers of coverage of the House of Commons, comment on the relatively small attendance of members in the Chamber. Objective measures are hard to come by, but average attendance in the Chamber has certainly fallen over the last fifteen years or so, although the Chamber is packed weekly for Prime Minister's Questions and at other times for major debates or statements. The level of attendance is influenced by various factors: there is continuous television coverage over the annunciator system, and there have been improvements in members' office accommodation, both of which have limited the tendency to 'drop in' to the Chamber rather than planning to be there for a particular item of business. When debate is predictable and the outcome certain – especially if it is by a large majority – this too will have an effect.

However, it will be clear from the description of an MP's day that members are also drawn away from the Chamber simply because there is so much else to do. For most of the day, there is a great deal of formal parliamentary activity going on elsewhere – in Westminster Hall, and in standing or select committees – in addition to the huge variety of party and group activity, as well as constituency work. Much is sometimes made of 'activity statistics': how many times an MP has voted, or how many times he or she has spoken in debate. These give a rather two-dimensional picture and can be misleading. Whips will score highly on divisions, because they are on the premises most of the time the House is sitting. But they will not feature in debates, because by convention they do not speak. Members with distant constituencies may not score as highly as London members; other MPs may decide that they can do more through select committee work than by interventions in the Chamber.

Sittings and use of time in the House of Lords

The House of Lords usually sits from Monday to Thursday, and on Fridays in the latter part of the session. In the 1999–2000 session – a very busy session – it sat for 177 days, an average of 7 hours 29 minutes each day (the Commons sat for 170 days, averaging 8 hours 29 minutes per day). In 1995–96, by contrast, it sat for 136 days, averaging 6 hours 53 minutes each day. On Mondays, Tuesdays and Wednesdays the Lords meets at 2.30 p.m., and on Thursdays at 11 a.m., adjourning at 1.30 p.m. for one hour if legislative business is being taken (Thursday morning sittings began in the 2002–03 session on a trial basis.) On Fridays, sittings begin at 11 a.m. and continue without interruption until the business before the House has been completed. As in the Commons, Saturday and Sunday sittings have taken place only at times of national crisis. The length of Lords' sittings has grown gradually – in the 1974–75 session, the average sitting lasted under six hours.

As in the Commons, the day begins with *prayers*. In the Lords, prayers are read by a bishop, and members kneel on the benches. Immediately after prayers, new peers go through their ceremony of introduction and take the oath, as does any peer who has not yet taken the oath in this parliament. The business starts with a short *question time*. Four questions – known as 'starred questions' because they are marked with a star on the order paper – are taken on Mondays and Thursdays and five on Tuesdays and Wednesdays. Private notice questions are very rarely allowed in the Lords but, when they are, they come immediately after starred questions. *Business statements* – indicating the limitations on speaking time to be observed in time-limited debates, or the hour of adjournment for dinner during a particularly long piece of legislative business, for example – follow. *Ministerial statements* in theory come next, but only if the minister making the statement is a lord. Most statements are made in the Commons and repeated in the Lords. Occasionally statements to be made in the Commons are deemed by the usual channels not to be sufficiently important to the Lords to be repeated. When they are important, they are usually delivered in the Commons at 12.30 p.m. and in the Lords as soon after as is convenient. In the Lords, brief comments and questions for clarification from the opposition front benches and from back-benchers of all parties are allowed for a total period not exceeding forty minutes following the end of the statement. Members clearly value this opportunity to comment and probe the government further on statements, and an attempt by the Lords Procedure Committee to restrict comment to front-bench spokesmen of the main political parties received very short shrift from the House.

The substantive business then begins. Discussion of *private legislation* comes first, followed by *Business of the House motions*, usually moved by the Leader of the House and signifying a change in the order of business. Then, when necessary, comes *Chairman of Committees' business*. This usually relates to the discussion of any reports by committees for which the Chairman of Committees has responsibility – such as reports of the House Committee on some matter of internal management, or the Procedure Committee. Discussion of *public bills, delegated legislation and reports from select committees* come next, followed by other motions. At the end of business, any *questions for debate that have been tabled for oral answer* by the government may be taken. These are called 'unstarred questions' (to distinguish them from the questions put at the commencement of business, which do not give rise to debate, they are not prefixed by a star on the order paper). Proceedings on unstarred questions are time-limited to one and a half hours. They are somewhat akin to adjournment debates in the Commons. Indeed, so popular have they become that, if time permits, they are now sometimes taken during the adjournment for dinner of proceedings on a major bill.

The order of business is slightly different on Wednesdays, when by standing order motions have precedence over bills and other business. The practical effect of this is to make Wednesday a day of debates. Any other business has to come last.

It would be very unusual to find all the different kinds of business set down for any one day. A typical day might begin with prayers, followed by starred questions and business statements; proceedings on a private bill might come next but would usually be very brief (discussion of a controversial nature will, at the Chairman of Committees' discretion, usually be deferred until later in the day); there may then come a business motion; then would follow the legislative stages of one or more bills. If the principal business consists of a lengthy stage of a major bill requiring constant attendance, then at 7.30 p.m. that stage may be adjourned for an hour, in which time short items of business – like an uncontentious piece of delegated legislation or a private member's bill or, as has recently become the practice, an unstarred question – might be taken. The adjourned proceedings on the major bill will then be resumed and the House might adjourn at any time between about 9 p.m. and 11 p.m. If it is likely that business will finish earlier in the evening, an unstarred question may have been set down as last business.

A day's business in the Lords is illustrated by the Order Paper reproduced overleaf. After questions, a motion relating to the establishment of a joint select committee was moved: this was followed by a government motion (an 'instruction') to provide on a later day for a bill to be considered by a committee of the whole House in a particular order; a motion was next moved discharging a committee stage of a private member's bill because no amendments had been tabled; then we find the main business of the day, a debate moved by the government on the Convention on the Future of Europe (this debate was held jointly with that on the relevant report of the European Union Select Committee, which is the subject of the motion in the name of Lord Grenfell, its chairman); after the debate comes a motion to approve an item of delegated legislation requiring the approval of the House (an affirmative instrument); and business ends with the committee stage of a Commons private member's bill, to which amendments had been tabled. The House rose at a quarter to midnight!

In July 2002, the Procedure Committee endorsed the recommendation of a working group chaired by the then Leader of the House, Lord Williams of Mostyn, that it should be a firm convention that the House should rise by about 10 p.m. on Mondays to Wednesdays and that on Thursdays any business should be completed by 7.00 p.m. It remains to be seen whether this 10 p.m. convention becomes established. By the latter part of the 2002–03 session, pressure of business meant that the 10 p.m. convention was often simply not observed.

The sitting time of the House of Lords in the 1995–96 and 2001–02 sessions broke down approximately as shown in Table 6.3.

We conclude this chapter with four topics that are ever-present in a parliamentarian's day: parliamentary papers, voting, the media and the broadcasting of Parliament; and two that form a preface to the more detailed examination of some of the functions of Parliament that follows: privilege and procedure.

Parliamentary papers

The parliamentary process generates a great deal of paper. Much of it is private and relates only to a particular group – for example the working papers of a select committee – but there is also a central core of printed material that

NOTICES AND ORDERS OF THE DAY

TUESDAY 9TH SEPTEMBER

At half-past two o'clock

*The Lord Dormand of Easington—To ask Her Majesty's Government when they expect to introduce legislation to deal with excessive payments to company chairmen and executives.

*The Lord Campbell of Croy—To ask Her Majesty's Government whether the English language tests, required to be taken by foreign doctors intending to practise in the United Kingdom, are to be abolished.

*The Baroness McIntosh of Hudnall—To ask Her Majesty's Government whether they consider that significant expansion of airport capacity in South-East England will be in the long term interests of the residents of the area and their environment.

*The Lord Hannay of Chiswick—To ask Her Majesty's Government how much worse off the universities would be if they received no income at all from tuition fees rather than the fees set out in the January White Paper; and whether there is any viable alternative for financing higher education other than the raising of tuition fees.

*The Viscount Bridgeman—To ask Her Majesty's Government whether the proposed drug testing for police officers in England and Wales could be considered intrusive and a breach of their civil liberties.

Gambling—The Chairman of Committees to move, That the Commons message of 10th July be now considered, and that a Committee of eight Lords be appointed to join with the Committee appointed by the Commons, to consider and report on any draft Gambling Bill presented to both Houses by a Minister of the Crown;

That, as proposed by the Committee of Selection, the Lords following be named of the Committee:

L. Brooke of Sutton Mandeville	B. Golding
L. Donoughue	L. Mancroft
V. Falkland	L. Wade of Chorlton
L. Faulkner of Worcester	L. Walpole;

That the Committee have power to agree with the Commons in the appointment of a Chairman;

That the Committee have leave to report from time to time;

That the Committee have power to appoint specialist advisers;

That the Committee have power to adjourn from place to place within the United Kingdom;

That the reports of the Committee from time to time shall be printed, notwithstanding any adjournment of the House;

That the Committee do report on the draft Bill by 8th April 2004;

And that the Committee do meet with the Committee appointed by the Commons on Tuesday 16th September at half past nine o'clock in Committee Room 3.

Anti-social Behaviour Bill—The Baroness Scotland of Asthal to move, That it be an instruction to the Committee to which the Anti-social Behaviour Bill has been committed that they consider the bill in the following order:

Clauses 1 to 14	Clauses 41 to 66
Schedule 1	Schedule 3
Clause 15 to 40	Clauses 67 to 71.
Schedule 2	

National Lottery (Funding of Endowments) Bill—Committee [The Lord Walpole]
   The Lord Walpole—To move, That the order of commitment be discharged.

The Baroness Symons of Vernham Dean—To move, That this House takes note of the draft Constitutional Treaty produced by the Convention on the Future of Europe.

The Lord Grenfell—To move, That this House takes note of the Report of the European Union Committee on The Future of Europe: Progress Report on the draft Constitutional Treaty and the IGC (35th Report, HL Paper 150).

Vienna Document 1999 (Privileges and Immunities) Order 2003—The Baroness Symons of Vernham Dean to move, That the draft Order laid before the House on 3rd July be approved. [26th Report from the Joint Committee]

Fireworks Bill—Committee [The Baroness Ramsay of Cartvale]   [23rd Report from the Delegated Powers Committee]

Notices and Orders of the day: the House of Lords Order Paper
Source: The House of Lords 2003

Table 6.3 Comparisons of sitting time breakdowns in the House of Lords, Sessions 1995–96 and 2001–02

	Percentage of time spent	
	1995–96	*2001–02*
Prayers	1.2	1.2
Introductions	0.5	0.3
Starred questions	6.7	6.4
Private bills	0.1	0.2
Statements	3.1	4.8
Public bills (government)	47.8	47.4
Public bills (private members)	4.3	4.3
Statutory instruments	5.7	4.6
Debates	25.1	22.2
Unstarred questions	3.0	6.8

provides MPs with their bread-and-butter information and that is also available to people outside Parliament.

The Vote bundle

Every MP receives a daily bundle of papers known as 'the Vote'. This will be no more than a few pages in the first few days of the session, but for many sitting days it may be as much as 200 pages. The front page is the *Summary Agenda*, which lists the titles of business to be taken in the House and Westminster Hall. Then follows the *Order of Business* or Order Paper, a detailed agenda that gives all the items for which notice is required; so, for example, the texts of oral questions and of any motions to be debated (or to be put for decision without debate), in the order in which they will be taken. The Order Paper 'freezes' at the moment when the House adjourns on the previous sitting day; nothing can be slipped in thereafter (although of course some things are permitted to be done without notice). Statements and urgent questions are not included; they are notified by way of the television annunciators before the start of the sitting. The Order Paper tries to be informative without being misleading (for example, by implying that a practice normally followed will necessarily be followed). After all, it is often the opposition's aim not to achieve the agenda; and the government does not have to proceed with every item of business simply because it is on the Order Paper.

There is then a list of *standing and select committee sittings that day*, giving the time and place of each, and the witnesses for public sittings of select committees, followed by *standing committee sittings for the next week*. The next section is *future business*, section A of which covers *the provisional business announced by the Leader of the House* for the next week or more; B is *business for Westminster Hall*; C is *remaining orders and notices*, which covers future business (although each item is set down formally for that day, it is not expected to be taken); D, *other future business*, gives items scheduled for particular future days (normally ten-minute rule motions and private members' bills) and E gives notice of *written ministerial statements* to be made that day (for less important announcements, an alternative to making an oral statement to the House). Then follows the *Order Paper for Westminster Hall*.

Other items in the Vote bundle are *lists of amendments* put down to bills to be debated that day, both on the floor of the House and in standing committee; and the *Votes and Proceedings*. This is the formal legal record of what the House *did* the previous day rather than what was said: decisions on motions, amendments made to bills, papers laid before the House, the record of reports from select committees, and so on. Many of the papers listed above are available on the parliamentary website (www.parliament.uk).

Also in the Vote bundle are the parliamentary questions and amendments to bills that were tabled the previous day, and new early day motions (or those up to a fortnight old to which new signatures were added the previous day). These are all printed on blue paper to show that they are new notices rather than papers for the current working day. All parliamentary questions already tabled for that day or for a future day are contained in the separate *Question Book*.

Hansard

T.C. Hansard was the nineteenth-century printer and publisher whose daily record of the Commons was published privately. From 1909, staff of the House took on the recording of debates, but the name 'Hansard' stuck and was officially adopted in 1943. Properly called *the Official Report*, Hansard is the record of what is said in the House. It is verbatim; *Official Report* staff tidy up obvious mistakes and repetitions, but they do not allow any change of substance.

Hansard contains not only everything that is said in debates in the House and Westminster Hall the previous day but also lists of MPs voting in divisions and a large section devoted to the answers given by ministers to written questions, motions awaiting debate, questions for written answer, bills and orders of various kinds in progress, and forthcoming meetings of committees. A *Weekly Bulletin* of meetings of select committees for up to one month ahead is published by the Committee Office. There is also a sessional journal, the formal record of proceedings.

The House of Lords also has its own *Hansard*, and nearly all the papers presented to the Commons are also laid before the House of Lords.

Voting

Votes are called 'divisions' because MPs 'divide' physically, going through different lobbies depending on which way they are voting. Although during a sitting day many things are decided without a division, disagreement between government and opposition (or dissent by a smaller group of MPs on either side of the House) will produce a vote. And forcing votes as a means of taking time and disrupting or delaying the business is a tactic used in every parliament.

Voting in both Houses of Parliament is on the basis of approval or disapproval; there is no provision for formally recording abstentions and no means of ranking competing choices in a single decision (which might have led to a rather different outcome on the future composition of the House of Lords); the only exception is in the new procedure for the election of a Speaker.

When a proposition has been put before the House for debate (for example, when a member has moved that a bill 'be now read a second time', or that an amendment be made), when the mover sits down, the Speaker *proposes the Question* – in other words, says formally to the House 'The Question is, that the Bill be now read a second time' or whatever, making clear exactly what it is that the House then has to decide or debate. This may seem a pointless duplication, but it is important as a formality – and vital if the House is proceeding rapidly through a flock of amendments (or, for example, the eight different options for the future composition of the House of Lords). At the end of a debate the Speaker *puts the Question*, saying 'The Question is, that the Bill be now read a second time. As many as are of that opinion say "Aye". Of the contrary, "No"'. If the matter is uncontroversial, the only response he hears is a muffled 'Aye' from the government whips, and the matter is decided without a vote.

But if there is disagreement and the opposition as a whole, or a group of back-benchers, wants to press the matter to a vote, the two sides will shout out 'Aye' or 'No' in response to the Chair. The Speaker, in what is known as *collecting the voices*, says, judging what he thinks is the louder cry, 'I think the Ayes/Noes have it'. If his decision is challenged by the other side still shouting

as well as written statements by ministers. Unlike many parliaments, V
does not allow speeches prepared but not delivered to be put into i
The full text of every day's *Hansard* is published at 7.30 a.m. the
morning and put on the parliamentary website at 8.00 a.m. *Hansard*
record all the debates in standing committees; these appear a little m
than the Chamber *Hansard*. Evidence given by witnesses before selec
tees is recorded not by *Hansard* but by the private firm of W.G. Gu
founder of the firm invented his own form of shorthand), which has d
more than 150 years. Select committee evidence appears either with
mittee's eventual report or in 'daily parts'; transcripts of the more ii
hearings are put on the website in uncorrected form.

Other parliamentary papers

A wide range of papers are presented to Parliament, which MPs may o
hard copy from the House's Vote Office, and members of the public n
from the Stationery Office. Most papers generated by Parliament itself ;
available at www.parliament.uk; those produced by government depai
are usually on their own websites.

   Bills are published when they are first introduced and again at subs
stages if they are amended. More than 300 *Command Papers* (so called b
they are formally presented by the government 'by command of Her Ma
are presented each year. These may be treaties and other agreements
foreign governments, reports of non-parliamentary committees of investig
or Royal Commissions, 'White Papers' (statements of government poli
'Green Papers' (documents for consultation on possible policy opt
Act Papers are laid before Parliament because an Act of Parliament req
it; the majority are Statutory Instruments (see page 228) – about 1,5
year – but this category also includes reports and accounts of a wide r
of public bodies, government statistics, and reports by the Comptroller
Auditor-General (see page 253).

House of Lords working papers

The most important of these is the *Minute*. The Minute is, broadly speaki
the Lords equivalent of the Commons Order of Business, Votes and P
ceedings and other notices rolled into one. It is compiled each day and sent c
to peers overnight. It begins with a formal record of the business conducted
the Chamber that day, including the judicial decisions of the House; next con
the motions and orders of the day for the coming month in so far as busine
will have been set down (the next day's business is also printed separate
as the *Order Paper* (see page 152) each day); and finally there are liste

'Aye' or 'No' then he says 'Division. Clear the Lobby' (in the singular, this refers not to the division lobby but to Members' Lobby beyond the Chamber, which the doorkeepers now clear of all but members and officers of the House to allow MPs easier access to vote). The division bells ring throughout the parliamentary precincts (and in nearby flats, pubs and restaurants whose owners pay to be connected to the system), and a division is under way.

After two minutes, the Speaker *puts the Question again* to check that there is still disagreement between the two sides. He then *names the tellers*. These are usually two whips on each side, although any MP may act as a teller. 'The Ayes to the right, the Noes to the left [referring to the two division lobbies]. Tellers for the Ayes, Mrs Cheryl Gillan and Mr Mark Hoban. Tellers for the Noes, Mr Dan Norris and Mr Jim Fitzpatrick' (or whoever it may be). If no teller (or only one) has come forward on one side, the Speaker declares the result in favour of the other side.

The tellers, one from each side so that they agree on the numbers, then go to the exit door of each division lobby and count MPs as they emerge (whips will be at the other end of the lobby to encourage their own MPs to vote the right way). Inside the lobby their names will have been taken by the division clerks, and the lists that result will be published in *Hansard* the following day. After eight minutes from first calling the division the Speaker says 'Lock the doors'; the doorkeepers lock the doors leading into the lobbies and no more MPs can get in to vote. When every member has passed the division clerks and then the tellers, the results are reported to one of the Clerks at the Table, who writes them on a 'division slip', which is handed to one of the tellers on the winning side. The tellers then form up at the Table, by the Mace and facing the Speaker, with the Clerk at the despatch box to one side, and the teller with the division slip reads out the result to the House – a soundbite often used on the television news when a major vote has taken place. The Clerk takes the slip to the Speaker, who repeats the result: 'The Ayes to the Right, 348. The Noes to the left, 174. So the Ayes have it, the Ayes have it. Unlock'. The doorkeepers unlock the doors to the division lobbies, and the House moves on to the next part of the business of the day. From start to finish, the division has taken anything from twelve to fifteen minutes.

This may seem unnecessarily complicated, but there is a lot of common sense about it. Collecting the voices allows an expression of disagreement but does not commit the House to a division unless the disagreement is persevered with. Putting the question again after two minutes allows for second thoughts; and if no disagreement is expressed then (or if it is not enough to provide two tellers for one side or the other) the matter is decided. This avoids unnecessary votes (and in complicated proceedings allows for the occasional mistake, for example when a group of MPs actually wanted a vote on the next amendment rather than this one). Requiring tellers on each side to agree on the number of votes they have counted also means that the numbers are unlikely to be challenged.

If the result of a division shows that fewer than forty MPs were present (that is, fewer than thirty-five actually voting, plus the two tellers from each side and the occupant of the Chair) then the division is not valid and the House proceeds to the next business. In fact, many MPs may be present but not voting; staging an inquorate vote in this way is, for example, a very good way of killing a private member's bill.

Electronic voting?

But for many people the idea of taking a quarter of an hour of valuable parliamentary time on a vote is inexplicable. Why not vote electronically? There is a good case for it, but also some powerful arguments against. From a practical point of view, the fact that MPs do not have individual seats in the Chamber means that there would have to be voting stations outside the Chamber. Then, because MPs would have to come to the Chamber to vote, perhaps from offices some distance away, and queue up at the voting stations, not a lot of time might be saved after all. Remote electronic voting is canvassed by some – after all, if you can pay your London congestion charge by text on your mobile phone, why couldn't you vote? However, for many proponents of electronic voting, this goes too far. The public perception of MPs not even having to come to the Chamber to vote on some vital issue, at a time when Parliament is struggling to 'reconnect' with the public, might not be favourable. The same might go for a more modest solution, such as voting stations in more distant parts of the precincts.

There is also the question of security; how do you ensure that in every case a vote is registered only by an MP entitled to do so? Swipe cards may not be enough and may need validation by biometric systems such as palmprints or iris recognition. After all, what is at stake is not whether or not you can get £100 out of a cash machine. A vote 'to take note' of a particular EU document may not be of huge significance, but the House of Commons also votes on the biggest national issues – whether a government survives a vote of confidence, or, in March 2003, whether there should be a war. Any system of electronic voting has to deliver the same confidence in the result as the present system; and it is interesting to note that, in the later days of the Major government, with close results on important votes and even the government's survival in the balance, the accuracy of those votes was never challenged.

However, for many MPs, a powerful argument for the present system is that it collects large numbers of members together for a few minutes, often at a predictable time. This brings back-bench and front-bench MPs together (and many back-benchers may not actually see very much of those in government) and is a valuable opportunity to buttonhole ministers, or to gather support for some initiative or signatures for an early day motion. For most MPs, this adds a great deal of value to the otherwise often mundane business of voting.

Deferred divisions

In June 2000, the Modernisation Committee recommended a new procedure to 'reduce the number of occasions on which [the House's] judgements have to be delivered in the small hours of the morning' and to allow debate without requiring other members to be on hand for a vote that might in the event not take place. In July 2001, the House agreed to introduce deferred divisions experimentally for the 2001–02 session; the experiment has been continued for the 2002–03 and the 2003–04 sessions.

The procedure does not apply to bills or to motions that authorise expenditure or charging in relation to bills; nor does it apply to consideration of Estimates and to some types of motion to regulate the business of the House. But where it does apply, if after the moment of interruption (see page 143) an attempt is made to force a vote, that vote is held between 12.30 p.m. and 2.00 p.m. on the next sitting Wednesday. In one of the division lobbies members mark 'Aye' or 'No' on a form that lists all the votes to be taken, the numbers are totalled by the clerks, and the Speaker announces the result to the House later during that sitting.

The procedure is a departure from the practice of the House of taking a decision immediately following a debate (although this could already happen on Estimates and on some amendments to bills (see page 181), and it has some strong critics. To an extent it reduces the power of the opposition (or dissenters anywhere in the House) to force votes on the spot to demonstrate disagreement and to have that disagreement reflected in inconvenience for the government. Others see it as preserving the opportunity to vote, but at a more sensible time (although the fact that the change in sitting hours means that on three days of the week votes that are now able to be deferred would have taken place in the early evening has somewhat weakened this argument).

Voting in the Lords

Voting is very similar in the Lords, the principal difference being one of terminology. Three minutes elapse before the question is put a second time, and eight minutes pass before the doors are locked. Generally speaking, the numbers of members voting in divisions in the Lords are fewer than in the Commons, but a vote can still take ten minutes or more from beginning to end. Because party discipline is weaker in the Lords, there is no tradition of pairing. But the whips nevertheless try to keep their members in the House as long as they can when important divisions are likely. In a busy session this can be fatiguing: there were 250 divisions in 1985–86, compared with 165 in 1992–93, 110 in 1995–96 and 172 in the unusually long post-election session of 2001–02. There are no deferred votes in the Lords, and the same considerations apply to electronic voting as in the Commons.

The media

The gallery and the lobby

The relationship between politicians and journalists has always been, and will always be, an equivocal one. Politics is about publicity; opinions will gather force and support if they are positively presented to a mass audience. But good political reporting has to be critical; it must show up weaknesses as well as strengths, which politicians find less attractive. And political disasters make the best copy of all. There is a partnership – or perhaps a fatal attraction; journalists need the stories that politicians provide, and politicians need the oxygen of publicity to further their own aims.

For many years, the House of Commons treated reporting of its proceedings with the gravest suspicion. In 1694, the writer of a newsletter that carried an account of debates was summoned to the Bar of the House and there – on his knees – was rebuked by the Speaker. In 1738 the House resolved that:

> It is a high indignity to, and a notorious breach of privilege of, this House for any news writer, in letters or other papers . . . or for any printer or publisher . . . to give . . . any account of debates or other proceedings of this House . . . ; and that this House will proceed with the utmost severity against such offenders.

However, by the end of the eighteenth century, although the resolution still stood, reporters were starting to appear in the gallery of the House (where they had to compete for space with members of the public). The 'press gallery' was established 200 years ago, when in 1803 Speaker Abbott directed that seats should be reserved for the press. In the eighteenth and nineteenth centuries, literary luminaries appear as parliamentary reporters: Johnson, Hazlitt, Coleridge, Cobbett and Dickens, as well as (before note taking was permitted) 'Memory' Woodfall, a prodigy who could remember hours of debate verbatim and would later return to his office to dictate from memory.

Today there are about 170 print, radio and television journalists in the gallery and some 200 in the lobby. Many of these represent national papers or channels, but others report for a regional audience; given their constituency focus, MPs are particularly keen to establish good relations with these. All journalists must be accredited by the Serjeant at Arms before they get a pass

– and they too must make a declaration of their interests. Members of the gallery used to report proceedings in the House and in committees, and members of the lobby were more concerned with interpreting parliamentary and political events to the outside world; but in practice the distinction has disappeared. Most national newspapers also have sketch writers, who contribute satirical – and more or less witty – pieces about one or two events the previous day. When they are at Westminster, journalists inhabit cramped and somewhat Dickensian quarters behind the actual press gallery in the House.

The lobby have access to a number of places around the palace frequented by MPs but denied to the general public: principally the Members' Lobby and some of the bars. They will also receive advance copies of documents, such as government White Papers or select committee reports 'under embargo', which allows them a vital twenty-four or forty-eight hours to write their stories on what may be a complex subject in time for publication. More importantly, lobby correspondents have access to MPs and ministers in both Houses on 'lobby terms'; the journalists are given information on the basis that it may be disclosed but not attributed. Politicians will use this channel in a number of ways: a secretary of state whose policy has proved damagingly unpopular may be able to hint at a U-turn; public opinion may be prepared for some new initiative; or disenchantment with the party leadership may be aired, and a warning shot fired, without actually putting a head over the parapet.

There are more formal ways in which the lobby is briefed and ministers and others may be questioned. On sitting days, the Prime Minister's press secretary holds twice-daily briefings (since May 2002, the morning briefing has been open to other journalists as well). On Thursday afternoons, the Leader of the House holds a briefing, mainly covering the parliamentary business for the following week, and his Lords opposite number does the same on Fridays. The Leader of the Opposition gives a briefing on Thursdays, and press conferences are held by ministers and others as occasion demands.

The lobby system has its critics; it is alleged to be too cosy and open to manipulation by those – especially governments – eager to spin the best story. Partly in response, after the 2001 general election the No. 10 briefings became attributable (although not by name, but as the Prime Minister's official spokesman (PMOS)), and summaries of these briefings are now put on the No. 10 website. The Prime Minister also holds regular televised press conferences.

The days when every reputable newspaper devoted many column-inches and even pages to detailed reporting of Parliament are long gone; but serious parliamentary reporting hit a low point in the late 1980s and early 1990s, illustrated by the decision to abandon the parliamentary page in *The Times* (and to save a dozen staff). MPs criticise what they see as the press's lack of interest in the institution of Parliament; journalists (and newspaper proprietors) respond that they report what is newsworthy and relevant, and that they cannot be expected to report Parliament only because it is Parliament. Interestingly, in the build-up to war against Iraq the amount of straight reporting greatly increased. In its coverage of the decisive debate on 18 March, *The Times* report ran to 7,500 words, including a 2,500-word account of the Prime Minister's speech, and there was lengthy coverage in most other papers.

However, most reporting is political rather than parliamentary; Westminster is more often part of the backdrop than the main focus. And although much political reporting is sharp and insightful, it sometimes displays an ignorance of the workings of Parliament even on occasions when knowledge is crucial to a real understanding of what is happening.

Politicians and journalists each have something the other wants – information on one side, and a national or local platform on the other – but journalists can also exercise a great deal of influence on politics. MPs and, more important, senior ministers take notice of Andrew Marr's stylish dissection of an issue, of Peter Riddell's magisterial analysis, or of the results of a mugging in an interview by John Humphrys or Jeremy Paxman. Sometimes the media are partisan; *The Sun*, the UK's biggest selling daily at over four million copies, headlined the Conservative victory in the 1992 election with 'IT WAS THE SUN WOT WON IT'. Yet following the Labour victory in 1997, many observers have seen Trevor Kavanagh, the political editor of *The Sun*, as especially influential with No. 10. But whether the relationship is by turns supportive or critical, suspicious or friendly, the media are an integral part of British politics and so of the Westminster Parliament.

Broadcasting Parliament

Although it was as long ago as 1923 that the BBC sought unsuccessfully to broadcast the King's Speech at the State Opening of Parliament, it was not until 3 April 1978 that regular sound broadcasting of both Houses and their committees began. The Lords has been televised since 23 January 1985 and the Commons since 21 November 1989. Both Houses began with an experiment, which was then made permanent. The initial reluctance to be televised – the Commons rejected it in 1966, 1971, 1975 and 1985 – is slightly reminiscent of the House's view of journalists in previous centuries. Even when the Commons approved televising, the majority was not overwhelming: 320 in favour and 266 against; but only fifteen years later it is very hard to imagine Parliament not being televised.

Committees of the two Houses have drawn up rules of coverage concentrating on what is actually being said rather than distractions elsewhere in the

Chamber: 'a full, balanced and accurate account of proceedings, with the aim of informing viewers about the work of the House'. This means that the use of cutaway shots is limited, which can be frustrating to broadcasters who want more atmospheric coverage; but the pictures ('the clean feed' – in other words, with no captions or other material added) are also used by broadcasters who want brief inserts for a news bulletin and so need pictures of MPs speaking rather than reacting. The rules for the use of material prohibit it being used for comedy or satire, or for advertising.

Proceedings in both the Commons and the Lords are covered gavel to gavel by remote-control cameras in each Chamber operated from a control room across the road at 7 Millbank – eight cameras in the Commons and five in the Lords. All sittings in Westminster Hall are televised, but coverage of committees, either live or recorded (or in sound only) is decided (and charged) on the basis of how many of the broadcasting organisations want to take the feed. These arrangements, and the rules of coverage and use, are supervised by the Director of Parliamentary Broadcasting, who is an officer of both Houses.

The opening of Portcullis House, with six camera-equipped rooms (four of which are primarily for select committees) and two permanent control rooms, brought in digital broadcasting for the first time. All parliamentary broadcasting is now digital and is available in widescreen format. BBC Parliament, the digital channel, carries the House of Commons Chamber live, time-shifted coverage of the House of Lords and unedited coverage of about ten committees each week. BBC 2, BBC 24 and Sky News take Prime Minister's Questions live together with some ministerial statements and committee evidence. The main domestic channels, regional companies and some international organisations use recorded extracts.

All material is archived by the Parliamentary Recording Unit, which keeps tapes for about two years before they are deposited at the National Film Archive. This is developing into a fascinating historical record; many will regret that televising or filming was not permitted many years before, and that the archive does not show us debates at the time of Munich, during the Second World War or during the Suez crisis; and that we have only the written word and contemporary recollections to tell us how Chamberlain, Churchill, Bevan, Macmillan, Wilson and many others performed in the House of Commons.

In January 2002, the two Houses launched experimental webcasting, transmitting audio and audio-visual coverage of proceedings over the Internet (www.parliamentlive.tv). This was made permanent in May 2003, also covering select committees, and is likely to develop extensively in the years ahead.

The microphones used in the Chambers are highly selective and directional to reduce extraneous noise, especially in the often noisier Commons.

Perversely, this makes the coverage slightly less realistic. A minister may be under a great deal of pressure, being barracked as he or she winds up a debate; but if the minister keeps going, talking directly at the microphone, it sounds as though the ride is fairly smooth. The one-liners that spice proceedings are often lost: in one statement during the Iraq war, the Prime Minister was asked about arranging a surrender. He was replying that one of the difficulties was finding someone with authority to surrender, when a wag behind him shouted out 'George Galloway?' The House collapsed with laughter; but the intervention was almost inaudible on the television.

It is understandable that broadcasters should make the most use of moments of confrontation on the floor of the House, but a good contrast is provided by coverage of select committee hearings, which can be compelling television (it is interesting to speculate what additional political impact the Defence Select Committee's hearings on Westland, some of the most high-profile in recent years, might have had on television). The televising of proceedings is now a fact of parliamentary life, and its effect on proceedings and behaviour, feared by its original opponents, is to that extent an academic question. What is certain is that it has made Parliament and its proceedings much better known and more accessible to the country at large.

Privilege

The privilege of Parliament allows the Houses, and their members, to perform their duties without outside threat or interference: rights absolutely necessary for 'the due execution of [Parliament's] powers' as the eighteenth-century Clerk of the House of Commons John Hatsell described them. 'Privilege' is an unfortunate term, as it implies a special advantage rather than a special protection. 'Public interest immunity' would be a better description.

The privileges of Parliament, and especially of the House of Commons in its struggle for power with the sovereign, have been established over many years in a series of cases that are charted in *Erskine May*. In later years, assertion of privilege became less important, and in the nineteenth and twentieth centuries these cases became more a matter of defining the limits of privilege – actions to which it did or did not apply.

From 1997 to 1999, the whole question of privilege was examined by a joint committee of both Houses, chaired by a law lord. The committee made a number of detailed recommendations, which have not yet been implemented, including setting out the extent of privilege clearly in an Act of Parliament; its overall approach was that privilege was needed for the proper functioning of Parliament in the public interest, but that it should be limited to what was essential in practice. It is worth noting that Westminster MPs are in any event less protected than those of many other parliaments, where a parliamentary immunity from arrest or civil suit exists.

There are two key elements in modern parliamentary privilege: the first is *freedom of speech*. The classic statement of this is in Article 9 of the Bill of Rights 1688–89: 'That the freedom of speech, and debates or proceedings in Parliament, should not be impeached or questioned in any court or place out of Parliament'. This means that no MP can be sued or prosecuted for anything he or she says as part of the proceedings of the House or any of its committees. This ensures that a Member of Parliament can speak up on behalf of constituents, or can express any opinion on a public issue, without fear of legal action. Rich and powerful individuals or companies cannot use the threat of writs to silence criticism. Anyone giving evidence to a committee of the House also has the absolute protection of privilege; no civil or criminal action can be brought against them on the basis of what they have said. In a recent case in which a constituent sought to bring an action against her MP for identifying her family in the House as socially disruptive, the European Court of Human Rights acknowledged the public interest of free speech in a national parliament, and the attempt to bring the action failed.

The protection of privilege is balanced by a need for it to be used responsibly, as has been emphasised by successive Speakers (and the Chair, both in the House and in committees, does have some control over MPs' opportunities to speak). Nevertheless, it does happen that individuals are unfairly criticised, or even unjustly accused of a crime, but as Robert Blackburn and Andrew Kennon (see page 417) comment:

> As in the courts themselves, the House of Commons could not work effectively unless its Members were able to speak and criticise without having to account to any outside body. Freedom includes the freedom to make mistakes. There would be no freedom of speech if everything had to be proved to be true before it was uttered.

However, this freedom of speech is limited to *proceedings*. This includes anything said in debates on the floor or in standing or select committees; it also includes anything put in writing that forms part of a proceeding, such as the text of any question (or a minister's written answer), amendment or early day motion, and, by virtue of the Parliamentary Papers Act 1840, any document published by order of the House (select committee reports, *Hansard* and potentially sensitive reports by outside bodies that are the subject of a motion 'for an unopposed return' (see page 138)).

The privilege of freedom of speech does not include press conferences, letters to constituents or to ministers, or words said at ordinary public meetings (even if they are held within the parliamentary precincts). Strictly speaking, it does not even include distributing a speech from *Hansard*, as the protection applies to the whole of the document rather than excerpts; but, unless the excerpts were selected and edited in a distorting and malicious way, it would be very unlikely that any action would succeed.

Exclusive cognisance

The second key element in modern parliamentary privilege is *the freedom of each House to regulate its own affairs* – to use the language of the Bill of Rights, not to have its proceedings questioned. This freedom is sometimes known as 'exclusive cognisance', and in practice it means that the validity of what one House or the other has done, whether in making amendments to a bill, deciding not to proceed with some matter or in regulating the conduct of its own members, cannot be adjudicated upon by any other body.

Parliament and the courts

The scope of exclusive cognisance has contracted in recent years, as Parliament has made certain legislation – for example the Freedom of Information Act 2000 – applicable to itself. It is also the case that the courts may find legislation incompatible either with the Human Rights Act 1998 or with EU law; but both these possibilities arise as a result of decisions by Parliament itself, and in both cases what is at issue is the final content of the legislation rather than the way in which Parliament has passed it. In addition, following the *Pepper v. Hart* case in 1993 (where the Inland Revenue interpreted a piece of tax law in a way at odds with what a Treasury minister had said about it when the bill was before Parliament), the courts may try to resolve ambiguities in law by looking at ministerial statements and speeches setting out the intention of a piece of legislation.

   With the exception of these closely defined categories, the courts are careful to follow the principle set out by the jurist Blackstone in 1830, that 'the whole of the law and custom of Parliament has its origin in this one maxim, that whatever matter arises concerning either House of Parliament, ought to be examined, discussed and adjudged in that House and not elsewhere'. The rules of both Houses seek to return the compliment, through the rules on matters *sub judice* (see page 274) and on criticism of judges.

   If the extent of parliamentary privilege were to be set out in an Act of Parliament, as recommended by the Joint Committee on Parliamentary Privilege, the courts would have an interpretative role (as they do in Australia, for example), which might not make the relationship easier.

Complaints of privilege

Until 1978, complaints that parliamentary privilege had been infringed could be made by any MP in the Chamber, and this became a regular slot (rather like the 'bogus point of order') for raising political matters that had nothing to do with privilege. Now MPs have to write privately to the Speaker; in the exceptional cases where he agrees that there has been a serious breach, he makes a statement to the House and allows the MP the opportunity to move a motion relating to the matter, normally the following day, and usually referring the matters to the Committee on Standards and Privileges for detailed examination.

Contempts

The privileges of free speech and exclusive cognisance protect the proceedings of Parliament in the public interest. Attempts to interfere with proceedings in Parliament, or to obstruct or threaten MPs in the performance of their parliamentary duties, are known as 'contempts'. Examples of contempts might include disrupting a sitting, giving false evidence to a select committee or threatening an MP on account of something he or she had said, or intended to say, in the House – or for voting in a particular way. A contempt may also be committed by an MP: examples in the last twenty years are the leaking of a draft select committee report to a government department and agreeing to ask parliamentary questions in return for payment.

There is no automatic definition of whether something is a contempt or not. Only if the Committee on Standards and Privileges finds that a contempt has been committed, and its view is endorsed by the House, is the matter decided.

Punishment

From early times, both Houses have had the power to imprison, fine or reprimand anyone (including an MP), and to suspend or expel MPs from the House. The last time the Commons imprisoned someone was in 1880, and it is difficult to see the House attempting to do so in modern times. The last time the House fined someone was in 1666; but the power has never been formally discontinued, and indeed select committees in 1967 and 1977 recommended that a power to fine should be put on a statutory basis, although nothing was done.

The sixteenth to eighteenth centuries are dotted with expulsions of members from the House, from the rather grand crime of 'being in open rebellion' through forgery, fraud and perjury to the social discrimination of 'having behaved in a manner unbecoming an officer and a gentleman'. Expulsion became less frequent in the nineteenth and twentieth centuries; the last occasion was in 1954, for a criminal conviction. Suspension, on the other hand, is used more frequently; when an MP is named by the Speaker in the House (usually for disorderly conduct challenging the authority of the Chair), the House suspends the member for five sitting days on the first occasion, twenty sitting days on the second occasion and indefinitely on the third.

Suspensions are also used as punishments for other offences: twenty days for damaging the Mace (1988); ten and twenty days for 'cash for questions' (1995); three, five and ten days for leaking a draft select committee report (1999); three weeks for not disclosing a financial interest (2002); one month for non-disclosure and for obstructing an inquiry (2002); and three weeks for claiming an allowance without entitlement (2003). An MP who is suspended is not paid during the period of the suspension.

Procedure

Procedure regulates the proceedings of the House and its committees. It has four sources. *Practice*, sometimes called 'ancient usage', refers to matters so clearly established over centuries that there is no need to set them down formally – for example the process of moving a motion, 'proposing the question' on it to the House, debating that question, and then deciding it by 'putting the question'.

Standing orders are general rules for the conduct of business and are amended or added to as the House alters its procedures. They govern matters as diverse as the election of the Speaker, the appointment and powers of most select committees, and the length of debate on different types of business. As *Erskine May* remarks, 'their chief characteristic is that they are intended to expedite the progress of business by reducing the opportunities for debate and checking its luxuriance'; and it is probably not a coincidence that standing orders became significant in the early nineteenth century when the government began to exert more control over the time of the House. Today 163 standing orders occupy 138 pages of the blue booklet which these days is republished annually – sometimes more often – to keep up with changes. Some standing orders (another twenty-two pages) are temporary, perhaps for a session or until the end of a parliament; the experiments on new sitting hours and deferred divisions are examples.

Rulings from the Chair are an important part of the case law of procedure. These usually arise because the view of the Speaker is sought on a point of interpretation, or some new matter not otherwise covered. The rules on admissibility of parliamentary questions, motions and amendments to bills have grown up in this way. Rulings have a close relationship with precedent – that which has been done before, and judged to have been in order by the Speaker of the day. Rulings and precedents are distilled in successive editions of *Erskine May*.

Finally, some parliamentary proceedings are regulated by *Acts of Parliament*, covering such things as the way Royal Assent to bills is signified to Parliament, how secondary legislation (see page 227) is dealt with, and making an affirmation or taking an oath.

Like the Commons, the House of Lords derives its procedure from practice, from standing orders, and to some limited extent from Acts of Parliament. But as the House has no Speaker with powers of order, there are no Speaker's rulings in the Lords. Instead, procedure is developed and refined by the House itself by agreeing recommendations from its Procedure Committee. Sometimes these may result in amendments to standing orders, but more usually they are set out in the House's own procedural handbook, the *Companion to Standing Orders*.

Why procedure? And why is it complicated?

Every deliberative body, from a parish council to the General Assembly of the United Nations, needs rules to a greater or lesser extent. Rules regulate how business is initiated; they provide a framework for consideration; and they define how a valid decision is reached.

Many organisations can manage with simple rules, and perhaps no great damage is done if even those rules are not followed very closely. The procedure of Parliament is not simple, for three main reasons.

1. *Contention*. If a group of people are in complete agreement about something, rules are barely necessary. The Supreme Soviet in the old USSR had little need of procedure. The Westminster Parliament is a forum where often profound disagreements on politics and principles are argued out and decided. Procedure thus has to provide a means of focusing points for decision, allowing challenge to take place, and balancing the will of the majority against the arguments of the minority.

   In addition, procedure has to protect the rights not only of the opposition parties but also of groups of MPs, or individual members, wherever they may sit in the House. In a House the size of the Commons, this is especially important; one MP out of 659 may be in a very small minority, but he or she may have constituents whose interests might be threatened by a decision of the majority.

   Where the balance should be struck between the will of the majority (in effect, the government of the day) and the arguments of those who disagree is controversial. There has always been an understanding that a government that has a majority will get its way in the end; but governments are always impatient. In the 2001 parliament, for example, both the Conservative official Opposition and the Liberal Democrats have been highly critical of the effect of programming of bills (see page 179) upon scrutiny of legislation. The debate on hunting perfectly encapsulates the tension between the wishes of a majority and the interests of a minority.

2. *Control.* The standing orders are about setting limits – defining what powers select committees may have, how long various types of business may be debated, when certain things happen, and so on. The more tightly those limits are drawn, and the more circumstances that have to be controlled, the more complex the rules. For example, the temporary standing orders on the programming of bills run to twelve pages.

3. *Complexity of business.* Parliament has to deal with a huge range of material: every issue for which the government is responsible, and legislation on any subject, often extremely detailed. It approves taxation and grants the government the money required to run the country. At the same time, it must try to fulfil its role of calling government to account. Small wonder that procedures to regulate this business are often complicated.

Consistent, certain and clear

We have seen why there have to be rules, and why they are complicated. But rules are not an end in themselves. As the United Kingdom has no written constitution, and as the way Parliament operates cannot be reviewed by any other body, its rules must be robust. Good procedural rules have three qualities:

1. They must be *consistent*; things of the same type must be dealt with in the same way; when something is not, that must be on the basis of a formal decision to handle it in a different way.

2. They must be *certain*, with notice given of matters for substantive decision and rules enforced firmly but fairly. Punctuality is an important part of this; if the moment of interruption is 7.00 p.m., the Speaker will say 'Order, order' precisely on the stroke of seven o'clock, not a moment earlier or later.

3. Rules may be complex, but they must be *clear*. Vagueness will mean that the rules themselves, not what they regulate, will become a source of disagreement; and it will also tend to cast doubt on the validity of what has been done.

7 Making the law

If asked 'Who makes the law in the UK?' most people would instinctively reply 'Parliament'. It seems to be an obvious feature of our democracy that the law under which it operates has been decided by elected representatives in Parliament. And if we were asked 'Where can one find the law?' we might point to the long series of volumes entitled 'Statutes' or 'Acts of Parliament'. As we saw in Chapter 2, each of these Acts of Parliament begins with the formula:

> Be it enacted by the Queen's Most Excellent Majesty, by and with the consent of the Lords Spiritual and Temporal, and Commons, in this present Parliament assembled, and by the authority of the same, as follows . . .

However, if we look at any particular instance of the law in operation, the picture is less simple. The way the law works in practice may differ from the intentions of Parliament when the law was passed, or the application of the law may vary in different parts of the country.

For example, the driver of an antique lorry used in a funfair is stopped by the police as he drives the wrong way down a one-way street. The police find that he has no tachograph in his cab, and they take the view that this is required by law to record his hours of work and the miles he has travelled. The driver is charged with driving the wrong way down the street and with not having the tachograph and is convicted by the magistrates on both counts. He accepts the first but goes all the way to the Court of Appeal on the second, on the grounds that his lorry is an exhibit and is not used for commercial haulage purposes, so it is not required to have a tachograph. The appeal court judges agree and quash the conviction.

What has Parliament to do with this process? The enforcement of the law was the duty of the police. The interpretation of the law was a matter for the courts. The street was not designated as one-way by Parliament but by the district council. The law about tachographs was set out in regulations made by the Secretary of State for Transport, not by Parliament. And all the Secretary of State for Transport had done was to give effect in the UK to European Union legislation brought forward by the European Commission and agreed by the Council of Ministers and the European Parliament.

However, all the actors in this drama have been operating within a framework that derives from statute law as made by the Westminster Parliament.

The district council was able to make the street one-way because an Act of Parliament gave it the power to do so; the European Union was able to legislate because an Act of Parliament – in this case the European Communities Act 1972 – provides that such legislation shall apply to the UK; and the Secretary of State for Transport was able to make regulations because the same Act of Parliament allows the translation of general EU legislation into detailed domestic law. The Westminster Parliament retains the power to repeal the European Communities Act 1972 and end the power of the EU to make any law applying to the UK; and although such a thing might be politically highly unlikely, it remains possible.

This chapter will look in detail at these Acts of Parliament and how they are made. It will also examine delegated legislation: that is, legislation made directly by the government and other bodies that have been authorised by Parliament to do so.

Types of legislation

First, some definitions. The *Acts of Parliament* we have been talking about are a level of legislation known as *primary legislation*. A piece of draft primary legislation is a *bill*. When a bill is passed, it becomes an *Act* and part of *statute law*. An Act is referred to by its title and the year it was passed.

There are two types of bill and Act: *public* and *private*. The majority, and by far the more important, are public. They affect the public general law, which applies to everyone in the UK – although some Acts may apply specifically to England, Wales, Scotland or Northern Ireland, and the Scottish Parliament has power to make primary legislation for Scotland on a range of subjects defined by the Westminster Parliament in the Scotland Act 1998.

Private Acts confer private and particular rights or are local and personal in their effect. A private Act might allow a local authority to close a cemetery, or to confer powers to manage and control access to areas of common land. A private Act may also allow an exception to the general law: for example, the Birmingham City Council Act 1985 allows motor racing – when authorised by the City Council! – on public roads in Birmingham. In recent years, the rare cases of personal legislation (once used for divorces) have been to allow people to marry who otherwise would be prevented from doing so (for example stepfather and stepdaughter).

Sometimes a public bill contains provisions that do not apply generally but affect particular individuals or bodies differently from others who would otherwise be in the same situation. If these were the only provisions in the bill, it would be a private bill; but combining them with changes to the general law turns the bill into a *hybrid bill*. Different procedures apply to public bills, private bills and hybrid bills.

Private members' bills are sometimes confused with private bills, but they are public bills to change the general law; their title comes from the fact that they are brought forward by a private member (that is, a back-bencher) rather than by the government.

Bills of all types may start their parliamentary passage in either House, although those whose purpose is mainly or entirely financial will start in the Commons. At the beginning of a parliamentary session, the government business managers will try to maximise the use of parliamentary time available by deciding which bills will start in the Lords and which in the Commons. A bill that begins in the Lords has [Lords] suffixed to its title when in the Commons and [HL] when in the Lords.

Delegated legislation is made by a minister (or occasionally a public body) under powers conferred by an Act of Parliament. Individual pieces of legislation may be called *orders*, *rules*, *regulations*, *schemes* or *codes*, depending on what the original Act (called the 'parent Act') says; but they are generally known as *delegated legislation*, *secondary legislation* or *Statutory Instruments* (SIs). A special type of order, an *Order in Council*, requires the approval of the Queen in the Privy Council.

Delegated legislation is normally used for detailed arrangements that flesh out broader provisions in the parent Act, or to specify things – such as, for example, the arrangements for licensing some activity – the details of which may need to be changed and for which an amending bill would be a poor use of time. But the balance between what is contained in primary legislation, which can be examined in detail during the passage of a bill, and what is left for ministers to determine in much less scrutinised secondary legislation, is an important issue. We deal with delegated legislation in greater detail on pages 227 to 237, which also covers *regulatory reform orders*, *remedial orders* and *Church of England measures*.

Government bills

Origins

After a general election, the legislative programme is dominated by *bills reflecting commitments that the winning party has made in its manifesto*. Reversing the policy of the previous government on a key issue may be a priority, as for example when the Labour government introduced a bill soon after it was elected in 1997 to repeal legislation passed seventeen years before under a Conservative government that provided for some pupils at independent schools to have their fees paid by local authorities. In the same way, the incoming Conservative government in 1979 repealed the previous Labour government's

Education Act 1976, which had compelled local education authorities to introduce comprehensive schools.

Examples of 'manifesto' bills for the incoming Labour government in 1997 were the Human Rights Bill, legislation to devolve power to the Scottish Parliament and the National Assembly for Wales and to create the Greater London Authority and Assembly, and the Firearms (Amendment) Bill, fulfilling a manifesto pledge to allow a free vote on the banning of handguns. Following the 2001 general election, 'manifesto' bills included the National Health Service Reform and Health Care Professions Bill, which sought to decentralise power in the NHS; the Transport Bill to establish a Strategic Rail Authority, regulate bus services and set up a public/private partnership to run air traffic control; and an Education Bill, which sought to promote diversity and higher standards.

During a government's term of office, its legislative programme will *reflect new and developing policies* as a result of changing circumstances, subjects moving up the general political agenda or sometimes – even though agreed by Cabinet – the personal priorities of a senior member of the Cabinet in his or her area of policy. In the 2002–03 session, such bills included the Health and Social Care (Community Health and Standards) Bill, which would allow the setting up of foundation hospital trusts and introduce new healthcare and social care inspectorates, and the Criminal Justice Bill, which sought to reform court procedure and sentencing and to speed up the process of trial.

Financial bills are required both to raise revenue and to authorise how it is spent. The Finance Bill, introduced following the Budget, authorises taxation as well as embodying the Chancellor of the Exchequer's proposals for tax changes; and Consolidated Fund Bills authorise government spending.

Bills may be needed to *give effect to international commitments*, such as the European Communities (Amendment) Act 2002 to implement the Treaty of Nice in UK domestic law, or the European Union (Accessions) Bill to do the same for the Treaty of Accession for the ten new member countries of the EU. Treaties are not required to be approved by legislation, but in the case of EU treaties bills are necessary to incorporate their provisions into domestic law.

Government bills may *respond to events*. The growth of organised crime and terrorism led to the Terrorism Act 2000, which gave ministers new powers against organisations involved in terrorism, and the Anti-terrorism, Crime and Security Act 2001 followed the events of 11 September 2001. Sometimes specific events lead to legislation, for example legislation on the safety of sports grounds following the Hillsborough disaster, or on firearms after the Hungerford and Dunblane massacres, or on dangerous dogs after incidents in which children were attacked. Legislation may also be needed *to respond to court decisions*, which may perhaps demonstrate that ministers do not have a power they thought they had, or which otherwise show that the law needs clarification.

In addition, most government departments will want what might be called *housekeeping bills*. These may or may not be substantial, are often not controversial in party political terms and are about keeping the business of government and public affairs up to date. Thus the Representation of the People Act 2000 among other things introduced rolling electoral registration (see page 23), made it easier for the homeless to vote and allowed local authorities to try out innovative electoral procedures. The Government Resources and Accounts Act 2000 introduced the system of resource accounting and budgeting to the public sector, while the Limited Liability Partnerships Act 2000 created a new form of corporate entity, combining features both of limited companies and partnerships.

Also in the housekeeping category are *consolidation bills*, which set out the law on a particular subject in a clearer and more up-to-date form without changing its substance, and *tax law rewrite bills*, which with some greater latitude do the same for tax law.

From proposal to bill

Political pressures and day-to-day departmental pressures – to say nothing of the proposals from special interest groups for changes in the law – ensure that no government department is ever short of ideas for legislation. When those ideas have been formulated, a process of consultation begins, the length and detail of which depends on what sort of legislation is being considered and how quickly it is needed. Inside government, the Treasury will be consulted as well as other departments with an interest, together with the devolved administrations in Scotland, Wales and Northern Ireland. Outside government, the views of the pressure groups, public bodies, industries or trade unions affected will be sought.

The process of consulting outside government is sometimes open to criticism. Political pressures may mean that there is in fact little time for effective consultation. The process also focuses on 'the usual suspects' – those organisations with a national profile – rather than opinion more widely. Consultation often has to be on the broad intentions of a proposal, but 'the devil is in the detail', and some important elements of a proposal may be decided only when the business of drafting begins. Finally, consultation often takes place in private, although the results are generally made public if those consulted do not object.

These criticisms are met to a certain extent if legislation follows a Green Paper, where the government has sought views on various legislative options, or a White Paper, where is has made its intentions clear. Increasingly, though, the use of draft bills (see page 182), where a complete legislative proposal can be considered in detail before it begins its formal parliamentary stages, is seen as a way of allowing the widest consultation as well as resulting in better legislation.

In due course the sponsoring government department will have proposals to put before a policy committee of the Cabinet. This will often be done by correspondence, and only if disagreements arise or if major issues are at stake will the subject need to be discussed at a meeting of the committee itself. There are twelve ministerial policy committees of the Cabinet, covering broad areas such as Domestic Affairs, Economic Affairs, Productivity and Competitiveness, and Defence and Overseas Policy. Sub-committees cover specific areas of policy within those fields; thus Domestic Affairs has sub-committees on drugs, equality, communities, rural renewal, social exclusion and regeneration.

But even if the relevant ministerial committee endorses a proposal, this does not mean immediate legislation. A minor change may have to wait until a more extensive bill in that subject area comes along. A major policy development, or a series of related proposals, may need a whole bill and so a place of its own in the government's legislative programme.

Parliamentary time is scarce, so further decisions need to be taken centrally about priorities and about balancing the programme of bills for each session of a parliament. This is the task of the Cabinet Committee on the Legislative Programme – known as 'LP' – which includes the Leaders and government Chief Whips in both Houses. That committee recommends to the Cabinet what proposals will actually find a place in the next Queen's Speech. As the new session approaches, LP will decide which bills will start in the Commons and which in the Lords, and which should be published in draft; it makes an assessment of how much parliamentary time will be needed for each and any difficulties on the way – perhaps dissenting government back-benchers in the Commons, or a critical reaction in the Lords; and it decides on the phasing of bills, in order to make the best use of the time available.

Meanwhile, those proposals that have been approved for the next session's programme have been moving from concept to detail. The sponsoring department prepares drafting instructions for parliamentary counsel. These instructions will set out what the bill needs to do but not the detail of how it will do it. This is the job of parliamentary counsel, an élite group of lawyers specialising in legislative drafting. They are servants of the government rather than of Parliament, and they draft all government primary legislation (secondary legislation is normally drafted by lawyers in the government department concerned).

In converting a department's instructions into a bill, parliamentary counsel have a number of tasks. They must achieve clarity and precision, not only so that the bill's provisions will be tightly defined but also so that, once it is passed, the possibility of legal challenge is minimised. They must ensure that the bill fits with legislation already in existence – both the statute book of primary legislation and any relevant EU or delegated legislation. This may mean that the bill must amend or repeal provisions of UK legislation that may be scattered through a number of Acts of Parliament. Finally, they must ensure that the provisions of the bill work – in terms of logic rather than political policy. To take a simple example, if you make something illegal you need to ensure that there is a penalty for doing it, and you also need to define what will constitute evidence that the offence has been committed.

This process of turning instructions into drafting often throws up new questions of policy, and for most bills there will be a continuing dialogue between the sponsoring department and parliamentary counsel while the bill is being drafted. Even then the bill may go through several further drafts before it is finally approved by its sponsoring department and minister, agreed by LP, and is ready to begin its parliamentary journey.

Just before it does so, the text must be submitted to the authorities of the House in which it is to start. In the Commons, the Clerk of Legislation ensures that the bill complies with the rules of the House; that everything in it is covered by the long title – the passage at the start of a bill that says that it is 'A Bill to . . .' and then lists its purposes; that any provisions that would require expenditure or would levy charges or taxes are identified (and are printed in italics); whether the Royal Prerogative is affected (in which case the Queen's or Prince of Wales's Consent will be required); whether any uncertainties exist as to what sort of amendments might be relevant to the bill; whether it conflicts with or duplicates a bill or part of a bill that has already been introduced; and whether it relates exclusively to Scotland (in which case special procedures are followed). In the Lords, the Public Bill Office offers advice on the same range of issues, except on financial matters. Once these consultations are complete, the bill is ready for introduction.

Is a government bill really draft legislation?

Every textbook of parliament and politics says that a bill is a draft Act of Parliament, but governments tend not to see it like that. For each bill, there has been a lengthy process of development and debate between departments and ministers; the government has consulted those it feels have an interest; the contents of the bill have been minutely considered by officials and by parliamentary counsel; and the bill has been through a series of drafts.

Small wonder, then, that by the time the bill reaches parliament it is not so much draft legislation for discussion and amendment as word for word what the government of the day wants to see on the statute book. Moreover, ministers identify personally with major bills; 'their' bills are part of their political achievements as ministers, and significant amendment of a government bill would generally be seen as a loss of face.

The pressure of legislation

This might matter less if there were more time to consider legislation and the lead times were longer. However, governments of both parties are always in a hurry: to demonstrate their dynamism; to seek to deliver on commitments; and to put their stamp on key areas of policy. This means in turn that the machinery for preparing legislation is frequently overloaded. The result is that the consultation process is rushed or curtailed; too many large and complex bills are attempted in a session; policy is sometimes not settled well in advance of drafting (and sometimes it changes after introduction of a bill); and instructions from departments to parliamentary counsel are sometimes late.

This often leads to 'drafting on the hoof', when significant amendments to a bill are made not because of effective criticism inside or outside Parliament but in order to reflect the government's changing views. Some government amendments are brought forward to meet such criticism (and one of the strengths of a bicameral system is that it allows an undertaking to amend to be given in one House and the time to bring forward the amendment in the other House).

However, although it is difficult, if not impossible, to be sure of the genesis of every amendment that a government puts down to one of its own bills, a large proportion are the result of second thoughts rather than a response to a measured critical process. To give examples of the general and the particular: in the 1999–2000 session, 3,892 government amendments were made in the Lords to government bills coming from the Commons; and in the 2002–03 session, the government tabled at the report stage of the Criminal Justice Bill thirteen new clauses introducing additional provisions, some of them major matters of policy. That bill was being considered under a programme order (see below), which meant that there could be little or no substantive consideration in the Commons. Drafting on the hoof has an additional perverse effect in that it occupies the time of parliamentary counsel, who could be working with a longer lead time on the next session's bills.

Looking at the 1997–98 session, Blackburn and Kennon (see page 417) observe that fifteen of the twenty main government bills ended up with more sections than they had clauses when introduced, with the Finance (No. 2) Bill more than tripling in size. The 131 clauses of the Crime and Disorder Bill attracted 558 government amendments and the ninety-clause Competition Bill 343 government amendments. In the 1999–2000 session, the total page count of government bills increased from 2,760 to 3,600, an increase of 30 percent. Blackburn and Kennon comment: 'This shows that in many cases the legislative process is really a mechanism for the government of the day to tidy up under-prepared bills'.

Programming and guillotines

In the Lords, the intervals between the different stages of the passage of a Bill are prescribed by a recommendation of the Procedure Committee in 1977: two weekends between introduction of a bill and second reading, fourteen days between second reading and committee, fourteen days between committee and report for large and complex bills, and three sitting days between report and third reading. Intervals in the Commons are governed by practice and a degree of negotiation between the two sides but are usually much shorter than in the Lords. The 1985 Commons Procedure Committee recommendation for two weekends between introduction and second reading, and ten days between both second reading and committee, and committee and report, was never adopted.

Bills may need little – or sometimes no – debating time if they are narrow and technical or if they command support on all sides (although all-party agreement may not make for good legislation, as was shown by the Dangerous Dogs Act 1991 and especially the Child Support Act 1991). However, for most bills there is pressure, both from the opposition and from government back-benchers, for more debating time than the government is prepared to concede. The purposes and motives of such debate are varied: to set out a contrary political position; to seek explanation and clarification from the government; to explore and criticise the details of the legislation and its likely effects, and to make alternative proposals; and, in the case of the more contentious bills, to make opposition clear, and to inconvenience the government, by delaying the bill.

There are various ways in which debate may be limited. We have already looked at the closure (see pages 45 and 143), where, after what in the view of the Chair is a reasonable period of discussion, the use of the government's majority can bring debate to an end and have the particular question before the House at the time put; but this is of little practical use to the government where legislation is concerned. A more draconian power was introduced into the Commons in the nineteenth century following the disruption of proceedings over several sessions by Irish MPs campaigning for Home Rule. It was generally recognised that the rights of the majority needed to be pre-served and, despite considerable reservations at the time, the 'guillotine' or 'allocation of time order' was introduced. This has been modified over the years, but in essence it allows the House to agree, at any stage in pro-ceedings on a bill, strict time limits for the remainder of its progress. A timetable is set out in a motion that is put to the House. If it is agreed, then delaying tactics are of no use; committee and report stages come to an end after a fixed period whether all amendments selected by the Chair have been discussed or not, and sometimes with many clauses of a bill not having been debated at all.

At one time the guillotines were considered wholly exceptional and could arouse outrage both inside and outside the House. The procedure was thus used just over seventy times in the ninety years 1881–1970. However, from the late 1970s its use increased under governments of both parties, and it was routine for three or four, or more, bills to be guillotined each session. In recent years, the highest numbers were in 1988–89 (ten guillotines out of thirty-seven government bills passed), 1998–99 (eleven out of twenty-seven) and 1999–2000 (thirteen out of thirty-nine).

One of the problems with a guillotine is its undiscriminating nature; the knife falls to conclude a stage of a bill, such as its consideration in standing committee, without taking account of how much of that bill has been considered. From the government business manager's point of view, the solution to this is in the hands of MPs on the committee; a degree of self-control would allow the time to be used more effectively. But with a contentious and complex bill this simply does not work – not least because in some cases in the past there has been political mileage for the opposition in spinning out proceedings in standing committee in the knowledge that the government will respond with a guillotine and can be criticised for that response.

In 1985, the Procedure Committee argued that the weapon of delay probably does nothing to change a government's mind, and that the guillotine response usually meant patchy scrutiny. It recommended that for controversial bills (those likely to need more than twenty-five hours in standing committee) there should be a timetable agreed by a Legislative Business Committee on which all parties were represented, which would allocate time in committee and on report to reflect the importance of different parts of the bill. This proposal had a good deal of support on the back benches but not on the front benches, and in February 1986 it was defeated in the House by 231 to 166. The Jopling Committee (see page 132) returned to this in 1992 and endorsed the earlier approach. In the event this was introduced in an informal way, with some timetabling agreed through the usual channels and guillotines avoided whenever possible (and indeed from 1994 to 1997 there were only six guillotines).

In 1997, the newly established Modernisation Committee returned to the issue. It recommended a halfway house between informal agreement and guillotine, to be known as 'programming'. When a bill was selected for programming, there should be discussions that would take account of representations from all sides of the House, including back-benchers. In the light of those discussions, the government would move an amendable motion immediately after second reading specifying the type of committee to which the bill should be sent and the day by which it should be reported. The committee would then decide how to use that time.

A programme order differs from a guillotine in that a standing order (at the moment renewed each session rather than being permanent) contains most of the detailed provisions that previously were contained in each guillotine. A programme order thus picks up these provisions and applies them to the particular bill in question. It is also imposed on proceedings on a bill immediately after second reading rather than later, when the speed of progress (or extent of delay) is known, and, if taken immediately after second reading, is not debatable (guillotines were debatable for three hours). And, as noted above, unlike a guillotine it specifies the type of committee to which the bill should be sent. The programme order may be amended later, for example if the opposition persuades the government to provide more time.

When under a programme order the time allotted for part of a bill expires, only certain specified questions may be put to the standing committee or the House: in particular, the question already under discussion, the question on any amendment selected by the Chair for separate division (in practice, amendments on which the opposition parties particularly want to register their disapproval); thereafter, government amendments and new clauses may be taken *en bloc*. The selection list for the report stage of the bill on page 199 is an example of the number of amendments that may have to be dealt with in a short time under a programme order.

If a programming order applies to the Committee of the Whole House, report stage or third reading, a programming committee (consisting of the Chairman of Ways and Means and up to eight MPs nominated by the Speaker) proposes how the available time should be allocated. The House may debate the proposal for up to forty-five minutes (and may amend it). When a programme order applies to proceedings in standing committee, the allocation is proposed by a sub-committee comprising the chairman of the committee and seven of its members and may be debated by the committee for half an hour (and may be amended). A standing committee can also make proposals to the House for changes in the date for reporting a bill, or in the programming of the report stage and third reading.

Since their introduction early in the 1997 parliament, programming arrangements have been fine-tuned following further reports from the Modernisation Committee. In the early days of programming, the system operated on a fairly consensual basis, even when applied to controversial bills such as the devolution measures, but from 2000 onwards they have increasingly become a matter of contention, indeed bitter contention, between the two sides. In a debate in 2001, Eric Forth, the then shadow Leader of the House, said 'The Government seem determined to minimise or dispose of all opportunities for proper scrutiny of legislation', and in April 2003 he referred in the House to 'the systematic, routine and vicious timetabling of bills'; and the former Chancellor Kenneth Clarke has described programming as 'pernicious'.

There are various reasons why programming of bills is now a source of such strong disagreement. The original proposals were seen as something of a compact, in which constraints on time would be balanced by more effective means of scrutiny, with a greater use of special standing committees (see below), as the Modernisation Committee had recommended. In the four sessions 1998–2002 there were forty-eight programme motions; but only one bill was sent to a special standing committee.

Second, although programming offers the prospect of more effective use of time, it can do nothing to increase the total time available; nor in itself can it reduce the pressure of the government's legislative programme. In a letter to the Modernisation Committee in June 2000 Speaker Boothroyd observed that 'Government legislation introduced in this House or brought from the House of Lords in the session to date comprises a total of 2,537 pages (excluding consolidation bills). The equivalent figure for the long 1997–98 session was 1,901, and for session 1998–99 was 1,590'. And as long as the pressure of the legislative programme leads to the 'drafting on the hoof' described in the previous section, any means of allocating time to the consideration of legislation will come under strain. One way of improving scrutiny – and perhaps of saving time in the long run – might be the use of draft bills.

Draft bills

It has been the case for many years that a bill may be sent to a select committee for detailed examination after second reading. The select committee format has several advantages. The committee is not just a debating forum but can take oral and written evidence, involving many more people in a formal process of consultation and making the legislative process more accessible to those outside Parliament. A select committee has to return to the House the text of a bill just as a standing committee (see page 191) does, but unlike a standing committee it can also report its views and the reasons for its decisions. Even on highly contentious issues, select committees have a long history of operating in a consensual rather than an adversarial way, which is likely to make for more effective scrutiny of legislation.

Scrutiny of bills in draft by select committees (or joint committees of both Houses) goes several steps further. A draft bill has not begun its formal parliamentary progress, and it really is draft legislation in a way that a bill, once introduced, is not. Ministers have invested less political capital in it, and changes will not necessarily be seen as defeats. The Liaison Committee, consisting of the chairmen of all select committees, described the scrutiny of bills in draft as 'a development of great significance. It offers the prospect of properly examined, better thought out and so higher quality legislation'.

The present government has made a commitment in principle to bring forward more bills in draft, but the numbers have varied: there were three in session 1997–98; eight in 1998–99; three in 1999–2000, two in 2000–01 and five in 2001–02. There were nine in 2002–03, and the 2003 Queen's Speech foreshadowed seven for 2003–04. These figures are against the background of forty to fifty government bills a session.

However, draft bills are not a panacea – at least, not for governments. They add to the time before a proposal passes into law (and circumstances may change during that time); they tie up more resources in the preparation and drafting of bills, as substantial changes may be needed in the bills eventually introduced; and, as there is the opportunity for criticism well supported by argument and evidence, they may make it harder for the government of the day to get its way. However, unless a way is found of slackening the *overall* pressure on a government's legislative programme, the contribution that draft bills can make may be limited.

The scrutiny of the draft Communications Bill in session 2001–02 is a case in point. This was a major and complex bill that proposed significant changes to the regulation and ownership of the media in the UK. The joint committee had two months to examine the draft bill. In that time it took oral evidence from more than fifty organisations, received 200 written submissions, set up an on-line forum for consultation, held three seminars and had thirteen deliberative sittings on the contents of the bill itself. Only extraordinary efforts by the members and staff of the committee produced an effective piece of pre-legislative scrutiny.

We return to these issues in Chapter 13. We now follow the passage of a government bill (formally introduced into the Commons and not a draft bill) through Parliament. (A chart showing the stages of legislation in the two Houses is overleaf.)

The form of a bill

The European Union (Accessions) Bill of the 2002–03 session, whose purpose was to incorporate into UK domestic law the treaty enlarging the EU, is reproduced on pages 185 to 188 and shows some of the main features of any bill. Every bill has a *short title*, which is the title by which it is known during its passage and which will normally be the same as the title of the Act that will result. Also on the cover page of the bill will be a statement by the relevant minister as to whether the provisions of the bill are compatible with the European Convention on Human Rights. After the cover page will be a list of contents, if the bill is long enough to need one. At the start of the bill is the *long title*, which

STAGES *of* LEGISLATION

HOUSE *of* COMMONS

		TIMING
First Reading	• Formal reading out of title of the Bill by Clerk. • Ordered to be printed.	
Second Reading	• Main opportunity to debate the Bill. A division at this stage represents a direct challenge to the principle of the Bill. • After Second Reading, Government Bills are timetabled by Programme Motions.	Usually two weekends after *First Reading.*
Committee Stage R	• Chance to vote on the detail, clause by clause. • Amendments **selected** by Chairman (advised by Clerk). • All Bills go to one of four Committee types: (i) *Committee of the Whole House:*- for constitutional Bills and parts of the Finance Bill; (ii) *Standing Committee* - most usual procedure. 16-50 Members, in proportion to overall party strengths. (iii) *Select Committee* [Infrequently used]. (iv) *Special Standing Committee* [Rarely used] - has powers to send for persons, papers and records; holds 4 sittings and hears oral evidence in private and public.	Usually starts two weeks after *Second Reading* and can take anything from one meeting to several months.
Report Stage	• A further chance to consider amendments, new clauses and, for MPs not on the Committee, to propose changes.	Usually two weekends elapse between end of *Committee Stage* and *Report Stage.*
Third Reading	• Final chance to debate the Bill. • A vote gives chance to show dissatisfaction with amended Bill. • The Bill now goes to the Lords.	Usually immediately after *Report Stage* on the same day.

HOUSE *of* LORDS

		No significant delay in the transfer of a Bill between the two Houses.
First Reading R	• Formal. • The Bill is reprinted in the form finally agreed by the Commons (*see note below*).	
Second Reading	• Debate on general principles of the Bill. • **Government Bills included in the election manifesto are, by convention, not opposed at the Second Reading,** but "reasoned" amendments may be tabled as a means of indicating dissent and can be voted on.	Two weekends must elapse after *First Reading.*
Committee Stage R	• Bills usually go to a Committee of the Whole House or Grand Committee away from the Chamber and rarely to other types of committee (*See over*). • Detailed line by line examination. • **Unlike the Commons, there is no selection of amendments – all can be considered.** • **No programme, unlike the Commons, and debate on amendments is unrestricted.**	Usually start at least fourteen days after *Second Reading.* Often spread over several days.
Report Stage R	• Further chance to amend Bill. • May be spread over several days.	Usually start at least fourteen days after the end of *Committee Stage.*
Third Reading and Passing	• **Unlike in the Commons, amendments can be made** provided the issue has not been voted on at an earlier stage. • Passing: The final opportunity for peers to comment and vote on Bill.	Usually at least three sitting days after the end of *Report Stage.*

Consideration of Amendments	• Depending on which House the Bill started in, each House now considers the other's amendments. • Bills with contentious amendments pass back and forth between the Houses until agreement is reached. If each House insists on its amendments, a Bill is lost. • Bills with agreed amendments await Royal Assent.
Royal Assent	• Queen's assent formally notified to both Houses. • Bill becomes an Act.

Notes
(1) For the purpose of this chart, the Bill is assumed to have started in the Commons. Bills may equally be introduced first into the Lords. There are no differences in the stages followed by a Bill starting in the Lords.
(2) **R** = Bill is reprinted at these points if amended at previous stage.
(3) To follow the progress of a Bill, **Contact:** Information Office: (Lords) 020 7219 3107 (Commons) 020 7219 4272
        Consult: Weekly Information Bulletin (*see Progress on Bills*)
        Visit: Parliament website at www.parliament.uk

The stages in the passing of a public bill
Source: The House of Lords 2002

sets out the purposes of the bill; all the provisions of the bill must fall within the long title. This is followed by the words of enactment: 'Be it enacted by the Queen's Most Excellent Majesty . . .'.

Clauses are the basic units of a bill; they are divided into *subsections, paragraphs and sub-paragraphs*. This particular bill contains only three *clauses*, but a long bill may contain fifty to 500 clauses or more and be divided up into several *parts* or *chapters*. When a bill becomes an Act, the clauses become known as *sections*. To reduce complexity, the *schedules* to a bill fill in some of the fine detail (for example, one of the schedules will usually list amendments and repeals affecting existing legislation). A schedule is always dependent on the clause that introduces it and has no effect unless the clause is agreed to. Any provisions that would cost public money (other than routine administration by the government department concerned), or that would impose taxes or levy a charge, are printed in italics.

The last page of the bill is the *backsheet*, which repeats the long and short titles, gives the bill number and the session it was introduced, and lists the MP introducing the bill (the 'Member in charge') and his or her 'supporters'. For a government bill, the member in charge will be the secretary of state heading the relevant department, and the supporters will be senior ministers with an interest in the subject matter.

European Union (Accessions) Bill

EXPLANATORY NOTES

Explanatory notes to the Bill, prepared by the Foreign and Commonwealth Office, are published separately as Bill 98–EN.

EUROPEAN CONVENTION ON HUMAN RIGHTS

Mr Secretary Straw has made the following statement under section 19(1)(a) of the Human Rights Act 1998:

In my view the provisions of the European Union (Accessions) Bill are compatible with the Convention rights.

A

BILL

TO

Make provision consequential on the treaty concerning the accession of the Czech Republic, the Republic of Estonia, the Republic of Cyprus, the Republic of Latvia, the Republic of Lithuania, the Republic of Hungary, the Republic of Malta, the Republic of Poland, the Republic of Slovenia and the Slovak Republic to the European Union, signed at Athens on 16th April 2003; and to make provision in relation to the entitlement of nationals of certain acceding States to enter or reside in the United Kingdom as workers.

B E IT ENACTED by the Queen's most Excellent Majesty, by and with the advice and consent of the Lords Spiritual and Temporal, and Commons, in this present Parliament assembled, and by the authority of the same, as follows:—

1   Accession treaty

(1)   In section 1(2) of the European Communities Act 1972 (c. 68), in the definition of "the Treaties" and "the Community Treaties", after paragraph (p), insert "and

> (q)   the treaty concerning the accession of the Czech Republic, the   5
> Republic of Estonia, the Republic of Cyprus, the Republic of
> Latvia, the Republic of Lithuania, the Republic of Hungary, the
> Republic of Malta, the Republic of Poland, the Republic of
> Slovenia and the Slovak Republic to the European Union,
> signed at Athens on 16th April 2003;".   10

(2)   For the purpose of section 12 of the European Parliamentary Elections Act 2002 (c. 24) (ratification of treaties), the treaty concerning the accession of the Czech Republic, the Republic of Estonia, the Republic of Cyprus, the Republic of Latvia, the Republic of Lithuania, the Republic of Hungary, the Republic of Malta, the Republic of Poland, the Republic of Slovenia and the Slovak   15 Republic to the European Union, signed at Athens on 16th April 2003, is approved.

2   Freedom of movement for workers

(1)   The Secretary of State may by regulations provide that a specified enactment relating to—   20

    (a)   the entitlement of a national of an EEA State to enter or reside in the United Kingdom as a worker, or

    (b)   any matter ancillary to that entitlement,

applies in relation to a national of a relevant acceding State as it applies in relation to a national of an EEA State.   5

(2)   Regulations under this section in respect of a specified enactment may apply that enactment subject to specified exceptions or modifications.

(3)   Regulations under this section—

    (a)   may include incidental, supplementary, consequential or transitional provision;   10

    (b)   may make different provision for different cases.

(4)   Regulations under this section do not have effect so as to apply an enactment in relation to a national of a relevant acceding State which has not ratified the treaty mentioned in section 1(2).

(5)   The power to make regulations under this section is exercisable by statutory instrument subject to annulment in pursuance of a resolution of either House of Parliament.   15

(6)   In this section—

    "EEA State" means a State (other than the United Kingdom) which is a contracting party to the Agreement on the European Economic Area signed at Oporto on 2nd May 1992, as adjusted by the Protocol signed at Brussels on 17th March 1993;   20

    "enactment" includes an enactment comprised in subordinate legislation (within the meaning of the Interpretation Act 1978 (c. 30));

    "relevant acceding State" means any of the following—   25

        (a)   the Czech Republic,

        (b)   the Republic of Estonia,

        (c)   the Republic of Latvia,

        (d)   the Republic of Lithuania,

        (e)   the Republic of Hungary,   30

        (f)   the Republic of Poland,

        (g)   the Republic of Slovenia,

        (h)   the Slovak Republic;

    "specified" means specified in regulations under this section; and

    "worker" means the same as it does for the purposes of Article 39 of the Treaty establishing the European Community.   35

3   Short title

This Act may be cited as the European Union (Accessions) Act 2003.

European Union (Accessions) Bill

A

B I L L

To make provision consequential on the treaty concerning the accession of the Czech Republic, the Republic of Estonia, the Republic of Cyprus, the Republic of Latvia, the Republic of Lithuania, the Republic of Hungary, the Republic of Malta, the Republic of Poland, the Republic of Slovenia and the Slovak Republic to the European Union, signed at Athens on 16th April 2003; and to make provision in relation to the entitlement of nationals of certain acceding States to enter or reside in the United Kingdom as workers.

Presented by Mr Secretary Straw
supported by
The Prime Minister, Mr Secretary Prescott,
Mr Chancellor of the Exchequer,
Mr Secretary Blunkett, Secretary Margaret Beckett,
Mr Secretary Hoon and Ms Secretary Hewitt.

Ordered, by The House of Commons,
to be Printed, 30th April 2003.

© Parliamentary copyright House of Commons 2003
Applications for reproduction should be made in writing to the Copyright Unit,
Her Majesty's Stationery Office, St Clements House, 2–16 Colegate, Norwich NR3 1BQ

PRINTED BY AUTHORITY OF THE HOUSE OF COMMONS
LONDON: THE STATIONERY OFFICE LIMITED

Printed in the United Kingdom by
The Stationery Office Limited

£1·50

Bill 98   (850755)   53/2

ISBN 0–215–70260–3
9 780215 702609

The European Union (Accessions) Bill, passed by Parliament in session 2002–03
Source: The House of Commons 2003

Explanatory Notes are a separate document that accompanies a government bill. They set out the bill's intention and background, explain the clauses in lay person's language and give an assessment of the bill's effects on public service manpower and costs and on business in the private sector (for example, if a bill were to introduce a new system of regulation or licensing).

Commons stages

Introduction and first reading

The most usual method of introducing a bill is by the member in charge giving notice of the bill's long and short titles and of the intention to introduce it on a particular day. This notice appears on the Order Paper for that day, the MP is called by the Speaker at the commencement of public business (see page 142), and brings the so-called 'dummy bill' (merely a sheet of paper with the short and long titles and the names of up to twelve supporters) to the Clerk of the House at the Table. (In the case of a government bill, a 'dummy bill' is not brought to the Table.)

The Clerk reads out the short title and the Speaker says 'Second reading what day?' For all government bills the response is 'tomorrow' (or the next sitting day if there is a break for a weekend or recess) as the government can bring any of its bills forward on any sitting day. For a private member's bill, however, naming a day can be a matter of careful tactics (see page 207).

The bill is now said to have been read the first time; it is recorded in the Votes and Proceedings as having been ordered to be printed and to be read a second time on whichever day has been named. A bill introduced in this way is known as a *presentation bill*; bills may also come before the House by being *brought from the Lords*, by being *brought in upon a resolution* (the Finance Bill is founded upon the resolutions agreed by the House to give effect to the Chancellor's Budget proposals) or when an MP gets *leave to bring in a ten-minute rule bill*.

Second reading

This is the first time the bill itself is debated, and it is a discussion of the principle of the bill rather than the details of individual clauses. It is considered good practice for second reading to be delayed until at least two weekends have passed since the bill's introduction (although, if the bill has not been seen before in draft, even this does not give much time to assess it). The government does not always comply with the 'two weekends' convention; nor, less importantly, do back-benchers with private members' bills.

A second reading debate on a major government bill will normally take a day (in practice about six hours; on a Wednesday, for example, from about 1.00 p.m. to 7.00 p.m.). Less important bills will get less time, and wholly uncontroversial measures (including some private members' bills) can receive their second reading 'on the nod' – that is, without any debate at all. It is also possible – but unusual – for uncontroversial bills to be referred either to a *second reading committee* 'upstairs' or, in the case of a bill relating to Wales, second reading may be taken in the Welsh Grand Committee. The Scottish and Northern Ireland Grand Committees may in theory consider bills in relation to their principle, but following devolution this is now less likely, certainly for Scotland. Second reading committees are also used for bills prepared by the Law Commissions; but these are usually technical reworkings of the law and will normally have started in the Lords and have been considered by a select committee there.

Some major bills have in the past had lengthy second reading debates on the floor of the House. In 1972, the bill to enable the United Kingdom to join the then EEC was debated over three days on second reading, and the 1976 bill on Scottish and Welsh devolution (which eventually failed) was debated for thirty-two hours over four sitting days.

A second reading debate on a government bill takes place on a motion moved by a minister 'That the bill be now read a second time'. At the end of this debate, on bills which are opposed, a vote is taken. This can be a straight vote against second reading, or a vote on what is known 'a reasoned amendment' (if it has been selected by the Speaker). This spells out the reasons why the bill's opponents do not wish it to have a second reading. If the reasoned amendment is carried, or the House votes against second reading, the bill can go no further – nor can exactly the same bill be reintroduced in the same session. It is extremely rare for a government bill to be defeated on second reading; the last example was in 1986, when the Shops Bill, which had been intended to relax the law on Sunday trading, was passed by the Lords but defeated in the Commons by a majority of fourteen. However, as we saw in Chapter 5, voting against the second reading of a controversial bill may be a powerful way for government back-benchers to register dissent.

These days, the second reading of a bill will normally be followed immediately by a *programme motion*, which is decided without debate (although almost always with a vote), followed if necessary by a motion to authorise government expenditure in relation to the bill (*a money resolution*) or the raising of a tax or charge (*a ways and means resolution*). These also give the committee on the bill authority to consider any provisions that would require expenditure or impose a tax.

Expedited procedures

Certain types of bill are dealt with on a 'fast-track' procedure. *Consolidation bills* are prepared by the Law Commissions as a sort of housekeeping of the statute book. These bills draw together the law on a particular subject, which may be in a series of Acts of Parliament, and present it in a more logical and user-friendly way. *Statute law repeal bills* remove parts of the law that have become redundant. Bills of both sorts are checked by a joint committee of both Houses to ensure that no change of substance has been made in the process of restating the law, and that no 'live' legislation is to be repealed. If no amendments are put down, such bills are passed without debate. There is also a fast-track procedure for *tax law rewrite bills*, which are considered by a separate joint committee. *Consolidated fund bills*, which authorise government spending, have no committee or report stage; the questions on second and third reading are put successively without debate.

Committee

As soon as a bill has had its second reading, it is sent to a committee for a detailed examination of the text. The choices are *standing committee, Committee of the whole House, select committee* and *special standing committee.* The Finance Bill is routinely divided between Committee of the whole House for its most important provisions and a standing committee for the rest, and since 1998 the Hunting Bill (the version in session 2000–01), the Greater London Authority Bill and the Political Parties, Elections and Referendums Bills have been treated in the same way. As standing committees are the default setting – if no other decision is taken, a bill goes automatically to a standing committee – we begin with this method of consideration.

Standing committees

To begin with, the very name is misleading. Standing committees are not permanent; new members are appointed to a committee specifically for each bill; and, when the committee has reported the bill back to the House, it is effectively dissolved. When standing committees were first introduced at the end of the nineteenth century as a means of saving time spent in Committee of the Whole House, the intention was actually one that modern advocates of reform would applaud; there were to be four permanent committees, each specialising in broad areas of public policy, which could develop expertise and deliver better scrutiny. However, it took only a few years for this to fall victim to expediency.

Standing committees are set up as bills receive their second readings. Each is designated by a letter; in session 2001–02 Standing Committees A, B, C, D, E,

F and G sat, but there is no limit on the number (apart from the practical one of MPs available to sit on them). Standing Committee C is reserved for the committee stages of private members' bills; but once a standing committee is set up it remains available for other bills, and, as we shall see, this can be tactically important for private members' bills.

To take a typical standing committee dealing with government bills, in session 2001–02, Standing Committee B dealt with

▲ the Export Control Bill (which occupied six sittings from 9 July to 18 October);
▲ the Proceeds of Crime Bill (thirty-nine sittings from 30 October to 5 February);
▲ the Employee Share Schemes Bill (one sitting on 27 February);
▲ the Enterprise Bill (eighteen sittings from 10 April to 16 May); and
▲ the Housing Benefit (Withholding of Payment) Bill (two sittings in July).

Standing Committee B was sitting for a good proportion of the session, but for each bill its membership was different (numbering eighteen, twenty-five, sixteen, twenty-one and sixteen MPs, respectively) and it had a different chairman or chairmen for each bill.[5]

Membership

A standing committee on a bill must have between sixteen and fifty members, but in practice the membership is usually between sixteen and thirty. Its members are chosen by the Committee of Selection, which includes whips of the three main parties. Membership of a standing committee reflects the party proportions in the House as closely as possible. Where there was a free vote on second reading (as on the Hunting Bill in the 2002–03 session), the membership reflects the numbers of supporters and opponents in the House on the second reading vote. The Committee of Selection appoints members directly to a standing committee; the names do not have to be approved by the House, unlike the membership of select committees.

At least one government minister will always be a member of a standing committee (including standing committees on private members' bills), together with a government whip, and front-benchers from the other parties are also appointed. The remaining back-benchers are a combination of those who are interested in the subject (and who spoke in the second reading debate) and those who are drafted on by the whips but are ready loyally to support their party's line on the subject. Obviously the strength of the second group becomes more important when very contentious legislation is being considered, but the Committee of Selection has generally appointed a spread of MPs, so that dissent within a party is represented as well.

The Law Officers (Attorney-General, Advocate-General and Solicitor-General) may, if they are members of the Commons, attend a standing committee and speak (but not vote), although this is in practice very rare. Any minister may do the same in the committee on the Finance Bill, but in practice this is handled by Treasury ministers. Other MPs not appointed to a committee on a bill may not take part in its proceedings.

Chairmanship

Each standing committee is chaired by a member of the Speaker's Panel of Chairmen. This is a group of thirty to thirty-five senior MPs chosen by the Speaker to chair standing committees. It also includes the Deputy Speakers (and is itself chaired by the Chairman of Ways and Means), thus connecting the business of chairmanship in the House with that of standing committees. The panel meets from time to time as a committee to consider matters affecting standing committees generally (for example, whether MPs should be allowed to use laptops and palmtops in committee).

If a standing committee is taking a big bill, there may be two or three chairmen sharing the duties. The chairman has most of the powers to control proceedings that the Speaker has in the House, including power to select amendments (see below). As in the House, he or she does not vote unless there is a tie, and then strictly according to precedent (see page 46).

Meetings

Standing committees meet in the suite of committee rooms on the riverside first floor of the Palace of Westminster (hence a bill in standing committee is sometimes referred to as having been 'sent upstairs'). The room is laid out very much like the Chamber, with the two sides facing each other across the floor. The chairman sits on the dais at one end, with the clerk on his or her left (see the plan overleaf).

Meetings of standing committees are open to the public and, as in the House, debates are recorded verbatim by the *Official Report* and published and placed on the parliamentary website. Standing committees may meet on any day on which the House sits, but committees on government bills normally meet on Tuesdays and Thursdays from 8.55 a.m. to 11.25 a.m., breaking then to allow members to attend Question Time in the House and resuming at 2.30 p.m. Depending on how keen the government is to make progress with the bill, and how contentious it is, the committee may then go on until late in the evening (and it may be subject to the provisions of a programme order: see page 181).

The normal first business of a standing committee is to consider the resolution of the *programming sub-committee* (the chairman of the committee and

1 CHAIRMAN
2 CLERK
3 HANSARD SUB-EDITOR
4 CIVIL SERVANTS
5 MINISTER(S)
6 OPPOSITION FRONT-BENCH SPOKESMAN

7 THIRD PARTY SPOKESMAN
8 GOVERNMENT BACK-BENCHES
9 OPPOSITION BACK-BENCHES
10 PRESS
11 PUBLIC

The layout of a Standing Committee Room

seven members), which makes proposals about the time to be allotted to the various parts of the bill and sometimes the order in which parts of the bill are to be taken.

Amendments, selection and grouping

The committee deals with the clauses of the bill one by one. Any MP may put down an amendment to a bill in standing committee (or an entire new clause or schedule), but only a member of the committee may actually move it.

Amendments can serve a variety of purposes. If the bill is highly contentious in party political terms, many amendments will be pegs for debate to give publicity to government and opposition viewpoints – although this is more the case in Committee of the Whole House (see below) as standing committees get very little media coverage. So-called 'probing amendments' are used to get the minister to clarify provisions of the bill and outline the thinking behind them. However, for the reasons we have seen, it is extremely unlikely that the opposition will table an amendment, convince the government of its merits and have it agreed to.

The chairman of a standing committee, like the Speaker in the House or the Chairman of Ways and Means in Committee of the Whole House, has the power of *selection and grouping* (which does not exist in the House of Lords). This is crucial in allowing an orderly and logical debate on amendments, and it also prevents the proceedings of the committee being clogged up by hosts of amendments being tabled for their own sake.

Amendments are tabled on the days before the committee first meets (usually, at this stage by the opposition parties and possibly government back-benchers, but as we have seen, the government may even at this stage want to modify its own bill, and amendments may go down in the name of the minister in charge of the bill). The day after they are tabled, amendments will appear on blue paper in the Vote bundle (see page 153); but on the day the committee first meets, it will have before it a *marshalled list*, printed on white paper, of all the amendments that have been put down up to and including the previous day. This list of amendments is the committee's order paper.

The marshalled list sets amendments down by reference to where they apply to the bill. As each amendment is tabled, it is given its own unique reference number, so the numbering will jump about: for example, if the very first amendment tabled was to the last schedule, it will still be 1; and if, after 500 amendments have been tabled, an amendment is put down to the first line of the bill, it will be 501.

The process of selection and grouping, in which the chairman is advised by the clerk of the committee, begins with weeding out amendments that are *out of order*. Disorderly amendments include those that are irrelevant or outside the scope of the bill (or of the clause to which they are tabled);[6] inconsistent with a decision that the committee has already taken (or that the House has taken in approving second reading – so-called 'wrecking' amendments); ineffective or incomplete; tabled to the wrong place in the bill, or to a part of the bill that the committee has already considered; 'vague, trifling or tendered in a spirit of mockery'; or that would impose charges outside the scope of the money or ways and means resolutions agreed to by the House. These rules are sometimes quite complex in their application, but they are a common-sense way of clearing out amendments that are irrelevant or ineffective (although an MP whose pet amendment is ruled out of order may not always see it like that).

Then begins the process of *selecting* from among the remaining amendments those that will be debated. Selection in standing committee is fairly generous (at report stage it is not), and unless an amendment is fairly trivial, or one of a multiplicity on the same point, it is likely to be selected. Amendments proposed by the member in charge of a bill, whether a minister or a private member, are normally selected automatically provided they are in order. An amendment that has been tabled only the previous day (and is marked by a star against it on the marshalled list), rather than the minimum two days in advance, will usually not be selected, although the chairman has power even to select a 'manuscript' amendment put forward within the previous few minutes if the circumstances warrant it.

At the same time, the chairman and clerk will be looking for themes that will help to *group* amendments. There are three main ways of doing this: the first is to group amendments that offer *alternative proposals on the same point*. An example might be where the bill proposes that a search can be authorised by any police officer. The opposition think that this is not stringent enough and so have put down an amendment that would require the authorising officer to be of the rank of inspector. Back-benchers on the committee (on both sides) would like to go further, and amendments are down variously specifying a superintendent, a magistrate and a High Court judge. If the 'inspector' amendment were selected on its own, the debate would take place only on the issue of whether the minimum authority should be constable or inspector. Separate debates would have to take place on the other proposals – and if the 'inspector' amendment were to be agreed to, then that would rule out debate on any alternative as being inconsistent with the decision the committee had reached. So all the amendments about the level of authorisation are grouped.

The second method is to group *interdependent amendments*. An example here might be where the opposition has an amendment early in the bill to appoint a statutory investigator of complaints. It has a raft of other amendments throughout the bill that specify how different types of case will come to this investigator. If the principle of appointing an investigator is defeated early on, all the later amendments will fall, so it is sensible to debate them together.

The third method is to *group amendments on a theme*. For example, there might be a number of amendments designed to require the secretary of state to make a regulatory impact assessment before using any of a number of powers that the bill would confer. Grouping these together allows a debate on the principle of requiring such an assessment. If the amendments were not so grouped, the result would be a series of very similar debates as the committee got to each of the clauses that would give the secretary of state each of those powers.

The result of this is a *selection list*, a new edition of which appears for each sitting day. The chairman gives no reasons for his or her decisions on selection, and there is no appeal to the Speaker. Two examples of selection lists appear on pages 198 and 199: one for the first day of a standing committee's consideration of a bill; and one for part of the report stage of a bill in the House. Both bills are programmed.

How the committee goes through the bill

Once the recommendations of the programming sub-committee have been considered, the committee begins with the first clause of the bill. Let us suppose that the first amendment in the first group – *the lead amendment* in that group – is to Clause 1. That amendment is moved, and the debate on the question 'That the amendment be made' then includes debate on any other amendment (or new clause) that is grouped with it. At the end of the debate the question is decided, on a vote if necessary: after a short interval the doors of the committee room are locked, the clerk rises and reads out the names of members of the committee. MPs say 'Aye' or 'No' or 'No vote'; the clerk totals the votes and hands the list to the chairman. She or he declares the result, says 'unlock' and moves on to the next question to be decided.

If a second group has its lead amendment to Clause 1, that group will be dealt with in the same way. But if not, the chairman proposes the question 'That Clause 1 stand part of the bill'. This gives the opportunity of a 'stand part debate' on the clause as a whole. If debate on a number of amendments to a clause has covered the ground, the chairman can put the question on clause stand part without further debate.

An important feature of this way of going through a bill – and one that often causes confusion – is that the *amendments are decided not in the order in which they are grouped for debate but in the order in which they apply to the bill.* This can mean that an amendment to a clause near the end of the bill may be debated with the first group at the first sitting; but it will be put to the vote only when the committee gets to that clause, which may be after many hours of consideration. If amendments have already been debated (unless they are in the name of the member in charge of the bill), they are often passed over in silence when they are reached. But if the opposition or a back-bencher wants

Standing Committee B

SEXUAL OFFENCES BILL

Tuesday 9th September at 8.55 am and 2.30 pm

Chairmen's Provisional Selection of Amendments: 9th September
(Arranged in accordance with the terms of the resolution of the Programming Sub-Committee)

[Programming motion - max 30 minutes]

Clause 1
35 + 34
36 + 25 + 29 + 26 + 30 + 27 + 31 + 28 +
    32
37
1 + 2 to 6 + 8
22

Clause 3
39

Clause 4

Clause 5

Clause 76
Govt 41 + 33

Clause 77
38

Clause 78

Clause 2
23 + 24 + NC1

**Proceedings to be concluded at 6.55 p.m.
on Tuesday 9th September**

Clause 6

Clause 7

Clause 8

Clause 9
Govt 43 + Govt 93 + Govt 94 + Govt 95 +
    Govt 96

Clause 10

Clause 11

Clause 12
Govt 44 + Govt 50 + Govt 56 + Govt 66 +
    Govt 80 + Govt 97 + Govt 98 +
    Govt 99 + Govt 103

Clause 13
Govt 45 + Govt 47 + Govt 51 + Govt 59 +
    Govt 69 + Govt 85 + Govt 92 +
    Govt 100 + Govt 102

Clause 14
11

Clause 15
Govt 46 + Govt 48 + Govt 49

Clause 16

Clause 74

ROGER GALE
CHAIRMAN
[1]

A typical selection list for the first day of a Commons standing committee's consideration of a bill under a programme order

Source: The House of Commons 2003

CRIMINAL JUSTICE BILL, as amended

Consideration of Bill [Third Day]

The Speaker's provisional selection of amendments

(Arranged in accordance with the Criminal Justice (Programme) (No. 5) Motion
in the name of Mr Secretary Blunkett and Dr John Reid)

Part 12: Life sentences, road traffic offences, firearms offences
Govt NC30 + Govt NC31 to Govt NC38 + Govt NC39 + (a) + Govt NC46 + (a) + (b) +
Govt NC47 to Govt NC50 + Govt NC51 (a) + (b) + NC7 + NC9 + Govt 426 to Govt 429 +
Govt 223 + Govt 430 + Govt 224 + Govt 436 + Govt 437 + Govt 228 + Govt 229 + Govt 438
to Govt 440 + Govt 431 + Govt NC41 + Govt 325 to Govt 330 + Govt 338 + Govt 342 +
Govt 225 + Govt 432 + Govt 441 + Govt 303 + Govt 305 + Govt 442 + Govt 230 + Govt 226
+ Govt 434 + Govt 435 + Govt 227 + Govt 259 + Govt NS2 + (a) to (j) + Govt NS3

Two and a half hours after the commencement of proceedings

Part 12: Sentencing
Govt NC28 + NC6 + NC10 + Govt 233 + 31 + Govt 234 + Govt 235 + 482 + 483 + 67 +
Govt 236 + Govt 197 + 175 to 177 + Govt 198 + (a) + (b) + 178 + Govt 199 + 181 + 179 + 183
+ 184 + 180 + 25 + 182 + 26 + 186 + Govt 200 + Govt 201 + 188 + Govt 262 to Govt 271 +
Govt 237 + Govt 238 + Govt 239 + Govt 272 to Govt 275 + Govt 240 + Govt 241 + 488 +
Govt 242 + 484 + Govt 243 + 489 + 485 to 487 + 490 + Govt 244 to Govt 247 + 191 + Govt 248
+ Govt 249 + 492 + 496 + 494 + Govt 276 + 493 + 497 + 495 + Govt 277 to Govt 280 + 192 +
120 + 193 + Govt 281 + 491 + 68 to 70 + Govt 282 to Govt 284 + Govt 250 to Govt 252 +
Govt 285 to Govt 298 + 194 + Govt 202 + Govt 253 + Govt 254 + Govt 301 + Govt 302 +
Govt 304 + Govt 306 to Govt 313 + Govt 255 + Govt 315 + Govt 256 to Govt 258

Part 6: Allocation and Transfer of Offences
Govt 317 + Govt 318 to Govt 324 + Govt 260 + Govt 331 to Govt 337 + Govt 339 to Govt 341
+ Govt 343 to Govt 351 + Govt 261 + Govt 352 to Govt 354 + Govt 316

Part 13: Miscellaneous – jury service
Govt 299 + Govt 300 + Govt 314 + NC21

Part 14: General
Govt 355 + Govt 458 to Govt 461 + Govt 356 + Govt 212 + Govt 455 to Govt 457

Four hours after the commencement of proceedings

Terrorism
Govt NC45 + (a) + NC56

Criminal records certificates
Govt NC26 + Govt NS1 + (a) + Govt196

Public decency
Govt NC40

Five and a half hours after the commencement of proceedings

By Order of the Speaker

19 May 2003

The selection list for part of the report stage of a bill in the House of Commons, under a
programme order
Source: The House of Commons 2003

a vote – a separate division – and the chairman agrees, a vote on a specific amendment may take place, but without further debate. Government amendments that are reached in this way are called formally whether or not a vote is expected; the minister says 'I beg to move' and the question on the amendment is put to the committee.

If no lead amendment is down to any clause, the committee must nevertheless agree whether or not the clause should stand part of the bill. When the committee has got to the end of the bill, any new clauses and new schedules (and any amendments to them) are decided upon (and debated if they have not been grouped with earlier amendments).

When the committee has completed its consideration of a bill, the members of the committee are discharged, the formal report of the bill appears in the Votes and Proceedings for that day, and the bill – if it has been amended – is reprinted for the *report stage* (see page 203). The process of going through the bill may have taken only a few minutes at a single sitting, or it may have taken a hundred hours of often fierce debate over thirty or forty sittings in the space of several weeks.

Scrutiny by debate and amendment

Richard Crossman, Labour Leader of the House in the 1960s, wrote 'The whole procedure of standing committees is insane . . . under the present system there is no genuine committee work, just formal speech-making, mostly from written briefs'. Consideration in standing committee occupies a great deal of time: in the four sessions 1998–99 to 2001–02 standing committees on bills held 219, 353, 126 and 269 sittings, respectively, and it is reasonable to ask how good a use of the time of the MPs involved this was, and how effectively the legislation was scrutinised.

Unlike select committees, standing committees have no research or staff resources of their own (the concern of the clerk of a standing committee is the conduct of the proceedings, not the merits of the bill). MPs have to rely on briefings from outside pressure groups (which are naturally often advocacy for a particular point of view). However, the minister taking a bill through standing committee has the support of the 'bill team' of civil servants, and behind them the substantial resources of his or her own department.

It is rare for the government to accept opposition (or individual back-bench) amendments in standing committee; when the other side feels that it has won the argument this is dispiriting and fuels pressure for a more consensual, evidence-based scrutiny, perhaps by select committee. However attractive measured, non-partisan scrutiny of that sort may be, one should not lose sight of the role of the Commons as a place where political ideologies clash and where deep divisions between parties (often reflecting different views in the country at large) are played out in an adversarial way. However, there is no reason why select committee-type scrutiny (and especially the use of draft bills) should not be complemented by the full-dress political occasion, either in Committee of the whole House or at report stage.

Committees of the whole House

At one time, almost all bills were considered in Committee of the whole House. As its name suggests, it consists of all MPs (although of course a relatively small proportion of those will be present during its proceedings) and takes place in the Chamber during part of a normal sitting of the House. The only evident differences are that it is presided over by the Chairman of Ways and Means and his deputies and not by the Speaker, that he sits at the Table beside the Clerk and not in the Chair, and that the Mace is placed on brackets below the Table rather than on it. Votes are taken in the same way as in the House.

The manner of going through a bill is similar to that in standing committee; and, as in standing committee, an MP may speak more than once in any debate. Selection and grouping of amendments is the responsibility of the Chairman of Ways and Means.

In recent years, Committees of the whole House have been confined to three types of bill. For convenience, *uncontroversial bills* (for which there would be no point in setting up a separate sitting of a standing committee) are considered in this way to save time. Also taken in Committee of the whole House are *bills of great urgency* that need to become law quickly, such as, in session 2002–03, the Northern Ireland Assembly Elections Bill to postpone the elections to the Northern Ireland Assembly following the breakdown of political cooperation in the province.

The third category is of major *bills of first-class constitutional importance*. Since 1945, governments have been committed to having such bills dealt with in this way, but there is no formal definition. Legislation to incorporate EU treaties into domestic law, to devolve powers to Scotland and Wales, or to reform the House of Lords clearly fall into this category. In the 1997–2001 parliament, the European Parliamentary Elections Bill, the Human Rights Bill and several Northern Ireland Bills were taken in this way; but the Bank of England Bill of 1997–98, which shifted the responsibility for setting interest rates from the Treasury to the Bank, was taken entirely in standing committee.

It may thus be a matter of argument (or negotiation) as to what measures are treated in this way. The opposition will want time on the floor of the House and the higher profile of Committee of the whole House, but the government business managers will generally be reluctant, not only to take floor time on a bill they feel could be dealt with in standing committee, but also to have the burden of votes taking place in a forum of 659 MPs when they could take place in a committee of twenty or thirty members upstairs. And, historically, Committees of the whole House have presented problems for government business managers: the Parliament (No. 2) Bill to reform the House of Lords was considered for twelve days before it was dropped; and devolution to Scotland and Wales took up thirty-four days in Committee of the whole House in the 1976–77 and 1977–78 sessions. Nowadays, the prospect of being able to programme proceedings and so make them much more predictable and controllable may make government business managers slightly less reluctant to take committee stages on the floor of the House.

Select committees

We considered earlier the advantages of scrutinising *draft* legislation in a select committee. A bill that is on its *formal* passage through the House may be committed to a select committee after second reading, although this is rare. The main example is the bill every five years to renew disciplinary law for the armed forces, although in 2000–01 and 2001–02 the Adoption and Children Bill was considered by a specially appointed select committee.

More frequently it happens that a select committee seizes the moment and conducts a swift inquiry into a bill and reports in time to influence later proceedings upon it. In 2001, for example, three departmental select committees and the Joint Committee on Human Rights examined the post-9/11 Anti-Terrorism, Crime and Security Bill and reported upon it in time for the second reading debate; and in 2002 the Home Affairs Select Committee produced reports on the Police Reform Bill and the Criminal Justice Bill (the latter was squeezed into a week and a half between introduction and second reading). However, if the bill has not been formally referred to a select committee by the House, the committee cannot make amendments to it.

Special standing committees

This provides a hybrid procedure; a special standing committee may have four sittings in select committee mode (one private deliberative session and three to take evidence, often with the chairman of the relevant departmental select committee in the chair) and then turns into a standing committee debating the bill formally in the way described above. The advantage of this is that the committee is able to hear outside expert opinion on the bill, which will inform debate, and the committee will probably work more cooperatively as a result.

However, a special standing committee is more constrained than a select committee; the procedure is less flexible; and, although its members are likely to work more cooperatively, the majority of its proceedings will be in the usually adversarial debating format of a standing committee. It is perfectly possible for a bill to be examined by a select committee (perhaps by an existing committee specialising in the subject area that is used to working on a cross-party basis) and then given the standing committee treatment.

From the government's point of view, the disadvantage is that the process will take more time and that the party with the majority has less control. This may be why the special standing committee procedure has been used fairly infrequently, and mainly for non-controversial and fairly technical bills. The procedure was established in 1980 but used for only seven bills in the four years to 1984 and then not again for eleven years until two Scottish bills in 1995 and 1996. Although the Modernisation Committee recommended greater use of special standing committees, only the Asylum and Immigration Bill was so referred in the 1997 parliament, and only the Adoption and Children Bill (an earlier version of which had already been considered by a select committee) in the 2001 parliament.

Report stage

Except for bills that are considered in Committee of the whole House *and* are not amended there, all bills come back to the floor of the Commons for their 'report stage', properly called 'consideration'. The bill returns in the form in which it left committee, and report stage is a further opportunity for amendments to be made. The important difference (unless the bill has been to Committee of the whole House) is that all MPs have an opportunity to speak to amendments on report.

Most report stages of bills starting in the Commons occur in the period after Easter. Even for major bills the programme order is unlikely to give them more than two days on report (in May 2003, the Criminal Justice Bill had three days, but this was a major and complex measure, some of whose provisions – especially on the limitation of the right to trial by jury – were contentious with government back-benchers as well as with the Conservative and Liberal Democrat parties). Many government bills complete their report stage and third reading in a single sitting. Report stages of government bills in the four sessions 1998–99 to 2001–02 occupied between 8 and 15 percent of the total time on the floor of the House.

New clauses and amendments for debate on report are selected by the Speaker on the same principles as in standing committee. However, selection is much tougher than in standing committee; the Speaker is unlikely to select amendments on a topic that has been fully aired in committee, unless the government indicated in committee that it was prepared to think again. However, major matters of public policy that were debated in committee may reappear, on the grounds that the House as a whole rather than a small group of MPs in committee should have the opportunity of expressing a view.

Procedure on report is somewhat different from Committee of the whole House. The Speaker (or one of the deputies) is in the Chair, and the Mace is on the Table. New clauses and schedules are normally taken first (although as in committee the minister may propose a particular order in which proceedings should be taken). The House is now revising the bill as a whole rather than going through it clause by clause, so there is no 'clause stand part', and the amendments are set out in a slightly different way.

Third reading

When all the selected amendments have been disposed of (or when the time allotted to report stage under the programme has expired), the House moves on to the third reading (usually at the same sitting). If there are no amendments on report, that stage is omitted and the third reading is taken immediately.

Third reading is the final review of the contents of the bill (debate is limited now to what is actually in the bill rather than, as at second reading, what might have been included). Except on highly controversial bills, where the opposition has the opportunity to fire some last shots, third reading debates tend to be quietly valedictory affairs in which those most closely involved (front-benchers and other MPs who were on the standing committee) look back rather sentimentally on the bill's progress through the House. Since the introduction of programming, however, the opposition front bench has often taken the opportunity to express hopes that the House of Lords will deal in more detail with this or that provision which they feel has had inadequate scrutiny in the Commons.

The procedure is akin to second reading: a minister will move 'That the bill be now read the third time', and a debate takes place on that question. As at second reading, it is possible to move a reasoned amendment (if selected by the Speaker), but this is very rare. Third readings occupy relatively little time on the floor of the House: between 1 and 2 percent of the total over the last four complete sessions.

Once the third reading has been agreed to, the bill has been passed by the Commons. One of the Clerks at the Table, in wig and gown, then 'walks' the bill to the Lords. The doorkeepers shout 'Message to the Lords', the doors are thrown open, and the clerk proceeds in stately fashion through the Members' Lobby, the Central Lobby and eventually to the Bar of the House of Lords. There the bill, tied up in Commons green ribbon (known as 'ferret', from *fioretti*, a sixteenth-century Italian name for a kind of silk), is handed over to one of the Lords clerks.

This may seem a somewhat archaic way of taking a bill from one House to the other, but bills are compiled and amended using highly sophisticated software, and at the same time an electronic version of the bill text has gone from the Public Bill Office in the Commons to its counterpart in the Lords. It can happen, though, near the end of a session, with the 'ping-pong' of amendments between the Houses, that the exact moment of a bill's formal arrival is of some importance. Handing it over in the Chamber makes this publicly evident in a way that its electronic appearance in a distant office does not.

Private members' bills

Before we move to the other end of the building to see how the House of Lords considers legislation, let us look at a category of legislation that often attracts publicity even though many more bills in this category fail than ever find their way on to the statute book: private members' bills.

These are not private bills but public bills that aim to change the general law of the land. They are introduced in one of four ways: as *presentation bills*, (described on page 189), sometimes called 'back of the Chair bills'; when leave is given under the *ten-minute rule*; the first private members' bills in each session appear following the *private members' bill ballot*; and private peers' bills that have been passed by the House of Lords may be *brought from the Lords* and taken up by a private member in the Commons.

Ballot bills

Ballot bills are introduced in the same way as presentation bills, but an MP gets the right to introduce such a bill through success in the ballot, a sort of legislative prize draw. On the Tuesday and Wednesday in the second week of each session MPs sign a book kept in the No Lobby, being allotted a number in the process. On the Thursday at 12 noon in Committee Room 10, normally televised live, the Clerk Assistant draws twenty numbers from a despatch box. The Chairman of Ways and Means matches the numbers to the MPs who have signed in and calls out the names. The twenty MPs get priority in introducing their own bills – but absolutely no guarantee that any of those bills will become law.

Some MPs are enormously keen to win the ballot; others strenuously hope not to be successful, as they have a good idea of how much sponsoring a private member's bill may interfere with their daily work. However, the reluctant are 'encouraged' by their whips to sign in, as the whips would prefer to see their own people successful rather than the other side. In most sessions 400 MPs will enter the ballot. Those whose names are drawn – especially those in the first seven places – are immediately mobbed in person, by post, telephone and e-mail by pressure groups who hope to persuade an MP to take on their special cause (and who may just happen to have a bill ready for the MP to adopt).

The ballot bills are presented on the fifth Wednesday of the session; and each of the twenty MPs has up to the rising of the House the previous day to decide what sort of bill to introduce. For some this will be a simple matter; this may at last be the opportunity to introduce legislation for which they have spent much of their parliamentary careers campaigning. For others, there are choices to be made. Should they accept that any bill is unlikely to become law and so produce a sort of manifesto on a subject they think important, hoping that as a bonus they might get a chance to debate it? Or should they temper their ambitions and go for a narrow bill that is likely to be uncontroversial but could make a modest but worthwhile change to the law?

One of the factors that will help an MP to come to a decision is the extent of outside support likely to be available. A pressure group may be a large and influential body, with resources including lawyers who can help with drafting the bill and people who can write speeches and briefings on hostile amendments. In these circumstances, an MP will feel a little less like David pitted against Goliath.

In a sense, the ultimate pressure group is the government itself. We saw earlier that it can be difficult for a government department to get its bills included in the legislative programme for any session. Persuading a friendly MP (not always from the government party) to take on one of its smaller hoped-for bills can be another route to the statute book. If an MP decides to take on one of these so-called 'hand-out bills', he or she will act rather like a minister, supported by departmental civil servants; and the bill itself will have been drafted by parliamentary counsel. However, the bill itself will proceed just like any other private member's bill and will get no special treatment (unless it is one of the very small number of private members' bills to which the government of the day is prepared to give some of its own time).

By the evening before the fifth Wednesday of the session, the MPs successful in the ballot must have given in the short and long titles of their bills (the latter will limit the scope of the bill when drafted), and they will have collected the names of their supporters for the back of the bill. At the commencement of public business the next day, the twenty MPs form a queue at the back of the Speaker's Chair, and as their names are called they come forward and hand their bills to the Clerk, who reads the title. The Speaker says 'Second reading what day?' and the MP names a day.

Tactics and procedure

It is at this point that the tactics essential for success in private members' legislation begin. There are normally seven days for private members' second readings. Obviously it is best to be the first bill on any day, because that means a full day's debate and the prospect (if 100 MPs can be found to vote for the closure) of getting a second reading and going into committee; and the earlier one can do that, the better. So if the twenty MPs name the days strictly according to those criteria, the bills will come on like this (the dates of the Fridays below are illustrative):

9 January	16 January	23 January	6 February	20 February	12 March	19 March
1	2	3	4	5	6	7
8	9	10	11	12	13	14
15	16	17	18	19	20	

However, it may be that the sponsor of bill 5 is not too concerned about her bill and cannot be in the House on 20 February anyway. So she names 9 January, which leaves a first-place slot open on 20 February. A quick-witted MP with a much lower-placed bill may then be able to get the first slot on 20 February, and a full day's debate. And unless the sponsor of bill 8 has those quick wits, and when it comes to his turn he names 9 January as he had planned, he will find that he is now the third bill on that day and not the second as he had hoped. And once a day is named, there is nothing to be done; a bill can be deferred but not advanced. The picture may be further complicated by MPs guessing that a particular bill will be fairly uncontroversial and may get through quickly and so putting their bill on for that day rather than the earlier day they could have taken (but when they would have been behind a fiercely contested bill and would have had no chance of getting debating time).

The next step for all the MPs successful in the ballot is to get their bills drafted. They may have the help of an outside body, of parliamentary counsel for a hand-out bill, or a kindly Public Bill Office (although this is not a formal part of the office's role). The drafting does not have to be perfect at this stage. If a bill gets into committee and looks to have a chance of getting further, the government will normally put down amendments so that if the bill is eventually successful it will be in properly drafted and workable form.

For those in the top slots on the second reading days, it will not be enough simply to have a majority of those in the House on the Friday in question. Even a few opponents can 'talk the bill out' by continuing to debate it up to the moment when the Deputy Speaker says 'Order, order' at 2.30 p.m. It will be important to muster at least 100 supporters, so that when the sponsor of the bill claims the closure just before 2.30 p.m. by saying 'I beg to move that the Question be now put', the closure is agreed with at least 100 MPs voting in the majority. With most MPs wanting Fridays for constituency work, this may take some silver-tongued persuasion – private members do not have the armoury of the whips at their disposal.

The rule that financial initiative rests with the Crown means that only a minister may bring in a bill whose main purpose is to create a charge. However, if a private member's bill that gets a second reading would incidentally involve an increase in public spending, the government will normally put down a money resolution to authorise such expenditure and to allow the bill to be considered in committee.

As with government bills, the next stage after second reading is standing committee, where opponents may seek to delay the bill by putting down a great many amendments, or – more subtly – may hurry the bill through to report because they can put amendments down at that stage, not to kill this bill but to deny time to the bill that is behind it on report.

The astute MP can get an advantage when going into committee. Standing Committee C is the one reserved for private members' bills, and as they get their second readings they join the queue for this standing committee. However, if a government bill comes out of one of the other standing committees and there is no government bill waiting to go in, the MP can ask to have his or her bill assigned to that standing committee. If the Committee of Selection can be encouraged to nominate the members of the standing committee before another government bill has appeared, the MP has overtaken the Standing Committee C queue on the inside lane.

The next hurdle will be the six 'remaining stages' days. On these Fridays the bills are ranked with the most advanced stage first: so, Lords amendments, third readings, report stages, Committee of the whole House (which is an option, although a high-risk one, for the private member) and second readings, in that order. Much the same tactics (and the need for closures) will apply, but at this stage it is much easier for opponents to take up time with amendments rather than on the single question of second reading, and so easier to kill the bill. The MP who is successful at this stage and secures third reading will rely on a colleague in the Lords to sponsor the bill there, and he will hope that that House does not amend the bill as this will produce another chance of 'sudden death' when the Commons considers those Lords amendments.

When a stage of a private member's bill is on the Order Paper on any of the first twelve private members' days but is not completed (because it is talked out or objected to after 2.30 p.m.), the member in charge may name one of the later private members' days for continuing with the bill. As the session proceeds, unsuccessful bills are put off from Friday to Friday, until on the thirteenth and last day (widely known as 'the massacre of the innocents') there may be fifty or sixty to be 'called over' at 2.30 p.m. Even if an MP is lucky enough to get third reading at this stage, eventual success will depend on the Lords agreeing to the bill without amendment in the relatively little time that then remains in the session.

Presentation, ten-minute rule and Lords bills

Much of what we have said about the procedure and tactics of ballot bills also applies to ordinary presentation bills, to ten-minute rule bills and to bills brought from the Lords. However, all of these have more of a hill to climb, as none may be proceeded with until the ballot bills have been presented (and those will have taken up two or three slots on each of the days devoted to second readings).

Both presentation bills and ten-minute rule bills are thus used more often to make a point than seriously to seek to change the law. Ten-minute rule bills have the additional advantage that an MP has the opportunity to gauge opinion in the House. Beginning in the seventh week of the session, on every Tuesday and Wednesday before the main business of the day, one MP is called to make a speech of not more than ten minutes setting out the case for a bill and seeking the leave of the House to introduce it. Other MPs are alerted to the subject matter by a brief description on the Order Paper. If there is objection to the proposal, one opponent may speak against, again for a maximum of ten minutes; and, if necessary, there is a vote. If the proposer is successful, the bill is introduced in a little ceremony that involves the MP walking from the bar of the House to the Table, bowing three times *en route*.

Ten-minute rule bills are very popular with MPs. They could of course introduce exactly the same bill by the ordinary presentation method, without seeking the leave of the House. However, ten-minute rule bills come on at prime time immediately after questions and statements, and they are often a high-profile way of floating an idea and getting media attention – and perhaps laying the foundations of a later successful attempt. The right to introduce them is on a first come, first served basis. Sometimes an MP will spend the night in a room next to the Public Bill Office in order to be the first to give notice fifteen sitting days before the slot comes up; but there are often informal arrangements between the parties to avoid this 'January sales' tactic.

Success and failure

Even with government backing, the success of a private member's bill is not assured. Against government opposition, failure is virtually certain; and even half a dozen determined back-bench opponents can make it exceedingly difficult to get a private member's bill on the statute book. An additional obstacle may be encountered every four years or so: a spring or early summer general election will probably kill all the private members' bills that are not on the point of being passed, even if they are entirely uncontroversial.

In the twenty-five years 1977–2002, exactly 300 private members' bills became law. In the last four complete sessions, the figures have been rather lower than the 25-year average of twelve, as shown in Table 7.1.

It is difficult to categorise successful back-bench legislation. Many are minor pieces of tidying up of the statute book to remove generally recognised anomalies, and a number of these will have been suggested to sympathetic private members by government departments. Other Acts have dealt with small social

CHAPTER 7 MAKING THE LAW

Table 7.1 Bills dealt with by Parliament, 1998–2002

Session	1998–99	1999–2000	2000–01 short session (general election)	2001–02 long session
Passed	8 (27)	6 (39)	0 (21)	8 (39)
Not passed	96 (4)	(98) 1	(61) 7	(115) 0

Figures for government bills are in brackets.

reforms, particularly in areas affecting the rights of the disabled; marriage, children and the family; gaming and alcohol; care and control of animals; and the environment.

Overall, though, the scope has been very wide. Examples include the British Nationality (Falkland Islands) Act 1983, which gave British nationality to the inhabitants of the islands; the Pet Animals Act 1951 (Amendment) Act 1983, which made the sale of pets from market barrows illegal; the Race Relations (Remedies) Act 1994, giving industrial tribunals new powers in cases of racial discrimination; the Dogs (Fouling of Land) Act 1996, which gave local authorities new means of dealing with this problem; the Law Reform (Year and a Day Rule) Act 1996, which abolished the old rule of law that a person could not be found guilty of murder if the victim died more than a year and a day after being attacked; the Building Societies (Distributions) Act 1997, which removed some of the anomalies in the distribution of shares when building societies were 'demutualised'; the Protection of Animals (Amendment) Act 1999, which dealt with the welfare of animals when a prosecution for cruelty had been brought; and the Private Hire Vehicles (Carriage of Guide Dogs etc.) Act 2002, which made it illegal to refuse to take a person in a taxi or similar vehicle on the grounds that he or she had a guide dog. Although the scope of these private members' bills may have been relatively small compared with major government bills, they have had important consequences in particular areas.

Some private members' bills have had a much wider application; they have brought about the abolition of the death penalty, the legalisation of abortion and homosexuality and the end of theatre censorship. More recently, the Knives Act 1997 prohibited the carrying of knives as offensive weapons; the Video Recordings Act 1984 regulated the sale of 'video nasties'; the National Audit Act 1983 established the National Audit Office and introduced important reforms to make government more accountable to Parliament; the Housing (Homeless Persons) Act 1977 placed requirements on local authorities to house the homeless; and the Unsolicited Goods and Services (Amendment) Act 1975 regulated the sending of unsolicited material to private citizens.

Success can be measured in other terms. Sometimes the government will take over the intention of a private member's bill, and it will appear in a subsequent session as a government bill. In 1994, the then government's embarrassment following its blocking of a private member's bill on disability discrimination led to a government bill being introduced, which became the Disability Discrimination Act 1995. The Wild Mammals (Hunting with Dogs) Bill failed in the 1997–98 session but appeared in the 2000–01 session as the Hunting Bill; was passed by the Commons but overtaken by the dissolution of Parliament in 2001; and a similar bill was introduced by the government in 2002–03 but was not passed by the Lords.

It is possible for the government to give a private member's bill government time in the same session that it began as a private member's bill. This was done in the 1950s and 1960s on such subjects as the abolition of the death penalty and the legalisation of abortion, but it is now very unusual – no doubt because of the 'me too' principle; the government would find it hard to pick and choose among worthy bills. In 1976 the Sexual Offences Bill, which provided for anonymity in rape cases, was given government time; so too was the Census (Amendment) Bill [Lords] in 2002. A slightly different case occurred in 2002, when the Tobacco Advertising and Promotion Bill [Lords], a private peer's bill, was taken over as a government bill when it arrived in the Commons. (The bill, or rather a bill identical to it, had originally been introduced in the 2000–01 session as a government measure but had been lost at the general election for want of time.)

Success may have nothing to do with eventual legislation. The former Labour cabinet minister Tony Benn used substantial presentation bills to put forward his ideas on a Commonwealth of Europe to replace the European Union, on giving Parliament control over Crown prerogative, and on the reform of Parliament. None of these had a chance of succeeding, but setting out these detailed political proposals was an end in itself (and an MP whose bill is printed can receive up to 150 free copies of it).

The MP who seeks leave to bring in a ten-minute rule bill rarely expects that his or her bill will get onto the statute book (although ten did so in the period 1992 to 2002); and many bills for which leave is given are never actually printed. The ten-minute rule slot is a way of attracting attention to a subject, gauging opinion and putting it on the future political agenda. In the seventeen-month 2001–02 session, sixty-six bills were brought in under the ten-minute rule. One (the Divorce (Religious Marriages) Bill, which enabled a court to require the dissolution of a religious marriage before granting a divorce) did become law; but the others gave an opportunity to air subjects for possible legislation such as compulsory voting and voting at 16, controls on fireworks, reducing the rate of VAT on energy-saving materials, and (later taken up by the government) prohibiting the use of handheld mobile phones when driving.

Should it be easier?

Private members' bills are fragile vessels. The sponsor of a bill from scratch (rather than a government hand-out) will have to compromise on what is desirable to achieve what is realistic; he or she has to be an astute tactician; must try to ensure that the government is at the least neutral on the proposal; will have to persuade doubters and potential saboteurs; and needs a bit of luck. And even then success is by no means guaranteed.

This process can be frustrating – perhaps never more so than when a bill gets a second reading by a large majority but is then defeated by guerrilla warfare in standing committee and on report. The Wild Mammals (Hunting with Dogs) Bill is an example; it received a second reading by 411 votes to 151, a majority of 260 on a vote of 86 percent of MPs, but it did not become law. It may be said that the principle is one thing but the details another, and that scrutinising those is what the committee and report stages are for. And even if the degree of scrutiny – as opposed to obstruction – that a bill gets in those circumstances is open to question, many would argue that protecting the rights of the minority to disagree is especially important in the case of private members' legislation – in contrast to the assumption that a government with a majority will get its bills in the end.

Most proposals for making it easier for private members' bills to pass into law centre on providing more time, although, to make real difference, a substantial amount of time would have to be provided (and in a House that already sits for longer than many other parliamentary chambers). Another suggestion has been to make a few bills, perhaps the first five in the ballot, subject to a form of programming that would allow them to be voted upon at all their stages and would prevent their simply being 'talked out'.

But opinion is divided, even among MPs themselves. Some believe that taking initiatives to change the law should be a key part of an MP's role, and one in which MPs generally could act more independently of government; others are reluctant to see the amount of legislation already made every year increased, and they take Churchill's view that 'not every bright idea which occurs to a Member of Parliament should necessarily find its way onto the statute book'.

Lords stages

Bills can begin the parliamentary process in either House, and they have to pass through both Houses before they can be presented for Royal Assent. A bill introduced in the Commons, and passed by that House after it has completed the various stages just described, is sent to the Lords. A bill introduced in the Lords will, after going through its stages in that House, be sent to the Commons for similar treatment. Consideration by the two Houses is – unlike the practice in the United States – never simultaneous, although on very rare occasions, to save time, identical bills are introduced in both Houses. One is later dropped, but the other can then proceed more quickly because its main points have been discussed already by both Houses.

The Lords spend a great deal of their sitting time discussing bills. All stages are normally taken on the floor of the House, although the House has in recent years developed the grand committee procedure with a view to considering more bills in committee off the floor. Indeed, a greater proportion of time is spent on bills in the Chamber in the Lords than in the Commons – between 50 and 60 percent of the total sitting hours as opposed to one-third.

Bills in the Lords go through the same stages as in the Commons – a formal first reading, a substantial debate on second reading, detailed amendments at committee stage and report, and further debate (and, in the Lords only, consideration of amendments) at third reading. But outward appearances hide substantial differences in procedure, many of which reflect the more flexible and less constrained procedures that have survived in the Lords long after their demise in the late nineteenth-century House of Commons.

Differences in Lords procedure

The principal difference between Lords and Commons procedure is that bills are mostly considered at committee stage by a Committee of the Whole House. For many years, the only means of considering a bill in a committee off the floor was to commit it to a Public Bill Committee, roughly the equivalent of a Commons standing committee. But these committees have seldom been considered a success except for considering wholly uncontentious bills. Thus their scope for saving time on the floor of the House is limited. Their chief problem is that, as currently composed, it is virtually impossible to recreate the House in microcosm to form a committee in which only those named on the committee can vote in divisions. Only nine bills have been subjected to this procedure since 1968.

Since 1995, it has been possible to consider bills in a grand committee. The committee considers the bill, and amendments are tabled in the usual way; all Lords can attend and participate, but no divisions may take place. In 2001–02, five bills were subjected to this procedure. Although used at first for relatively uncontroversial measures, it has proved a potentially useful way of saving time on the floor and has recently been used for longer and more substantial bills like the Adoption Bill and the Employment Bill in 2001–02. Indeed, this was the intention of the 1994 Group on Sittings of the House (the Rippon Committee), which had originally recommended the procedure, and endorsed by the Group on the Working Practices of the House in 2002.

In 1994 the Lords adopted a procedure akin to special standing committees in the Commons: a special public bill committee may take written and oral evidence on a bill within twenty-eight days of its appointment. Thereafter, these committees proceed as public bill committees. Originally devised to expedite Law Commission bills, the procedure was used only in 1994–95 and may now be considered defunct.

It has always been possible for a bill to be committed to a select committee at any stage between second and third reading, usually after second reading, for consideration of its merits (see also page 342 below). The committee undertakes detailed investigation of the subject matter and reports on the main provisions, recommending whether the bill should proceed or not, and if so in what form. If a bill is to proceed it is recommitted to a Committee of the whole House. The procedure is often used as a way of considering controversial issues raised in private members' bills, like the Dangerous Dogs (Amendment) Bill in 1995. Nevertheless, despite vigorous efforts in the 1990s to move legislative work off the floor, the norm is for the committee stage of bills containing any controversial material to be taken in Committee of the whole House.

A second difference between the Lords and Commons legislative procedures is that there is no selection by a chairman of amendments to be discussed. All the amendments that have been tabled may be considered. Third, there is no guillotine or programme procedure, so in theory proceedings could be very protracted indeed. Fortunately, filibustering is rare. Most members – and especially the party whips – realise that the excellent opportunities that arise in the Lords to consider all clauses and to take all amendments could not long survive persistent abuse by any one member or any one party.

Another substantial difference is that in the Lords it is possible to move amendments at third reading. The principal purposes of amendments at this stage are to clarify remaining uncertainties, to improve drafting and to enable the government to fulfil undertakings given at earlier stages of the bill. It is not permissible to raise an issue that has been fully debated and decided upon at a previous stage. A general debate may also take place on the motion 'that the bill do now pass', after any amendments have been considered, although this practice is now discouraged.

Since 1992, all government and some private members' bills are considered by a Lords Select Committee on Delegated Powers and Regulatory Reform, which reports to the House whether the provisions of any bill inappropriately delegate legislative powers to ministers using Statutory Instruments; or whether they subject the use of any delegated powers to insufficient parliamentary scrutiny. All bills are considered – usually on the basis of memoranda supplied by the government – after Lords first reading; and the committee reports quickly so that its findings can if necessary be acted upon by the House at committee stage. There is no equivalent committee in the House of Commons. All bills, whether introduced in the Lords or Commons, are also scrutinised by the Joint Committee on Human Rights in respect of any human rights issue; and by the Lords Constitution Committee for any constitutional issue. Reports are published by these committees on the issues raised, but the bills themselves are not committed to them and they cannot amend them.

It is worth noting that the government has no formal priority over other peers in introducing or debating legislation. In practice, government business is recognised to take priority, but at the same time – possibly as a *quid pro quo* – generous provision is made for private members' bills in the Lords. Because there is no limitation on the number of days on which they can be considered, the government has little control on the number of these bills that will actually be considered on the floor of the House. Ultimately this does not cause any trouble for the government, because a private member's bill to which the government is opposed and which survives in the Lords can always be blocked in the Commons.

Lords impact on legislation

House of Lords practice and procedure give a persistent back-bench (or opposition front-bench) peer a far better chance of getting a point of view across than the equivalent MP in the House of Commons. And these advantages, when combined with the comparative political independence of members of the House of Lords, can result in opposition to the elected government of the day, to the extent of sometimes radical amendment of bills. Until the passage of the House of Lords Act in 1998 the House of Lords was a predominantly Conservative body. All the more remarkable, then, that between 1979 and 1997 the Lords were often highly critical of aspects of government policy. During the Conservative administration of 1970–74, the government was defeated twenty-six times on a vote in the House of Lords but between 1979 and 1997 these occasions became more frequent (see Table 7.2).

Table 7.2 Government defeats in the House of Lords, 1979–97

Parliament	Number of defeats
1979–83	45
1983–87	62
1987–92	72
1992–97	56

Most of these amendments were accepted by the government either as they stood or with modification when the bills returned to the Commons. But if reversed, the Lords only rarely insisted upon their disagreement. In the 1984–85 session, for example, the government suffered seventeen defeats in the Lords. Of these, sixteen related to amendments to bills; only two were reversed by the government in the Commons (we describe later what happens when the two Houses disagree). Some of these amendments made substantial dents in government policy.

Some writers have contended – usually in the context of discussions of Lords reform – that the Lords should have done more to modify or even curb the more radical Conservative policies of the 1979–97 era; and the fact that they did not showed that the House was on the whole content to acquiesce in those policies. While it is true that on certain major issues the government was, with strong whipping, able to carry the day, it is perhaps unfair to censure the Lords for not doing more. Political composition aside, the House of Lords, however composed, will always need to be mindful of its secondary position in relation to the Commons and use its remaining – and in theory still very considerable – powers sparingly. Under our current constitutional arrangements, Parliament, as a bicameral legislature, would rapidly become inoperable unless the upper House continued to be sensitive to the delicacy of its position.

Ironically, since the election of a Labour government in 1997, the Lords have continued to inflict defeats over unwelcome provisions in bills – notwithstanding the exclusion of many opposition hereditary peers in late 1998 (see Table 7.3).

One such bill was the Criminal Justice (Mode of Trial) Bill in 1999–2000, a Lords bill that sought to abolish trial by jury in so-called 'either way' cases. The provisions on jury trial were removed by the Lords and the bill abandoned. Reintroduced in the Commons as a No. 2 bill later that session, it was rejected by the Lords at second reading. It was not reintroduced, although somewhat different provisions limiting the right to jury trial reappeared in the strongly contested Criminal Justice Bill in 2003. The Sexual Offences (Amendment) Bill, which lowered the homosexual age of consent for males from 18 to 16, was rejected at second reading by the Lords in the 1998–99 session, reintroduced

Table 7.3 Government defeats in the House of Lords, 1997–2002

Parliament/session	Number of defeats
1997–2001	128
2001–02	57

in the following session and received Royal Assent under the Parliament Act at the end of the session.

Other bills have been heavily amended. A provision in the Local Government Bill in the 1999–2000 session that sought to repeal the now infamous 'section 28' of the Local Government Act 1986 (preventing local authorities from 'promoting' homosexuality) was removed by the Lords and not insisted upon by the government. (The Lords finally assented to the repeal of this section in 2003!) An amendment to the Transport Bill in the same session had the effect of delaying the proposed privatisation of the National Air Traffic Service until after the expected general election in 2001; and safeguards on privacy relating to e-mail interceptions were written into the Regulation of Investigatory Powers Bill. There were many other such examples as the pressure of time at the end of that very crowded session made the government receptive – perforce – to Lords amendments.

Since the 2001 election, no bill better illustrates the influence of the Lords as a chamber of legislature than the Anti-Terrorism, Crime and Security Bill – a 126-clause bill containing measures in response to the terrorist attacks in New York and Washington on 11 September 2001. Although proceedings were accelerated, the Lords spent fifty-three hours seeking to amend this bill. As a result, changes were made in key areas, in some cases after the Lords had insisted on their amendments. Thus, among other things, an appeal mechanism against deportation was provided for; the additional police powers conferred by the bill were confined to anti-terrorism and national security matters; the offence of inciting religious hatred was struck out; and a 'sunset clause' was inserted to time-limit many of the bill's provisions.

Of other amendments made to bills, those on vaccination and import controls to the Animal Health Bill and on academic freedom and sustainable development to the Export Control Bill had a noteworthy effect on the resulting legislation. In the 2002–03 session, Lords opposition focused on Lord Puttnam, the Labour back-bencher, and the prospect of certain defeat in the lobbies led the government to amend its Communications Bill at third reading so as to protect UK television channels from undesirable foreign or multimedia ownership.

Lords independence

Why has the House of Lords been ready on occasion to impose its will on both Conservative and Labour administrations? The chief reason is that over the last twenty years or so neither party has been able consistently to control the House at critical moments. Table 7.4 shows how neither of the two major parties has, in terms of actual attendance of its members, held an absolute majority in the House in recent years.

Table 7.4 Average daily attendance in the House of Lords by party (%)

Session	Conservative	Labour	Liberal	Cross-bench	Other
1988–89	46.6	22.1	11.7	18.0	1.7
1998–99	37.0	34.4	10.6	15.9	2.0
1999–2000	35.3	36.0	11.4	15.4	1.9

The Conservative administrations, despite the relative strength of the Conservative Party in the pre-1998 House, were vulnerable to defeat on a vote if Labour, Liberal and cross-bench members united in opposition. Similarly, in spite of the strengthening of the Labour group in the House by the new peerage creations following the 1997 general election and the expulsion of the hereditary peers in 1998, the Labour Party has proved vulnerable in the same way.

But in addition to simple arithmetic, a number of other factors are at play. Party discipline is weaker in the Lords than in the Commons and back-bench rebellion more frequent. There are a number of reasons for this. As the House is not elected, its members are not directly accountable – as are members of the House of Commons – to an electorate and a party manifesto. Moreover, professional politicians or former politicians are in a minority, and even they may on occasions be out of sympathy with certain aspects of their party's policy. Furthermore, the payroll vote (of office holders) is very small in the Lords (see page 117), so caution in voting is less influential with members of the House, many of whom are in the twilight years of their political careers, than it is with aspiring MPs.

Why, then, does the government not reverse in the Commons every Lords amendment with which it disagrees? Some of the defeats are on matters of principle that command some support from the ranks of back-benchers in the Commons and from the country at large. So the government accepts amendments of this kind graciously rather than risk unnecessary unpopularity for itself among its own supporters both inside and outside Parliament. As in the Commons, compromise amendments will be accepted by a government to expedite a bill's progress, and any government may even admit defeat on part of its bill in order to get the other provisions through on time.

But amendments to bills following the defeat of the government on a vote are a very small element in the total number of amendments made in a session, for the fact remains that most of the Lords' work is of a revising character – revising bills received from the Commons. Whichever party is in power, this aspect of the Lords' legislative work continues unchanged. In recent heavy legislative sessions, between 2,000 and 3,000 amendments have been made to bills in any one session. The majority of them are drafting amendments of no real significance, amendments introduced by the government to meet points made in either the Commons or the Lords, or to introduce new provisions of its own into bills. One study (Shell and Beamish 1993) analysed proceedings in the Lords on eight bills in the 1988–89 session. It traced the origins of the amendments made and showed that the vast majority were made by the government itself, with, relatively speaking, a few more being made with government approval but on the initiative of others. Thus, of the 1,164 amendments moved by the government, 1,161 (99.7 percent) were accepted: of the 1,047 moved by non-government members, only sixty-five (6.2 percent) were accepted. A further look showed that, of these sixty-five, only four followed defeats in the lobbies (in fact two of these were later reversed in the Commons). Of the remaining sixty-one, thirty-nine were consequential or drafting amendments and only twenty-two involved matters of substance that the government accepted without a vote. Of the amendments moved by the government, about thirty-five were identified as arising out of ministerial undertakings to look again at aspects of the bills following criticisms in the Lords in the early stages.

Disagreement between the Houses: the balance of power

Ping-pong

In the previous section, we saw that on occasion there is disagreement between the two Houses on a bill. We now explore this more fully. We also consider constraints on the Lords' powers to amend bills. A bill that passes without amendment through the second House then needs only the Royal Assent – or formal approval by the Queen – before it becomes law. It does not go back to the House where its progress began. However, if the second House makes amendments to a bill, those amendments (but no other part of the bill) must be considered by the first House. If they are agreed, the bill is ready to become law. If they are not, the second House looks at the matter again and can either insist upon its amendments or attempt compromise proposals. Theoretically, alternative compromises can be shuttled between the two Houses indefinitely. Each time, messages are exchanged between the two Houses. These can become fiendishly complicated. For example, in the final stages of the controversial Licensing Bill 2003, which had started its life as a Lords bill, the Lords received the following message from the Commons after it had been considered by that House a second time:

> My Lords, the Commons do not insist on certain of their Amendments to the Licensing Bill to which the Commons have disagreed; they agree to an Amendment made by the Lords in lieu of words left out of the Bill by a Commons Amendment; they do not insist on an Amendment but propose Amendments in lieu thereof, to which they desire the agreement of the Lords; and they insist on the remaining Amendment and disagree to the Amendment proposed by the Lords in lieu thereof, but propose an Amendment in lieu of that Amendment, to which they desire the agreement of the Lords.

Eventually disagreements are ironed out, and the bill goes forward for Royal Assent in the form in which it was agreed by both Houses. If a compromise were not reached, the bill would be lost, as happened to the House of Commons Distribution of Seats Bill in 1969 (which was not reintroduced); and to the Trade Union and Labour Relations Bill and Aircraft and Shipbuilding Industries Bill in 1976 (reintroduced in 1977 and enacted in the conventional manner following compromise). The point of final disagreement is normally thought to have been reached when each House has taken up its position and insisted upon it.

Limitations on Lords powers: ancient practice and the Parliament Acts

The Lords do not have free rein in amending certain types of Commons bill. By ancient practice set out in Commons resolutions dating from the late seventeenth century, the Lords may not amend bills 'of aids and supplies' – a type of bill that includes the annual Finance Bill, which implements the tax proposals made by the Chancellor of the Exchequer in his Budget, and Consolidated Fund Bills, which sanction government expenditure.

If the Lords insist on their amendments to any other public bill in a manner that renders the bill wholly unacceptable to the majority in the Commons and to the point that the bill is lost by the close of the session, or if they reject altogether a bill passed by the Commons, the procedures of the Parliament Acts 1911 and 1949 may be invoked. These Acts were passed to ensure that important reforming legislation introduced by the Liberal and Labour governments of the time was not frustrated by the then overwhelming Conservative majority in the Lords.

The severest restrictions in the Parliament Acts apply to 'money bills'. These are bills that deal only with certain specified central government finance matters. The most important of them are pure taxation bills or the Consolidated Fund Bills that formally vote money to the government. These will be described in more detail in Chapter 8. (The annual Finance Bill, which implements the budget proposals, is often not a money bill because it contains wider provisions than those defined in the Parliament Act. This is somewhat paradoxical, since the 1911 Parliament Act was passed as a reaction to the Lords' rejection of the 1909 Finance Bill.) Under the Parliament Acts, money bills passed by the Commons are allowed one month to pass through the Lords. If the Lords do not pass them within a month, they can be sent for Royal Assent without the Lords' approval. The provisions relating to money bills have never had to be invoked for the purpose of giving Royal Assent.

All other public bills passed by the Commons may be delayed for a minimum effective period of thirteen months by the Lords. The rule is strictly as follows: any bill (except one to extend the life of a parliament – that is, to postpone a general election) that passes the Commons in two successive sessions (whether or not a general election intervenes) can be presented for Royal Assent without the agreement of the Lords, provided that (1) there has been a minimum period of one year between the Commons giving it a second reading for the first time and a third reading for the second time, and (2) the Lords have received the bill at least one month before the end of each of the two sessions.

The rigours of these provisions of the Parliament Acts have on only three occasions been taken to their final stage since the 1949 Act (which reduced by one year the delaying time of the 1911 Act) was itself passed without the agreement of the Lords. In 1991, the War Crimes Act received Royal Assent under these provisions after the bill had been passed by the Commons and rejected by the Lords at second reading in two successive sessions. This bill sought, retrospectively, to create a new criminal offence so as to enable charges to be brought against alleged perpetrators of atrocities, chiefly against Jews, in continental Europe during the Second World War. Many lords felt that such prosecutions would be difficult to secure and that too many legal principles were offended by the proposed legislation. As the bill was not a manifesto commitment by the government, the Lords felt entitled to reject it. In 1998, the European Parliamentary Elections Bill was lost following disagreement over the electoral system proposed. The Lords rejected the reintroduced bill at second reading in the following session, thus enabling Royal Assent to take place in time for the elections to proceed notwithstanding the initial delay. In 2000, Royal Assent was also given under the Parliament Acts to the Sexual Offences (Amendment) Bill, which lowered the age of consent for homosexual activity and buggery to 16.

The Parliament Act procedures are the fundamental limitation on the legislative power of the Lords. They enable any administration with a majority in the Commons to exert its will and ultimately to pass its legislation without Lords agreement. But its procedures are akin to a nuclear deterrent, and of course they involve delay. For practical reasons, government business managers often find it easier to accept Lords amendments than to attempt to overturn them every time, let alone threaten the use of the Parliament Acts.

The Salisbury convention

Members of the House of Lords accept that the elected government of the day must be allowed to get its business through. The nearest that this idea has come to formal expression is in the Salisbury convention – an understanding reached between the Conservative opposition in the House of Lords (led by the fifth Marquess of Salisbury) and the Labour government immediately after the Second World War in 1945. The convention is that the Lords should not reject at second reading any government legislation that has been passed by the House of Commons and that carries out a manifesto commitment – that is to say, a commitment made to the electorate in the government party's election manifesto. However, this convention does not extend to the amendment of bills; nor can it be held, strictly, to apply to government bills that do not reflect a manifesto commitment. So even this self-denying ordinance leaves the Lords with considerable room for manoeuvre.

The convention had its origin in the doctrine of the mandate developed by the third Marquess of Salisbury in the nineteenth century. He argued that the will of the people and the views of the House of Commons did not necessarily coincide and that the Lords had a duty to reject – and hence refer back to the electorate – contentious bills, particularly those with constitutional implications. Like the doctrine of the mandate before it, the Salisbury convention is perhaps more a code of behaviour for the Conservative Party when in opposition in the Lords than a convention of the House. Indeed, it is a moot point whether, following the passage of the House of Lords Act 1999, the expulsion of the hereditary members and the ending of the overwhelming numerical advantage of the Conservative Party, the Salisbury convention as originally devised can have any continuing validity. But the notion that Government bills (whether in fulfilment of a manifesto commitment or not) should not be denied a second reading – whatever the party of government – certainly persists.

In spite of the Parliament Acts, and historical conventions on matters of supply, and more recent conventions on manifesto commitments, in practice – and under certain conditions – the Lords' powers to amend bills other than money are real and influential. What is more, these powers have recently been reconfirmed by the Joint Committee on House of Lords Reform in December 2002; and by the Royal Commission on Reform of the House of Lords in 2000.

Royal Assent and implementation

A bill passed by both Houses needs the Royal Assent – from the sovereign as the third element of Parliament in addition to the Lords and the Commons – before it can become law. The Queen's agreement is automatic (Queen Anne in 1707–08 was the last monarch to refuse to accept a bill passed by both Houses). Although in theory the Royal Assent can be given by the sovereign in person, this was last done in 1854, and in 1967 it was decided to stop the procedure by which Black Rod would interrupt the proceedings of the Commons, summoning them to the Lords Chamber to hear the Lords Commissioners announcing Royal Assent. This now occurs only at prorogation. At other times, the Speaker in the Commons and the Lord Chancellor in the Lords announce the Royal Assent at a convenient break in each House's proceedings.

Although Royal Assent to a bill turns it into an Act and makes it law, the law does not necessarily come into force immediately. The Act will normally contain a commencement provision. Typically, this allows the secretary of state concerned to make an order at some future date to bring part or all of the Act into force, although a date may be specified, for example three or six months after Royal Assent. Sometimes the appropriate date never comes: the Employment of Children Act 1973 has never been brought fully into effect. In response to a recommendation of the House of Lords Procedure Committee, in March 1997 the government listed sixty-nine Acts passed between May 1979 and December 1992, parts of which had for a variety of reasons never been commenced.

The question of whether it was legal for a minister simply not to bring into force something that had been decided by Parliament was considered by the Court of Appeal in 1994. That court decided that as Parliament had not set a time for commencement the minister had not acted illegally; but the then Master of the Rolls, in a dissenting judgement, suggested that the power given to the minister was to decide *when* rather than *whether* an Act should come into force. However, it is a moot point as to when delay becomes long enough to regard the Act passed by Parliament as ineffective.

If there is no commencement provision (whether a date, or a power given to a minister), the Act comes into force from midnight at the beginning of the day on which Royal Assent was given.

What is the law?

Acts of Parliament are available in bound copies of the statutes for any particular year (and Acts from 1988 are available on the parliamentary website). However, these sources will not show whether an Act is wholly or partially in force, or whether it has been amended (or even repealed), or what delegated legislation has been made under its authority. The picture is complicated when an Act legislates 'by reference' – not setting out the law anew but changing it by inserting new material in a series of other Acts. UK legislation is not codified; in other words, there is not a single Act covering, say, gaming law, that is republished every time there is an amending bill. To some extent, the work of the Law Commissions addresses this problem by compiling consolidation bills that bring together the existing law in a more logical and convenient form. For want of resources, the programme of consolidation has produced very little in recent sessions of Parliament. So the reader who wishes to know what a particular Act says needs to be careful to consult a fully revised and updated version, or to go to a publication such as Halsbury's *Laws of England* for a statement of how the law stands, and then look up the individual statutes or delegated legislation. The Internet is now an invaluable source too. Law publishers like Halsbury and Butterworth offer an on-line subscription version of the statute book, as does the government's own statute law database.

Private legislation

The reader of the House of Commons Order of Business will often see at the beginning of the day's agenda on Mondays to Thursday references to private business. Occasionally the words 'At four o'clock [or three o'clock or seven o'clock] private business set down under Standing Order No. 20' can be seen. The private business is not private in the sense of being confidential or related to the internal affairs of the House; it is business related to private legislation.

As we saw earlier in this chapter (pages 172 and 173), private bills are nothing to do with private members' bills. Private members' bills seek to change the general law, but private bills affect individuals, groups of individuals or corporate bodies in a way different from other individuals, groups or bodies. Their effect is private and particular as opposed to public and general. For example, the Dartmoor Commons Act 1985 was promoted by Dartmoor farmers to give powers to stop the overgrazing of the moors; the Southampton International Boat Show Act 1997 allowed a park in Southampton to open for one extra day a year; and the City of London (Ward Elections) Act 2002 made changes to the franchise for local elections in the City. In the 2002–03 session, the Hereford Markets Bill sought to allow a livestock market that by royal charter had to be held within the city limits to be moved outside and so release a prime site for other uses.

The first step in private legislation is for the person or group seeking the legislation to petition for the bill. Private bills are not presented by MPs or peers but by the promoters of the legislation, who are represented by special lawyers known as parliamentary agents. Throughout the bill's passage – but especially before it is even introduced – the promoters will be working to ensure that the bill attracts as little opposition as possible. Promoters need to comply with an elaborate set of standing orders, which try to ensure that interested parties (who may know nothing of the promoters' intentions) are given notice of the bill. When this has been done, the bill is allocated to one House or the other for first consideration, and, after second reading, is sent to a special committee. Private bill procedure is particularly complex and is set out in detail in *Erskine May*, but the main elements are described here.

Anyone who is aggrieved by the bill's provisions has the right to petition against it, but only those directly affected by the bill (who have what is known as *locus standi*) have the right to be heard. If the bill is not opposed by petitions, or if all the petitions are withdrawn because the promoters have been able to meet the petitioners' wishes, the bill is considered by a committee on unopposed bills, through which it usually passes swiftly after a explanation of its purposes by the promoters. Opposed private bills are considered much more elaborately over many days by a committee of four MPs (or five peers), who must have no personal interest in the matter.

The committee acts in a semi-judicial capacity, examining witnesses and hearing barristers who appear for and against the bill. In effect, it displays the character of Parliament both as a court, inquiring into and adjudicating on the interests of private individuals, and as a legislature safeguarding the public interest. The committee has to decide whether the promoters have demonstrated that the bill is necessary, whether those affected by it have been treated fairly, and whether there is any objection to it on public policy grounds. The committee has the power to make amendments, or even to recommend that the bill should not proceed (as happened with the Crossrail Bill in 1994, which failed).

After their committee stage, private bills are considered on report (in the Commons, but not the Lords), read a third time and passed to the other House for similar stages to be taken. It is quite usual for a private bill not to complete all its stages in one session; an order is made that allows it to be taken up in the following session at the stage it had reached. By contrast, the carry-over procedure for public bills has been used only three times. Private bills are not covered by the Parliament Acts, so there is no restriction on the power of the Lords to delay them.

Most private bills do not encounter sustained opposition from MPs or peers, but the opportunities for delay are considerable. Each stage of a bill's progress is advertised on the Order of Business 'at the time of unopposed private business' and can be stopped from proceeding further by an MP shouting 'Object!' or by the tabling of a 'blocking motion'. If this objection is sustained on each appearance of the bill on the Order of Business, the bill cannot proceed without time being found for a debate. This is in the hands of the Chairman of Ways and Means, who has a general responsibility for the way that private bills are handled (but not for the success or failure of any bill). He can set a bill down for a three-hour period (on a Monday, from 7.00 p.m. to 10.00 p.m.; on a Tuesday or Wednesday, from 4.00 p.m. to 7.00 p.m.; or on a Thursday from 3.00 p.m. to 6.00 p.m.).

The government business managers are naturally anxious not to have much scarce parliamentary time taken up with opposed private business, so an MP who objects to an aspect of a private bill has a strong bargaining counter with the promoters. Unless they go some way towards meeting the MP's wishes, he or she can delay the bill by insisting on a debate at each stage, and this may eventually mean that the bill is lost.

In the Lords, private bills that have been reported from a select committee are not usually opposed further on the floor. The Chairman of Committees oversees private legislation proceedings in the Lords in the same way as the Chairman of Ways and Means in the Commons.

The amount of private legislation has fallen dramatically in recent years, especially following the Transport and Works Act 1992. This removed from the parliamentary process private bills dealing with matters such as railway, tramway and harbour building, and other types of development. These were often the most controversial private bills. Nowadays, parliamentary involvement in such projects will occur only when a project is seen by the government as being nationally significant, when a single debate on its desirability will take place on the floor of the House. An example is the debate on the proposal to build a new railway from Leicester to the Channel Tunnel via Rugby, which was rejected by the Commons in 1996.

Table 7.5 shows the numbers of new private bills in the four sessions before the passing of the Transport and Works Act 1992 and in the last four complete sessions, together with the numbers that attracted opposition and so were petitioned against.

There will no doubt be private bills in the future that do not deal with transport and works but that will still prove controversial, as for example did the City of London (Ward Elections) Bill, which encountered opposition on the grounds that it provided for a weighted franchise, and which took nearly four years to get through Parliament. And any private bill may be of great importance both for its promoters and for those who will be affected. But, compared with their nineteenth-century heyday, private bills have become something of a parliamentary backwater.

Table 7.5 Private bills presented and petitioned against, 1988–92 and 1998–2002

Session	Number of bills	Number petitioned against*
1988–89	39	12
1989–90	32	12
1990–91	28	11
1991–92	24	10
1998–99	10	1
1999–2000	3	3
2000–01	2	0
2001–02	5	1

*which includes those suspended from a previous session, but petitioned against in the session shown.

Hybrid bills

These bills – which are fairly unusual – combine characteristics of a public bill and a private bill. Bills that are introduced by the government but that would otherwise be private bills are also treated as hybrid. Examples of hybrid bills include the Channel Tunnel Bill in 1987, the Cardiff Bay Barrage Bill (which was enacted in 1993 after starting out as a private bill and then being taken over by the government), and the Channel Tunnel Rail Link Bill in 1994, which became law in 1996. One of the classic examples of a hybrid bill was the Aircraft and Shipbuilding Industries Bill of 1976, which was intended to nationalise these two industries. It was discovered that this bill did not apply to one shipbuilding company that otherwise fulfilled the bill's criteria for nationalisation. Because this company was thus being treated differently from all other companies in the same class, the bill was ruled by the Speaker to be hybrid. Although this ruling was set aside by the Commons, the bill was committed to a select committee in the Lords.

Hybrid bills are treated as public bills, except that the promoters do not need to prove the need for the bill. Bills are examined to see whether they comply with the standing orders that relate to private bills, and there is an additional stage – they are referred to a select committee in each House, which can hear petitions from those affected. This may be a major exercise; the committee on the Channel Tunnel Bill received several thousand petitions.

Delegated legislation

Definitions

Delegated legislation is law made by ministers or certain public bodies under powers given to them by Act of Parliament, but it is just as much part of the law of the land as are those Acts. The volume of delegated legislation is huge, and this presents particular challenges for parliamentary scrutiny.

Individual pieces of delegated legislation, often called *secondary legislation* to distinguish them from primary legislation contained in Acts of Parliament, or *subordinate legislation*, are found under many different names. They can be *orders*, *regulations*, *Orders in Council*, *schemes*, *rules*, *codes of practice* and *statutes* (of certain colleges rather than in the sense of Acts). Even the Highway Code is a form of secondary legislation.

Delegated legislation may be made by any person or body empowered to do so by an Act of Parliament ('the parent Act'); and although some institutions and professional bodies have this power in particular cases, the bulk of such legislation is made by ministers.

Before the Second World War there was very much less delegated legislation, and parent Acts prescribed a variety of different parliamentary procedures, often designed for the particular case. Most of these were unified by the Statutory

Instruments Act 1946, which describes what a statutory instrument is and prescribes the principal procedures for parliamentary approval. Not all pieces of delegated legislation are *Statutory Instruments*, but this general term (abbreviated to SI, with individual instruments numbered in an annual series, for example 'SI 2003/875') will serve. About half of the 3,000 or so Statutory Instruments made have only a local effect and may be for only a temporary purpose. Our concern is with the general instruments that form part of the law of the land.

Purpose

The original idea of an SI was to supplement what was set down in an Act of Parliament, for two particular purposes. The first was to prescribe things that were too detailed for inclusion in an Act of Parliament. The second was – again, for fairly minor matters – to provide the flexibility to change the law to meet changing circumstances without the sledgehammer (and the delay) of new primary legislation.

As long as this remained the guiding principle, one would expect there to be little difficulty. However, over the years the boundaries of delegated legislation have been tested.

Table 7.6 Statutory instruments laid before Parliament, 1955–2002

Year	Number of statutory instruments
1955	657
1960	733
1965	899
1970	1,040
1975	1,362
1980	1,197
1985	1,204
1990	1,408
1995	1,666
2000	1,373
2001	1,502
2002	1,325

The increase over the last thirty years has been of the order of 50 percent, although it appears that the upward trend may have levelled out. However, the *volume* of delegated legislation is huge: the 1,373 SIs in 2000 took up 10,755 A4 pages.

The second area of strain has been in the *use* of SIs. Ministers naturally find it more convenient to be able to legislate in a way that is subject to more limited parliamentary scrutiny than primary legislation, and there is thus a temptation to leave to delegated legislation matters that arguably should be set out in a bill and so in an Act. The most extreme examples of this have been in so-called 'skeleton' or 'framework' bills, where the use of delegated powers is so extensive that the real operation of the bill would be entirely by the regulations made under it. The Education (Student Loans) Bill in 1990, the Child Support Bill in 1991 and the Jobseekers Bill in 1995 all attracted criticism on these grounds, as have 'Henry VIII powers', which allow ministers to amend primary legislation by the use of secondary legislation (see also page 234).

The speed of the legislative process encourages an overuse of delegated powers. A minister may want to put a new provision into a bill during its passage, but the limited time available to settle the details may lead to the provision being drafted in very general terms, with even quite significant matters being left to delegated legislation. There is also the question of where the threshold should be set between the more important *affirmative instruments*, which Parliament must approve explicitly, and *negative instruments*, which have effect unless Parliament says otherwise.

Since 1992, the House of Lords has sought to address the balance between delegation and control through the work of the Delegated Powers and Regulatory Reform Committee (formerly the Delegated Powers and Deregulation Committee). For each bill introduced into the Lords (and for substantial government amendments), this committee examines the powers to make delegated legislation that are proposed to be given to ministers. It reports on both whether those powers are justified and whether the level of parliamentary control is appropriate (in other words, which powers should be exercised through negative instruments, which through affirmative instruments, and which should be matters for an Act of Parliament rather than delegated legislation). The vast majority of the committee's recommendations have been accepted, and it plays an important role in striking a balance between executive freedom and parliamentary control.

Two other features of the system should also be mentioned. The first is that the vast majority of SIs are not amendable. This is inevitable in that both Houses must take the same view on an SI, and amendable instruments would be like another class of bills going back and forth for both Houses to agree on any amendments. But it also means an element of 'take it or leave it', especially when an SI is substantial or complex.

The second is that the way the threshold is set between affirmative and negative instruments can become out of date with changes in society. For example, in an Act passed in 1950 it might have been thought essential to require a minister to come back to Parliament for permission to exercise a power that by 2003 would be thought to be a matter of routine. But the requirement remains in the 1950 Act, and only further primary legislation will remove it. The phenomenon may also work the other way – something routine in 1950 may have taken on a different significance fifty years later.

Parliamentary control

There are four levels:

1. Delegated legislation that may be made and come into effect *without any reference to Parliament*. This category includes a large number of SIs with only local effect, and many of these will be printed only if the responsible minister wishes them to be.
2. Delegated legislation that may be made and come into effect, and that *must be laid before Parliament, but on which there are no parliamentary proceedings*. These are really for information; commencement orders bringing an Act of Parliament into effect are typical.
3. *Negative instruments*: these are *laid before Parliament* and may *come into effect* immediately or on some future date *unless either House resolves that the instrument be annulled*.
4. *Affirmative instruments*: these do not normally (except in cases of urgency) come into effect until they have been *approved by resolution of each House*.

The third and fourth categories are the most significant; in the last four complete sessions, they averaged 186 affirmatives and 1,173 negatives a year (see Table 7.7).

Procedure

When an instrument has been laid before Parliament it is examined by the Joint Committee on Statutory Instruments, which is supported by specialist lawyers and which reports on various technical aspects: whether in making the instrument the minister has exceeded the powers given by Parliament (this is also something that can be challenged in the courts); whether the drafting is defective or unclear; whether the instrument has retrospective effect, and so on. The committee reports its conclusions but, even if it finds fault, the progress of the instrument is not automatically halted. Some instruments, on finance and taxation, are laid before the Commons only and are examined by the Select

Table 7.7 Statutory instruments considered by Parliament, 1998–2002

	Affirmative	Negative
1998–99	178	1,266
1999–2000	180	1,241
2000–01, short session	123	717
2001–02, long session	262	1,468

Committee on Statutory Instruments, which consists of the Commons members of the Joint Committee.

Negative instruments

In the case of a negative instrument, nothing will happen unless an opposition party, or a group of back-benchers, tables what is known as a *prayer*. This has nothing to do with religious devotion but is so called because of the form of the motion; because the instrument has been made by one of Her Majesty's ministers, it is the sovereign who has to be asked to undo what has been done. To take a real example from the 2001–02 session, the motion would read:

> That an Humble Address be presented to Her Majesty, praying that the Social Security (Jobcentre Plus Interviews) Regulations 2001 (S.I., 2001, No. 3210) be annulled.

Any annulment of an instrument must take place during a period of forty days (excluding time when both Houses are adjourned for more than four days) from the laying of the SI; this time is unsurprisingly known as *praying time*.

In the Commons, debate on a prayer on the floor of the House is unusual; most are taken upstairs in a *standing committee on delegated legislation*, which is very like a standing committee on a bill but which debates the prayer on a motion 'That the committee has considered' the instrument, for a period of one and a half hours (two and a half hours in the case of Northern Ireland instruments). Only a minister can move a motion in the House to refer a prayer to a standing committee, so even debates of this sort are in the gift of the government and are normally only granted to the principal opposition parties, and almost never to back-benchers. Moreover, the standing committee cannot reject the instrument, so any vote that is not on the floor of the House is purely symbolic; and on the floor of the House no prayer has been carried since 1979.

In the last four complete sessions, the numbers of prayers taken in standing committee have been twenty-eight, sixteen, six and forty-one; for the rarer debates on the floor of the House, the numbers were one, four, four and three.

Affirmative procedure

Because any instrument in this category must be explicitly approved, a decision of each House is required. In the Commons, affirmative instruments are automatically referred to a standing committee on delegated legislation. These operate in exactly the same way for affirmative instruments as for prayers against negative instruments, and they offer an opportunity for debate rather than substantive decision. Affirmative instruments are occasionally considered in the Northern Ireland Grand Committee (two in the four years 1998–2002). When an affirmative has been debated in standing committee it returns to the floor of the House for decision, and a vote if necessary, but without further debate.

It is also possible for an affirmative to be 'de-referred': that is, so that it is both debated and decided on the floor of the House. The automatic referral to standing committee has existed since 1995; it was introduced as part of an effort to reduce sitting time on the floor of the House, but there was an understanding that the government would accede to a reasonable request to take particular affirmatives on the floor of the House.

Although, to begin with, substantial numbers of affirmatives were taken on the floor (seventy-three in 1994–95, forty-seven in 1995–96 and forty-two in 1996–97), there was a sharp decline thereafter, and in the four sessions 1998–2002, the numbers of affirmatives considered in the House have been twenty-one, seventeen, eleven and twelve. Subjects taken on the floor in the 2001–02 session included EU extradition regulations, amendments to the list of proscribed terrorist organisations, arrangements for elections to the Northern Ireland Assembly, local government finance and the financing of police authorities.

Every sitting week, the Journal Office in the House of Commons produces a *Statutory Instrument List* showing the state of play on all affirmative and negative instruments and, in the latter case, the number of 'praying days' remaining on each. It is available on the parliamentary website.

Lords proceedings on Statutory Instruments

Although delegated legislation is not subject to the Parliament Acts, the House of Lords rarely opposes negative or affirmative instruments. As we have seen, they are not amendable, so if the House pressed its opposition to a vote the result could be the wholesale rejection of the instrument. As the Lords usually consider instruments after they have been taken in the House of Commons, this has constrained opposition parties from pressing their disagreement. Between 1955 and the end of the 2001–02 session there were seventy-five divisions on statutory instruments, but such was the unease of the two major parties while in opposition about using the House's powers to the full that thirty-two of those divisions were on motions that would not, if carried, have proved fatal to the instrument in question.

Only three times has the government of the day ever been defeated on a vote directly on an order. The Conservative opposition divided the House against the Southern Rhodesia (United Nations Sanctions) Order 1968 and defeated the government, so provoking a constitutional furore. A virtually identical version of the order was approved a few weeks later. The two other instances occurred in February 2002 on a prayer to annul the Greater London Authority Election Rules 2000 and a motion to approve the Greater London Authority (Election Expenses) Order 2000. In addition, since 1955 one order has been withdrawn following debate with no vote taken and another – the Town and Country Planning General Development Order 1977 – was not proceeded with after the government lost a vote on a motion inviting it to withdraw the order.

The Royal Commission on Reform of the House of Lords recommended that the Statutory Instruments Act 1946 be amended to enable the Commons to override a Lords rejection of an affirmative or negative instrument. By diminishing the theoretical powers over delegated legislation slightly, it was argued, the House might make more use of the powers that remained to it. But there are no indications that this recommendation will be taken up.

Improving parliamentary control

Parliament's control of secondary legislation has been criticised on a number of grounds. The remit of the Joint Committee is limited to technical issues of *vires* and drafting; opportunities for debate, particularly in the Commons, are limited; and SIs are unamendable in either House.

Both the Royal Commission on Reform of the House of Lords in 2000 and more recently the Group on the Working of the House in 2002 have recommended that the House of Lords should establish a committee to consider the merits of statutory instruments, and to identify or sift those of political significance from the rest. In February 2003, the House of Lords Liaison Committee agreed that such a committee be established with effect from the beginning of the 2003–04 session.

The Commons Procedure Committee has twice recommended a similar sifting committee (in 1996 and 2000), saying that 'the existing system of scrutinising delegated legislation is urgently in need of reform'. The committee also recommended that praying time for negative instruments should be increased from forty days to sixty; that no decision on an SI should be taken by the House until the Joint Committee on Statutory Instruments had completed its consideration; and that the most substantial and complex SIs should be given a super-affirmative treatment, being subject to pre-legislative scrutiny in the same way as a draft bill. The government has not so far taken action on these recommendations. We return to this in Chapter 13.

Regulatory reform orders

There are some Acts of Parliament that allow a minister to amend primary legislation by secondary legislation – to amend an Act by an SI. Such a provision in a bill is known as a 'Henry VIII clause' – reflecting that monarch's somewhat broad-brush approach to his powers. It is generally undesirable for a minister to be able to change what normally only Parliament may decide; however, in 1994 the Deregulation and Contracting Out Act gave ministers just those powers, but subject to a stringent system of parliamentary control.

As part of the then Conservative government's wish to lighten the weight of regulation, the 1994 Act allowed ministers to amend or repeal primary legislation that imposed a burden affecting any person carrying on a trade, business or profession. It introduced an entirely new parliamentary procedure whereby a minister had to consult on a proposal, which would then be laid before Parliament and examined by Deregulation Committees of both Houses, which could suggest amendments before the deregulation order was laid as a formal draft for approval. Nearly ninety deregulation orders were made under the 1994 Act, ranging from greyhound racing to the registration of marriages to the selling of salmon roe; but it is in the nature of deregulation that after the early quick hits it becomes harder to find areas to deregulate.

The scope of the procedure was then widened by the Labour government's Regulatory Reform Act 2001 to cover 'burdens affecting persons in the carrying on of any activity'; and some other limitations in the 1994 Act were relaxed. A power to make 'subordinate provisions' (a sort of further delegated legislation, but also to be considered by the committees) was introduced. The committees were renamed: that in the Commons became the Regulatory Reform Committee, and the Lords committee became the Delegated Powers and Regulatory Reform Committee.

Before a minister may make a regulatory reform order, he or she must *consult widely with those who would be affected*. This is part of the procedure on which the committees have been particularly insistent. After the consultation, the minister may lay before Parliament *a proposal for an order, together with an explanatory statement*. There is then a period of sixty days for consideration by the committees (as with praying time, not including recesses). They test the proposal against fourteen criteria, including whether this is the right method of changing the law; the adequacy of the consultation; whether the right balance of burdens and benefits has been struck, and whether the proposal would continue any necessary protection for those affected; whether it would limit any reasonable rights or freedoms; and whether the minister is acting within the powers given by the Act.

In assessing the proposal, the committees often take written or oral evidence, both from the government and from those who might be affected, and they then report separately on whether the proposal should go forward, with or without amendments.

At the end of the sixty days, the minister is able to lay before Parliament *a draft order*, taking into account the views of the committees and of anyone else who has commented during the sixty-day period, and setting out what changes have been made, and why. The committees look at the draft order within fifteen sitting days and report to each House upon it. In the Commons, there is then a graduated procedure. If the committee has unanimously recommended that the draft order be made, it is put to the House without debate; if the committee had a vote on the matter, there is an hour and a half's debate in the House; but if the committee recommends that the draft order not be approved there must be a debate of up to three hours on a motion to disagree with the committee. If that motion is successful, the question on approval of the draft order is put without further debate.

Once the draft order has been approved by both Houses, the minister may *make it* and so bring it into law. A list of regulatory reform business, and the stages each proposal or draft order has reached, is published weekly. At the beginning of the 2001 parliament, the government identified fifty changes to the law that it planned to address through the regulatory reform procedure.

This procedure, under both the 1994 and the 2001 Acts, has been innovative and effective. It has all the advantages of pre-legislative scrutiny: detailed, evidence-based scrutiny and analysis; wide consultation and public access to the legislative process; and the testing and amendment of proposed legislation to produce a better quality of outcome. Moreover, it is systematic; it is not up to the government of the day to decide, as with bills, whether they should be examined in draft before being formally introduced. If the regulatory reform route is taken, then the procedure outlined above applies automatically.

It has been rigorous; indeed, so much so that several government departments decided early on that they would not take this route but wait for an opportunity for the easier ride of primary legislation. It has been effective and has allowed back-benchers to have a real influence on the content of legislation; governments of both parties have almost always accepted the committees' recommendations. And it has been consensual; the committees have worked in a remarkably non-partisan way. The procedure is seen by many as offering lessons that could be applied more widely.

Remedial orders

The Human Rights Act 1998, which came into effect in October 2000, allows ministers to make a new form of delegated legislation known as 'remedial orders'. These come about when a UK court finds that some provision of an Act of Parliament is incompatible with the Human Rights Act. A remedial order may amend primary legislation; the procedure for considering it is similar to that for a regulatory reform order, except that it is the task of the Joint Committee on Human Rights, rather than the two Committees described above, to consider and report on proposals and draft orders. Once it has been considered by the Joint Committee on Human Rights, and the statutory periods have passed, a draft order is treated in the same way as any other affirmative instrument.

If swift action is required, a minister may make an order, laying it before both Houses. It has immediate statutory effect, but it must be confirmed by both Houses approving it within 120 days of its being laid (as for praying time, excluding times when both Houses are in recess). During the first sixty of those days, representations may be made to the minister; and if as a result the minister decides to make a new order, it must be approved by both Houses within the remaining sixty days.

A list of proposals, draft remedial orders and any urgent procedure orders, together with time remaining on each, is published with the Vote bundle every sitting Wednesday. There has so far been only one remedial order, in 2001, to amend the Mental Health Act 1983 in respect of the burden of proof for detaining someone under that Act.

Devolution: Northern Ireland

The principal post-devolution source of delegated legislation considered at Westminster is Northern Ireland. Under the Northern Ireland Act 1974, which introduced direct rule from Westminster, legislation is in the form of Orders in Council; these have normally been a version of legislation enacted for England and Wales. The Northern Ireland Act 1998 requires that proposals for Orders in Council dealing with matters reserved to Westminster (such as public order, criminal law, firearms, police, the Civil Service and emergency powers) should be referred to the Northern Ireland Assembly for its views during a sixty-day consultation period. At the end of that time, the government may lay before Parliament a draft order for approval, together with a report on representations made and any changes as a result – a form of super-affirmative instrument that has similarities with the regulatory reform procedure. If the Northern Ireland Assembly is suspended, then Orders in Council are dealt with as straightforward affirmative instruments.

During the 2003 suspension, the House of Lords started to debate such Orders in grand committee off the floor so as to increase the time available for consideration. The motions for approval continued to be taken in the House, but with shorter debate.

Church of England measures

As the established church of the state, the Church of England has to have its legislation approved by Parliament, including the Royal Assent of the sovereign. These *measures* are a form of delegated legislation, although they eventually form part of the statute book. They are first agreed by the Church's parliament, the General Synod, which has procedures for debate and amendment very similar to the Commons and Lords. A draft of the measure is then sent to the Ecclesiastical Committee, which consists of fifteen peers nominated by the Lord Chancellor and fifteen MPs nominated by the Speaker. This is not a conventional joint committee appointed by the two Houses but a statutory body set up under the Church of England (Assembly) General Powers Act 1919.

The purpose of the Committee is 'to determine whether or not the measure is expedient'. The committee cannot amend the measure. To assist the Committee in coming to a view, comments and explanations are submitted by the General Synod, and members of its Legislative Committee assist the Ecclesiastical Committee in its deliberations. On difficult issues a conference with the full membership of the Legislative Committee may be held, but this is rare. The committee presents a short report on each measure, together with its decision on whether the measure in question is expedient. The measure is at the same time laid before each House of Parliament for approval.

The role of Parliament in the governance of the Church is sometimes a cause of controversy. After all, the General Synod as the Church's own representative body has already approved a measure by the time it reaches Parliament. It is arguable that in its consideration of a measure Parliament should not seek to second guess the Synod. Very occasionally, the Ecclesiastical Committee has, on some point of principle, suggest that a measure be laid in a slightly different form. Once the Ecclesiastical Committee has found a measure expedient the proceedings in the two Houses are uncontroversial, although in 1989 a measure dealing with the ordination of divorced men was actually rejected by the Commons.

8 Parliament and the taxpayer

Total government expenditure in 2002–03 was expected to be £466 billion, or about £7,700 for every man, woman and child in the United Kingdom. Taxation and public spending touch everyone's daily lives, from the amount of income tax we pay to the levels of social security and old age pensions we receive, and from standards in our local hospitals and schools to the quality of the environment and the number of police on the beat. It is not surprising, then, that the nation's finances are always at the heart of political controversy. Are the economic prospects hopeful? Is the taxpayer getting good value for money? Should a project be financed through a public/private partnership? Should we be spending more on schools? On the NHS? On the police? If we do, what will that do to taxation?

These questions are central to much of the work of Parliament but, as we shall see in this chapter, although the big issues are always in debate, Parliament exercises little detailed control over public spending.

The constitutional principles

The modern role of Parliament (and especially the House of Commons) in financial matters reflects the ancient relationship with the Crown. The sovereign needed the authority and agreement of the Commons for taxes and for spending; but from early times the House required the redress of grievances before granting through taxation (*ways and means*) the money (*supply*) that the Crown sought, and this was the basis of its growing influence.

It is still a basic constitutional principle that it is for the Crown (in fact, the government of the day) and not for Parliament to propose expenditure and taxation. This *financial initiative of the Crown* means in practice that only ministers may make proposals for spending and taxes. If Parliament agrees to those proposals, then they are given authority through legislation.

The House of Commons has a special role in financial matters, based on a resolution of 1671, which stated 'That in all aids given to the King by the Commons, the rate or tax ought not to be altered by the Lords', reinforced seven years later by a resolution that said in splendidly comprehensive language:

all aids and supplies, and aids to his Majesty in Parliament, are the sole gift of the Commons; and all bills for the granting of any such aids and supplies ought to begin with the Commons; and that it is the undoubted and sole right of the Commons to direct, limit and appoint in such bills the ends, purposes, considerations, limitations, and qualifications of such grants, which ought not to be changed or altered by the House of Lords.

Despite the language, this did not put things permanently beyond doubt and it was arguable that the Lords retained a power to reject a supply bill outright. Thus in 1860 the Lords rejected the Paper Duty Repeal Bill and, more seriously in 1909, the Finance Bill, which gave effect to Lloyd George's controversial Budget. In the latter case, the result was the passing of the Parliament Act 1911 and the permanent restriction of the powers of the House of Lords to thwart the legislative will of the Commons.

Today the practical results of the *financial privilege* of the House of Commons are that *bills of aids and supplies*, principally the Finance Bill, which authorises the government's taxation proposals, and the Consolidated Fund Bills, which authorise government spending, originate in the Commons and are not amended by the Lords. Although in normal circumstances they must be passed by the Lords in order to become law, the stages are taken formally in that House.

However, if the Commons passes what the Parliament Act 1911 defines as a *money bill* – that is, a bill whose *only* purpose is to authorise expenditure or taxation – it is certified by the Speaker as a money bill. If such a bill is sent to the Lords at least one month before the end of the session and has not been agreed by the Lords within a month, it may be sent directly for Royal Assent. Although it remains in theory possible for the Lords to amend money bills – and such amendments have in the past been made – the Commons are not obliged to consider them, and it is now inconceivable that any amendment would be attempted. As with supply bills, the stages of money bills are taken formally in the Lords. And in fact no money bill has ever had to be presented for Royal Assent under the terms of the 1911 Act.

A bill whose provisions involve an increase in public expenditure or taxation may begin in the House of Lords, but it may proceed in the Commons only if a minister takes charge of it. In such a case the constitutional niceties are preserved by a *'privilege amendment'*: a subsection at the end of the bill that says 'Nothing in this Act shall impose any charge on the people or on public funds' or vary any such charge. This is a fiction, of course; and the privilege amendment is routinely removed when the bill is in committee in the Commons.

Another practical effect of Commons financial privilege is that any Lords amendments to a Commons bill that involve a charge upon the public revenue not sanctioned by the Commons money resolution in respect of that bill are deemed disagreed to upon the Speaker's declaration, by reason of privilege. A privilege reason for disagreeing to such amendments is now not questioned by the Lords.

The financial pre-eminence of the Commons in matters of legislation does not mean that the Lords are inhibited in discussing or investigating financial subjects. Both in debate and through the work of select committees such as the Economic Affairs Committee and the European Union Committee, such matters are frequently pursued. Indeed, in 2003 a sub-committee of the Economic Affairs Committee was established specially to consider certain policy aspects of that year's Finance Bill. It is interesting to speculate whether the climate of Lords reform may encourage that House to seek a more formal role in financial matters.

The annual cycles

Financial procedure is complex; this is partly because of the complexity of the subject matter but is also because the process takes place in three largely separate cycles. The *Budget cycle* deals with broad financial issues, the management of the economy and the authorisation of taxation. The *estimates cycle* covers the authorisation of public spending; and the *reporting cycle* provides information on what money has been spent and how effectively it has been used. We will examine these one by one; but Table 8.1 on pages 255 and 256 shows how events in all three relate. The fact that the parliamentary year (the session, normally from November to the following October) does not coincide with either the calendar year or the financial year is a further complication.

It should also be remembered that some important economic factors are reported to Parliament but are not under parliamentary control: interest rates are set by the Bank of England rather than by the government; and the level of the public sector borrowing requirement – in which the House of Commons might reasonably have a say – is, at least in theory, under government control.

The Budget cycle

The word 'budget' comes from the archaic French *bougette*, a little bag, which in English had its literal meaning from the fifteenth century; later, 'to open one's budget' meant 'to speak one's mind'. In 1733, Sir Robert Walpole, then Chancellor of the Exchequer as well as Prime Minister, was depicted in a satirical pamphlet as a quack doctor opening a bag of pills. The term rapidly became applied to the Chancellor's review of the national finances, given annually from Walpole's time onwards.

The Chancellor of the Exchequer normally delivers his Budget in March, although the 2003 Budget statement was given on 9 April. There will also usually be a Budget not long after a general election if there has been a change of government. In recent decades, the Budget statement has been on a Tuesday, but in 2001, 2002 and 2003 the statement was on a Wednesday. Budget day is always something of a media event, with the Chancellor being photographed outside his residence at No. 11 Downing Street before leaving for the Commons holding up the despatch box containing his Budget speech. For 140 years Chancellors used a battered red box first used by Gladstone in the 1860s; in 1997, for his first Budget, Gordon Brown used a new box made by young trainees in his constituency.

The Budget speech comes immediately after Question Time; in order not to upstage the Chancellor, the ten-minute rule bill slot (which is normally on Tuesdays and Wednesdays) for Budget day is deferred to the following Monday. Before the Chancellor begins his statement, the Speaker's place in the Chair is generally taken by the Chairman of Ways and Means, a tradition reflecting the fact that between 1641 and 1967, when it was abolished, taxation proposals were made in the Committee of Ways and Means.

The Chancellor begins with the review of the nation's finances and the economic situation, which might be recognised in form – although not always in content! – by his predecessors over three centuries. In the later part of his speech – in which he does not usually take interventions – he moves on to his taxation proposals. Modern Budget statements have lasted an hour or so: a far cry from Gladstone's four-and-three-quarter-hour marathon in 1853. When the Chancellor has completed his statement, the motions to give effect to the proposals he has announced – fifty to sixty of them (sixty-five in 2003) – are made available to the House. Strict secrecy is maintained on the Budget proposals until the Chancellor announces them – not least because of their market sensitivity – so, exceptionally, no notice is given of these motions.

The Chancellor then usually moves a motion to give immediate legal effect to certain of his proposals (ten in 2003) to forestall the speculation that might take place if it were known that the duty on cigarettes or whisky, for example, would be raised, but not for days or weeks. Under the Provisional Collection of Taxes Act 1968, when this motion is agreed to the proposals it covers have the force of law, but the House must agree to the motions on the individual proposals within ten sitting days. This procedure may apply to any proposal continuing a tax or altering its rate, but not to new taxes.

The Chancellor then moves what is known as the 'amendment of the law' motion. This is a general statement that 'it is expedient to amend the law with respect to the National Debt and to make further provision in respect of finance', and it is the vehicle for the very broad budget debate that follows. The Chancellor is followed not by the shadow Chancellor but by the Leader of the

Opposition, who must make some shrewd guesses in advance so that he can react swiftly to what the Chancellor has said, in addition to setting out his own party's economic policies.

The Budget debate normally lasts for four or five days, and at its conclusion all fifty or sixty motions are put to the House, providing the opposition parties with an opportunity to vote against – usually three or four – individual proposals with which they particularly disagree. The Finance Bill is then formally introduced on the basis of what have now become the *founding resolutions*. Budget secrecy has meant that consultation on many specific provisions has not been possible, so the bill is not finally printed and published for three to four weeks after the Budget statement.

The Finance Bill

The Finance Bill is a substantial document, often running to 250 or more clauses. Its provisions combine changes to levels and types of taxation with much detailed administration of the tax system, which makes for greater complexity. It also provides for the renewal for that year of taxes already in force. In 1992–93, the Commons Procedure Committee suggested that the process be simplified, with one bill making tax changes and a taxes management bill doing the rest. In the event, no change has been made.

The Finance Bill's second reading debate will be a single day, providing a further opportunity for a general debate on the government's taxation strategy. The bill is then divided; clauses dealing with the major, or most controversial, proposals are taken in Committee of the whole House; the wishes of the opposition parties will be influential in this division. The rest of the bill is committed to a standing committee. The report stage and third reading usually occupy a further two days on the floor of the House.

Standing committees on the Finance Bill have a character rather different from those on other bills. They are larger, often with thirty to forty members rather than twenty or so; because of the regularity of Finance Bills, and of debates on economic affairs, the participants will know each other well and be old sparring partners; and the level of expertise is high. Both the opposition parties and government back-benchers will be extensively briefed by groups that will be affected by the Chancellor's proposals and assisted by them in drafting amendments to the often highly complex provisions of the bill. In addition to the usual rules about the admissibility of amendments (see page 195), MPs' ability to propose changes is restricted by the scope of the resolutions to which the House has agreed and, where the resolutions simply said 'that provision may be made about the level of' such and such a tax or charge, the levels actually proposed in the bill. For example, in 2003 the House agreed to a resolution that said that the rate of corporation tax for small companies should be 19 percent. Amendments seeking to raise that rate would not be in order, although it would be possible to move to reduce it.

Governments are usually even less willing to accept substantial amendments to the Finance Bill than they are in the case of other legislation, although disquiet among back-benchers can cause changes, whether following defeat on a vote, as with the scrapping of the second tranche of VAT on domestic fuel in December 1994, or by the government altering its proposals to head off possible defeat, as in the halving of the increase in petrol duty that was proposed in the 1981 Budget. However, to a great extent the Budget is a package and, for MPs of the government party in particular, voting to defeat one proposal implies voting to increase revenue elsewhere – or to reduce public expenditure. However, less dramatic changes are not unusual as a result of the committee stage of the Finance Bill. One example in 1998 was the proposal to tax agricultural earnings applied to the upkeep of historic houses. The Historic Houses Association briefed MPs on the standing committee, they took up the case, and the taxation was phased in rather than being introduced immediately, with considerable benefits for the national heritage.

The Finance Bill then goes to the Lords. As we have seen, Lords stages of supply bills, like the Finance Bill and any money bill, are taken formally. However, a general economic debate is often held on second reading of the Finance Bill. Remaining stages are then taken formally forthwith.

Budget information

On Budget day the Treasury publishes the *Financial Statement and Budget Report* (FSBR), now a glossy-covered production but often known as the Red Book, from its former plain red cover. The FSBR is now combined with an *Economic and Fiscal Strategy Report*. The document is a substantial one, in 2003 running to nearly 300 pages. It sets out the features of the national economy in a global context, reports on a wide range of economic and financial measures, and seeks to integrate financial and taxation proposals into a broader context of policy across government. It is accompanied by a raft of press releases, and fifty to sixty notes by the Inland Revenue and Customs and Excise on specific proposals, setting them out in less technical language. In 2003, the Treasury also published three consultation papers: on residence rules for taxation purposes; on productivity in the public services; and on access to growth capital for small businesses.

An important part of the 'Budget bundle' is the report, by the Comptroller and Auditor-General provided for in the Finance Act 1998, on those conventions and assumptions underlying the Treasury's fiscal projections which the Chancellor has asked him to validate. In 2003, the C&AG examined the likely extent of tobacco smuggling, the possible result of measures to counter tax and national insurance contribution fraud, and expected proceeds from privatisation.

The papers published on Budget day make up a bundle between five and ten centimetres thick, on a wide range of measures and policies, often of great technicality and complexity. Their audience is of course much wider than Parliament, and the proposals and analysis are closely examined in the financial, commercial and industrial sectors. Nevertheless, the Budget proposals and information set the House of Commons a substantial task of scrutiny, which the lengthy Finance Bill committee stage (usually between fifty and 100 hours of debate) struggles to perform.

However, the Treasury Committee reports rapidly upon the Budget in order to inform consideration of the Finance Bill. It takes oral evidence not only from the Chancellor himself but also from the Permanent Secretary and senior officials at the Treasury, as well as from outside financial and economic experts. Despite a government majority, it often provides a critical counterweight to the government's proposals. In 2003, for example, the committee suggested that Treasury growth forecasts might be too optimistic, and that tax revenues might not recover as quickly as the government assumed; it also expressed concern about the effect of fluctuations in public sector investment.

The unified Budget

One of the features of financial procedure in the House of Commons has been that taxation – the Budget cycle – is dealt with separately from public spending plans and the related estimates cycle. From 1993 to 1996 under the Conservative government the Budget statement was made in November of each year, and it covered not only taxation proposals for the forthcoming financial year but also public spending for the next three years.

The pre-Budget report

In the first Labour Budget statement in July 1997, the new government announced a return to the separate approach, but with the introduction of a 'pre-Budget report', sometimes called the 'Green Budget' (as in 'Green Paper', because of its consultative character). The first of these was published in November 1997; the Chancellor described its purpose as to report the government's assessment of the economy, to outline the government's budget aims and to encourage an informed debate on the issues.

This too is a substantial document; the November 2002 edition ran to 225 pages, with twenty-seven tables. As with the Budget report itself, it places economic assessments in the context of policy priorities (in 2002 these included productivity, employment opportunities, high-quality public services, and protecting the environment), so there is some element of read-across to detailed spending plans. The pre-Budget report provides an opportunity for select committees other than the Treasury Committee to examine implications for their areas of interest; for example, the Environmental Audit Committee has in the past reported on the environmental implications of particular policies.

The estimates cycle

The process of voting 'supply' has its origins in a time when monarchs needed to spend money that the Crown did not have, usually on wars. Parliament then had to be asked to supply the funds. Even though state expenditure is now on a very different scale and for a multitude of different purposes, the sovereign's government must still ask the Commons for the money it needs. This request is conveyed through the *estimates*. Expenditure for which supply is voted is not the whole story. There are large areas of public expenditure that the supply estimates do not cover – for example, national insurance, expenditure by local authorities and net payments to the European Union.

Resource accounting

From 2001–02, as a result of the Government Resources and Accounts Act 2000, the estimates are now presented to Parliament on a resource accounting basis (although they still also contain cash figures). Resource accounting records the economic costs of the provision of services and the consumption of assets (including depreciation, the cost of using capital assets, and future liabilities such as those for compensation for early retirement). It is designed to give a more accurate picture of how resources are being used and makes government accounts much more like company accounts. It also allows a better assessment of how resources have been applied to the achievement of policy objectives. Cash accounting, by contrast, just tracks the movement of cash.

Public spending plans

Over the last five years, government spending reviews have taken place every two years. They are run by the Treasury, and government departments put in proposals for extra resources (or for not cutting existing budgets), which Treasury ministers then evaluate. The result of this process – in which Parliament has no role – is the *three-year spending plans* published in July.

These give for each government department a brief summary of key objectives (including *public service agreements* – see page 251) and a short report on progress so far. Then follows total planned expenditure for that department for the next three financial years, expressed as a *departmental expenditure limit* (DEL) (split into a resource budget and a capital budget). DELs are totals of expenditure that departments can control, even though some elements may be demand-led.

The spending plans also bring together broader and cross-cutting policies and show how resources are to be applied to their achievement. A statistical annex sets out the figures across government and gives figures for new allocations and net investment. It also shows planned *total managed expenditure* for each of the next three years: that is, the totals of all the DELs plus expectations of *annually managed expenditure* (AME). AME covers expenditure that is less predictable or controllable than DELs: for example, social security and Common Agricultural Policy payments.

This government-wide forward look, which provides an opportunity for debate on the floor of the House as well as material for examination by the departmental select committees, is followed each spring by a *departmental report*, which reports annual progress against the three-year spending plan, with any adjustments.

Votes on Account

These come before the House in November. They cover about 45 percent of the estimated expenditure of each government department in the coming financial year and are in effect to tide the government over until the main estimates are approved in the following July. Votes on Account must be agreed by the House by 6 February.

Ministry of Defence Votes A

These are published in February. The Bill of Rights 1688–9 prevented the Crown from maintaining a standing army in time of peace without the approval of Parliament, so these 'Votes A' laid before the House by the Secretary of State for Defence invite the annual authorisation by the House of Commons of the maximum numbers of personnel in the armed services.

Main estimates

These estimates, one for each government department (and for other bodies such as the Office of the Rail Regulator and the NHS Pension Scheme), are published at roughly the same time as the departmental reports. The Treasury aims to issue main estimates within three weeks of the Budget, which means that they are usually published in late March or early April. They form the principal request from the Government to the House of Commons for the resources required to run the state in the following financial year. They vary from small departments such as the Cabinet Office, which in 2002–03 sought £235 million to run its operations, to major areas of government expenditure: in 2002–03, the National Health Service was set to cost £74 billion.

The key elements of each estimate are, in Part I, the net amount sought. It is the headline 'request for resources' figures in Part I of the estimates that are presented for parliamentary approval. Even though government accounting is on a resource basis, the amount sought is expressed in cash terms as well as in resource terms. This is because resources are an accounting concept in which amounts may not be finally determined until the books are audited after the end of the financial year, and there is in the meantime a need to control the cash flowing out of the Consolidated Fund (the government's account at the Bank of England).

Each estimate also contains a formal description of the services to be financed from the estimate (known as the *ambit* of the estimate). When the estimate has been approved by the House, this part will be reproduced in the Appropriation Act. The ambit is an important part of the authorisation; it provides the statutory description of the purpose for which the money is sought, and expenditure must fall within that description.

Part I also says who will account for the estimate; for each estimate there must be an *accounting officer*, usually the Permanent Secretary of the government department concerned or the chief executive of an executive agency. Accounting officers have a personal responsibility for the regularity and propriety of expenditure – including ensuring that money is spent only on purposes authorised by Parliament – as well as for the quality of internal financial controls in the department concerned. Finally, Part I of the estimate notes any amounts already allocated in the *Vote on Account*.

Part II of the estimate shows the resource requirement from Part I, broken down into more detail of what is going to be provided with the money. This breakdown forms the basis for in-year control of expenditure by the Treasury. If there is an underspend in one area and a requirement in another, funds may be moved between these subheads with Treasury approval but without further parliamentary authority (a process known as *virement*). The rationale for this is that Parliament approves the headline figures but not the detailed breakdown. The flexibility that *virement* gives also means that there is less need to build in a contingency into each subhead, which would encourage an over-provision in the estimate as a whole.

Also in Part II is a detailed reconciliation between a department's net resource requirement and the cash it needs (its 'net cash requirement'). Part III sets out any additional income that the department expects to receive in the course of the year, but which it will surrender to the Consolidated Fund and not use to finance its own expenditure.

Each estimate is accompanied by a *forecast operating cost statement*, which shows net administration costs and net programme costs. It also notes any 'contingent liabilities': commitments that, if they were to be called upon, would require further expenditure. Although ministers may give guarantees or indemnities, Parliament is not bound in advance to honour any liabilities arising unless by law the liability is charged on the Consolidated Fund. Any other type of liability of more than £100,000 must be reported to Parliament.

Estimates days

In each session, three days are allotted for the House to consider the estimates. Given the huge sums involved, and the myriad purposes for which they are used, this may not seem much, and the process is indeed highly selective. The Liaison Committee, consisting of all the chairmen of select committees, proposes an estimate (or part of an estimate) for debate on each of these days or half-days. However, rather than inviting the House's detailed examination of the particular part of the estimate concerned, there is normally a reversal of the process. The estimate is used as a peg for a debate upon a select committee report that may be as much – or more – about policy than about the money the government is seeking from the House of Commons.

The three estimates days are usually taken close to the other supply deadlines of 6 February, 18 March and 5 August (see the chart on page 255), but they must all happen before 5 August. The arbitrary date of 5 August was fixed in 1896, reportedly when A.J. Balfour suggested that the House of Commons was 'not in its best parliamentary form' after the August Bank holiday.

Because of the financial initiative reserved to the Crown – in effect to ministers – any amendment proposed to an estimate may only reduce the total of a request for resources, not increase it. In order to allow debate on the maximum number of select committee reports, estimates days are almost always divided into two halves, each with a different subject.

At the end of an estimates day, those estimates selected by the Liaison Committee for debate, and any amendments selected by the Speaker (usually such amendments indicate disapproval by means of a formulaic proposal to reduce an estimate by £1,000 or £10,000), are put to the House for approval. Immediately thereafter the question is put on outstanding estimates (that is, those that have to be approved before the next deadline); but these are put not in a detailed department by department form but as totals of resources and cash sought. For the winter and spring deadlines, this specifies only the total sums to be paid out of the Consolidated Fund.

Supplementary estimates

The *spring supplementary estimates* are presented shortly before the main estimates for the following year are published, allowing up-to-date figures for expenditure in the current year to be compared with that for the next year. The *summer supplementary estimates* are published in the early summer, usually in May. They seek authority for any additional funds that government departments have found to be necessary since the main estimates were prepared. The government tries hard to ensure that these are for an identifiable new requirement rather than as a result of poor estimating; but, either way, a supplementary estimate focuses attention on a particular area of a department's spending and can trigger an inquiry by a select committee. The *winter supplementary estimates* provide for adjustments that may be required later in the financial year. *Revised estimates* may be presented in the early summer; the purpose of these is not to seek additional funds but to change the ambit of an estimate if it seems that funds authorised via the main estimate may have to be spent on something that would otherwise be outside its scope.

If emergencies arise, the government can have recourse to the contingencies fund. This is limited by law to 2 percent of the previous year's total authorised supply expenditure, and any money drawn out of the fund must be repaid. Alternatively, the House may be asked to agree an emergency supplementary estimate at any time; although, as for any supplementary estimate, seven clear days must elapse between presentation and approval.

Consolidated Fund Bills

When the House by resolution approves the estimates at the winter and spring deadlines, in each case a 'Consolidated Fund Bill' is brought in on those resolutions in order to give them legislative authority. Again, the bill does no more than specify the overall totals. On the basis that debate on the estimates has taken place on the items chosen for debate by the Liaison Committee, on a subsequent day the questions on second and third reading are put without debate; and there is no committee stage. Consideration in the Lords is purely formal, and these bills receive Royal Assent as Consolidated Fund Acts.

However, in the summer the bill brought in after approval of the estimates to be decided before the summer deadline (the 'Consolidated Fund (Appropriation) Bill') is a much more detailed legislative authority for supply. As noted above, it sets out the ambit of each request for resources and the amount to be 'appropriated' – that is, paid – in respect of each. It also shows any receipts to be set against expenditure, and the numbers of personnel authorised for the armed services (the 'Votes A' covered above). This bill, too, is passed without debate and is dealt with only formally by the Lords. Upon Royal Assent it becomes the Appropriation Act. Except for any 'excess Votes', the cycle of estimates and supply for the current financial year is almost over.

Excess Votes

These seek retrospective authorisation when a department's spending in a financial year has exceeded what Parliament authorised (or has been incurred for a purpose that was not authorised), and there was not enough time to have a supplementary estimate approved in the course of the year (or if the over-spend came to light only after the end of the financial year). Excess votes are examined by the National Audit Office, which advises the Public Accounts Committee; no excess vote may be put to the House for approval unless that committee has no objection.

The reporting cycle

We have seen so far how the government seeks authorisation for the taxes it wishes to levy and the different stages by which its proposed spending is approved. What about the other side of the process: how does the government account for how it has spent the money?

Departmental annual reports

These are normally published between March and May. They have been produced since 1991 and have developed substantially since then through initiatives by departments themselves, recommendations by select committees and, most recently, the additional transparency provided by the introduction of resource accounting. The Treasury exercises general supervision and lays down guidance. Departmental annual reports vary widely in format and presentation, but all contain core elements. They set out the names and responsibilities of the department's ministers and senior officials and the department's structure and purpose, and they survey the principal activities of the previous year. Departments also take the opportunity to explain to Parliament and the public how they go about their tasks and the main problems and challenges they face.

Departmental reports also give figures for each department's planned spending over the next three years (which are much more detailed than those in the government-wide spending plans published the previous July), together with the estimated spending for the current year and the actual spending for the four previous years. Other elements include changes to previously published plans, value-for-money initiatives, and departmental running costs and staffing.

A crucial part of every departmental report is its assessment of how it has delivered on its objectives and how it has used the resources provided by Parliament. This may be in terms of reporting on objectives and the extent to which they were achieved, often through formal *public service agreements* (PSAs). These are undertakings to deliver in the form of measurable targets over the period covered by the spending plans. In 2003, for example, the Home Office had a target to reduce the level of recorded robbery in principal cities by 14 percent against the figures for 1999–2000. The Foreign and Commonwealth Office had a PSA target to create 'a new partnership between the UK and the Overseas Territories embracing constitutional arrangements and citizenship, which yields improved standards of governance, human rights, the environment, sustainable development and the security of the territories'.

Progress towards the Home Office target ought to have been easily measurable in objective terms, but it was reported in a way that made it difficult to compare with the original objective: 'In the 12 months to December 2002 recorded robbery fell by 3 percent compared with the previous year, and fell by 23 percent (adjusted for National Crime Recording Standard) in the 3 months to December 2002 compared to the same three months in December 2001'.

The FCO target was – perhaps inevitably – framed in a somewhat impressionistic way. One may be able to identify that standards of governance have improved, or that sustainable development has been supported, but objective measurement is more difficult. Against this target, the FCO reported spending on law and order, progress on constitutional reviews, the setting up of a new legislative council, a study to help to improve human rights, the preparation of disaster management plans, and an FCO-funded project to restore endangered seabirds to Ascension Island, which was described as having made 'tangible progress'.

An obsession with measurement can become an end in itself and get in the way of the activity concerned. Again, some activities – improving the state of diplomatic relations with a particular country, or the Cabinet Office's Objective 1 ('to support the Prime Minister in leading the government') – are difficult to measure in any exact way. The process of measurement becomes more one of totting up positive and negative factors. And there is a tendency for departments to report inputs (what they are doing) rather than outcomes and outputs (what they have got for it). Nevertheless, much of what the government does is capable of fairly rigorous measurement, and departmental reports represent an important opportunity to do this.

In October 2002, the House of Commons approved a set of core tasks for departmental select committees (see page 328). One of those core tasks was to monitor performance against targets in the PSAs. Select committees, assisted by the new Scrutiny Unit (see page 328), have increased their efforts in this area. They have focused especially on the need for targets to be both consistent year by year – measuring achievement is impossible if the goalposts move – and more consistent across government. Objectives also need to be realistically challenging and precise. For example, the 2003 report of the Department for Work and Pensions has a key objective to 'sustain a higher proportion of people in work than ever before, while providing security for those who cannot work'; the first part of the target might in literal terms be met if one more person found work as a result of the department's efforts.

Select committees' examination of departmental reports, and assessments of the way that PSAs are formulated, measured and reported, seems likely to be an increasingly significant way of judging what the money voted by Parliament has actually bought.

Resource accounts

Resource accounts must be laid before Parliament by 31 January following the financial year to which they relate (although there are plans to speed this up; the more up-to-date the information, the more use it is). Resource accounts are prepared according to GAAP (Generally Accepted Accounting Practice) and in some respects are similar to annual accounts of private sector businesses. They have the following elements: a foreword sets out the aims, objectives and main activities of the department. This is followed by statements of the accounting officer's responsibilities and on the system of internal financial controls that is in place.

All government departments (and many other public bodies, with some controversial exceptions, such as the BBC) are audited by the National Audit Office, headed by the Comptroller and Auditor-General. The C&AG's certificate and report then sets out how the NAO has audited the accounts, and whether they represent a true and fair statement of the position. The *summary of resource outturn* compares actual expenditure with the estimate; there have been some substantial differences in the early stages of resource accounting, as departments have little historical experience on which to build, and some items (for example valuation of capital assets) have been difficult to forecast. The *operating cost statement* shows the resources consumed during the year; the *balance sheet* shows the assets and liabilities at year end; and the *cash flow statement* gives the cash flows during the year, including operating activities, capital expenditure and financing. Finally, there is an analysis of the department's expenditure to show what resources have been used in supporting each of its principal objectives.

The Comptroller and Auditor-General and the National Audit Office

Resource accounts provide departmental select committees with more material in their monitoring of government departments; however, across government and other public bodies as a whole, audit and control is the task of the Comptroller and Auditor-General backed by the Committee of Public Accounts.

The full title of the officer usually known simply as 'the C&AG' is 'Comptroller General of the Receipt and Issue of Her Majesty's Exchequer and Auditor-General of Public Accounts'. He heads a staff of about 800 (about two-thirds of whom are either professionally qualified or training for professional qualifications) in the National Audit Office, whose main buildings are about a mile from the Houses of Parliament. The C&AG has a direct responsibility to Parliament and works closely with the Committee of Public Accounts (usually known as 'the PAC'). This relationship is recognised by the C&AG's personal status as an officer of the House of Commons.

The C&AG's work has three elements. In relation to his Comptroller function, the Bank of England releases money to the government from the Consolidated Fund only on the authority of one of the C&AG's officials, who certifies that the release does not exceed the amount voted by the House. The C&AG also carries out an audit of the propriety and regularity of accounts – a total of some 600 accounts examined every year, including government departments, executive agencies and associated public bodies. Finally, the National Audit Act 1983, which established the NAO (previously the Exchequer and Audit Department), also gave the C&AG the task of examining the economy, efficiency and effectiveness of public spending. This side of his work is represented by about fifty value-for-money studies each year. Examples from 2003 are the English National Stadium project at Wembley and the procurement of vaccines by the Department of Health; and, more broadly, improving service delivery and the role of executive agencies. The C&AG's reports are laid before Parliament and published.

The C&AG is not subject to operational direction from the PAC, or even from the House of Commons itself. He alone decides what to investigate and what conclusions he will reach. The great majority of his reports are taken up by the PAC, which enhances his status, while the committee's work is made more credible by the very substantial back-up of the C&AG and his staff.

The Committee of Public Accounts

The PAC was first established at Gladstone's instigation in 1861. The committee has sixteen members and is always chaired by an opposition MP. It meets twice a week while the House is sitting, and its principal witnesses are accounting officers. The standing orders give it the narrow task of 'the examination of the accounts showing the appropriation of the sums granted by Parliament to meet the public expenditure, and of such other accounts laid before Parliament as the Committee may think fit'; but for some years the committee has ranged more widely, principally following up the value-for-money reports of the C&AG but also moving into areas of policy, which leads to overlap with departmental select committees. The PAC publishes some fifty reports a year. In combination, the C&AG and the PAC are an important means of checking the propriety of government expenditure – that money has been properly expended on authorised purposes – and, in selected areas, the extent to which value for money has been achieved.

The annual pattern

Table 8.1 shows the main events in each of the Budget, estimates and reporting cycles. Dates are indicative rather than exact (except for the approval deadlines). The financial year beginning in April is designated year 3; during the session the House will consider business relating to year 1 (the financial year that ended seven months before the start of the new parliamentary session) and year 2 (the financial year that is about halfway through when the session begins).

Conclusion

We said at the start of this chapter that Parliament (in practice, the House of Commons) exercises very little control over the details of public spending. The examination of tax proposals is far less criticised – although the time available for debate on the Finance Bill is always a source of tension. Parliamentary examination of expenditure after the event, through the work of the C&AG, the PAC and other select committees, is seen as fairly effective. However, such examination always risks being somewhat academic; mistakes may have been made, or value for money may have been achieved, but either way, even though lessons have been learned, the money has been spent. Control over proposed spending is intrinsically more important.

The House of Commons has the ultimate deterrent of voting down the estimates – refusing supply – but that would be tantamount to a vote of no confidence in the government of the day and would almost certainly precipitate a general election. Nor would such an action really be one of *control*, which most people would see as analysis of each request for expenditure, followed by a decision on whether requests should be approved, or sums increased or reduced.

Table 8.1 The annual parliamentary cycles

	Budget cycle	Estimates cycle	Reporting cycle
			(throughout year, continuous programme of VFM inquiries and reports by C&AG and PAC)
Start of parliamentary session			
October/ November	Pre-Budget report published Treasury Committee and other select committees report	Winter supplementary estimates (for year 2) presented (must be approved by 6 February) Votes on Account (for year 3) presented	Resource accounts (for year 1) presented Departmental performance reports (for year 1) published.
December		Consolidated Fund Bill (Consolidated Fund (No. 2) Act) (for year 2) passed	Select committees review and report
January		First estimates day (debates on select committee reports)	
February		Spring supplementary estimates (for year 2) presented (for approval by 6 February) Excess Votes (for year 1) presented (for approval by 18 March) Ministry of Defence Votes A presented (for approval by 18 March) Second estimates day (debates on select committee reports)	
March	Budget statement and debate	Main estimates (for year 3) presented (for approval by 5 August) Consolidated Fund (No. 2) Bill (Consolidated Fund Act) passed (must be approved by 18 March)	

Table 8.1 (cont.)

	Budget cycle	Estimates cycle	Reporting cycle
Start of financial year 3			
April	Finance Bill published		Departmental reports and spending plans (for years 3, 4 and 5) published. Select committees review and report
	Second reading (Treasury Committee reports in time for second reading)		
May	Finance Bill in Committee of the whole House and standing committee	Summer supplementary estimates (for year 3) presented (for approval by 5 August)	
June	Finance Bill report stage and third reading	Third estimates day (debates on select committee reports)	
July	Formal consideration by Lords (Finance Act)	Consolidated Fund (Appropriation) Bill (the Appropriation Act) passed (must be by 5 August)	
		Spending plans (for years 4, 5 and 6) published (if a biennial spending review is taking place that year)	

Source: Adapted from Paul Evans (2002) *House of Commons Procedure*, 3rd edition, p. 108, Vacher Dod Publishing Ltd, London

Because money is voted only on the initiative of the Crown, on the ancient principle that the Commons did not volunteer the money – the monarch had to ask for it – increasing estimates is not permitted. There is no fundamental reason why this should be so; increases are allowed in Germany, for example; and in France individual estimates may be varied up or down provided that the total remains the same (thus preserving the government's overall 'package' of income and expenditure). Suggestions that the practice in the Commons should be altered have been resisted by successive governments but, as a select committee examining the problem in the early 1980s pointed out, increases would have to be met by additional taxation. However, this would not apply to the 'tax-neutral' approach of keeping *total* expenditure the same.

In theory, estimates can be reduced, but here too effective power is limited. This is because the majority of money is voted, not line by line but on three occasions during the year, as a total of resources and cash for all the estimates before the House. True, there are the three estimates days, when specific estimates selected by the Liaison Committee are debated. But this does not provide effective control: first, the selected estimates represent a small proportion of the total; and, second, they are usually selected because they relate to a policy matter that merits debate, not a request for funds that needs to be analysed and challenged. And it is interesting to note that when in 1981 the Procedure Committee sought to address 'the myth of effective control' it recommended that there should be *eight* estimates days rather than the three that were conceded by the government of the day.

Select committees have traditionally been less interested in the spending that supports policies than in the policies themselves, although when the departmental select committee system was established in 1979 examination of expenditure was the first duty laid upon them, before examination of departments' administration and policies. The fact that the 'core tasks' now required by the House of all departmental select committees include examination of annual expenditure plans and outturns, as well as monitoring delivery against public service targets, may mean an increase in detailed examination. The increases in staff support for such committees has also been partly with the aim of better equipping them to carry out those core tasks.

However, even if committees major on the estimates, they have – especially for the often significant supplementary estimates – little time to carry out their work, a point on which the Liaison Committee was especially critical in 2002. Moreover, the opportunities for connecting the analysis and judgements of a select committee with the decisions taken in the House are very limited.

In 1998–99 the Procedure Committee, speaking as had its predecessor twenty years earlier of the House's power over expenditure as 'if not a constitutional myth, very close to one', asserted that:

the House and the government would both gain from a system in which the House could engage directly in identifying priorities and examining the effectiveness of spending. The House would have an opportunity to influence the Government's plans; the Government would have the opportunity to explain those plans to Members and ensure that the House understood the constraints in which they worked.

The Procedure Committee put forward a package of reforms. It wanted to circumvent the restriction imposed by the financial initiative of the Crown through debates on motions that 'in the opinion of this House' increases in expenditure or transfers between budgets should be made. It also wished to see automatic referral of the estimates to the relevant departmental select committee, with no vote taking place on the estimate concerned until the committee had reported (within a limit of sixty days), and the ability of select committees to put forward motions relating to estimates or departmental plans or reports, rather than the often artificial link between a select committee report and an estimate.

No action has yet been taken on the Procedure Committee's proposals. We return to the subject in Chapter 13.

9 Debates

The *Oxford English Dictionary* defines the principal meaning of 'debate' as 'to dispute about, argue, discuss, especially to discuss a question of public interest in a legislative or other assembly'. Most proceedings in Parliament, whether on legislation or any other matter, take the form of debates. The main exceptions are questions and the examination of witnesses by select committees. In this chapter, we look at how debates take place on the floor of the House and elsewhere, how motions are moved and amended, and at some of the conventions of parliamentary debate.

Substantive motions

A substantive motion is one that expresses an opinion about something. The subject matter may range from 'That this House takes note of the Fourteenth to Thirty-Seventh Reports from the Committee of Public Accounts, Session 2002–03', for which there may be a dozen MPs in the Chamber (and probably no journalists in the Press Gallery) to 'That this House has no confidence in Her Majesty's Government', which will be a full-dress occasion, with intense media interest and the Chamber packed, perhaps to see the Prime Minister of the day fighting for his or her political life and the survival of the government.

A motion is *moved*, or proposed, by an MP who sponsors it. No seconder is required in the House of Commons; the seconding of the motion for the reply to the Queen's Speech is a tradition rather than a requirement.

If the motion requires notice, then the names of that member and any others who are putting the motion forward will appear on the Order of Business. The MP moving the motion argues for its approval by the House. When he or she sits down, the Speaker will *propose the Question*, stating to the House what must be decided. Rather than read out a long text, he will normally say 'The Question is, as on the Order Paper'. A debate then takes place, with the Chair normally calling MPs alternately from one side of the House and then the other.

If an *amendment* is down to the motion and is *selected* by the Speaker (see page 45) then at some point in the debate the Chair will ask one of the MPs whose names are to the amendment on the Order of Business to move it. It is possible for the Speaker to select a *manuscript amendment* – that is, one that was not tabled before the rising of the House at the previous sitting and so does not appear on the Order of Business, but this is very unusual.

Once the amendment has been moved, the Speaker proposes the Question upon it, saying 'The original Question was [as on the Order Paper]. Since when an amendment has been moved [as on the Order Paper]. The Question is, that the amendment be made'. Strictly speaking, the debate then takes place on the amendment rather than on the motion that was first moved, but in most cases the scope of debate covers both.

When the time for the debate has elapsed, because the Question must be put at the moment of interruption (see page 143) or at any particular time, or because the closure (see page 45) has been moved and agreed to – or simply because there are no more MPs wishing to speak – the Speaker *puts the Question* on the amendment first ('The Question is, that the amendment be made') and the House decides that question, if necessary, by dividing (see page 156). Once the House has made its decision on the amendment, the original motion – whether or not amended – is decided, again by dividing if necessary. If an amendment was moved, the original motion is also known as *the main Question*.

If the motion is agreed to, it becomes a *resolution* or an *order* of the House. The distinction is that a resolution expresses an opinion (for example, 'that this House has no confidence in Her Majesty's Government'); an order is something on which the House can exercise power directly ('that a select committee be appointed to examine . . .').

The Iraq debate

As an example of the House dealing with a substantive motion – in this case a very high-profile one – let us take the debate on war with Iraq on Tuesday 18 March 2003. A 390-word motion stood on the Order of Business in the names of the Prime Minister and other senior ministers. Carefully crafted to attract the maximum support from wavering government back-benchers, it began 'That this House notes its decisions of 25th November 2002 and 26th February 2003 to endorse UN Security Council Resolution 1441 . . .', and, after a rehearsal of the circumstances, it contained the crucial words 'and therefore supports the decision of Her Majesty's Government that the United Kingdom should use all means necessary to ensure the disarmament of Iraq's weapons of mass destruction . . .'.

Other amendments stood on the Order of Business, including one in the name of the former Labour cabinet minister Chris Smith and a number of other government back-benchers. At 12.35 p.m., the Deputy Speaker, Sir Alan Haselhurst, announced the main business of the day and informed the House that the Speaker had selected Chris Smith's amendment. The Prime Minister then rose to move the government's motion. He spoke for forty-eight minutes and gave way twelve times to interventions, eight of those from his own back benches. At 1.23 p.m., the Leader of the Opposition then spoke, for twenty-one minutes, giving way four times.

At 1.44 p.m., Peter Kilfoyle, a former Labour defence minister and one of the signatories to Chris Smith's amendment, was called to move it. He had only eight minutes in which to do so; after the Leader of the Opposition's speech, the Speaker had announced that he had imposed an eight-minute limit on back-bench speeches in the debate. Then the leader of the Liberal Democrats (to whom the time limit did not apply) spoke for twenty-one minutes. In the debate fifty-one MPs spoke (a remarkable number because the debate was to be extended by three hours and because the eight-minute time limit had been imposed): twenty-six Labour, seventeen Conservative, five Liberal Democrats, and the leaders of the Scottish National, Ulster Unionist and Democratic Unionist parties. Back-bench MPs who spoke included William Hague, the former leader of the Conservative Party, John Denham, the Home Office minister who that morning had resigned from the government on the issue, and the chairmen of both the Defence and Foreign Affairs Select Committees. The Chair called MPs alternately from each side of the House, but on this question being much less able than usual to predict whether they would support the government's line or not. In the winding-up speeches at the end of the debate the shadow Foreign Secretary spoke for seventeen minutes and the Foreign Secretary for twenty-eight minutes.

At 10.00 p.m., the amendment was put to the vote and defeated by 396 votes to 217. The government motion was then approved by 412 votes to 149, and the House had agreed to a resolution that, among other things, authorised the use of military force. The votes had taken twenty-nine minutes; and, as soon as the numbers in the second vote had been announced by the Speaker, the House moved on to the daily half-hour adjournment debate (see below), a very different parliamentary occasion for which only four MPs and the Deputy Speaker were present.

This was for many reasons an unusual debate, but it contained all the key elements of debate on a substantive motion. As we saw in Chapter 7, debate on legislation is structured in much the same way: a member moves 'that the such and such Bill be now read a second time'; it is possible to move a 'reasoned amendment'; and at the end of the debate the amendment and the main question are disposed of. Similarly, when an amendment to the text of a bill (or a new clause or schedule), is proposed in Committee of the whole House or standing committee, or in the House on report, the amendment is moved, and the question is proposed and debated. Amendments to amendments or to new clauses or schedules are treated in the same way as amendments to motions.

The moving of an amendment, whether in the House or in committee, is subject to the Chair having selected it. As we saw in Chapter 3, this is a power through which the Chair exercises great influence on the shape of proceedings, However, the power of selection does not exist in select committees (when, for example, they consider draft reports).

Disposing of a motion

Once a motion has been moved and the question proposed, it may be disposed of by being decided one way or the other, as outlined above. It may also lapse because the moment of interruption arrives and there is no provision for it to be debated beyond that hour. It will then have been 'talked out' (see page 143). A motion may also be *withdrawn* or *superseded*.

Withdrawal

Once a motion of any sort has been moved, and before it has been put to the House or a committee for decision, it is possible to seek to withdraw it. But because the motion has been moved, it is in the possession of the House or committee and may be withdrawn only 'by leave' – that is, by unanimous consent. The MP who moved it says 'I beg leave to withdraw the motion [or amendment]'; and the Chair says to all and sundry 'Is it your pleasure that the motion [amendment] be withdrawn? . . . Motion [amendment], by leave, withdrawn'. But even one objection is enough to prevent this happening, and in that case the motion or amendment must eventually be put to a decision.

Superseding

It is possible to supersede debate on a question before the House or committee by what is known as a *dilatory motion*. This may be a motion for the adjournment of the debate, or of the committee, or of the House. In consideration of legislation, it may also be a motion that further consideration of the bill be adjourned, or 'that the Chairman do report progress'. The moving of such a motion is subject to the permission of the Chair, who must be satisfied that it is not an abuse. If it proceeds, however, debate upon it supersedes the original debate, which is not resumed until the dilatory motion has been decided (or, indeed, which will not be resumed at that sitting if the dilatory motion is successful).

A rare and old-fashioned form of dilatory motion is *the previous Question*: a motion 'that the Question be not now put'. If it is agreed to, the House immediately moves on to the next business; but if it is not agreed to, whatever matter was interrupted must be decided immediately (as when a closure is agreed to).

Debate may also be interrupted by a motion 'that the House sit in private'. This might be in earnest if extraordinary circumstances arose during some national emergency; the House sat in secret several times during the First and Second World Wars. Modern use of the motion (formerly in the words 'that Strangers do now withdraw') has been to attempt to disrupt business or express strong objection to some proceeding. The Chair must put the motion immediately to the House for decision; but it may not be moved more than once during a sitting. It is rarely successful; the most recent occasion was in December 2001, during proceedings on the Anti-Terrorism, Crime and Security Bill (as an expression of objection rather than to allow some confidential matter to be discussed). The government was unprepared for such a motion to be moved, the motion was agreed to, and the House sat in private for nearly an hour. As the *Hansard* reporters withdraw when the House sits in private, there is no record of what was said during that time.

Quorum

A motion to sit in private may also be used to test whether a quorum is present, which in the House or Committee of the whole House can be demonstrated only when a vote takes place. If the result of the vote shows that fewer than forty MPs are present (thirty-five voting, two tellers on each side and the occupant of the Chair), then the business that was under discussion beforehand stands over until the next sitting of the House. If the business is not government business, this may well be fatal, and this tactic is used from time to time to attempt to kill private members' bills.

In standing committees and select committees no such procedure exists; the specified quorum must be present throughout or the chairman must suspend the committee. In select committees, the quorum is three or a quarter of the membership; in standing committees, it is one-third of the membership. In both cases fractions are rounded up. Somewhat illogically in standing committees, the chairman is not counted in calculating what the quorum is but does count towards whether a quorum is present. In Westminster Hall (see page 268) the quorum is three.

If the number of members present on the government side of a committee alone does not provide a quorum, the opposition sometimes uses the tactic of removing its own MPs from the room and thus stopping the business. The rule of the business standing over does not apply 'upstairs', however, and as soon as a quorum is again present (provided it is within twenty minutes), debate proceeds.

We now look at several different types of motion.

Motions on opposition days

Each session twenty days are set aside for debates initiated by the opposition parties. Seventeen of these are allocated to the official opposition and three to the Liberal Democrats as the second-largest opposition party. One of these latter days is often shared between two of the smaller parties; in 2001–02, half of one day was taken by Plaid Cymru and the other half of the day by the Scottish National Party. Opposition day debates represented about 9 percent of the total time of the House.

These days are ring-fenced opposition time; but, although their scheduling is normally agreed through the usual channels (see page 88), exactly when opposition days are taken is formally in the gift of the government. Each is the main business of a parliamentary day, so usually about six hours' debate – although ministerial statements can cut into this (often producing objections from the opposition). Days are often informally divided into two halves so that two subjects can be debated.

These days are a key opportunity for the opposition parties, and especially for the official Opposition, to try to expose the government over an issue on which it may be vulnerable, or to provide a shop window for one of its own policies. Among the subjects selected by the Conservatives in 2001–02 were the conduct of Jo Moore (the special adviser to Stephen Byers as Secretary of State for Transport, who came under heavy criticism for advocating 'burying bad news' by announcing it on the day of the '9/11' terrorist attacks in the USA); the countryside; asylum seekers; the Northern Ireland peace process; truancy and discipline in schools; the funding of public services; and Zimbabwe. Among subjects selected by the Liberal Democrats were post office closures and Royal Mail deliveries; the Johannesburg summit on sustainable development; and affordable housing. Plaid Cymru selected the domestic steel industry and the support that the government had been seen to give to a company belonging to a Mr Mittal, whose steel manufacturing was largely outside the UK; while the Scottish National Party's subject was the process of consent for the siting of nuclear and other power stations.

The motion moved in the House is usually a strongly worded criticism of government policies; the government tables an amendment that normally seeks to remove all the words of the motion after 'That this House' and substitute a warm endorsement of what the government is doing. The front-bench speakers will be the relevant shadow secretary of state and shadow minister, and their counterparts in government. The debate is often combative. Some can be testing for ministers as well as a proving ground for opposition front-benchers; and opposition days can give newer MPs an opportunity to shine and perhaps catch the selectors' eye as possible ministerial material.

At the end of an opposition day debate, the Question is put in an old-fashioned form that survives only in this case. Normally, the government amendment would be decided first and would no doubt be approved. The next Question would be the main Question, as amended; so both votes would take place on the government's words, not those of the opposition. The device that is used to avoid this is that the first Question put is 'That the original words stand part of the Question' – in other words, a vote on keeping the opposition motion as it is. When this proposition has been defeated, the second Question put is 'That the proposed words be there added' – a vote to approve the government's amendment. When this is agreed to, the Chair declares the main Question, as amended, to be agreed to, without a further vote (which would be pointless, as it would be a second vote on the government's text).

This may seem a rather complex minuet, but it is important to opposition parties to be able to put their own proposition to the House rather than to be forced simply to vote upon the government's counter-proposition.

Government substantive motions

Most of the occasions on which the government needs to seek the approval of the House of Commons are on legislation or spending. Exceptionally, as in the debates on Iraq, it may wish to have the backing of an explicit resolution of the House of Commons. On most substantive motions in a session, the government is in the position of defending or explaining in the face of opposition challenge. However, there are some occasions when the government puts a substantive motion before the House for debate. These are often when procedural changes are being proposed (as in the packages of Modernisation Committee recommendations on 14 May and 29 October 2002); when the Standards and Privileges Committee reports on the conduct of an MP; the annual 'take note' debate on the reports of the Public Accounts Committee; domestic business such as approving arrangements for the summer opening for visitors; or money and ways and means motions that are taken other than immediately after second reading. The four or five days of debates on the Queen's Speech and on the Budget – although each is very much a special case – may also be counted as government substantive motions.

Back-benchers' motions

Until 1995, four half-days and ten Fridays were set aside for motions moved by back-benchers chosen by ballot. As part of the Jopling reforms (see page 132), these were abolished and replaced by extra opportunities for back-benchers to raise subjects on the adjournment on Wednesday mornings (later moved, with increased time, to Westminster Hall). Private members' motion days gave individual MPs an opportunity to put a proposition to the House – which could be as controversial as they wished. Their passing is still regretted by many MPs; the only similar (but much more limited) opportunity that now exists is the chance under the ten-minute rule (see page 209) to put a proposal for legislation to the House for decision.

Adjournment motions

It may seem rather strange that the House of Commons apparently spends so much time deciding whether to adjourn or not (20 percent of the total time in the 2001–02 session). In fact, adjournment motions are not really about whether to end the sitting (which would be brought to an end anyway under the standing orders); they are vehicles for debate.

Government adjournment motions

From the government's point of view, these have the advantage of avoiding substantive decisions; there is no need to put any form of words before the House other than 'That this House do now adjourn' and indicating the subject for debate. On matters where the government may feel vulnerable to back-bench dissent, this allows debate but avoids a motion whose terms might encourage disagreement. It also prevents hostile amendments being tabled, either by the opposition parties or by its own back-benchers, because a motion for the adjournment is not amendable.

On contentious subjects, the minister replying to the debate will normally try to speak right up to the moment of interruption (see page 143), so that the motion lapses, having been 'talked out'. However, the opposition – or any individual back-bencher – can force a vote by moving the closure, usually in the last few seconds before the motion would lapse. This does provide an opportunity for the expression of views, but as it is only on the question of adjourning – what the media normally call 'a technical motion' – even a significant vote against loses much of its sting.

Some debates on adjournment motions are great parliamentary occasions. One such in 1940 led directly to the replacement of Neville Chamberlain by Winston Churchill as Prime Minister. In recent years, the debates at emergency sittings of the House (for example, on the invasion of the Falkland Islands and on the 11 September 2001 terrorist attacks in the USA) have been on motions for the adjournment.

Less controversially, government adjournment motions are used to provide opportunities for general debates, often more to ventilate a subject and to allow the expression of individual MPs' opinions than to provide a set-to between government and opposition. Some examples in 2003 were debates on armed forces personnel, developing a national skills strategy, flood and coastal defence policy, International Women's Day, and Welsh affairs. Government adjournment debates are also used to test the view of the House before more formal proposals are brought forward (for example, in the early stages of Lords reform). About 12 percent of the time of the House is taken up by government adjournment motions in an average session.

The daily half-hour adjournment motion

Every day, after other business has been disposed of, back-benchers have an opportunity to raise a subject in the half-hour adjournment debate. The government whip on duty formally moves 'That this House do now adjourn', and the back-bencher then has fifteen minutes or so to speak, followed by a minister replying for the remainder of the time. Brief interventions from other MPs are allowed with the permission of the initiator of the debate and the minister.

MPs apply to the Speaker for an adjournment slot (by the end of a Wednesday for the following week), and their applications are put into a ballot. The Speaker himself chooses the subject for the Thursday slot, often picking an MP who has an urgent constituency matter to raise or who has been consistently unlucky in the ballot.

Any subject can be raised, provided that it falls within the responsibilities of the government so that a minister can reply to the debate. MPs are not allowed to use the half-hour adjournment primarily to call for legislation, but in practice this rule is not especially restrictive. As an illustration of the topics raised, five successive sitting days in 2003 produced debates on the closure of a children's hospital in Manchester, the closure of a post office in Dunstable, accidents on the A36, the whereabouts of Tariq Aziz (the former Deputy Prime Minister of Iraq), and the effects of illegal development on a community in Kent.

The half-hour adjournment is a sought-after opportunity for back-benchers, providing about 150 to 160 mini-debates a year and occupying about 6 percent of the total time of the House. Unlike the Westminster Hall debates (see below) the timing of the half-hour adjournment is not always predictable; but many MPs see such debates in the Chamber as having a higher status.

The half-hour adjournment often shows the extraordinary flexibility of the House of Commons. Some great matter may have been decided at the end of the day's main business, eagerly reported by the media; but as MPs stream out of the Chamber after a dramatic vote, the House – albeit much depleted – may turn to a very specific local problem: perhaps the difficulties faced by a single constituent.

Recess debates

Before each recess, there is a debate of three hours on 'matters to be considered before the forthcoming adjournment'. This gives an opportunity for back-benchers to raise topics similar to the half-hour adjournment debates, although in this case they are replied to not individually by the departmental ministers responsible for the subject but in an omnibus reply given by the Leader or Deputy Leader of the House. This is nevertheless parliamentary time valued by back benchers, as evidenced by the number of takers, which often means that a time limit on speeches is imposed.

Emergency adjournment debates

In Chapter 6 (page 140), we described how an MP can make a case for an emergency debate; if granted by the Speaker, a three-hour debate takes place on a motion for the adjournment. However, such debates are very rare; there have been only two in the last ten years. Debates during a recall of the House (see above and page 132) also have the character of emergency adjournment debates, although these happen on the initiative of the government.

Westminster Hall

Much of the business in Westminster Hall takes place on the adjournment, so this may be a convenient place to describe this important procedural innovation.

Following the House's approval of a recommendation from the Modernisation Committee, from the beginning of session 1999–2000 a 'parallel chamber' was established, known as Westminster Hall but in fact in the Grand Committee Room, a large committee room off the northern end of Westminster Hall. The idea had its origin in the 'Main Committee', a parallel but subordinate chamber used by the Australian House of Representatives in Canberra.

The Westminster parallel chamber was intended to allow debates, open to all MPs, on less contentious business for which it would be difficult to find time on the floor of the House. Such business was to be referred by agreement through the usual channels, and decisions in Westminster Hall would be taken only by unanimity. The more consensual approach of Westminster Hall was emphasised by a seating layout closer to the hemicycle found in many other parliaments, with two rows of seats on each side as in the Chamber but with two more rows in a semicircle at the end, facing the Chair.

The Modernisation Committee was keen to avoid two possible disadvantages of a parallel chamber; that the additional time available should not simply provide an outlet for more government business – and especially not more legislation – and that the Chamber of the House itself should remain clearly pre-eminent.

Westminster Hall sittings take place on Tuesdays and Wednesdays from 9.30 a.m. to 11.30 a.m., when they are suspended to allow MPs to attend the main Chamber, resuming at 2.00 p.m. until 4.30 p.m. On Thursdays the sitting time is 2.30 p.m. to 5.30 p.m. Sittings in Westminster Hall are suspended for any votes in the House but have 'injury time' to compensate.

On Tuesdays and Wednesdays, Westminster Hall is given over to back-bench adjournment debates, two of one and a half hours each – which are intended for broader subjects on which a number of MPs will want to speak – and three of half an hour each. Two ballots are held on the Wednesday of the previous week for each category of debate; MPs may enter for both but cannot be successful in both. To minimise the disruption to ministers' work, each government department is on call to respond to debates every other week rather than (as in the House) whenever a relevant debate comes up. The business for Thursdays may include debates on government adjournment motions and, from the 2002–03 session, cross-cutting oral questions (see page 289). Westminster Hall Thursdays also provide an important opportunity for debates on reports from select committees, giving the work of those committees a higher profile. In session 2001–02, more than sixty hours of debate was devoted to select committee reports. Forthcoming business in Westminster Hall is set out in Part B of *Future Business* (see page 154).

In a typical week in May 2003, broader ninety-minute subjects included economic activity in former mining communities, the mid-term review of the Common Agricultural Policy, fly-tipping and the European Year of Disabled People. Half-hour subjects included the shellfish industry in Devon, the future of Newcraighall village post office near Edinburgh, a planning case affecting Cranham Road, Little Waltham, near Chelmsford, and house-building levels in West Sussex.

In Westminster Hall, the chair is taken by the Chairman of Ways and Means (who has overall responsibility for proceedings in the same way as the Speaker in the House), his two deputies (see page 49) and by four senior members of the Chairmen's Panel appointed as additional Deputy Speakers for the purpose, as well as by other members of the Chairmen's Panel. The proceedings are recorded in *Hansard* and published in hard copy and on the parliamentary website in the same way as proceedings in the Chamber. Westminster Hall sittings are also televised in their entirety.

Decisions in Westminster Hall may be taken only by unanimity; if a decision is challenged it is referred to the House. In addition, if six MPs object to further proceedings a debate stands adjourned. This has not yet happened, as no substantive business has been taken in Westminster Hall; all debates have been on the adjournment.

Table 9.1 Sitting time in Westminster Hall compared with sitting time in the House, in hours and minutes

Session	1999–2000	2000–01	2001–02
On subjects selected by:			
The government	45.28	18.51	48.15
Back-benchers	249.20	142.07	360.52
The Liaison Committee	53.44	21.58	61.06
(debates on select committee reports)			
Total	348.32	182.56	470.14
Time the House itself sat	1442.41	690.27	1540.46

In the three full sessions since the introduction of sittings in Westminster Hall, they have provided the additional debating time on the adjournment shown in Table 9.1.

In each of three sessions, Westminster Hall has thus provided an additional 24, 27 and 31 percent of the total time available in the House, largely to the benefit of back-bench debates on the adjournment. In an average year it is likely that there will be 320 such debates, about 130 of the longer ninety-minute slots and 190 of the half-hour debates.

Debates in the Grand Committees and the Standing Committee on Regional Affairs

The Scottish, Welsh and Northern Ireland Grand Committees (not to be confused with the select committees on each of those parts of the UK) consist of all the MPs sitting for constituencies in each country. Additional MPs from elsewhere may be added to the Welsh and Northern Ireland committees from time to time. In the years immediately before devolution, the roles of all three committees were widened, allowing them to hear statements from ministers (including ministers in the Lords), to hold sessions of oral questions, to consider bills and delegated legislation, and to hold adjournment debates. Post-devolution, the committees have met less frequently (although the suspension of devolved government in Northern Ireland has revived the role of the Northern Ireland Grand Committee). All three committees may, with the leave of the House, meet away from Westminster in their respective parts of the UK.

In the last four complete sessions, these committees have met on the numbers of days shown in Table 9.2.

The majority of sittings in the Scottish and Welsh committees have been for general debates on subjects such as health in Scotland, the Budget and the

Table 9.2 Meetings of grand committees, 1998–2002 (meetings away from Westminster in brackets)

Session	1998–99	1999–2000	2000–01	2001–02
Scottish	4 (4)	4 (1)	1	4
Welsh	2 (1)	5	3	4
Northern Ireland	6	4	3	3

Scottish economy, the government's legislative programme as it relates to Wales, and the Welsh economy. The Northern Ireland Grand Committee has held similar types of debate (for example on the review of the criminal justice system in Northern Ireland) but has considered more legislation.

The Regional Affairs Committee consists of thirteen MPs sitting for constituencies in England, although any MP with a seat in England may attend and speak. The committee considers matters referred to it by the House and with the leave of the House may sit away from Westminster. A sitting of the committee may begin with a ministerial statement, followed by questions, for one hour; then a debate for three hours. The committee has met only four times in the last four complete sessions, debating such matters as regional governance and regional economic imbalances.

Early day motions

Every sitting day an average of ten motions are tabled 'for an early day' – that is, for debate on an unspecified day. Almost all these 'early day motions' (EDMs) are tabled by back-benchers (although 'prayers' – see page 231 – first make their appearance as EDMs), so the chances of their being debated are negligible. Very occasionally, as in the case of the 1989 EDM on war crimes, a really significant EDM will be given debating time by the government or may figure in an opposition day debate.

An EDM is simply an expression of a view that could be debated by the House (they all begin 'That this House . . .'). They may be tabled by any MP, must not be longer than 250 words and must conform to other rules of order (for example, no unparliamentary language, and no reference to matters *sub judice*). An EDM appears in the Vote bundle, printed on blue pages, the day after it is tabled, and is reprinted for the rest of that week and the following week if any other MPs add their names to it. It is reprinted on any Thursday thereafter if names have been added during the preceding week; but it falls at the end of the session.

EDMs are used for a wide variety of purposes; an MP may want to put on record the success of his local football team (perhaps attracting only the signatures of his constituency neighbours – and perhaps a hostile amendment from supporters of a rival team), or criticise somebody's opinion or action – almost like writing a letter to a national newspaper. EDMs are also used by MPs to defuse pressure from constituents and others by being seen to be doing something about an issue, or to put material on the parliamentary record under the protection of parliamentary privilege. EDMs are also used to test and gather support on major issues (recently, on hunting, foundation hospitals and Iraq), and they are a useful source of political intelligence for the whips.

A random selection of EDMs from May 2003 stressed the need for autism awareness, welcomed the re-election of the First Minister in Scotland, drew attention to a threat to the UK system of hallmarking silver and gold, encouraged the Queen to visit Gibraltar, warned against the effect of an anti-depressant drug, urged the placing of a statue of Nelson Mandela in Trafalgar Square, and expressed concern about the merger of Bristol and Bath rugby clubs. One cross-party EDM with 140 signatures on its first appearance called for more comprehensive and effective equality legislation.

Some 1,500 EDMs are tabled each session and may attract four or five hundred signatures from MPs on a single sitting day. The number of EDMs, and the fact that many are on relatively trivial matters, have led to criticism of them as 'parliamentary graffiti'; but they do act as a safety valve, and MPs (and many outside the House) value them as a means of expressing and testing views. Apart from the 'prayers' referred to above, none will ever get debated, although it is sometimes suggested that time should be found for those with substantial numbers of signatures (see page 382).

The rules and conventions of debate

An MP is called to speak by the Speaker (or by the chairman in a committee). MPs who want to take part in debates in the House (but not when a bill is in Committee of the whole House or at report stage), or in the ninety-minute debates in Westminster Hall, write to the Speaker beforehand. This is not to say that those who do not write cannot be called, but those who do write have preference.

When there is great pressure to speak in a particular debate, the Speaker may impose a time limit on speeches, as in the Iraq debate described earlier. This does not apply to the two front benches (nor to one MP speaking on behalf of the Liberal Democrats). The minimum time limit is eight minutes. In order to preserve the exchanges of debate, MPs get 'injury time' for the first two interventions they take from other members; the clock stops while the other Member is intervening, and then the MP speaking gets an extra minute so that he or she can reply to the intervention. This injury time can be profitable if the reply to the intervention is very short!

Unlike the practice in the House of Lords and in many other parliaments, no list is made available of those who are to speak (although there is some pressure for the introduction of such a list). When the previous MP sits down, all those in the Chamber wanting to speak will bob up, hoping to 'catch the Speaker's eye'. The Speaker then says 'Mr Smith' and Mr Smith begins his speech. It is said that the practice of calling out a Member's name originated with the corrupt Speaker Trevor at the end of the seventeenth century (see page 111). Up to then, the Speaker merely looked meaningfully at the Member he wished to call; but Speaker Trevor had a truly grotesque squint, which is supposed to have led to widespread misunderstanding as to which Member he had intended to call. This may be apocryphal; but Trevor's portrait confirms the squint, at least.

MPs must address the House through the Chair, referring to other Members in the third person, and by their constituency or the office they hold rather than by name. So an MP cannot say to another 'what do you mean by that?' but must say 'what does the honourable Member for Loamshire East mean by that'; and an MP cannot talk about 'Charles Kennedy' or 'you in charge of the Liberal Democrats' but must instead refer to 'the right honourable member for Ross, Skye and Inverness West' or 'the leader of the Liberal Democrats'. All MPs are referred to as 'honourable members' or 'the honourable lady' or 'the honourable gentleman'; those who are Privy Counsellors (usually present or former senior ministers) are styled 'right honourable'. This may sound rather antique, but it avoids the direct confrontation of two MPs addressing each other as 'you' and often helps to lower the temperature.

The practice of referring to QCs as 'honourable and learned' and officers retired from the armed forces (or still in the reserves) as 'honourable and gallant' is no longer a convention of debate, but the terms are still used by traditionalists.

When they enter or leave the Chamber, MPs are expected to give a slight bow to the Chair as a gesture of respect to the House itself. They should not cross the line of sight between the Speaker and the member who has the floor; and – very important – should sit down as soon as the Speaker or a deputy rises. Dress conventions – jackets and ties for men – are generally upheld. Eating, drinking, the use of mobile phones and smoking are forbidden: the House of Commons has been a no-smoking area since the resolution of 1696 'That no Member do presume to take tobacco in the gallery of the House or at a committee table'.

MPs must speak from the place where they are called, which must be within the formal limits of the Chamber (so not from the cross-benches below the Bar of the House or from the parts of the galleries reserved for members). MPs may refer to notes, but they should not read questions or speeches at length

– although notes tend to be used to a greater degree than was the case a few years ago. An MP should be present for the opening and winding-up speeches of the debate in which he or she takes part, and after speaking should stay in the Chamber for at least the next two speeches. The Speaker will not call an MP to ask a question following a ministerial statement (or an urgent question) unless he or she has been there for the whole of the opening statement.

The House of Commons has a long tradition of MPs seeking to intervene in each other's speeches, to ask a question or to make a point. This – different from the practice in many other parliaments – makes debate much more lively than would otherwise be the case and is easier in the relatively intimate style of the Chamber than it would be in a large hemicycle (see page 14). Interventions must be brief; and they may be made only if the MP who has the floor 'gives way', although the expectation is that the MP speaking will indeed give way. The Chair will stop an MP whose speech is irrelevant or tediously repetitive, although with a certain amount of ingenuity most things can be made relevant and unrepetitive.

In most debates MPs may speak only once, but this does not apply, for example, in a committee on a bill. The *sub judice* rule prevents any MP referring to a current or impending court case (more precisely, when someone has been charged in a criminal case or, in a civil action, when a case has been set down for trial). This is to avoid debate in the House – under the protection of privilege – possibly influencing the outcome of a case; but it also reflects the relationship between Parliament and the courts (see page 166). However, the rule may be relaxed at the Speaker's discretion, and it need not prevent the House considering legislation.

The language of debate must be restrained. An MP may not accuse another of lying, or of misleading the House; the Chair will intervene immediately to require the withdrawal of the charge. *Erskine May* no longer lists the words ruled to be 'unparliamentary', although the lists in earlier editions are entertaining. 'Villains' got a red card in 1875, as did 'Pecksniffian cant' in 1928. Rather surprisingly, so did 'rude remarks' in 1887. Animal words of all sorts ('jackasses', 'swine', 'rats' and even 'stool pigeons') have always been required to be withdrawn. However, the important thing (and the reason why *Erskine May* no longer lists examples) is the context in which language is used. In February 2003, in a letter to all MPs reminding them of the conventions and courtesies of the House, Speaker Martin echoed the words of several of his predecessors when he said 'Members should bear in mind Erskine May's dictum that good temper and moderation are the characteristics of parliamentary language. It is important that exercise of the privilege of free speech is tempered with responsibility'.

MPs are expected to inform their colleagues when they intend to refer to them in the Chamber; when they table parliamentary questions that specifically affect the constituency of another MP; and when they intend to visit another constituency (except in a purely private capacity).

All these conventions and constraints may sound a little like school rules, and some occasionally come in for criticism from new MPs and others. But where political views clash and passions can run high a little formality can make the House more dignified and tolerant. It is a pity that many people judge the House of Commons from what they see on television of the gladiatorial Prime Minister's Questions; the House is actually a much more courteous place than many might think, while still allowing challenge and lively disagreement. At a time when Parliament is seeking to reconnect with the people, this is no bad thing.

The purpose of debate

As the previous pages show, the House of Commons itself, Westminster Hall and a variety of committees provide a great many different occasions and circumstances where debate takes place. What is the purpose of the millions of words spoken as a result?

Much of debate is, in one way or another, about deploying political argument: seeking to make the case for a particular philosophy or interpretation and applying it to the issue of the moment. Although many in the country at large see a clash of ideologies as rather sterile and negative, it is part of political reality.

But debate is also about challenge, testing and explanation. Parliament is a place where the government should be forced to justify its policies and actions. That process is part of checking an executive that will always tend to be over-mighty. It is also a process that crosses political divides, and it involves both the shadow minister who aspires to be in government and the government backbencher who is uneasy about a course that the government is taking. In these circumstances, debate provides the opportunity to point out the weakness in a case, to offer alternative solutions and to ask 'why?'

Debate is also about exposure. One purpose of this is to force – or provide an opportunity for – the government to set out its view and its policy. This may be on some major issue – the reconstruction of Iraq, the achievement of peace in the Middle East or whether the UK should adopt the euro. It may be on something with a lower profile but of great importance to those affected; to take the earlier examples: fly-tipping, the shellfish industry in Devon or house building in Sussex. This will produce a statement of government policy, or a response to criticism, but it will also act as a mind concentrator, not only for the minister but also for the civil servants in his or her department, who should be asking 'Is this a reasonable line to take? How vulnerable are we on this? Should we do more?'

Exposure through debate is a way of putting subjects on the political (and media) agenda. It may be some abuse – perhaps a holiday timeshare scam – or perhaps an ethical or moral issue, such as stem cell research, battery hens or cluster bombs. It may also be a way of swinging the spotlight onto some injustice – sometimes affecting only one person or one family – perhaps children kidnapped by an estranged father, a disability pension denied or the perverse application of some planning law.

Debate is also about representation: industries, regions, constituencies, pressure groups and individuals have a parliamentary voice through MPs taking up causes, setting out the case and gathering support.

Does debate change minds? On the spot, rarely. On most matters that come to the House of Commons, the parties will already have their view; individual MPs will have their opinions. On a non-partisan issue, a compelling speech may be influential; on a highly charged issue, the trend of debate may change minds (a significant number of MPs said that they finally made up their minds which way to vote on war with Iraq only during the debate in March 2003). In the case of most debates, effective advocacy will indeed change minds, but more slowly. It may modify the government's view, influence public opinion and put new subjects on the agenda. How effectively it does this is very much down to MPs themselves.

Debates in the House of Lords

Unstarred questions

About a quarter of the House of Lords' time is taken up with debates. Some of these, as we have seen already, arise on 'unstarred questions' and take the form of short debates time-limited to an hour and a half at the end of the day's business, rather like adjournment debates in the Commons. A minister answers the question at the end of the debate, and there is no right of reply. These debatable questions can also be held during dinner adjournments in the course of legislative business, when they are limited to one hour. Unstarred questions are hugely popular and occupy about 7 percent of the House's sitting time. The availability of time for these debates varies widely from session to session.

Debatable motions

Most debates take place, as in the Commons, on a motion moved by the initiator. The form of the motion used will vary according to the purpose of the debate. Most debates in the Lords will take place on a neutral motion 'for papers', a procedural device that allows the mover to raise a subject with a right of reply for himself or herself. The motion is invariably withdrawn at the end of the debate. Debates initiated for the purpose of considering reports of committees, or documents, and debates initiated by the government itself will normally be on motions 'to take note', or if an opinion on the content is to be expressed, 'to approve'. Finally, when it is desired that the House express a view on the subject matter under debate, a motion 'for resolution' is moved – usually resulting in a vote at the end. Let us look now at the context in which these different debating tools are used.

Debates on reports of select committees

Select committees on public policy (see page 342) – like the Economic Affairs Committee, Science and Technology Committee or European Union Committee – make their reports to the House in the expectation that at some stage they will be debated. In recent sessions, 2 to 3 percent of sitting time was spent debating these reports, almost invariably on a motion to take note. Sometimes motions to take note of reports on similar subjects are debated together. The debate on the Economic Affairs Committee's report on the 2003 Finance Bill was debated as part of the second reading of the bill.

Chairmen and members of select committees are often critical that insufficient time is offered by the government Whips Office for debates on select committee reports or that time, when it is offered, tends to be at short notice or subject to last-minute change. On the other hand, there are those who point out that such debates rarely attract interest from the wider House and, save for a few members with knowledge of the subject matter, most of the participants tend to be members of the committee that made the report. In some ways this does not matter. The dialogue with the government over a committee's recommendations take place not only on the floor of the House but also in the direct exchanges between the committees and ministers.

Opposition and back-bench debates

Most debates on motions moved by opposition parties and back-benchers take place on Wednesdays, when motions have precedence over bills and other business. Most of these Wednesdays are given over to the political parties to initiate debates, usually on the neutral motion 'for papers' or occasionally a 'take note' motion. The days for these debates are allocated to the various parties by agreement between party whips, with by far the most going to the official Opposition. They are not time-limited. However, the mover of the motion can ask the Leader of the House to move a Business of the House motion limiting the time. This is often done by the political parties to create the opportunity for two debates to be held. The limit on a single debate is usually five hours:

the limits where two debates are held can vary but must not exceed a total of six hours.

In the earlier part of the session, up until the spring recess, one Wednesday a month is set aside for two short debates limited to two and a half hours each and initiated by back-benchers or cross-benchers. The subjects are chosen by a ballot conducted some weeks beforehand by the Clerk of the Parliaments in the presence of chief whips and the Convenor of the Cross Benches.

In recent sessions, 13 to 15 percent of sitting time was spent debating Wednesday opposition and back-bench motions. In the 2001–02 session, the debates included such themes as foreign affairs (Zimbabwe, Afghanistan, sub-Saharan Africa), public policy (from the London Underground to pensions, urban regeneration and crime reduction) and aspects of public administration (holding the executive to account, planning, local government, Wales, regulation).

Government motions

Sometimes the government will itself wish to initiate a debate on a matter of public concern or potential concern to the House. Thus debates on reform of the House in recent sessions have usually been held on government motions to take note. Debates on pressing issues of foreign policy fall into the same category. On 18 March 2003 the Lords, like the Commons, debated the situation in Iraq, but on a take note motion, in the full knowledge that war was probably imminent. Unlike the Commons, however, no vote followed the end of the debate.

But there have been occasions in recent sessions where the government has sought to test the opinion of the two Houses of Parliament on issues of policy, placing a series of options before each House. Thus in March 2002 the government itself tabled motions for resolution on a series of options relating to hunting with dogs; and in February 2003, although the debate had already taken place, a series of votes were held on seven motions to approve one or other of the options relating to the reform of the composition of the House that had been proposed by the Joint Committee on Reform of the House.

Conventions of debate

Certain conventions apply to all debate in the House, whether on legislative business or on the general motions that are the subject of this chapter. We have noted in Chapter 2 that the Chair does not call members to speak in the Lords. Peers usually give advance notice to the government Whips Office of their intention to speak in debates, and lists of speakers are prepared by the Leader of the House (in fact by the Private Secretary in the Whips Office) in consultation with the usual channels and published before the debate begins. Any lord not on the list may speak, but only after those already on the list and before the winding-up speeches, and then only briefly. So there is no problem in the Lords of 'catching the Speaker's eye'. And of course the House keeps its own order.

As in the Commons, there are conventions governing the way in which other members are addressed. Thus remarks are addressed to the House as a whole. Other participants are addressed in the third person, never as 'you'. And the style of address is always 'The Noble Lord, Lord . . .' or 'The Right Reverend Prelate, the Bishop of . . .'.

Generally speaking, a lord can speak only once in debate, except when the House is in committee on a bill, and must not read (although many do). Unless speaking from the front bench, where lords speak from a despatch box, members speak in their places. Speeches must be relevant and, indeed, in 1965 the House even resolved that they should be shorter. Today a fifteen-minute rule applies in debates that are not time-limited, with a twenty-minute limit for members opening or winding up. Members must avoid 'asperity of speech'. And relevant interests must be declared (see page 119).

In addition to these rules of debate various rules of conduct apply – like speaking 'uncovered' (without a hat!) or the custom of making obeisance to the Cloth of Estate behind the throne on entering the Chamber. Such customs help to lend the House a veneer of good, even courtly, manners which are sometimes sorely tested in the debates themselves.

Value of debate: the chamber of experts

It is no easier to set a value on Lords debates than it is for the Commons. We take it for granted that debate is free and open. It is of course protected by parliamentary privilege. That in itself is something to be cherished. But what purpose is served? Minds are certainly not swayed, especially where arguments follow party lines. Given that most speeches are pre-prepared, that is hardly surprising.

The value of debates is that they offer different opportunities and attractions to different participants. For a back-bencher initiating a debate, they offer the chance to air a policy matter of personal interest with the guarantee of a government response that is likely to represent the latest government thinking on the issue. For opposition parties, they offer the chance to set out their wares: to expose some aspect of government policy of which they do not approve, perhaps to say how things might be done better or differently, and to try to put the government on the spot. And for government itself they offer the opportunity to set out some new policy development or change in world events, and to test opinion across the parties.

Are the debates of good quality? Many are. And in most debates a few speakers can be deemed to have expertise that is relevant to the subject matter. This expertise stems in part from the fact that the House of Lords has never been a chamber of salaried members. Many, whether life peers or hereditary, have or have had full-time careers elsewhere. And life peerages have been bestowed on a wide range of men and women distinguished in their field – some irrespective of party, others because they have espoused a party cause. Thus in November 2001 a debate to call attention to the issues confronting medical teaching and research in the National Health Service attracted nineteen speakers: two former deans of university medical schools, a practising dentist, a consultant obstetrician, a consultant paediatrician, a former GP, a former professor of nursing, a former director of Age Concern, and the president of MENCAP, among others. Among the sixty-seven speakers in the debate on Iraq and weapons of mass destruction on 24 September 2002 there were three former Chiefs of the Defence Staff, three former Foreign Secretaries, two former Home Secretaries, six bishops, two former ambassadors and two former Secretaries of State for Defence.

Some commentators now view the House of Lords as a chamber of experts. This is perhaps to exaggerate the expert element in the House. Most of the peerages bestowed in the last fifty years have gone to politicians, active at either the national or local level. And many of the 'experts' have retired or are about to retire when they become members of the House. Their expertise might be thought a little dated. But the fact remains that the House of Lords as currently composed is a knowledgeable place in a way that distinguishes it from most other parliamentary assemblies in the world.

10 Calling to account: questions

In this chapter we will look at one of the best-known inquisitorial functions of Parliament: parliamentary questions, often known as PQs. This will also be a convenient place to look at public petitions and MPs' letters, which are other ways in which the actions of government can be influenced or exposed.

Questions in the Commons

By comparison with the processes of debate, legislation and examination by select committees, questions evolved relatively late in parliamentary history. Although the first recorded question to a minister was in the House of Lords in 1721, questions in the Commons did not develop until the nineteenth century, when all questions were asked orally; questions for written answer (now a major part of parliamentary activity) were not introduced until 1902.

What are questions?

Erskine May states that the purpose of a question is 'to obtain information or to press for action'. The people who have the information – and the ability to act upon it – are government ministers, and it is they who have to answer questions. Some questions are asked (or, in parliamentary language, 'tabled' or 'put down') of MPs who are not ministers but who speak on behalf of bodies such as the House of Commons Commission (see page 54) or the Church Commissioners. However, well over 99 percent of all PQs are asked of ministers by back-benchers, and this process is part of the way in which government can be held to account.

Questions are one of the best-known, but often misunderstood, features of the House of Commons, and it is on that House that we will concentrate. Questions are also asked in the House of Lords, but in much smaller numbers and less restricted by rules than in the Commons.

The rules for questions

First and foremost, questions must be about something for which a minister is responsible. In many cases this is clear-cut: the Secretary of State for Defence is responsible for ordering a new aircraft carrier, and the Secretary of State for International Development is responsible for how the UK's aid budget is spent. But, although the government has an overall responsibility for local government finance, it is not responsible for the detail of how local authorities spend their money. Nor, for example, is it responsible for what the courts do, for the operational details of policing or the actions of EU institutions (although it is responsible for its own policy towards them).

Ministers are responsible to Parliament for their own policies and actions, not for those of the opposition parties; so a government back-bencher could not table a question that asked 'What would be the effect on public services of the spending plans announced by the Conservative Party?' even if the minister was eager to answer. But if the MP were to ask the Chancellor of the Exchequer an oral question such as 'What factors does he take into account in allocating resources to public services?' then that is a matter for which he is responsible, and the reply may well take a side-swipe at the policy of the Conservative Party.

There are a variety of other rules. Matters that are *sub judice* (see page 274) cannot be raised. Questions must not offer information ('Is she aware that . . . ?') or be argumentative ('Does he agree that it is unacceptable that . . . ?'). They must have some reasonable basis in fact, rather than being purely speculative – they cannot, for example, ask whether a press report is correct. The government is treated as a single entity, so it is not in order to ask one minister to intervene with or influence another (although the same result may be achieved by asking the Prime Minister a question about improving coordination between two government departments).

A question that has been already been answered in the current session may not be asked again unless there is reason to think that the situation may have changed (although in practice this is often interpreted as allowing a question to be repeated after three months). This is a common-sense rule that prevents cluttering up both the question book and *Hansard* with identical exchanges. The tabling of numerous but very similar questions is not allowed for the same reason. A related rule prevents an MP asking for information that is readily available – for example, in official publications.

Since devolution to Scotland, Wales and Northern Ireland, ministers at Westminster may not be asked about things for which responsibility has passed to the devolved administrations. However, they may be asked about matters on which they have the power to require information from the administrations, or about concordats or liaison arrangements.

The rules about questions have developed over the years; for the most part, they either reflect other rules of the House (such as the *sub judice* rule) or try to ensure that questions keep to their principal purposes of obtaining information or pressing for action. MPs can find the rules frustrating; but it is remarkable how often a slightly different question – or the same question in a different form – avoids running foul of the rules and may even get closer to what the MP really wants to ask.

The answers

There is a rather hackneyed story of a minister and a senior civil servant being driven to some remote government establishment. The fog closed in, the car went slower and slower, and finally the driver, dimly seeing a passer-by, rolled down the window and said 'Where are we?' Back came the answer: 'You're in a car, in the fog'. 'Do you realise, Minister', said the civil servant, 'that's a perfect answer to a parliamentary question. It's short, it's absolutely true, and it tells you nothing you didn't know already'.

In Chapter 5 we quoted the 1997 resolution of the House of Commons on ministerial accountability, which states the duty of ministers to account for policies, decisions and actions. So far as questions are concerned, the key passages are those that require ministers 'to give accurate and truthful information to Parliament and to be as open as possible with Parliament, refusing to provide information only when disclosure would not be in the public interest'. Answers to PQs provide a huge amount of information on the whole range of government responsibilities, but attention inevitably focuses on occasions when answers are not given.

Ministers' judgement of 'not in the public interest' is normally based on the *Code of Practice on Access to Government Information*,[7] first introduced in 1994, which will be replaced by the provisions of the Freedom of Information Act which come into force in January 2005. The code lists fifteen categories of exemption to the provision of information, on grounds including harming international relations, or the frankness of discussion inside government, or the ability of the government to manage the economy, or the proper and efficient conduct of the business of a government department. There are some subjects on which few would expect information to be given in answer to a PQ, such as the operations of the security and intelligence services, or where an investigation into major VAT fraud might be under way.

However, on many other issues, interpretations and expectations can differ. In session 1999–2000, for example, details of experiments on animals were not given for reasons of commercial sensitivity. The same reason was cited for not revealing the government's estimate of the value of the Millennium Dome. Information about ministers' duty rosters and future engagements were withheld on the grounds that it was not the practice to publish them. It was also not the practice to comment on leak inquiries, or to reveal their findings. Although the future of small post offices was a hot political issue, the unit costs of processing benefits by voucher, girocheque and payable order, and the value to the Post Office of this business, were regarded by ministers as commercially confidential. Applications for the approval of pesticides were not published until that approval was given, which some might think was rather late in the day if there were public concern about a particular pesticide.

From a government perspective, it is easy to understand a reluctance to answer particular types of question – not least because answering one question may produce a flood of questions on a sensitive topic. Nevertheless, MPs find a minister's refusal to answer extremely frustrating when it prevents them pursuing a subject that they see as of political or constituency importance. If a minister refuses to provide information on a particular subject for a stated reason it usually also prevents the same question being asked for the remainder of the session, which adds to the frustration.

The Public Administration Select Committee reports from time to time on ministerial accountability through PQs, following up questions to which ministers refused to give an answer (its report of July 2002 contained a 35-page list of such questions) and asking for the relevant part of the code to be cited in each case.

However, the content of answers remains a matter for ministers; successive Speakers have refused to comment on the ways in which ministers answer – or avoid answering – and many back-benchers feel that it is unfair that ministers can decide without any independent check to refuse to answer particular questions that everyone accepts come within their responsibilities. There are also occasions when an answer is given that is rather less than helpful, as when a question seeks the timing of some publication or event, and the answer is 'shortly' or 'in due course'; or when a reply simply refers the questioner to a previous answer to a slightly different question.

It is important to set such concerns against the reality that, if questions really are a means of holding the government to account, one cannot expect them always to be a friendly volunteering of information. And, of course, questions – and especially oral questions – are an important dimension of the party clash between opposition and government.

Cost

Ministers may refuse to provide an answer to a PQ if the cost of doing so would exceed a certain amount, known as the 'advisory cost limit'. In April 2002, this was raised from £550 to £600. A minister's 'disproportionate cost' answer can be a source of annoyance to MPs: not only may they think that the expenditure of, say £800, is not excessive if it puts important information in the public domain; they may also suspect that estimating the cost of answering is a fairly rough and ready business, and that if ministers wanted to answer the question, they would do so (and indeed a minister may decide that a question is to be answered irrespective of cost). However, the government's internal guidance emphasises that even if to give a full answer would cost more than the limit, any readily available information should be given.

In April 2002, the Treasury estimated the average cost of answering a written question at £129 and of answering an oral question at £299. These figures are averages, not the price tag of each question; it does not cost very much to reply 'No' to a question asking for a particular document to be published, for example. The higher cost of answering oral questions is because of the additional research and briefing needed for possible supplementaries (see below), so the extra cost is more that of defending the minister's position than of actually answering the question.

The cost of answering is also often used against the more assiduous questioners. In the 2001–02 session, the Conservative MP for Buckingham, John Bercow, tabled only four oral questions but 4,206 written questions (the next place went to Andrew Turner, the Conservative MP for the Isle of Wight, who tabled fifteen oral and 1,337 written questions). It was perhaps not surprising that Mr Bercow's questioning was described by his opponents as 'costing the taxpayer half a million pounds' rather than 'calling ministers to account'.

Oral questions

Civil Service guidance for answering oral PQs describes Question Time as:

> usually the highest profile Parliamentary occasion of the month as Members can question Ministers on any topic for which they are responsible, to seek facts and to challenge and question Government policy. Supplementary Questions in particular are used by opposition Members to raise matters with the aim of putting Ministers on the defensive.

Many questions for oral answer receive a written reply, either because time runs out before they are reached or because the MP concerned cannot in the event be in the House that day and asks for a written rather than an oral reply.

But even though oral questions account for a relatively small part of the total, Question Time, when they are answered, is one of the liveliest parts of the parliamentary day, and Prime Minister's Questions (PMQs) each Wednesday is normally the highlight of the week.

Question Time

Question Time takes place every day except a Friday and begins immediately after prayers are over and any private business (see page 138) has been

Note: The shuffle of oral questions for answer on the following dates will take place on Monday 1 September:

Monday 8 September—Defence

Tuesday 9 September—Scotland; Advocate General; Constitutional Affairs; Leader of the House and House of Commons Commission

Wednesday 10 September—Northern Ireland; Prime Minister

Mon. 8 Sept	Tues. 9 Sept	Wed. 10 Sept	Thurs. 11 Sept
Defence	Scotland Advocate General[2] Constitutional Affairs[3] Leader of the House and House of Commons Commission[4]	Northern Ireland Prime Minister[5]	Education and Skills Solicitor General[6]
Last tabling at 12.30 for			
Education and Skills Solicitor General[1]	*Culture, Media and Sport Church Commissioners, Public Accounts Commission and Speaker's Committee on the Electoral Commission Wales*	*Health*	*Prime Minister*

Mon. 15 Sept	Tues. 16 Sept	Wed. 17 Sept	Thurs. 18 Sept
Culture, Media and Sport Church Commissioners, Public Accounts Commission and Speaker's Committee on the Electoral Commission[7]	Health	Wales Prime Minister[5]	Trade and Industry Minister for Women[8]
Last tabling at 12.30 for			
Trade and Industry Minister for Women			

Note: The shuffle of oral questions for answer on the following dates will take place on Wednesday 8 October:

Tuesday 14 October—Foreign and Commonwealth Office   **Wednesday 15 October**—International Development; Prime Minister   **Thursday 16 October**—Treasury

Tues. 14 Oct	Wed. 15 Oct	Thurs. 16 Oct
Foreign and Commonwealth Office	**International Development Prime Minister**[5]	**Treasury**
Last tabling at 12.30 for		
Work and Pensions	*Transport Cabinet Office*[9]	*Deputy Prime Minister Prime Minister*

Mon. 20 Oct	Tues. 21 Oct	Wed. 22 Oct	Thurs. 23 Oct
Work and Pensions	**Transport Cabinet Office**[8,9]	**Deputy Prime Minister Prime Minister**[5]	**Environment, Food and Rural Affairs**
Last tabling at 12.30 for			
Environment, Food and Rural Affairs Scotland Advocate General	*Home Office Northern Ireland*	*Constitutional Affairs Leader of the House and House of Commons Commission*[4]	*Prime Minister*

The House of Commons oral question rota for a typical fortnight
Source: The House of Commons 2003

disposed of. This means that on Mondays it runs from about 2.35 p.m. to 3.30 p.m., and on Tuesdays, Wednesdays and Thursdays from about 11.35 a.m. to 12.30 p.m.

The ministers from each government department answer questions every four weeks according to a rota that the government itself decides. Thus, when in May 1997 Tony Blair decided that he would answer questions for half an hour on Wednesdays rather than for a quarter of an hour on Tuesdays and Thursdays as his predecessors had done, it required no decision of the House to make the change. Similarly, when the Department of Constitutional Affairs was created in June 2003, the government simply revised the rota to provide a slot for the new department.

The change in the arrangements for PMQs was strongly criticised by the opposition, and indeed in June 2002 the Procedure Committee recommended that any future change should be open to debate and subject to the formal decision of the House, which will thus be seen to have 'ownership of its procedures'.

The rota for a typical fortnight appears on pages 286 and 287.

The day on which a department is top for questions can be a testing time for ministers answering at the despatch box, but it can also be a shop window for the department concerned, in which ministers have the opportunity of emphasising their successes and putting their interpretation of events on the record. The balance between the two depends on how quick ministers are on their feet, how well they prepare and how sharp opposition MPs are with their supplementaries.

Tabling oral questions

For many years, oral PQs had to be tabled ten sitting days (which usually meant a calendar fortnight) before the day for answer. However, in June 2002 the Procedure Committee concluded that this was 'a major barrier to the effective operation of questions' in that it often prevented Question Time dealing with the issues of the day; a question tabled a fortnight earlier might well be stale by the time it was answered. The committee thought that the only defence of the fortnight's notice was that it allowed civil servants longer to brief their ministers, and recommended that the period of notice should be reduced from ten to three sitting days. This was endorsed by the Modernisation Committee, approved by the House, and came into force in January 2003.

An MP can now table a PQ for oral answer any time after the previous Question Time for a particular department up to 12.30 p.m. three sitting days before that department's next Question time; so, if the department is top for questions on a Tuesday, questions have to be tabled by 12.30 p.m. the previous Wednesday. For questions to the Secretaries of State for Northern Ireland,

Scotland and Wales the notice period is five days because of the extra complication of there being devolved administrations in those parts of the UK. An MP may table only one oral question to a department on any one day, and no more than two in total on that day (which, for example, allows an MP to have a question to the Prime Minister as well as to the Secretary of State answering the same day).

Questions are tabled to the responsible Secretary of State or senior Commons minister in a department if the Secretary of State is in the Lords, rather than to an individual minister within a department, although there are other slots such as those for the Leader of the House and the Minister for Women.

As well as Question Time in the House, oral questions may be asked at some sittings of the Scottish, Welsh and Northern Ireland Grand Committees (see page 270), although these are not frequent occurrences. An interesting innovation has been the introduction of cross-cutting oral Question Times in Westminster Hall, in which questions are about a subject that involves a number of departments rather than about the responsibilities of a single department. On 17 July 2003, for example, a cross-cutting session on domestic violence involved ministers from the Home Office, the Department of Health, the Department for Education and Skills, the Department for Constitutional Affairs and the Office of the Deputy Prime Minister. Westminster Hall Question Times have also covered youth, drugs and older people.

Whatever the forum, MPs must table questions in writing, either personally with the clerks in the Table Office (a small room behind the Speaker's Chair), or by post. Since January 2003 they have also been able to send questions in by e-mail, using a system of authentication. By April 2003, 164 members had registered for this method of tabling questions, although only ninety-five had used the system. In its first three months of operation, electronic tabling accounted for 15 percent of questions, although half of the questions tabled in this way came from the fourteen MPs who had each tabled more than 100 questions electronically.

An MP's question is examined by one of the clerks, who checks that it does not breach any of the rules for questions (see page 282), and who will where possible suggest to the MP how to avoid breaching the rules, or perhaps how to put the question in a more effective form. As well as conforming to the rules that operate for all questions, an oral question must be a single question (rather than having two or more sub-questions); and, except in the case of questions to the Prime Minister (see below), they must be precise enough to give an indication of the intended supplementary – open questions are not allowed.

Just after 12.30 p.m. on the last tabling day, there is a random computer shuffle of the questions that have been tabled to the department or departments concerned. The successful questions are printed next morning in the blue pages of the Vote bundle (see page 153) in the order in which they will be called on the day. Not all questions tabled are printed; if a single department is to answer for the whole of Question Time (in practice fifty-five minutes) then twenty-five questions to that department will be printed. If the slot is for forty-five or fifty minutes, twenty will be printed, and so on down to a ten-minute slot, for which eight questions will be printed. The remainder are treated as 'lost', are not printed and do not receive answers.

If a question is put down to one government department but is more properly the responsibility of another, it will be transferred and answered by a minister from the second department. This does not matter for written questions, but an MP who has an oral question that is transferred after the shuffle has taken place will lose the opportunity to ask the question orally. When this happens it often produces a row; but it is a matter within the discretion of the government, and the Speaker will not intervene, although he has deprecated moving questions where there is some shared responsibility.

Both government and opposition parties are keen to get their MPs to table questions, because it shortens the odds of their party being successful in the shuffle and so beginning a question exchange with a friendly (or, for the opposition, a critical) supplementary. An opposition front-bench team will also identify themes it wants to raise in a forthcoming Question Time and encourage its back-benchers to table questions on these subjects.

Question Time: on the day

The Speaker announces 'Questions to the Secretary of State for the Home Department' (or whichever department is top), 'Mr Tony McWalter' (or whoever). Mr McWalter simply says 'Number One, Mr Speaker' (there is no point in reading out the question as it is printed on the Order of Business), and the minister gets up to give his reply. Mr McWalter is then called to ask a supplementary question, to which the minister replies. Two or three (or more) back-benchers (called alternately from each side of the Chamber) then ask supplementaries. If the subject is an important one, the opposition shadow minister may ask the final supplementary, and the Speaker calls the name of the next MP with a question down for answer. As we saw in Chapter 3 (page 44), the number of supplementaries called is entirely a matter for the Speaker; on a subject on which the government is vulnerable, calling more MPs to put supplementaries may put the minister under greater pressure; conversely, if fewer supplementaries are called, more questions on the Order of Business will be reached.

All the ministers in a department – in a large department, the secretary of state, two ministers of state and two junior ministers (parliamentary under-secretaries) – will be present for their slot at Question Time. Which questions

Oral Questions to the Minister of State, Department for International Development
continued

★14 **Derek Wyatt** (Sittingbourne & Sheppey):   What proposals the Secretary of State will put forward at the WTO meeting in Cancun to reduce tariff barriers between the EU and third world countries.   (124285)

★15 **Dr Nick Palmer** (Broxtowe):   What assessment the Secretary of State has made of progress in rebuilding Afghanistan.   (124286)

At 12 noon

Oral Questions to the Prime Minister

Unless otherwise indicated the Members listed below will ask a question without notice.

★Q1 **Mr Russell Brown** (Dumfries):   If he will list his official engagements for Wednesday 9th July.   (124287)

★Q2 **Michael Fabricant** (Lichfield):   (124288)

★Q3 **Hugh Bayley** (City of York):   (124289)

★Q4 **Mr Ian Liddell-Grainger** (Bridgwater):   (124290)

★Q5 **David Winnick** (Walsall North):   (124291)

★Q6 **Dr Andrew Murrison** (Westbury):   (124292)

★Q7 **Mr Crispin Blunt** (Reigate):   (124293)

★Q8 **John Barrett** (Edinburgh West):   (124294)

★Q9 **Tom Cox** (Tooting):   What plans he has to visit Cyprus to meet the President of Cyprus.   (124295)

★Q10 **Dr Doug Naysmith** (Bristol North West):   (124296)

★Q11 **Mr Andrew Turner** (Isle of Wight):   (124297)

★Q12 **Mr Hilton Dawson** (Lancaster & Wyre):   What plans he has to visit the Lancaster and Wyre constituency.   (124298)

★Q13 **Geraint Davies** (Croydon Central):   (124299)

★Q14 **Huw Irranca-Davies** (Ogmore):   (124300)

Oral Questions on the Commons Order of Business
Source: House of Commons 2003

Zimbabwe

5. **Chris Grayling** (Epsom and Ewell): What recent assessment he has made of the level of humanitarian aid reaching the people of Zimbabwe. [124276]

The Minister of State, Department for International Development (Hilary Benn): Most of the maize crop has been harvested in Zimbabwe and many areas of the country now have food. The maize crop is up 61 per cent. on last year but nevertheless remains at less than half the national requirement. The United Nations and non-governmental organisations are still feeding around 2 million people in areas where there has been no crop and those who remain vulnerable, including unemployed farm workers, children, the elderly and the chronically ill. These areas and groups will require food throughout the year. The UN predicts that 5.5 million people in Zimbabwe will require humanitarian assistance again by the end of the year.

Chris Grayling: Earlier this year, I raised with the then Under-Secretary during an Adjournment debate several concerns that had been put to me by aid workers in rural Zimbabwe. Since then, I have received a full response from both the Department and Save the Children, but none the less the concerns that were raised with me remain. Will the Minister, in his new brief, read what was said in that debate and keep a watchful eye on the situation to ensure that no further action needs to be taken in the future?

Hilary Benn: I am happy to give the hon. Gentleman that undertaking. If it would be helpful, I shall be happy to meet him so that we may discuss the issues.

Mr. Tom Clarke (Coatbridge and Chryston): Does my hon. Friend agree that some of the poorest people who live in the poorest countries should never be penalised because of some of the appalling people who lead them?

Hilary Benn: I do agree with my right hon. Friend. The UK has been playing such an important role as the second largest donor of humanitarian support to the people in Zimbabwe precisely because the collapse of the country and its Government, and the destruction that that Government have brought on the people of that country, should not stand in the way of our doing all that we can. It is a sign of the desperate state of affairs that two thirds of this year's humanitarian and food support will be provided by the international community. The Government of Zimbabwe will provide only one third because they are increasingly proving themselves to be incapable of meeting the needs of their people.

Several hon. Members *rose—*

Mr. Speaker: Order. There is a great deal of noise in the Chamber, which is unfair to hon. Members who are asking questions.

Dr. Jenny Tonge (Richmond Park): Some of us met the mayor of Harare last week for an appraisal of the humanitarian situation in Zimbabwe. He knew that he would be arrested on his return, and he was. The mayor and NGOs in Zimbabwe report not only that food is being distributed according to party loyalty, but that seeds and tools for next year's crops are not being distributed in areas controlled by the Movement for Democratic Change. Is it not time for us all to stop playing the white colonial card and to persuade the United Nations to send monitors to Zimbabwe to regulate the humanitarian situation and the abuse of human rights that is going on?

Hon. Members: Oh, come on!

Mr. Speaker: Order. I call the Minister.

Hilary Benn: I share the hon. Lady's concern about what has happened to the mayor of Harare. She will be aware that strict procedures are in place to ensure that the humanitarian aid that we and other members of the international community provide is not distributed for political purposes, although I understand her concerns about the way in which the one third that is distributed by the Government of Zimbabwe is used. If there are any complaints or concerns about the way in which our support or the multilateral support is distributed, I would be keen to receive them. I undertake to examine the matter for the hon. Lady.

David Taylor (North-West Leicestershire): The humanitarian relief has so far tended to be focused on rural areas. Will the Minister comment on the needs of the urban areas of Harare and Bulawayo in which the poorest people have neither the cash to buy food nor the prospect of crops in leaner times? That has an especially serious effect on many young people.

Hilary Benn: My hon. Friend is right to draw attention to the fact that there is a problem in cities as well as rural areas. Of the 5.5 million people who we estimate will need help with food again by the end of the year, 4.4 million will be in rural areas and 1.1 million will be in cities, which demonstrates that the crisis affects all Zimbabweans.

Mrs. Caroline Spelman (Meriden): Frankly, it beggars belief that the Government have now deemed Zimbabwe safe for asylum seekers to return to. The Minister just told the House that almost half the population still need food aid, and there are daily reports of violent oppression. How can the hon. Gentleman seriously expect asylum seekers to follow the Home Office advice to return voluntarily?

Hilary Benn: Well, returning voluntarily is, by definition, a matter of choice for the individuals concerned. They must make that judgment based on their assessment of the situation. I do not think that there is a contradiction in that. Because of the seriousness of the situation in Zimbabwe, we and the international community have taken steps, but in the end, the process of change has to come from within that country, because that is the only way in which a solution to the catastrophe will be found.

Hansard report of Question Time on 9th July 2003
Source: House of Commons 2003

PRIME MINISTER

The Prime Minister was asked—

Engagements

Q1. [124287] **Mr. Russell Brown** (Dumfries): If he will list his official engagements for Wednesday 9 July.

The Prime Minister (Mr. Tony Blair): This morning I had meetings with ministerial colleagues and others. In addition to my duties in the House, I will have further such meetings later today.

Mr. Brown: An excellent new Macmillan cancer centre is soon to open in Dumfries and Galloway Royal infirmary. At the last meeting of the all-party group on cancer, much was said about that kind of investment in cancer care. However, the group did express concern that we need additional cancer nurses or nurses who are better trained in cancer care. Keeping in mind that around 30 per cent. of the population will experience a cancer-related illness in their lifetime, does the Prime Minister feel that we need more training that includes a specific module on cancer care?

The Prime Minister: I agree entirely with my hon. Friend. I pay tribute to the excellent work by Macmillan Cancer Relief. He is right to say that we need to train more cancer nurses. That is why we are making such a huge investment in our national health service at the present time. As a result of that extra investment, people are being diagnosed quicker and treated quicker. More money is being invested. Over the past few years, cancer deaths in this country have fallen by almost 9 per cent. That is why it is important that that extra investment keeps going into our national health service.

Mr. Iain Duncan Smith (Chingford and Woodford Green): The Chairman of the Foreign Affairs Committee says that the Prime Minister should apologise to Parliament for misrepresenting the status of the second dossier. Will he do that now?

The Prime Minister: The Foreign Secretary has already apologised on behalf of the whole Government for the mistake that was made. I do not accept, in any shape or form, that the information in that second briefing was wrong. Actually, those parts of it that were based on intelligence were, indeed, based on intelligence.

Mr. Duncan Smith: Let me remind the Prime Minister what the report said. It said that the Prime Minister, in saying that the report was "further intelligence",

"misrepresented its status and . . . made a bad situation worse."

The Chairman went on to say that when a Minister misleads Parliament, even inadvertently, he should come to the House of Commons and apologise. Why is it that, for this Prime Minister, sorry seems to be the hardest word?

The Prime Minister: On 10 February, we made it quite clear that we acknowledged the mistake that one part of the briefing paper—one part of it—should have been sourced to a written record of a review that was published some time before. That part of it that was expressed to be based on intelligence was, indeed, based on intelligence. So I am afraid that I do not accept that Parliament was misled in any way at all.

Let me just say this to the right hon. Gentleman. The intelligence on which we based both the September dossier and that February briefing was intelligence that was specifically shared with him by our intelligence services. If he is now disputing any of that intelligence, perhaps he would say so.

Mr. Duncan Smith: The Prime Minister knows I was given no sight of that dossier. I was not even contacted about it. The first I knew about that dossier in February was when I found out about it in the newspapers, so he can retract that for a start. *[Interruption.]* Oh yes. Until the Prime Minister accepts that he misrepresented the status of the second dossier to Parliament and apologises, trust in him will plummet and no one will believe a word he says anymore.

The Prime Minister: First, my understanding is that the right hon. Gentleman was briefed on Iraq by the Chairman of the Joint Intelligence Committee on 18 September and again on 12 February. I have said to him that the intelligence that we put forward was shared with him.

Hon. Members: Retract!

Mr. Speaker: Order. Mr. Bacon, it is not for you to shout at the Prime Minister. *[Interruption.]* Order. I always pick out the one who is loudest.

The Prime Minister: I said that the intelligence on which we based both the dossier and the February briefing was shared with the Leader of the Opposition at briefings on 18 September and 12 February. That intelligence was not, as the shadow Foreign Secretary keeps saying, given to the Leader of the Opposition orally by me; it was given by the intelligence services. Perhaps he would just confirm whether that is right or wrong.

Hon Members: Up!

Mr. Speaker: Order. I call Mr. Khabra.

Mr. Piara S. Khabra (Ealing, Southall): In light of the recent case of Dame Shirley Porter allegedly owing Westminster council £37 million, may I ask the Prime Minister whether the Government are able to take any action to ensure that offshore assets can be made more transparent?

The Prime Minister: I want to be careful how I answer that because there may be legal proceedings on that subject, but I can simply say that I shall certainly look into the matter and get back to my hon. Friend.

Mr. Charles Kennedy (Ross, Skye and Inverness, West): On a previous occasion the Prime Minister replied to me that the nine UK citizens being held at Camp Delta could not remain there indefinitely, but he must recognise equally that he cannot give that reply indefinitely. How long must UK citizens be left to languish in this legal no-man's-land?

The Prime Minister: I agree that obviously there has to be a point in time when the issue is brought to an end. As the right hon. Gentleman knows, the United States is now talking about the right method by which to try anybody against whom charges would be brought. We will make active representations to the United States—indeed, we are already doing so—to make absolutely sure that any such trial will take place in accordance with proper international law.

Mr. Kennedy: Since I last raised the matter with the Prime Minister, those representations to the American authorities have fallen on deaf ears. Two of these British citizens may imminently face very serious charges but, he must surely acknowledge, they are not aware of what those charges are and they will be tried in a military tribunal. If they agree to plead guilty, they may be able to escape the death penalty, but if they do not, and are found guilty, they could face the death penalty. If they are not found guilty, the Americans could still choose to detain them as potential combatants. Just how long will the Prime Minister find that state of affairs acceptable, and what does that say for British influence, which he heralds, over the Americans?

The Prime Minister: It is of course important that the commission that tries these people is conducted according to proper rules. Those rules have not yet been drawn up, and it is precisely for that reason that we are making active representations, and our opposition to the death penalty is well known.

Geraint Davies (Croydon, Central): On that point, my constituent, Feroz Abbasi, has been held in Guantanamo bay for 18 months without charge, and he now faces the prospect of a military tribunal in which he will not be able to appoint his own defence lawyer or to cross-examine prosecution witnesses, and he may face the death penalty following a decision behind closed doors.

Have the Government applied for the repatriation of my constituent to face a fair trial in Britain, and will my right hon. Friend now press to have all the evidence against Feroz Abbasi supplied to the Government, so that we may press charges and apply for an extradition order under our terrorism legislation? Feroz Abbasi could then face a fair trial and be punished if guilty, and the rule of law and human rights would prevail.

The Prime Minister: What my hon. Friend says must be right. If charges are brought, they must be proved in accordance with proper rules of evidence. As he rightly says, the charges are serious. It is worth remembering that the allegations revolve around what happened in Afghanistan some time ago, when British and American troops were putting their lives at risk there. However, I entirely agree with my hon. Friend—there must be no question about this at all. Any commission or tribunal

that tries these men must be conducted in accordance with proper canons of law so that a fair trial takes place and is seen to take place.

Q2. [124288] **Michael Fabricant** (Lichfield): On another matter, when the Prime Minister talked about delivery targets last Thursday, he said:

"Maybe we have too many".

What delivery targets would the Prime Minister scrap, and what target has he set for delivering that?

The Prime Minister: Actually, we have reduced to a third the original number of targets in the first comprehensive spending review. I shall tell the hon. Gentleman about the targets that I would not scrap but which, apparently, the Conservatives would—[*Interruption.*] Oh yes, we will certainly not scrap targets for reducing waiting times and waiting lists for patients. We will not scrap our target for 50,000 extra nurses and we will not scrap our targets for extra investment in schools and hospitals. We will not do so because it is right that that investment is made.

Q3. [124289] **Hugh Bayley** (City of York): Given that so much crime is fuelled by drug addiction, even in a place like York, which has 250 drug addicts in rehabilitation at any one time, what are the Government doing to expand their range of policies to tackle drug abuse and fund the many agencies involved in delivering that strategy?

The Prime Minister: First, we are increasing investment by about half a billion pounds over the next few years. We are also increasing the use of drug treatment and testing orders, and are trying to make sure by increasing the number of people who receive drug treatment for their drug abuse that we reduce the prevalence of the link between drug abuse and crime. My hon. Friend is right—the link between drugs and crime is hugely important, which is precisely why we are making additional investment in both the criminal justice system and drug treatment—[*Interruption.*]

Mr. Iain Duncan Smith (Chingford and Woodford Green): They are cheering him now, but they will be voting against him tomorrow. After last night's massive Labour rebellion on foundation hospitals, can the Prime Minister say whether he intends to press ahead with the legislation on top-up fees?

The Prime Minister: We remain absolutely committed to the Government's position on that issue.

Mr. Duncan Smith: Well, can the Prime Minister now tell the House whether he intends to rely on the votes of Scottish Labour MPs, even though top-up fees, like foundation hospitals, have been rejected by his own party in Scotland?

The Prime Minister: I find it absolutely extraordinary that the right hon. Gentleman should say that Scottish and Welsh MPs are not able to vote on UK legislation passed in this House—[*Interruption.*] This is the UK Parliament, and if he is saying that the position of the Conservative party is that Scottish and Welsh MPs can no longer vote on English business, is it also his position that, if devolution is up and running again in Northern Ireland, Northern Ireland MPs cannot vote on it?

Mr. Duncan Smith: The Prime Minister is reduced to getting MPs who will not even be affected by this change to drive through his legislation for England. He is ploughing on, despite the fact that every single Labour MP stood on a manifesto that said that they would not introduce top-up fees. Is that not the reason why he has lost the trust of both the British people and, increasingly, his own party? Nobody believes a word he says any more.

The Prime Minister: We now have as official Conservative policy the belief that no one from Scotland, Wales or, indeed, if devolution is up and running, Northern Ireland, can vote on English issues—and they call themselves the Conservative and Unionist party. I think that the right hon. Gentleman needs to think that one through a little more carefully.

As for university finance, let me tell the right hon. Gentleman what would be a disaster—cutting £500 million off the university budget and, according to the higher education institute, having half a million fewer students by 2010. He wants fewer people going to worse-funded universities, which would be a disaster for the country.

they answer will depend on their particular responsibilities within the department, but the secretary of state will usually take the biggest political subjects.

The list of questions on the Order of Business may not be followed exactly. With the Speaker's permission, a minister may group similar questions for answer if they are reasonably close together on the list, and the MPs who tabled those questions are called first to ask supplementaries. If an MP is unable to be present, he or she may withdraw a question, or convert it from an oral to a written question (known as 'unstarring' because oral questions are denoted by a star against them on the Order of Business).

The art of the supplementary

If Question Time is seen as a duel, the tabling of the question and the minister's often low-key reply are rather like two fencers squaring up to each other before the swords clash. The real conflict of Question Time is in the supplementaries. Thus an opposition MP may table a question that simply asks the Home Secretary how many police officers there are in England. The Home Secretary gives the figure, and the MP then asks 'But is the right honourable member aware that in the police authority that covers my constituency police numbers have fallen by 9 percent over the last three years, and violent crime has increased by 13 percent? Doesn't that demonstrate that the government is soft on crime? Will the Home Secretary tell my constituents why he is not committed to improving their safety?' This not only makes the political point on behalf of the MP's party but will also play well in the MP's local press.

A government back-bencher may table exactly the same question, but the supplementary will be very different: 'Will the Home Secretary accept the thanks of my constituents for the government's commitment to beating crime, for extra officers on the beat, and for the reduction of [some category of crime that has gone down rather than up]?'

Short and sharp

By comparison with the *tabling* of oral and written questions, there are very few rules for oral supplementaries. If they are evidently wide of the original question, or if they refer to matters *sub judice* (see page 274), or if they clearly have nothing to do with the minister's responsibilities, the Speaker will call the MP to order. However, there is a Catch-22 about this: it is not easy to tell that a supplementary is out of order until the MP is a fair way through asking it, although one type of disorderly supplementary from the government side is usually spotted very quickly: inviting the minister to comment on the policies of the opposition. Ministers are responsible for the government's policies, not those of their opponents. Even in the more knockabout atmosphere of Prime Minister's Questions, the Speaker has stopped the Prime Minister responding overtly to supplementaries that seek criticism of Conservative or Liberal Democrat policies.

Question Time is above all a political exchange; it is not about seeking information, which is what written questions are for. Oral questions are about exposing and criticising, or helping and supporting. This means that there is a tendency for both supplementary questions and ministers' replies to be too long. In its major survey of parliamentary questions in June 2002, the Procedure Committee said:

> We strongly support Mr Speaker in his attempts to restrain the prolixity of some Members. Long, rambling questions are counter-productive, whilst long, rambling answers are an abuse of the time of the House . . . We believe that the Chair should take a pro-active role in seeking to change the culture of Question Time and foster more incisive, tightly focused exchanges.

The committee also felt that it was too easy for ministers to brush off awkward questions with vague answers, and it recommended that the MP who tabled the question should be able to ask a second supplementary after other MPs had been called.

Long supplementaries are tempting as a way of getting one's point on the record, but they also make things much easier for ministers. Not only is there plenty of time to turn to the relevant part of the briefing file for ammunition in reply, but long supplementaries are less focused and less likely to hit the target. Ministers are much less comfortable with the classic sharp supplementaries like 'Why?' or 'How much?' or 'How many?'

Preparing for Question Time

For the government, Question Time is an opportunity to tell the story the way ministers see it. It can also be a high-risk occasion, and government departments prepare very carefully for their 'top day'. Ministers will have had briefing meetings with their civil servants, and each minister will take into the Chamber a ring-binder with the answer he or she is to give to each question, together with a survival pack of information and briefing, according to a fairly standard template used by the Civil Service:

▲ *The reason for the question*: why is the MP asking it? Is there a particular constituency focus? What has he or she raised with the department recently?
[When a government MP puts down a question, he or she will often helpfully let the department know what is behind it, or what he or she plans as a supplementary question. Opposition MPs will also do this on occasion, especially if their intention is to flag up some issue of constituency concern rather than to attack the government.]
▲ *Elephant traps*: any information that the minister should know about potential gaps in the policy or problems with the figures on the main issues likely to be raised.
▲ *Positive/defensive*: three or four key best positive lines and three or four key defensive lines to take on the main issue covering government achievements and positive activity in the area of policy, and defending against the most likely lines of criticism.
▲ *Key background facts and figures* and, with a page for each issue, *other issues that may be raised* with bullet point lines to take.
▲ *Key quotes*: any useful third-party endorsements or supportive comments from members of the opposition.

The official Opposition team shadowing the government department will also lay its plans for Question Time, highlighting areas where it believes the government is open to criticism and seeking the help of back-benchers to reinforce the line being taken by the front-bench team.

When a government department answers oral questions, at least it knows what subjects are going to be raised, because specific questions have been put down. This is rarely the case in Prime Minister's Questions. Let us now look at one of the highest-profile parliamentary occasions.

Prime Minister's Questions

The Prime Minister answers for half an hour every Wednesday from 12 noon to 12.30 p.m. Only the top fifteen questions in the shuffle are printed, and the vast majority are in the form 'If he will list his official engagements for [Wednesday 9th July]'. Only the first such question is printed out in full on the Order of Business; if other MPs want to ask the same question, their names alone are printed alongside the question numbers.

Why the 'engagements question'?

It may seem strange that so many MPs want to ask the Prime Minister what he happens to be doing on a particular Wednesday. The reason is historical, but the habit persists even though in practice it is not really necessary. Thirty and more years ago, the Prime Minister of the day would transfer a specific question to the relevant secretary of state if the latter had ministerial responsibility for the subject, and the MP concerned would lose the chance of an oral question to the Prime Minister. Prime Ministers are in a sense responsible for everything, but there are relatively few things for which they have *specific* responsibility and a departmental minister does not; examples include coordination between government departments, sacking and appointing ministers, setting up Cabinet committees, and the intelligence services as a whole.

So the 'transfer-proof' question was devised: either to ask the Prime Minister his official engagements for the day, or a related open question – whether he would visit some particular place (usually the questioner's constituency) or country. When she became Prime Minister, Margaret Thatcher indicated that she would not transfer specific questions, as did John Major and Tony Blair when they came to office. However, the open question persisted for two reasons. It allowed MPs to raise the issue of the moment even though the question had been tabled a fortnight before; and it was easy – no thought had to be given to constructing some cunning question when it was odds-against that it would be successful in the shuffle. And even though the period of notice has shortened from ten sitting days to three with the express purpose of allowing more topical questions, the 'engagements question' still flourishes.

Prime Minister's Questions: on the day

As for departmental questions, the Speaker calls (say) 'Mr Crispin Blunt'; Mr Blunt stands up and says 'Number One, Mr Speaker'. The Prime Minister gives the standard response: 'This morning I had meetings with ministerial colleagues and others. In addition to my duties in this House, I shall have further such meetings later today'. Mr Blunt is then able to ask a supplementary on anything that is the responsibility of the government. After the Prime Minister has replied, the Speaker will call other MPs who were successful in the shuffle, interspersed with other back-benchers. Unlike departmental questions, MPs whose names are on the Order of Business simply ask their supplementary; they do not go through the process of calling out the number and having the Prime Minister repeat his original answer.

If the Leader of the Opposition rises, the Speaker will call him; he has a normal allocation of six questions in PMQs, which he may take in groups of three on two different themes. The leader of the Liberal Democrats gets two supplementaries.

Questions in PMQs are the usual mixture of the supportive and the critical, but the main event is the gladiatorial contest between the Prime Minister and the Leader of the Opposition. The House is full, noisy and partisan, which raises the stakes; and national newspapers carry 'post-match' comment the next day, sometimes rating the encounter in terms of goals scored or punches landed. The Prime Minister of the day has a built-in advantage; he is centre-stage for the whole play, while the Leader of the Opposition has only two scenes; and the Prime Minister can build on questions from his own back-benchers to project a positive presentation of government policy and achievements.

Even those who criticise PMQs often tend to be fascinated by the occasion; in a highly political House it distils the clash between government and opposition. However, PMQs are about putting the Prime Minister under political pressure rather than exploring policies and intentions; and, in this respect, the new format of the Prime Minister appearing before the Liaison Committee (see page 316) is a valuable innovation.

On pages 291–295, we reproduce the oral questions on the Order of Business for 9 July 2003, together with the *Hansard* report of the last oral to the Minister of State for Overseas Development (not the Secretary of State, as Baroness Amos was a member of the House of Lords) and the first few minutes of Prime Minister's Questions.

The international development oral on Zimbabwe was only the fifth reached in the twenty-five minutes available. After the Conservative Chris Grayling, the Speaker called Tom Clarke, who had been shadow Secretary of State for International Development when Labour were in opposition, then Jenny Tonge, the Liberal Democrat spokesperson on international development. After David Taylor from the government back benches, the Speaker then called Caroline Spelman, the shadow secretary of state. The House was filling up for PMQs, with the level of noise rising, as shown by the Speaker's intervention.

The first question to the Prime Minister was from the Labour member Russell Brown, who asked a non-partisan supplementary with a constituency basis. The Leader of the Opposition then intervened on an issue of the moment (this was shortly after the publication of the Foreign Affairs Select Committee's report on the decision to go to war in Iraq). After a question from the Labour back-bencher Piara Khabra, the leader of the Liberal Democrats asked his two questions. Two MPs (as it happened, one Conservative and one Labour) who had come out second and third in the shuffle for PMQs then got their chance before the Leader of the Opposition came back for his second trio of questions, on university top-up fees.

It was a fairly typical PMQs, with longish questions and answers making political points rather than seeking or providing information; the mixture of hot current issues and important but less contentious subjects; and the gladiatorial exchanges between the party leaders.

Urgent questions

On any sitting day, an MP can seek the Speaker's leave to ask an urgent question. These were formerly known as 'private notice questions' or PNQs because notice of them was given directly to the Speaker and not printed on the Order Paper as for other oral questions. The MP must make a request before 10.00 a.m. on a day when the House sits at 11.30 a.m. (before noon on a Monday), and the Speaker must be satisfied that the matter is of public importance and is genuinely urgent. If he grants the application, warning is displayed on the television annunciators around the parliamentary estate, and the MP concerned is called to ask the question at the end of Question Time (or, on a Friday, at 11.00 a.m., interrupting the business then under way).

The Speaker's power to grant an urgent question is a significant one. It brings a minister to the House at very short notice to answer on something on which the government may be in some disarray and is still deciding how to respond to a problem that may have arisen only a few hours before. The Speaker does not usually allow questioning to run for as long as for ministerial statements, but he has absolute discretion, and on major issues the minister concerned has been exposed to questioning for up to an hour.

In the 2001–02 session, the Speaker granted ten urgent questions. In 2003, subjects included the row in NATO over the impending war with Iraq, primary school tests and targets (where the secretary of state had announced changes in a press statement that morning, but the granting of an urgent question meant that he had to come to the House to answer questions), humanitarian aid in Iraq, and a security breach at Sizewell nuclear power station. In November 2002, the Leader of the Opposition was granted an urgent question on the firefighters' dispute, which brought the Prime Minister to the despatch box to answer.

The business question every Thursday at 12.30 p.m., in which the shadow Leader of the House asks the Leader of the House to announce forthcoming business in the House, is technically an urgent question, although of a specialised type. The Leader of the House lists the items of business, usually firm for the following week, more provisional for the week after, and then answers questions. Strictly speaking, these must relate to the forthcoming business, but they are often on more general political matters; and it does not take much ingenuity to ask for a debate on 'the government's failure to deliver on targets' or on 'the government's successes in carrying through public service reform'.

Questions answered at the end of Question Time

A minister may choose to answer an oral question not as it is reached during Question Time but at the end of oral questions (3.30 p.m. on Mondays, 12.30

p.m. on Tuesdays, Wednesdays and Thursdays). This is relatively unusual, but it tends to happen when a question on the Order of Business is a convenient hook for an announcement a minister wants to make but at greater length than would be permissible in answer to a conventional oral question. As this is in effect a mini-statement, the Speaker allows more supplementaries than during Question Time. A minister may answer an oral question in this way even though it would not have been reached during Question Time (and may even answer a written question in this way if it is down for answer on that day).

Written questions

In the long (seventeen-month) 2001–02 session, 2,203 questions received an oral answer in the House. By contrast, 72,905 written questions were tabled during that session, 13 percent of which – some 9,000 – were to the Department of Health. Three other departments (the former Transport, Local Government and the Regions, the Home Office and the Foreign and Commonwealth Office) answered more than 6,000 each (some 9 percent of the total in each case). Defence, Education and Skills, and Trade and Industry replied to more than 4,000 each (about 7 percent). At the other end of the scale, the Solicitor-General answered 400 and the Advocate-General for Scotland 100.

Written questions are of two types: *ordinary written questions*, which are put down for answer two sitting days after they are received, and which by convention the government answers within a week. There is no limit to the number of this type of question that an MP may table. *Named-day questions* are for answer on a stated day, with a minimum notice period of three sitting days (including non-sitting Fridays). The named-day system was originally intended for genuinely urgent questions, but it became greatly overused, and increasing numbers of question received holding replies ('I will reply to the hon. Member as soon as possible'). From January 2003, a limit of five named-day questions per member per day has been imposed.

Written questions have a wide variety of purposes. They are used by MPs to raise the profile of particular subjects, to tease out details of the government's policy on some issue with a view to deploying the material in political debate inside or outside the House, or to press ministers in an area where the government appears vulnerable. They are tabled to gather information in order to be able to respond to constituency concerns, or to give a constituent's case wider publicity. Shadow ministers use them to monitor what the government is doing in their policy areas. Outside organisations will ask MPs to put down questions in order to assist a campaign, or to obtain an authoritative statement on a situation or of the government's policy towards it.

Written questions have one great advantage over oral questions: they can be pursued much more relentlessly. Whereas in Question Time an MP gets one supplementary and the moment is past, with the ministers concerned not answering again until a month later, written questions can follow up in detail, almost as a barrister would in cross-examination, the precise conduct of government policy in a particular area.

Although, as we noted above, there are rubbing points when MPs see no good reason for the government refusing to answer, replies to written questions (which occupy forty to fifty pages of *Hansard* on a typical day) put a staggering amount of official information into the public domain. But there are signs that the increasing use of written questions is starting to devalue the currency. In the last three financial years, the total numbers of written answers published have soared: 32,821 in 2000–01, 42,088 in 2001–02 and 51,978 in 2002–03.

In June 2002, the Procedure Committee noted the concerns of a number of MPs that a further increase 'may lead to an erosion of the quality of responses and to delays in responding', but the committee believed that it would be 'wrong in principle' to impose any limit on the number of questions an MP could ask.

Written ministerial statements

It used to be the case that if the government wanted to put something formally on the record in the House that was not important enough for an oral statement (see page 139), a friendly back-bencher would be found to put down an 'arranged question' drafted in the department concerned, in answer to which the government could make the statement it wanted. These arranged questions or 'plants' were a rather opaque way for the government to make an announcement, and from October 2002 a system of written ministerial statements was introduced.

Statements to be made on any day are listed on the Order Paper at the end of the day's business, and statements on a future day appear in Section E of the *Future Business* part of the Vote bundle (see page 154). When made, the statements are printed before the written answers to questions in the next day's *Hansard* (and so are available on-line).

Are questions effective?

As part of its review of PQs in 2002, the Procedure Committee analysed the responses of 167 MPs to a questionnaire. One of the questions was 'How do you use the system of questions to assist in your work as a Member?' The responses confirmed the purposes of eliciting information (often about constituency matters), getting the government's position on the record, putting pressure on ministers, making a constituency point, researching an issue in depth and helping with a local campaign. One MP said 'It is one of the few areas where, as a back-bench MP, you can have a direct impact'; another said that it proved to constituents 'that you really are trying to get answers out of the government'.

MPs were also asked how effective they thought questions were in bringing information into the public domain, contributing to political debate and holding the executive to account. For oral questions, 43 percent replied either 'quite' or 'very effective' and 31 percent 'not very' or 'not at all effective'. Written questions scored better, with figures of 60 and 21 percent, respectively, and this probably reflects the different character of oral and written questions.

Of the sample, 57 percent received requests from outside organisations to table questions on their behalf, and about two-thirds 'occasionally' acceded to such requests. Over two-thirds of respondents said that their staff were involved in preparing questions for the MP to table, which may be seen by some to confirm their suspicions that staffers play too great a part in this area of parliamentary activity.

There is no doubt that, whereas thirty or forty years ago an MP would often first write to a government department for information or seek a meeting to put some point to a minister and would table a PQ only if he or she had to, in 2004 putting down a question is often the first step, not the last. As the Procedure Committee acknowledged, the scale of the increase in written questions risks a reduction in the quality of government replies – although this is not to suggest that, if there were half the number of questions, the answers would be twice as helpful!

The survey on pages 283–285 of reasons for refusing to answer questions may seem daunting, and it is certainly the case that competent ministers and departments have the odds stacked in their favour. However, as in so many areas of parliamentary life, the determination and hard work of an individual MP can produce remarkable results. For example, it was the written questions tabled by the back-bench Labour MP Tam Dalyell (now Father of the House) that led to the admission from Margaret Thatcher's government that during the Falklands War the Argentinian cruiser *General Belgrano* had been torpedoed when steaming away from British forces rather than towards them, as the government had previously implied.

The processes of oral and written questions are key functions of the House of Commons. Both can be means of exposing the government to criticism, and of requiring explanation and justification. Oral questions, although inquisitorial in theory, are also part of the political debate. Written questions, on the other hand, are a way of calling governments to account in detail, and they should be an important discipline on individual government departments and their ministers – the requirement to reply truthfully to a direct and precise question can mean that the spotlight swings onto something that the government would much preferred to have kept to itself.

Although, as we have seen, front-benchers use questions extensively, they are also one of the main opportunities for back-bench MPs on all sides of the House to pursue and expose issues, and to get the government of the day to put information on the public record. If the average costs of answering oral and written questions are correct, the system costs about £7 million a year, or about £12,500 for each MP who is not a minister and so is able to put down questions. Set against central government expenditure of some £466 *billion*, this does not seem excessive.

The great constitutional theorist Ivor Jennings described parliamentary questions as 'of the utmost constitutional importance'. The very existence of parliamentary questions, and the opportunities that they provide for the representatives of the people to question the government of the day, is undoubtedly of constitutional importance. Their effectiveness is very much down to the tenacity and skill of individual MPs.

Questions in the House of Lords

The House of Lords also has a variety of ways of scrutinising the actions of, and eliciting information from, the executive by means of questions. These questions are always addressed to 'Her Majesty's Government'. (Questions on domestic House of Lords matters are usually addressed to the Leader of the House or Chairman of Committees.) It follows that the government must have responsibility for the subject matter of the question. Fewer questions are tabled in the Lords than in the Commons, and the rules governing their content are less strict. It is ultimately for the House itself to determine what is in order and what is not. Nevertheless, there are some conventions. Questions casting reflections on the royal family or relating to the Church of England, or questions phrased offensively, are inadmissible. Questions that are *sub judice* (on matters awaiting decision by the criminal or civil courts) are also inadmissible – subject only to the discretion of the Leader of the House, who may allow such a question if the case is of national importance and there is no danger of prejudice to the proceedings. It is considered undesirable to table questions on nationalised industries except for those asking for statistical information or on matters of urgent public importance, but following successive privatisations this rule is of less significance than it used to be. It is also undesirable to incorporate statements of fact or opinion in the text of a question.

Questions for oral answer

Every day at the beginning of a sitting, questions for oral answer (starred questions) may be put to the government. They are marked on the Order Paper with an asterisk, and provided that they are not topical questions they may be tabled up to one month in advance. Four questions are allowed on Mondays and Thursdays and five on Tuesdays and Wednesdays. As in the Commons, questions in the Lords were losing their currency from being tabled too far in advance, and some members were, it was felt, hogging the Order Paper by tabling too many too far ahead. In recent years, the Procedure Committee has recommended that no member should have more than two on the Order Paper at any one time; that no lord may have more than one question on any one day; and that on Mondays and Tuesdays one, and on Wednesdays two, of the questions should be 'topical questions' selected by ballot by the Clerk Assistant two working days before they are to be asked. No starred question may be tabled less than twenty-four hours before it is to be asked.

Unlike the Commons, questions are not limited to any particular government department on any particular day, and there is no equivalent to Prime Minister's Questions. Every member asking a question is allowed one supplementary before other members' supplementaries are put. Supplementary questions must be in terms confined to the subject of the original question, but they frequently go wider. They must not give rise to debate. Question Time may not exceed thirty minutes on Mondays and Thursdays and forty minutes on Tuesdays and Wednesdays. In the 1999–2000 session 630 starred questions were asked. The effect of the increase in the number of questions allowed with effect from the 2002–03 session will be to raise the total annual figure by about 12.5 percent.

Questions for oral answer after debate

A question that may give rise to debate may be put down for any sitting day and is taken at the end of business. These debated questions are very popular with members. Such unstarred questions are time-limited to one and a half hours and are not marked by asterisks on the Order Paper. Any lord may make a speech upon the question, but after the minister has replied on behalf of the government there is no right of reply. Unstarred questions are normally taken when business appears to be relatively light and, although less frequent, they are in some ways akin to Commons adjournment debates (see also Chapter 9). Since March 1993, it has been possible to table unstarred questions for debate in the dinner break. An hour's time limit is imposed so that the resumption of legislative business is not delayed (see also page 150).

Questions for written answer

Members of the House may also obtain written answers by tabling questions on the Order Paper under the heading 'Questions for written answer'. The minister concerned will then write to the lord and the answer will also be published in *Hansard*. There is no limit to the number of questions a lord may ask in this way, although members are discouraged from tabling large numbers of questions or multiple requests for information masquerading as a single question, and no more than six a day may be tabled by a single member. Questions for written answer are answered within a fortnight. The government itself often uses the medium of a written answer to a question to make an announcement or publish information. In 1961–62, seventy-two questions for written answer were tabled; in 1998–99, 4,322; and in 2001–02, a long session, 5,798. Written answers on matters delegated to executive agencies are filtered through an appropriate member of the government and printed in the *Official Report* in letter form.

Private notice questions

A lord may seek to ask a question on a matter of urgency on any day, just as an MP may apply for an 'urgent question'. But it is the Leader of the House who, in the first instance, decides whether the question is of sufficient urgency to justify an immediate reply. Notice of such a question must be given by noon on the day it is proposed to ask it. Private notice questions are rare, and there are seldom more than one or two a session. They occur more frequently when a cabinet minister with major departmental responsibilities sits in the Lords and during those periods when the House sits while the Commons remains in recess. But answers to many Commons private notice questions are repeated as statements in the House of Lords if the opposition requests it.

Petitions

The right to petition Parliament is an ancient one, summarised in a resolution of the House of Commons of 1699: 'That it is the inherent right of every commoner in England to prepare and present petitions to the House of Commons in case of grievance, and the House of Commons to receive the same'. The first recorded petitions date from the reign of Richard II (1377–99); in 1571, a committee with the splendid name of the Committee for Motions of Griefs and Petitions was appointed to examine petitions.

Petitions were originally read at the start of a sitting, and debates could arise upon them. Huge numbers were presented during the nineteenth century; for example, 17,000 a year between 1837 and 1841; and 34,000 in 1893. The twentieth century saw a sharp fall in the numbers of public petitions, but they remain a way of giving local or more widespread concerns a higher profile.

Table 10.1 Petitions presented to the House of Commons, 1998–2002

Session	Petitions	of which presented formally	Government observations
1998–99	99	56	36
1999–2000	87	67	42
2000–01	35	28	22
2001–02	131	109	64

Petitions must be presented by an MP. They may have hundreds of thousands of signatures, or only one, but the procedure is the same in each case. The basic rules are that they should state from whom they come, should be in 'respectful language' and should ask for something that it is in the power of the House of Commons to grant. The MP has the petition checked by the Clerk of Public Petitions to make sure that it is in order, and he or she can then, at any time during a sitting of the House, simply put it in the green baize bag that hangs on the back of the Speaker's Chair. The MP can also present a petition formally in the House. Just before the daily half-hour adjournment debate (or, on Fridays, at the start of the day's business) he or she is called by the Speaker and briefly introduces the petition and reads the text. All petitions are printed and circulated with the House's working papers. Government departments may (but do not have to) make observations on them, and these observations are also printed. Recent statistics are given in Table 10.1 (bearing in mind that 2000–01 was a short session and 2001–02 a long session following a general election).

Petitions cover a wide variety of subjects, both national and local. In the summer of 2003, for example, subjects included the closure of local post offices, the proposed development of a piece of land in Stevenage used as a children's play area, the dangers of fireworks, the threat to local pharmacies as a result of opening up the market, the export of products made from dog and cat fur, and fairer methods of distributing local government grants.

Petitions are not formally taken up, either by a committee of the House, or by an outside authority such as the Ombudsman. In that sense, they are not a particularly effective way of making a case. But they can achieve a great deal of publicity and on a local issue can have a snowball effect. On national issues, either the sheer numbers of signatories to a petition or (as with the closure of local post offices and the threat to local pharmacies mentioned above) the fact that similar petitions from scores of constituencies are presented week after week can be a powerful statement of concern that for practical political reasons the government must heed.

Petitions may also be addressed to the House of Lords by a member of the House. No speech or debate takes place beyond the formal words of presentation, and they are not printed. Although largely defunct, petitions are very occasionally still presented there.

MPs' letters

MPs' letters to ministers can be seen as part of the questioning process, although they are not 'proceedings in Parliament' (see page 165). The level of correspondence between MPs and ministers is very high. The government's figures, from which Table 10.2 is drawn, include correspondence from peers,

Table 10.2 Correspondence received by government departments and executive agencies in calendar year 2002

Department for Culture, Media and Sport	4,747
Customs and Excise	1,616
Ministry of Defence	5,381
Department for Education and Skills	15,595
Department for Environment, Food and Rural Affairs	11,241
Foreign and Commonwealth Office	15,535
UK Visas	10,322
Department of Health	17,942
Home Office	27,320
Inland Revenue	3,592
Department for International Development	2,612
Lord Chancellor's Department	2,577
Office of the Deputy Prime Minister and Department of Transport*	19,699
Department of Trade and Industry	11,565
Treasury	4,657
Department for Work and Pensions	14,297
Child Support Agency	3,194
Others	12,175
Total	184,067

* Figures combined (departmental reorganisation). The Education and Skills and Customs and Excise figures also include letters from MEPs and members of the devolved assemblies.

but the vast majority of letters are from MPs (who in this case also include ministers and the Speaker in their constituency roles).

It is not surprising that the departments that deal with the things that touch people's lives most closely – health, law and order, education, transport, immigration – have heavy postbags.

Typically, an MP receives a complaint from a constituent, perhaps that he was discharged from hospital too soon, or that he has a fiancée who is not being allowed to settle in the UK from Pakistan, or that his son is being kept in poor conditions in a remand prison. It would be impossible for the MP to investigate these complaints personally. He or she could table parliamentary questions or apply for an adjournment debate; but usually the MP begins by forwarding the constituent's letter to the minister responsible for the subject and asking for comments. Not all letters are of complaint. A small firm may want to know what government or EU grants it can apply for or to seek the MP's help in negotiating some tangle of bureaucracy.

The constituent could have written directly to the department, whether with a complaint or a query, but the fact that the letter is coming from an MP means that the issue will be dealt with at a more senior level. The reply – usually from a minister personally, but also from officials with operational responsibility for the subject, or the chief executive of an executive agency – will be in a form that the MP can forward to the constituent as a response, but it may also give the MP useful background if similar cases arise.

Letters from members of the House of Lords to ministers are treated in the same way inside government departments as letters from MPs. No separate figures are published, but the numbers are much lower because peers have no constituency work.

Letters have several advantages over parliamentary questions. They can be sent at any time, whereas questions may be tabled only when the House is sitting or on non-sitting Fridays. They can raise confidential matters, or the personal details of a constituent's case, and can go into great detail about the point at issue. And, unlike questions, there are no rules restricting what an MP may say in a letter. The contents of letters between MPs and ministers are private unless one side or the other releases them; and although by convention the minister does not do this unless the MP does, ministers are always aware that the MP may go public and their letters are, whenever possible, written in a form that can be forwarded directly to the constituent.

One disadvantage of letters is that they are more prone to delay than the answers to PQs. All the departments in the table above have targets for replying to MPs' letters, usually between fifteen and twenty working days. In 2002, the Ministry of Defence replied to 83 percent of letters within fifteen working days; the Foreign and Commonwealth Office replied to 83 percent within twenty working days. However, the Department for the Environment, Food and Rural Affairs replied to only 47 percent of letters within fifteen working days, and the Department of Health had a bad year, responding to only 29 percent of MPs' and peers' letters within its twenty-working-day target.

Most matters raised by constituents and taken up by MPs with ministers are dealt with by correspondence. However, if the MP is unhappy with the government's response, he or she can seek a meeting with the minister, or put down parliamentary questions, or seek an adjournment debate, either in the Chamber or in Westminster Hall, to which a minister will have to reply. Proceedings in the House often start with a constituent's letter.

11 Calling to account: select committees

Select committees in the House of Commons

Introduction

People often associate select committees of the House of Commons with the system of departmental select committees set up in 1979; but in fact the House has used select committees for centuries to investigate, to advise, to consider complex matters – in fact for any task which is more effectively carried out by a small group of MPs than by the House as a whole. Indeed, the very name 'select committee' indicates that a task or function has been given, or *committed*, to that body, composed of MPs *selected* to sit upon it.

We have already encountered standing committees (see page 191) – strangely named because they are not permanent (with the exception of European standing committees (see page 359)): each one ceases to exist when it has finished considering the particular item of business committed to it. Some select committees are also appointed for a single purpose – to examine a draft bill, perhaps – and are dissolved when they have completed their work, but most are permanent institutions. They are appointed under standing orders and so do not die at the end of a session or the end of a parliament.

When the House meets after a general election, the permanent select committees are technically in existence but have no members. There is then a period of jockeying for membership of the most sought-after committees, and of negotiation between the parties for the chairmanships. Delays – sometimes of three months or more – in putting names to the House have been criticised as delaying the start of committee work and giving the new government a scrutiny-free run for the crucial early weeks after a general election. Largely due to the efforts of the new Leader of the House, Robin Cook, the delay at the start of the 2001 parliament was the shortest ever: the session began on 13 June 2001, and most select committees were nominated on 16 July.

The development of select committees

Select committees have long been a feature of the work of the House of Commons. If you look at the Journals of the House for the end of the sixteenth century, you will find select committees involved in, and advising the House on, some of the most sensitive political issues of the day. In 1571, there was a Committee for the Uniformity of Religion – a matter of life and death in Elizabethan England. The following year there was a Committee on the Queen of Scotts (*sic*) – in this case, a matter of death. In 1571, there was also a Committee for the Examination of Fees and Rewards taken for Voices (that is, votes) in this House – an early example of the House looking at appropriate standards of conduct. Just after the turn of the seventeenth century, select committees dealt with the Confirmation of the Book of Common Prayer and with the Union with Scotland (both in 1604).

Some committees were virtually permanent: committees on Grievances, on Privileges and on the Subsidy (the grant of money to the Crown) were regularly appointed. There were also select committees with wider responsibilities, such as the splendidly named Grand Committee for Evils (1623).

But most committees were ephemeral; something came up that the House wanted looked at, and it set up a committee. These would often operate very informally: the members nominated to the committee would go straight out of the House into another room, would deliberate, perhaps examine witnesses, and then come back to the House (possibly even later in the same sitting), when one of their members would report orally what view they had come to.

Until well into the twentieth century, most select committees were set up *ad hoc* to examine a particular issue of public policy, or often some disaster or scandal (and their appointment was often used as a political weapon). A classic case was the Sebastopol Committee, set up in 1855, which – with some resonances for the aftermath of the Iraq war in 2003 – investigated the conduct of affairs but also sought political scapegoats in the process. The committee sat almost every day for more than two months, asked some 7,000 questions of witnesses and was bitterly critical of Lord Aberdeen, the former Prime Minister (who gave evidence to the committee). Unlike a modern select committee, the Sebastopol Committee had no staff (the role of committee clerks then was largely to ensure procedural rectitude), and the final report was written by one of its members, Lord Seymour (the draft report proposed by the fiery chairman, Mr Roebuck, was rejected by the committee).

Unsystematic scrutiny

Committees such as the Sebastopol Committee played some part in calling governments to account (often after the event) but, with the possible exception of the Public Accounts Committee (see page 253), set up in 1861 to see whether public money had been properly expended, there was until the twentieth century little use by the House of Commons of select committees to monitor the detail of what the government of the day was actually doing.

A move in this direction was made with the appointment in 1912 of the Estimates Committee, which lasted until 1970, when it was succeeded (until

1979) by the Expenditure Committee. Both committees worked mainly through subject sub-committees, but their coverage of government activity, although occasionally influential, was very patchy. In the late 1960s and 1970s, a number of 'subject' select committees (for example, on agriculture, education and science, and overseas aid) were set up; but there was no real system of select committees; and the Agriculture Committee, for example, was wound up in February 1969 after a campaign of opposition by government departments.

The real change came with the election of the Conservative government in 1979. The new Leader of the House, Norman St John-Stevas, was quick to put before the House the recommendation of the Procedure Committee the previous year that there should be a select committee to shadow each government department. The committee had also recommended that eight days a year on the floor of the House should be devoted to debating the committees' reports (and that their chairmen should be paid a small additional salary). These latter recommendations were not adopted by the government, but the key principle of a system of select committees related to government departments was approved in June 1979.

It was widely thought that, had St John-Stevas not moved so quickly, the change would never have been made; by the autumn the Prime Minister, Margaret Thatcher (who had other things on her mind in the first few months of office), would have realised how inconvenient for the government these committees might be, and would have vetoed the proposal. But, for the first time, the House of Commons now had at its disposal a means of systematic scrutiny of the government of the day potentially much more rigorous than the traditional methods of debate and question.

Today these departmental select committees account for the majority of select committee activity; but they number less than half of the House's select committees. We now look at what select committees there are and what they do; then at their appointment and powers; and we will then use the example of a departmental committee to see how they work.

The committees

Departmental committees

There are eighteen of these:

- ▲ Culture, Media and Sport
- ▲ Defence
- ▲ Education and Skills
- ▲ Environment, Food and Rural Affairs
- ▲ Foreign Affairs
- ▲ Health

▲ Home Affairs
▲ International Development
▲ Constitutional Affairs
▲ Northern Ireland Affairs
▲ Office of the Deputy Prime Minister: Housing, Planning, Local Government and the Regions
▲ Science and Technology
▲ Scottish Affairs
▲ Trade and Industry
▲ Transport
▲ Treasury
▲ Welsh Affairs
▲ Work and Pensions.

They have a very broad remit: 'to examine the expenditure, administration and policy of [the relevant government department] and associated public bodies'. They are thus concerned not only with the doings of their department but also with any related executive agencies, and with regulators and inspectorates that operate in their field. Most departmental committees have eleven members; Northern Ireland Affairs has thirteen (to make the representation of different strands of Northern Ireland politics easier); and the Environment, Food and Rural Affairs Committee has seventeen (reflecting the fact that it was a merger of previous committees on the environment and on agriculture). All the committees have power to set up a sub-committee; the Environment and Rural Affairs Committee has power to appoint two sub-committees.

Because each committee shadows a government department, the system of committees has to change to match alterations in the structure of government. Thus, a Constitutional Affairs Committee was appointed in place of the Committee on the Lord Chancellor's Department, following the creation of the former department and the abolition of the latter (although it seems certain that the Scottish Affairs and Welsh Affairs Committees will continue). Similarly, when particular responsibilities move from one government department to another, the task of monitoring them moves from one committee to another.

'Cross-cutting' committees

The departmental committees look 'vertically' at all the responsibilities of a single department and its ministers (although the Scottish, Welsh and Northern Ireland Affairs Committees have a broader range of interests). The cross-cutting committees, on the other hand, look 'horizontally' across Whitehall at themes or actions in which all or most departments are involved:

▲ Environmental Audit
▲ European Scrutiny
▲ Liaison
▲ Public Accounts
▲ Public Administration.

The Environmental Audit Committee

This was set up in November 1997. It has sixteen members, and its task is 'to consider to what extent the policies and programmes of government departments and non-departmental public bodies contribute to environmental protection and sustainable development', and 'to audit their performance against such targets as may be set for them'. The committee inquires into a range of 'green' issues, including the environmental implications of the government's spending plans and international policies on sustainable development (and the agendas and effects of successive world summits). In the 2001 parliament, the committee's inquiries have covered subjects such as the use of environmentally friendly timber in construction, renewable energy sources, waste and the environmental implications of aviation. It has power to appoint a sub-committee.

The European Scrutiny Committee

This committee (formerly known as the European Legislation Committee) was established shortly after the United Kingdom joined the EEC in 1973. It examines a range of European Union business: not only European Union policies, spending and draft legislation, but also institutional issues – it reported in detail on the processes that led to the Maastricht, Amsterdam and Nice Treaties, and from 2001 to 2003 it monitored the work of the Convention on a New Constitution for the European Union. It has sixteen members and has power to set up as many sub-committees as it wishes. The work of this committee is covered in Chapter 12.

The Liaison Committee

This is an unusual committee whose work includes both detailed housekeeping (and so might be classed with the internal committees below) and some of the most high-profile hearings that any select committee holds. The committee consists of the chairmen of all the permanent select committees, plus two additional members, one of whom chairs the committee. The membership thus varies with the number of committees, but at present it stands at thirty-five. It has power to set up a sub-committee.

The Liaison Committee has the general task of considering 'general matters relating to the work of select committees'. This may be a change in the format of committee reports, for example, or the rules for putting uncorrected transcripts of evidence on the Internet, or adjudicating on overlap between the inquiries of two committees. The committee also decides how the budget for overseas travel by select committees is allocated, and it chooses reports for debate on the floor of the House on estimates days and in Westminster Hall (see pages 248 and 269).

In 2000, however, the committee changed its spots entirely and launched into a campaign to make select committees more effective. Its three reports, under the general theme of *Shifting the Balance* (between the executive and the legislature), put forward a reform programme that produced something of a confrontation with the government and with the then Leader of the House, Margaret Beckett. Her replacement by Robin Cook in 2001 led to the adoption of a number of the committee's proposals. The committee has followed up its work by publishing annual reports on the select committee system, assessing its effectiveness and examining innovations and problems.

One Liaison Committee recommendation produced an important result, although not immediately. In December 2000, the chairman of the committee wrote to the Prime Minister inviting him to give evidence to the committee on the government's annual report 'to spell out your policies in an atmosphere very different from that on the floor of the House'. The request was turned down on the grounds of precedent and what was described as 'the important principle that it is for individual Secretaries of State to answer to the House and its individual Select Committees for their areas of responsibility, and not the Prime Minister' – even though the Prime Minister answers on those areas of responsibility every week during Prime Minister's Questions.

However, just over a year later the Prime Minister did indeed offer to appear before the committee twice a year to discuss domestic and international affairs. The first session took place on 16 July 2002, with subsequent hearings in January and July 2003, and February 2004. The Prime Minister's appearances have become important parliamentary occasions, televised live and carefully analysed by the media. The size of the committee makes the normal style of examination more difficult, but questioning is focused on themes decided by the committee beforehand, each led by one MP. The Prime Minister is given notice of the themes but not of the detailed questions.

The calm questioning in depth at these sessions has been a valuable antidote to the knockabout of PMQs. They are opportunities for the Prime Minister as well as for MPs, but the fact that the PM now appears before a select committee in this way is symbolically important as well as making the head of the government more accountable. It is difficult to see a future Prime Minister being able to discontinue the practice.

The Committee of Public Accounts

The work of this committee, usually known as 'the PAC', and of the Comptroller and Auditor-General who supports it, is described in Chapter 8.

The Public Administration Committee

This committee was set up in 1997, taking on the functions of two previous committees, the Public Service Committee and the Committee on the Parliamentary Commissioner for Administration. In its public service role, the committee has conducted inquiries into matters that affect the government as a whole: for example, on the bill that became the Freedom of Information Act 2000, the ministerial code of conduct, the role of government special advisers, reform of the House of Lords and the exercise by ministers of the Royal prerogative. As we saw in Chapter 10, the committee also conducts regular reviews of ministers' refusals to answer particular types of parliamentary question. The committee has eleven members and the power to appoint a sub-committee.

In its other role, the committee considers the reports of the Parliamentary Commissioner for Administration (or Ombudsman, a Swedish name reflecting the fact that there were similar officials in Scandinavia in the nineteenth century; the concept was adopted by the UK in 1967, when the Parliamentary Commissioner Act was passed).

The Ombudsman is an entirely independent official who reports to Parliament. Assisted by a staff of 230, she investigates complaints about maladministration and the actions (or inactions) of government departments and other public bodies that seem to have caused injustice that has not been put right. Her main aim is to obtain a remedy for those who have suffered injustice, and her secondary aim is to ensure good standards of public administration. If she finds serious faults, she can recommend to the public body concerned what redress it should offer and the action it should take to avoid a repetition of the failure. The Ombudsman has no power to enforce her recommendations, but they are almost always accepted. Since 1994, she has also been able to investigate failures to provide information contrary to the relevant code on access to official information. She also holds the separate posts of Health Service Commissioner for England and for Wales, and Ombudsman for Administration in Wales. In the two latter roles she reports to the National Assembly for Wales. Her Scottish equivalent reports to the Scottish Parliament.

The relationship between the Ombudsman and the Public Administration Committee is not unlike that between the Comptroller and Auditor-General and the Public Accounts Committee (see page 253). The Ombudsman has the additional clout of the committee's backing, and the committee is able to draw on the work of the Ombudsman's office with its substantial resources. The committee considers the Ombudsman's annual reports (and those of her Northern Ireland equivalent); but, rather than following up the details of individual investigations, it draws more general lessons for public administration as a whole.

'Legislative' committees

Although most legislation is considered by standing committees, several select committees are concerned with different types of legislation:

- ▲ Consolidation, &c., Bills
- ▲ Human Rights
- ▲ Regulatory Reform
- ▲ Statutory Instruments
- ▲ Tax Law Rewrite Bills.

The European Scrutiny Committee might also be included in this list, but as it deals with a wide range of EU policy matters as well as legislation, we have treated it as a cross-cutting committee.

The *Joint Committee on Consolidation, &c., Bills* is a joint committee of both Houses on which both MPs and peers sit (we look at joint committees more closely on page 347). Established in 1894, the committee has twenty-four members, half from each House, and is traditionally chaired by a law lord, who does much of the scrutiny work. Its task is to examine bills that 'consolidate' the law – that is, restate it in a more logical and convenient form without changing its substance, although errors and ambiguities may be corrected. Such bills are always introduced in the House of Lords rather than in the House of Commons. The committee considers the form rather than the merits of legislation. It meets only when a bill is referred to it: only three times in the four sessions 1998–2002.

Following the enactment of the Human Rights Act 1998, the *Joint Committee on Human Rights* was appointed in 2001. It has a general remit to consider matters relating to human rights in the United Kingdom (but not individual cases), and among other things it has examined the case for a Human Rights Commission in the UK, the UN Convention on the Rights of the Child and the work of the Human Rights Unit. It also has an important role in legislation. It examines every government bill as soon as possible after introduction to see whether the bill, if enacted, might risk violating a human right, and it reports its views to both Houses. The committee also examines proposals for, and drafts of, remedial orders, which come about when a court finds that an Act of Parliament is incompatible with the Human Rights Act, and amendment of the legislation is necessary (see page 236).

This joint committee has twelve members, six from each House, and is chaired by a Labour MP (but the government does not have a majority on the committee). It is an active committee; in the long 2001–02 session it met thirty-two times and issued twenty-six reports. Its staff includes an eminent human rights expert as legal adviser.

The *Regulatory Reform Committee* is a Commons select committee (the Lords equivalent is the Delegated Powers and Regulatory Reform Committee), consisting of eighteen MPs. The committee considers proposals and draft orders under the Regulatory Reform Act 2001; this process is described in Chapter 7 (page 234). Its staff include legal advisers.

The *Joint Committee on Statutory Instruments* is responsible for examining the technical aspects of delegated legislation rather than its merits – unlike the new sifting committee in the House of Lords (see page 234). It has seven members from each House with an opposition MP as chairman; it normally meets weekly when Parliament is sitting, but it reports only when it wishes to draw the attention of both Houses to some defect in a statutory instrument. The analysis of well over a thousand statutory instruments each year is carried out by a staff that includes three specialist lawyers. Delegated legislation on financial matters, which is laid only before the House of Commons, is examined by the *Select Committee on Statutory Instruments*, consisting of the seven Commons members of the joint committee. Delegated legislation is described in more detail in Chapter 7 (page 233).

The *Tax Law Rewrite Committee* is another joint committee, consisting of seven members from each House, chaired by an opposition MP (the former Conservative Chancellor of the Exchequer, Kenneth Clarke). It was set up in January 2001 to consider bills that simplify the law on taxation but, as with consolidation bills, do not make changes of substance.

Internal committees

These committees are concerned with the way the House and its members work, both procedurally and administratively:

- ▲ Modernisation of the House of Commons
- ▲ Procedure
- ▲ Selection
- ▲ Standards and Privileges
- ▲ Accommodation and Works
- ▲ Administration
- ▲ Broadcasting
- ▲ Catering
- ▲ Finance and Services
- ▲ Information.

The Select Committee on the Modernisation of the House of Commons

The Modernisation Committee was set up in June 1997, a month after the general election at which the Labour government was returned. The Leader of the House, Ann Taylor, became chairman, and the committee of fifteen members also contained her Conservative and Liberal Democrat counterparts. The committee's task is 'to consider how the practices and procedures of the House should be modernised, and to make recommendations'. The committee was set up for the length of the 1997 parliament and was reappointed in 2001, again for the length of the parliament. On the grounds that there is already a wealth of opinion – perhaps too much! – expressed on the subject of reform of the House of Commons, the committee has proceeded largely through discussion and informal talks with MPs, clerks and others rather than taking formal oral and written evidence.

The Modernisation Committee has produced reports on various aspects of the legislative process, conduct in the Chamber, the scrutiny of European business, the parliamentary calendar, facilities for the media, sittings in Westminster Hall and select committees. The fact that – very unusually for a select committee – it is chaired by a cabinet minister has meant that its recommendations already carry some sort of government stamp of approval, although not all have been implemented (and its proposal of a more open and independent way of choosing members of select committees, backed by Robin Cook, was defeated in the House).

The committee took a noticeably more radical stance under the chairmanship of Robin Cook from July 2001; following his departure from the Cabinet in March 2003, the brief tenure of office of John Reid and the appointment of Peter Hain, it remains to be seen how active the committee will be in the future. We examine modernisation issues in greater detail in the final chapter of this book.

The Procedure Committee

Procedure Committees used to be appointed *ad hoc* to examine particular aspects of the House's business, or to address some problem. A Procedure Committee was appointed in each parliament from 1979, but the committee did not become permanent until 1997. The committee has thirteen members, and it has the job of considering the practice and procedure of the House in the conduct of public business (so not including private legislation – see page 224) and making recommendations.

The committee considers matters that are referred to it, usually informally by the Speaker or the government rather than formally by decision of the House. It also chooses its own subjects for investigation, although these are often picked because the committee is aware of a general feeling that some topic needs examination. There is inevitably an overlap with the work of the Modernisation Committee (although the chairman of the Procedure Committee is also a member of Modernisation). Over the last five years, the committee has reported on such things as the procedural consequences of devolution, debate on the government's expenditure plans, delegated legislation, parliamentary scrutiny of treaties, parliamentary questions and the method of election of a Speaker (after the day-long process to elect a successor to Betty Boothroyd in 2000). Its recommendations on the last two subjects were substantially implemented, but it does not have the fast track to implementation that the Modernisation Committee usually enjoys through its connection with government.

The Committee of Selection

The main task of this committee, which meets weekly while the House is sitting, is to select MPs to serve on standing committees on bills and statutory instruments and private bill committees. At the beginning of a parliament it also puts forward names of MPs to serve on the departmental select committees and domestic committees, and it nominates any replacements needed thereafter. It has nine members, six or seven of whom are whips. As we will see later (page 326), the involvement of government whips in the selection of MPs for committees that scrutinise government has been the cause of some criticism.

The Committee on Standards and Privileges

The committee was first appointed in 1996, combining the ancient institution of a Privileges Committee with the modern (from 1974) Committee on Members' Interests. The committee has eleven members and is chaired by a senior opposition back-bencher. Most of its work has been concerned with MPs' conduct, although it also investigates and reports on any complaint of privilege referred to it by the House (see page 167). It works closely with the Parliamentary Commissioner for Standards (see page 114), considers his reports on complaints against MPs, taking evidence if necessary, and recommends to the House what action (such as suspending an MP for a specified period or withholding salary) should be taken. The committee also oversees the operation of the rules of conduct, and the compilation and publication of the registers of interests.

Unusually, it has the power to order an MP to give evidence to it, or to produce documents; most committees have these powers only in respect of people who are not members of either House.

The Finance and Services Committee and the domestic committees

As we saw in Chapter 2 (page 55), the Finance and Services Committee (usually known as 'F&S') advises the House of Commons Commission on the financial and business plans of the House administration. The committee is chaired by a member of the Commission and has ten other members. The domestic committees (*Accommodation and Works*, *Administration*, *Catering* and *Information*) reflect the views of MPs generally in the planning and provision of services. Their role is to advise the Speaker and the Commission. A similar role is played by the *Broadcasting Committee*.

Ad hoc committees

The House can set up new committees at any time, although the formal initiative to do so is invariably a motion moved by the government (in the nineteenth century and earlier, this was not the case; the Sebastopol Committee described earlier was appointed in the teeth of ministerial opposition, and the approval of the motion to set it up finished the government led by Lord Aberdeen).

In the more recent past, such *ad hoc* committees have considered domestic matters such as MPs' pay (1980–82) the televising of the House (1988–90), the sitting hours of the House (the 'Jopling Committee'), and matters of public policy such as the royal family's pay and expenses (1971–72), a possible 'wealth tax' (1974–75), abortion (1974–75) and violence in the family (1975–76). The existence of the Modernisation Committee and the Procedure Committee means that select committees are now less likely to be set up to consider individual in-House issues; and the existence of the departmental committees (two or more of which are able to conduct joint inquiries if they wish) means that select committees are also less likely to be appointed to consider specific issues of public policy. However, from time to time, special circumstances arise, usually when a particular subject affects both Houses (see page 347 for the joint committees on parliamentary privilege and Lords reform).

However, most *ad hoc* committees are appointed to consider bills or draft bills. Thus in 1999 a joint committee was given the task of examining the draft Financial Services and Markets Bill, and a Commons committee scrutinised the draft Food Standards Bill. In 2002, a joint committee considered the draft Communications Bill, and in 2003 joint committees were set up for each of the draft Corruption, Mental Incapacity, Civil Contingencies and Gambling Bills.

The Intelligence and Security Committee

One committee is often referred to by the media as a 'select committee' or a 'parliamentary committee' but in fact is neither. The Intelligence and Security

Committee was set up under the Intelligence Services Act 1994. It consists of eight MPs and one peer, all back-benchers, and at present is chaired by Ann Taylor, the former Labour Leader of the House. Although its members are parliamentarians, they are chosen by the Prime Minister and not by Parliament, and it reports to the Prime Minister, not to Parliament (although its reports are presented to Parliament by the Prime Minister once sensitive material has been excised). The staff of the committee are civil servants and not servants of the legislature.

Although the committee has shown independence of view (for example in its December 2002 report on the intelligence background to the Bali bombings), there has been increasing pressure to have oversight of intelligence matters undertaken by a genuine select or joint committee directly responsible to Parliament. In its report on the decision to go to war in Iraq, the Foreign Affairs Select Committee recommended that the Intelligence and Security Committee be recast as a select committee of the House of Commons, and this was endorsed in principle by the Foreign Secretary in his evidence to the committee.

How committees work

Although in this section we have a departmental committee particularly in mind, most of it applies to most select committees.

Orders of reference and powers

A committee's task is set out in its 'orders of reference', which also define its powers and specify how many members it shall have. In the case of permanent committees, these orders of reference will be in the House's standing orders; but the House can set up a committee for as long or short a time as it sees fit and can give it other tasks or instructions (such as reporting by a certain date).

As the committee remits quoted in this chapter demonstrate, tasks are usually widely defined: 'to examine expenditure, administration and policy' or 'how the practices and procedures of the House should be modernised', although committees such as those on statutory instruments or regulatory reform are much more circumscribed. Most committees thus have a good deal of latitude; and it is also a basic principle that (subject to any instruction from the House) the interpretation of their orders of reference is a matter for them. Committees generally do not take kindly to being told by the government or by witnesses that they should not be looking at this or that subject; indeed, such comments are normally entirely counter-productive.

Committees are subordinate bodies of the House; they have only those powers that the House gives them and cannot exercise any power that the

House itself does not have. The normal menu is 'to adjourn from place to place', which means that they do not have to sit only at Westminster ('within the United Kingdom' is added for those committees that may not travel abroad); to report 'from time to time', which means that they may continue reporting on their subject area rather than making one report at the end of their work; to appoint specialist advisers; (in most cases) to appoint one or more sub-committees; to exchange evidence with other committees (and with the Scottish Parliament, the National Assembly for Wales and the Northern Ireland Assembly); and to meet jointly with any other committee of either House. This last power provides a good deal of flexibility when a subject affects several committees: for example, the Defence, Foreign Affairs, International Development and Trade and Industry Committees formed what was in effect a joint committee on arms exports.

The power of compulsion

A key phrase in a committee's powers is 'to send for persons, papers and records' (known as 'PPR'). This means that they have the formal power to compel witnesses 'within the jurisdiction' (that is, within the UK) to attend, answer questions and deliver up any papers that the committee may wish to see.

Most witnesses before select committees are willing, even enthusiastic; they want the opportunity to make their case on a very public stage. But some are not, for a variety of reasons from a generalised reluctance to answer a committee's questions to having something discreditable or damaging to hide. In such cases, the committee may make an order to attend (or produce documents), which is served personally on the witness. If he or she does not comply, the committee may report the matter to the House as a breach of privilege. But there are disadvantages to this: the matter is put into a wider political forum, which means that the committee loses control of events; the procedure is cumbersome; and – especially if the matter becomes a party political football – there is no guarantee that the committee in the end will get what it wants.

A select committee's strongest weapon is publicity rather than the use of formal powers. A recalcitrant witness looks as though he or she has something to hide; the trick is for the committee to make *not* giving evidence more embarrassing or awkward than acceding to the committee's request.

Ministers and civil servants have a special status that occasionally leads to conflict with select committees. Civil servants are agents of their secretary of state and carry out his or her instructions; they cannot be forced to divulge information against the secretary of state's wishes. A committee can ask a minister for information but (although the 'embarrassment factor' can come into play here as well) cannot demand it. The House could do so (technically by an address to the Crown, because the information is in the hands of Her Majesty's ministers), but the House does not delegate this power to select committees.

There have been celebrated tussles between investigating select committees and reluctant governments. In its investigation of the Westland Affair in 1986, the Defence Committee sought to interview the civil servants most closely involved with the selective leaking of an opinion by the Solicitor-General. The government refused to allow them to attend, but the Cabinet Secretary appeared twice before the committee, which – because of the political pressure building on the government – also secured internal government documents that had previously been refused. Although the government's internal guidance states that, when there is disagreement between a minister and a committee about the attendance of a civil servant, the minister should appear personally (and in 1990 the then Cabinet Secretary said that a civil servant called by a select committee had a duty to attend), this issue is still an occasional source of friction. In 2003, for example, in its investigation of the decision to go to war in Iraq, the Foreign Affairs Committee was critical of the government for not allowing intelligence personnel to appear before it.

It is sometimes suggested that committees should have unfettered powers of subpoena; we return to this in Chapter 13 (page 385).

Membership

Almost all members of select committee are back-bench MPs; the most notable exception is the Leader of the House as chairman of the Modernisation Committee. Committees normally consist of between nine and eighteen MPs in as near as possible the party proportions in the House as a whole; thus, in the 2001 parliament, a committee of eleven usually had seven Labour, three Conservative and one Liberal Democrat or other third party member. Once MPs are put on a committee, they remain on it for the whole of a parliament, unless they resign or become ministers or front-bench spokesmen.

The quorum of a committee – the number of members who must be present for business to be transacted – is three or a quarter of the number of members, whichever is the larger, with fractions counted as one.

MPs are appointed to committees by a motion put to the House (normally without debate). The names come either from the usual channels (see page 88) and the motion is in the name of the government Deputy Chief Whip; or (in the case of the departmental and domestic committees only) they are proposed by the Committee of Selection and the motion is in the name of a member of that committee. Either way, there has been suspicion that the whips exercise too much control over which MPs get onto committees; and criticism of the fact that government whips have a hand in selecting MPs whose job on the departmental committees is to scrutinise government – and would have an interest in picking MPs they thought would be less critical or independent-minded.

For many people, these suspicions were confirmed when, at the start of the 2001 parliament, the Committee of Selection did not put forward the names of two notably independent chairmen of committees in the previous parliament, the Labour MPs Gwyneth Dunwoody (Transport) and Donald Anderson (Foreign Affairs). This caused a row, and the names that were proposed for these committees were defeated in the House by substantial majorities. Dunwoody and Anderson were then reinstated.

However, a proposal from the Liaison Committee, later taken up by Robin Cook and the Modernisation Committee, that there should be an entirely open system in which the whips would not be involved, was narrowly defeated in the House in May 2002 – as some thought, as the result of an unholy alliance of the whips on *both* sides of the House. In fact, as we shall see, the way that committees work encourages MPs to be independent-minded, and it is remarkable how many conventional government supporters 'go native' when they are put on select committees.

Chairmen

Committees elect their own chairmen[5]; and although among the MPs put on a committee at the start of a parliament there is an obvious (or agreed) candidate for the chair, from time to time committees exercise their independence and elect someone else. Negotiation through 'the usual channels' results in a division of chairmanships between the parties that roughly corresponds to the party proportions in the House, although the governing party is always keen to have the chairmanships of committees that it sees as especially important: for example, Defence, Foreign Affairs, Home Affairs and Treasury. In the 2001 parliament, of the eighteen chairmanships of departmental committees, the Labour Party had thirteen, the Conservatives three and the Liberal Democrats two; and of the cross-cutting committees, the Labour Party had three chairmanships and the Conservatives two. Under a rule introduced in 2002, no MP may be elected chairman of a committee that she or he had chaired for the two previous parliaments, or for eight years, whichever is the longer.

The chairman is the key figure on any select committee. She or he takes a full part in the committee's work (unlike the chairman of a standing committee, who presides impartially over proceedings) and is usually the committee's spokesperson. The committee itself decides subjects for investigation and what witnesses to call, but the chairman's views will be highly influential; and, although chairmen have varying inputs into committees' reports, the draft considered by the committee is almost always in the chairman's name.

Styles of chairmanship vary: some are less interventionist 'chairmen of the board'; others are much more 'managing directors' driving the committee's work. Whichever style they adopt, the role of a good chairman is crucial in keeping the committee together: giving all its members a chance, promoting consensus, foreseeing political problems, establishing good – but not cosy – relationships with ministers in the relevant department, and providing leadership when the going gets tough.

The 1978 recommendation of the Procedure Committee that chairmen should be paid resurfaced in 2003 as result of a Liaison Committee recommendation that the matter should be examined by the Senior Salaries Review Body. The latter's report recommended that, in recognition of their additional responsibilities, the chairmen of the main investigative and legislative committees should be paid £12,500 a year in addition to their salaries as MPs. This was approved by the House; but some chairmen are strongly opposed to the principle, so it seems certain that a number will not draw the additional pay.

There is no formal post of 'deputy chairman'. If the chairman is absent, then the senior opposition MP (or government MP if the chairman is from an opposition party) often takes the chair; but the committee can decide to put any of its members in the chair on a temporary basis.

Staff

Select committees are supported by small teams of staff from the Department of the Clerk of the House; some twenty-five investigative committees are supported by about 130 staff in the Committee Office. A departmental select committee usually has five or six full-time staff. They are led by the *clerk of the committee*, usually a deputy principal clerk (equivalent to a Band 1 official in the senior Civil Service – what used to be called Assistant Secretary/Grade 5) with fifteen to twenty years of experience in the service of the House. In a nutshell, the clerk's job is to help the committee to be as effective as possible in doing the job the House has given it. He or she is the committee's principal adviser, manages the staff team and the specialist advisers, works closely with the chairman on all aspects of the committee's work, and will be responsible for some of the committee's inquiries. *The second clerk* manages inquiries and will usually clerk any sub-committee. One or two *committee specialists*, subject experts on short-term contracts, provide in-depth research and briefing. The *committee assistant* is primarily an administrator, supervising arrangements for hearings and committee visits, and overseeing printing and publication of evidence. The *secretary* is a specialist desktop publisher; even substantial committee reports are published extraordinarily quickly; sometimes agreed one afternoon and published by the Stationery Office, and posted on the parliamentary website, the next morning.

The permanent staff are augmented by *specialist advisers*, who work to the clerk of the committee. They are people, often of great eminence, who assist the committee part-time and are paid on a daily rate. This is a flexible and effective system; a committee can draw on a lifetime's experience in the precise area of what may be a very technical or complex inquiry. Some committees maintain panels of a dozen or fifteen advisers; others appoint one or two for specific inquiries. There are normally about 150 specialist advisers at any one time.

Committees also draw on the resources of the *Scrutiny Unit*, a group of eighteen staff who specialise in the analysis of estimates, departmental annual reports (see page 250) and other financial information; and also in the scrutiny of draft legislation (which allows a committee to deal at short notice with a draft bill without having its programme of work blown off course). Committee staff resources are being expanded to deal with the new 'core tasks' (see below).

A committee's work

Select committees always meet in private except when they are taking oral evidence; as we shall see later, this has advantages. When a committee meets for the first time at the start of a parliament, its members first make a formal declaration of their registered interests. The chairman is then elected, and the next business is to agree a programme of work. The clerk will put proposals before the committee: work outstanding from the last parliament; current and expected events in the subject area (including possible draft bills); previous recommendations on which the committee needs to maintain pressure; policies still in the process of formation, where the committee could have an influence; or perhaps some serious problem where the committee needs to keep up with developments. The chairman and committee members will have their own suggestions; and the committee will then agree and announce its programme of work.

In May 2002, on the recommendation of the Modernisation Committee, the House agreed a set of 'core tasks' for departmental select committees in each of their subject areas and approved some forty additional staff to help committees to carry them out. The Liaison Committee has refined these tasks, which are currently:

1. to examine policy proposals from the UK government and the European Commission in Green Papers, White Papers, draft Guidance etc. and to inquire further where the committee considers it appropriate;
2. to identify and examine areas of emerging policy where existing policy is deficient, and make proposals;
3. to conduct scrutiny of any published draft bill within the committee's responsibilities;

4. to examine specific output from the department expressed in documents or other decisions;
5. to examine the expenditure plans and outturn of the department, its agencies and principal non-departmental public bodies (NDPBs);
6. to examine the department's Public Service Agreements, the associated targets and the statistical measurements employed, and report if appropriate;
7. to monitor the work of the department's executive agencies, NDPBs, regulators and other associated public bodies;
8. to scrutinise major appointments made by the department;
9. to examine the implementation of legislation and major policy initiatives;
10. to produce reports that are suitable for debate in the House, including Westminster Hall, or debating committees.

Most committees were already doing most of these things, but the core tasks are aimed not only at a more methodical and less *ad hoc* approach to scrutiny but also at identifying areas where there was a lack of initiative from the government, or where existing policy was deficient. 'We thought it important', said the Liaison Committee, 'that committees should not have to limit themselves to an agenda of the government's making'.

A typical inquiry

Just as a departmental select committee has wide discretion about *what* it investigates, so it also has great flexibility about *how* it does so. Inquiries may range from an in-depth examination of a complex subject lasting several months to a short sharp inquiry carried out in a week, perhaps with five or six oral evidence hearings crammed into that time. Inquiries may aim to analyse and influence a developing policy, to review a whole subject area, to carry out a 'what went wrong' investigation, or to look at a topical issue of the moment.

Most formal inquiries lead to reports to the House, but a committee may take evidence without reporting; and most committees hold regular one-off evidence sessions with public bodies, chief inspectors or regulators within their area, or with ministers or senior officials on current issues. However, let us take as an example a typical 'subject area' inquiry.

The start of an inquiry

The committee decides on a subject – let us say the government's policy towards domestic violence. The committee approves terms of reference for the inquiry, which are really to help potential witnesses who want to know what the main areas of interest will be – they do not bind the committee. Indeed, once an inquiry is under way, its focus often changes as the committee identifies particular aspects as more important. The committee publishes a press notice about the inquiry, and it may also circulate an 'issues and questions' paper to stimulate debate and the submission of evidence. Both will be put on the parliamentary website.

As well as issuing a general invitation to submit evidence, the committee will make more specific requests for written evidence (often called 'memoranda'). Several government departments – the Home Office, the Department of Health, the Department for Education and Skills, the Department for Constitutional Affairs and the Office of the Deputy Prime Minister – are involved in different aspects of the subject. The committee may ask each department to prepare a paper on its own area of responsibility, or more likely (and to test coordination between the departments) will ask the government to provide a single paper addressing a series of written questions. At the same time, requests for evidence will go out to other key players: the NHS, the British Medical Association as representing GPs, the NSPCC, and national organisations representing social service providers, the police, and support groups for those who have suffered domestic violence.

The committee will at the same time draw up a list of likely witnesses. A programme of oral evidence often begins and ends with the responsible ministers; and there will be other obvious candidates to appear. However, committees try to make the process as open as possible, not limiting it to 'the usual suspects'; and on the basis of the written evidence that comes in – often not formal papers from prominent organisations but letters from local organisations or individuals who have heard about the inquiry – will select other people to give evidence. Several weeks after the call for written evidence first went out, the first oral evidence hearing takes place.

Taking evidence

The members of the committee sit around a horseshoe-shaped table with the chairman at the head and the clerk on his or her left (see page 332). Reflecting the more consensual approach in select committees, the members often do not sit by party affiliation (unlike standing committees). Witnesses sit at a table between the arms of the horseshoe. The shorthand writers who take a verbatim record of the evidence sit in the middle.

The MPs on the committee will have a detailed brief prepared by the committee staff. This will cover the background to the hearing, the key points from the witness's written evidence, including areas that could be explored further, anything that the committee especially needs to get on the record for its eventual report, and a list of suggested questions for the witness. The committee

The Work and Pensions Committee taking evidence in one of the modern Portcullis House committee rooms
Source: Deryc R. Sands; The House of Commons 2003

will often tell witnesses in advance the areas it wants to cover, but it does not normally give notice of particular questions unless some time for preparation would be needed to provide a full answer. The chairman opens the questioning, and other MPs follow. An oral evidence session usually lasts two to two and a half hours, but several witnesses, singly or in groups, may appear during that time. The hearing may be televised live, webcast, broadcast in sound only, or recorded. Seats are provided for the public and the press.

The vast majority of evidence is given in public, but committees can take evidence in private, usually if matters of personal or commercial confidentiality, or national security, are involved. Select committees, mainly the Defence Committee and the Foreign Affairs Committee, have dealt with national security or 'classified' material up to the highest levels of sensitivity.

Most hearings are fairly relaxed; the process is one of exploration and discussion of a subject about which the witnesses have special knowledge, on which the committee wants to draw. However, some hearings, usually if a committee is investigating something that has gone wrong, or where it believes that a government department or other witness is not being open, can be more adversarial. Committees can take evidence on oath if they wish, although this is extremely rare.

1 CHAIRMAN
2 CLERK
3 MEMBERS
4 SHORTHAND WRITER
5 COMMITTEE STAFF
6 PRESS
7 WITNESSES
8 PUBLIC

The layout of a select committee room

Those giving evidence before a select committee are taking part in a proceeding in Parliament (see page 165), so they are fully protected by parliamentary privilege – that is, neither their oral nor their written evidence may give rise to a criminal prosecution or civil action, nor, for example, to disciplinary action by an employer.

A few days after giving evidence, witnesses are sent a transcript to correct for accuracy; they can also add to answers in writing if they wish. Uncorrected transcripts are often published on the Internet as soon as they are available and are replaced with the final corrected version thereafter.

As the inquiry progresses, the committee will be following up oral evidence with requests for further papers, the staff will be researching other sources of information or possible evidence, and some thought will be given to possible visits.

Travel

Travel by select committees often gets a hard time in the media – but it contributes a great deal to a committee's effectiveness. In the inquiry example we have taken here, the committee will want to make visits within the UK, perhaps to see shelters for the victims of domestic violence in different parts of the country, to talk to social services, the police, GPs and support groups on their home ground, and possibly to take oral evidence as well. Visits make a select committee inquiry more accessible; not only do they bring the committee to a local community, but they also mean that people can talk informally to the MPs rather than giving evidence in the often daunting surroundings of Westminster.

Visits also mean that MPs see and hear for themselves; the often rather impersonal formal evidence is supplemented by the first-hand experience and opinions of the people actually involved, and a suggestion or criticism by a single individual often finds its way into the committee's final report.

Travel overseas plays a similar part. It may be that policy on domestic violence in Sweden, say, is better coordinated than in the UK; or that the Canadians have the most effective risk registers and techniques for early warning of violence. No amount of background reading and written evidence is a substitute for seeing for oneself, and finding out first-hand about the benefits and the problems.

The report

Towards the end of an inquiry, the clerk of the committee will usually prepare a 'heads of report' paper – identifying the possible main themes of the report and recommendations, and questions on which the committee itself will need to form a view. Thereafter the clerk will draft the report, perhaps with the assistance of other members of the committee staff or specialist advisers. The draft report will be submitted to the chairman and then presented to the committee in his or her name. In a contentious inquiry, other members may want an alternative draft report (and a clerk may be called upon to draft two entirely incompatible reports!). However, most select committee reports are unanimous and are the more effective for it.

Most committees go through draft reports very informally and then agree to the whole report as a single decision. However, if amendments are considered formally or there are any votes, these are set out in full in the formal minutes at the back of the published report. The same is true of any alternative draft report that may be put forward (although there is formally no such thing as a 'minority report', the same aim is achieved by publication in the formal minutes). When the report has been agreed, the chairman puts two questions for decision: 'That this be the [Fifth] Report of the Committee to the House' and 'That I do make the Report to the House'. One often hears in the media of MPs on a committee 'signing' the report; but this never happens.

Shortly after a report is agreed – and it may be in the next day or two, as even substantial reports can be produced by the committee staff and the Stationery Office at great speed – the report is published, together with all the public oral evidence and many of the written papers submitted during the inquiry. 'Embargoed' copies are often issued to the press beforehand so that they can have their stories ready for the moment of publication; and copies will usually go to witnesses and others who have contributed to the inquiry. The committee may hold a press conference; and the chairman and individual members of the committee will also give interviews to get their own perspective on the record. (In a sensitive inquiry, they may have to choose their words with care, as a press conference is not a proceeding in Parliament, and there is no protection of privilege.)

A type of report known as 'a special report' is used as a vehicle for publishing government replies to committees, or sometimes for informing the House of some difficulty encountered in the committee's work.

The government reply

Reports are made to the House, although the intended audience includes everyone concerned with the subject, the media and – crucially – the government. Every select committee report should receive a formal government reply within two months. This is a convention rather than a formal rule, but committees have found that asking the minister concerned to appear to explain a delay often means the rapid appearance of the reply.

No-one expects a government to put on sackcloth and ashes in this formal reply. If the committee has been highly critical, the government is more likely to be defensive and to restate its case than to say 'it's a fair cop'. If the committee has put forward challenging recommendations, the government is likely to be cautious rather than to accept them right away. But the 'delayed drop' effect of select committee reports should never be underestimated. Ambitious recommendations may change the whole public debate on a subject; they may be taken up by public bodies and pressure groups; and months (or sometimes two or three years) later they may contribute substantially to a major shift in government policy. Similarly, the effect of justified criticism may not be immediately apparent; but a department may be quietly changing its procedures to avoid making the same mistake again.

Whatever the contents of the government reply, committees are more influential if they follow up on their reports. Most departmental select committees have a 'continuous agenda' in which major policy issues recur, but returning to the detail of previous recommendations, and pursuing vague promises or non-committal responses through further inquiries, maintains the pressure and keeps the subject in the public eye.

Consensus

Select committees seem to be held in generally high regard – perhaps more than anything else that Parliament does. There may be several reasons for this: they provide access to the political process; they provide challenge and an alternative point of view; but probably most of all they show how politicians of different parties can work together.

There is no doubt that unanimous committees are more effective. They speak with a single voice, and it is much harder for governments to dismiss cross-party agreement. Some people see consensus as implying flabby compromise, but select committees show time and again that they can reach a tough agreed view on politically hot subjects. Given that select committees are made up of party politicians, how does this happen?

There are three main reasons. First, when they are not taking public oral evidence, select committees meet in private. Their discussions, working papers and draft reports are private. This means that it is much harder for party political pressure to be put on them – for example, by the whips – and it also means that the MPs can be remarkably frank with each other. For example, an individual back-bencher can put forward ideas totally at odds with party (or government) policy; and the readiness to see the other side of the argument is a key factor in getting cross-party agreement.

Second, the members of a select committee usually get to know each other well (even if, as can happen in a House of 659 members, they have never spoken to each other before the committee's first meeting). They will work together over many months, both formally and informally; there will be a good basis for trust; and they will then often see themselves as members of the committee more than as party representatives.

Third, select committees proceed on the basis of evidence (as shown by the wealth of footnotes in most select committee reports!). They do this because basing their conclusions firmly on evidence is part of the due process of investigation, but also because recommendations firmly grounded in fact, and explicitly supported by expert opinion, are much harder to challenge. This approach also helps to maintain consensus; a weight of evidence can lead MPs on a committee to agree on a conclusion even if it does not match their previous personal opinions.

Dealing with a select committee

As more and more people in all walks of life come into contact with the work of select committees, it may be helpful to say something about how to have an input into an inquiry (a fuller guide for witnesses is available on the parliamentary website).

First, make sure that what you want to say is relevant to the committee's work. Look at the press notice and any issues and questions (on the website), and see what ground the inquiry will cover. If you are submitting written evidence – and this goes for government departments and some major national bodies as well as individuals – do not simply top and tail a paper prepared for some other purpose; make sure it is tailored to the requirements of the inquiry. If the inquiry is already under way, look on the committee's home page at transcripts that have already been published to see what the government and other bodies are saying to the committee. You may also be able to follow an inquiry via the BBC Parliament channel or, increasingly, through webcasts.

Keep written evidence concise and to the point; number the paragraphs and, over two pages or so, begin with a summary of what the paper says (and a table of contents if necessary). Say if you want any part of the paper to be kept confidential. An address for written evidence will be on the committee's home page. Committees prefer if possible to have written evidence electronically (in MS Word or rich text format) by e-mail attachment to the committee's mailbox address (on the press notice), with a hard-copy letter validating the e-mail, or on disk. Once you submit written evidence it becomes a committee document and, if you want to use it publicly before the committee publishes it, you should seek permission (which is almost always given).

You can ask to give oral evidence, but remember that the committee will have a full programme for the inquiry and will certainly not be able to accommodate all those who wish to do so. A witness who submits a constructive written paper, which suggests solutions rather than simply rehearsing criticism, may be more likely to be called to give oral evidence. If you are called, the committee staff will talk to you about the details and will usually be able to give you an indication of the committee's likely areas of interest. Let them know if you need disabled access.

When you appear, do not expect to be able to make an opening statement; this is better done in writing in advance, as most committees want to get straight on with questioning. The MPs on the committee will all have name-plates in front of them, but it is best to address your answers to the chair. Remember that giving oral evidence (or submitting a written paper) is not the one and only chance to contribute. You can provide additional information in writing (for example if you feel you did not answer a question fully) or comment on the evidence given by someone else. If you want to give any of your evidence in private, talk to the clerk of the committee well before your appearance.

Whether you are contributing to an inquiry or not, you can attend the public hearings (subject to there being space; it is not possible to book seats in advance) either in the Palace of Westminster itself or in Portcullis House, or if a select committee takes evidence elsewhere in the UK.

Select committee activity

Activity is at a high level. There are more committees (recent additions include the Joint Committee on Human Rights, the Constitutional Affairs Committee and *ad hoc* committees on draft bills) and many more committees are able to set up sub-committees for particular inquiries or subjects. Formal meetings of select committees (not including informal meetings, seminars and visits) are running at over a thousand a year (1,037 in financial year 2002–03, including 497 sessions of public oral evidence). Seventy-two substantive reports were made in 2001–02, when work was interrupted by the general election, but 136 in financial year 2002–03. Over the last four years, an average of about 375 MPs have been members of select committees of one sort or another. With the advent of Westminster Hall (see page 269) there is more debate on select committee reports in addition to the three estimates days in the Chamber (see page 248); and there has been a noticeable increase in the use of committee reports in major debates in the House, as well as in Question Time, including Prime Minister's Questions.

Investigative select committees are also engaging in a wider range of activity. They hold seminars, often with outside experts, to focus and plan major inquiries; they undertake scrutiny of legislation (examples in the present parliament include the draft NHS (Wales) Bill (Welsh Affairs Committee), the Police Reform and Criminal Justice Bills and the draft Extradition Bill (Home Affairs Committee) and the State Pensions Credit Bill (Work and Pensions Committee), as well as a number of *ad hoc* committees); they have made a start on examining major public appointments (the Treasury Committee scrutinises appointments to the Bank of England Monetary Policy Committee) and, although there is resistance in government to this sort of process, it is likely to spread. Committees have also widened political debate, taking evidence from opposition spokespeople on their alternative policies as well as from government ministers.

Particularly in the context of the core tasks and with the help of the Scrutiny Unit, committees now conduct more financial scrutiny of government departments, including estimates, annual reports and performance targets, than ever before. There is more 'joined-up scrutiny', for example on European issues between the European Scrutiny Committee and the departmental select committees. Committees themselves have become more accountable, publishing annual reports on their work, and how they have tackled the core tasks.

At the same time, select committees continue to carry out investigations on every sort of subject and current issue. Examples of inquiries under way in the summer of 2003 included choice in maternity services, poultry farming in the UK, foreign policy aspects of the war against terrorism, the effectiveness of the government's target setting, the impact of direct payment on post offices and their customers, the UK biotechnology industry, and asylum applications: a mix of issues of national importance, many of which affect the lives of individual citizens.

What do select committees achieve?

In its March 2000 report *Shifting the Balance: Select Committees and the Executive*, the Liaison Committee said:

> The 1979 select committee system has been a success. We have no doubt of that. At a bargain price, it has provided independent scrutiny of government. It has enabled the questioning of ministers and civil servants, and has forced them to explain policies. On occasion, it has exposed mistaken and short-sighted policies and, from time to time, wrong-doing in both high places and low. It has been a source of unbiased information, rational debate, and constructive ideas. It has made the political process less remote, and more accessible to the citizen who is affected by that process – and who pays the bill. Its very existence has been a constant reminder to Ministers and officials, and many others in positions of power and influence, of the spotlight that may swing their way when least welcome. It has also shown the House of Commons at its best: working on the basis of fact, not supposition or prejudice; and with constructive co-operation rather than routine disagreement.

Objective measurement of the effectiveness or influence of select committees is impossible. Governments have accepted a great many select committee recommendations, even when they have not originally been disposed to do so, but it is always difficult to judge how far this has been down to the committee in each case and how far the committee has been the decisive advocate for a growing body of opinion. In 2002, for example, the government accepted the recommendation of the Home Affairs Select Committee to downgrade cannabis from a class B drug to a class C drug, but there was already some pressure for change. Had the committee come out against reclassification, on the other hand, the government would probably have used the committee's conclusion as the basis for *not* changing its policy.

Sometimes the mere fact of an inquiry leads to a change in government policy before the committee reports. To take another Home Affairs example, on the first day of hearings on the Criminal Records Bureau the government caved in on the main issue, that of charging volunteers for criminal records checks.

There is no point in trying to measure effectiveness by totting up how many recommendations are accepted by the government. This process makes no distinction between 'soft' recommendations, on which the door is already ajar, and 'hard' recommendations, which have no chance of being accepted now, but which change the whole nature of public debate, and which may end up as government policy – perhaps the policy of an incoming government after a general election – months or years later (the 'delayed drop' effect referred to above).

However, having even tough recommendations accepted is not what effective scrutiny is about (although it may be one of the results). Scrutiny of government is the process of examining expenditure, administration and policy in detail, on the public record, requiring the government of the day to explain itself to parliamentarians as representatives of the citizen and the taxpayer, and to justify its actions.

This process of accountability is never comfortable for those being scrutinised; and it should not be. But the fact that the government's actions can be put under the spotlight of public examination at any time makes for better decision making; as Robin Cook when Leader of the House said, 'good scrutiny makes for good government'.

A brief sample of some recent initiatives by just three of the departmental select committees gives a flavour of this process. Following the '9/11' terrorist attacks, the Defence Committee conducted a comprehensive inquiry into defence and security in the UK; a feature of the inquiry was the fact that it cut across the responsibilities of all the government departments concerned, addressing the key question of coordination between them. The committee also took up the case of Gulf War veterans who believed that they were suffering from 'Gulf War syndrome' and pursued the issue through a number of reports, forcing changes in policy upon administrations of both main parties. The recommendation of the Culture, Media and Sport Committee for a specific tax break for British films was accepted by the government and had a revitalising effect on the industry. In the context of the merging worlds of broadcasting and communications, the same committee first recommended the appointment of a single regulator for both – accepted by the government in the Communications Bill and the establishment of Ofcom. Three years before the 2002 Manchester Commonwealth Games, it also identified the need to have one minister taking responsibility for the event, later widely acknowledged to have been a critical factor in its success. The committee correctly identified the recipe for a viable Wembley Stadium in March 2000, which was rejected by the government immediately the report was published but accepted in September 2002. In another part of its responsibilities, the committee initiated a transformation of policy on illicit trade and repatriation of cultural items. In 2002, the Transport, Local Government and the Regions Committee published a report on empty homes, which the government accepted, setting up a substantial fund and a series of initiatives to deal with the problem. Finally, after the committee's responsibilities were split, successive reports of the new Transport Committee forced road user charging onto the political agenda.

In this chapter, we have described the role of Commons select committees largely in terms of scrutinising the government of the day. This accounts for much of their activity, but they also have a wider role. Their reports and recommendations may be aimed at particular public bodies, sectors of industry, or the professions. Select committees are often good at 'blue skies' thinking; they can examine some difficult topic of public policy and analyse possible courses of action – the relaxation of the law on drugs is a good example – that political parties would find more difficult. Where there is controversy about the factual basis of public debate, perhaps on a topic such as BSE or genetic engineering, a select committee is an excellent vehicle for analysing conflicting claims and setting out common ground. Like written questions (see page 301) but to an even greater degree, select committee written and oral evidence puts a mass of information, from both the government and other sources, into the public domain.

Whatever a select committee does, its effectiveness depends above all on its members. Their commitment and effort are crucial. As the Liaison Committee said in *Shifting the Balance*:

> no pain, no gain: there is no easy route to success. A determined and hardworking committee, in which Members are prepared to devote substantial effort and put the interests of the citizen and taxpayer first, can be extraordinarily effective.

MPs on select committees need an up-to-date understanding of the subject area. They do not have to be great technical experts – and indeed there is some reason for them not to be; it could be said that one of the strengths of select committees is that they are made up of well-informed lay people who can ask common-sense questions of the experts and make sure they get proper answers.

On individual inquiries, members of a committee need to keep up with the written and oral evidence and to prepare for oral evidence sessions. The committee staff supports the committee through briefing, and summarising and analysing evidence, but there is no substitute for individual MPs having command of the subject. Although, as we have seen in earlier chapters, there are many other calls on MPs' time, the most effective oral evidence sessions – especially with difficult and well-briefed witnesses – are those at which all the members of a committee are present throughout; are well prepared; divide up the areas of questioning between them; ask questions rather than make statements; and follow up each other's questions.

It is sometimes suggested that committees should have counsel to undertake part of the examination of witnesses. This misses the point on several counts; select committee work is a function of Parliament and should be undertaken by parliamentarians. It is also relatively rare that this sort of forensic examination is required: other types of inquiry are frequently more valuable and play to other select committee strengths.

But when forensic examination is required, a good many MPs are perfectly capable of extremely effective questioning. Anyone who saw or heard the clinical dissection of witness after witness by the Labour MP John Gilbert during the Defence Committee's inquiry into the Westland affair in 1986 will have a good idea of what is possible; but it cannot be done without hard work and a good deal of committee solidarity.

Being an effective member of a select committee is time-consuming. In its July 2003 report on pay for select committee chairmen, the Senior Salaries Review Body found that for most chairmen their select committee work occupied two days a week (or 50 percent of the time that they spent in the House) and that for some chairmen this occupied up to 70 percent of their time. The time commitment for members of a busy committee may not be much less. The average attendances each session for every committee are published in the Sessional Returns; it is noticeable that most of the committees generally seen as 'heavyweight' and effective have attendances around 80 percent or higher.

The Liaison Committee described the achievements of the select committee system as having been 'at a bargain price'. This is still the case. Some forty select committees, including twenty-five or so investigative committees, are supported by about 150 staff (the Public Accounts Committee and the Public Administration Committee also draw upon the resources of the Comptroller and Auditor-General and the Ombudsman respectively). Staff costs are about £5 million a year, and all other costs, including printing, shorthand recording and transcription of evidence, specialist advisers, travel, and work commissioned, amount to less than £4 million.

Select committees in the House of Lords

The committees

Since the early 1970s, the House of Lords has also developed an increasingly elaborate array of select committees reappointed every session to scrutinise various aspects of public policy. (For legislative committees, see page 213, and for domestic committees see page 67.) Some of these policy scrutiny committees enjoy a high reputation. Unlike the Commons, the Lords committee structure developed in a way that was thematic and cross-cutting rather than departmental, and there is now general acceptance that this enables Lords committee work to complement rather than compete with or duplicate that of the Commons.

The most elaborate of these committees is the European Union Committee, with its seven sub-committees, the work of which is described in the next chapter. A Science and Technology Committee, with two sub-committees, considers aspects of science policy and includes distinguished scientists among its members.

Since 2001, further committees have been established, not least because an expansion of select committee work has appealed to those interested in reform of the House. So, after the 2001 general election, an Economic Affairs Committee was established as a successor to what had originally been an *ad hoc* select committee on the Monetary Policy Committee of the Bank of England. In November 2002, this committee was empowered to set up a sub-committee in the expectation that it would consider policy aspects of the Finance Bill (other than the rates and incidence of tax). This was successfully done for the 2003 Finance Bill and is likely to continue.

A Constitution Committee was also set up in February 2001, both to carry out policy inquiries and to examine and report on all public bills for any constitutional implications.

In addition, the House from time to time sets up committees for specific purposes, either to consider the merits of bills (for example, the two Charities Bills in 1983, the Infant Life Preservation Bill in 1987–88 or the Dangerous Dogs Bill in 1995–96) or to consider policy matters. In 1985, a committee considered overseas trade, particularly the trade deficit in manufactured goods, and in 1993–94 another considered medical ethics, specifically euthanasia; in 2001, one committee examined embryonic stem cell research, while another considered animal experimentation; and in 2002–03 another looked at religious offences, and blasphemy in particular. Such committees are not normally expected to continue in existence for longer than one session and usually try to fulfil their orders of reference in that time. *Ad hoc* select committees on matters of public interest are now regularly appointed annually.

European Union Committee, sub-committee D (Environment, agriculture, Public Health and Consumer Protection)
Source: The House of Lords 2003, Terry Moore

One recent committee does not quite fit in with the general run of *ad hoc* committee activity and deserves brief mention by virtue of the oddity of both its subject matter and the manner of its being set up – the Select Committee on the Crash of Chinook Helicopter ZD576 on 2 June 1994. The pilots had been found grossly negligent by the RAF Board of Inquiry. On the motion of Lord Chalfont, a cross-bench member, the House agreed that the Liaison Committee (the work of this committee is discussed below) should consider appointing a select committee to consider the circumstances of the crash. Not surprisingly, the Liaison Committee took the view that select committees were not equipped to undertake quasi-judicial inquiries, and a precedent might be set. The Liaison Committee's advice was rejected by the House on a vote in March 2001, and a committee was then set up chaired by a Lord of Appeal. In January 2002, the committee found that the Board of Inquiry's finding could not be justified. The government rejected the committee's conclusion.

The process

How does the House decide when to establish a committee? Following a study of the House's committee work in 1991–92, a Liaison Committee chaired by the Chairman of Committees was set up to allocate resources between select committees and to make recommendations to the House on the appointment of committees. Discussions about committee work, which used to take place between the usual channels, now take place in the Liaison Committee, on which the party leaders, the Convenor of the Cross Bench Peers and a small number of back-bench members also sit.

The demand for establishing committees – usually temporary in the first instance – is strong. The initiative rests with the individual member promoting the idea, who now has to convince the Liaison Committee that the subject of inquiry is a suitable one for a Lords committee to consider. By no means all proposals meet with the approval of the Liaison Committee and, with the notable exception of the Chinook inquiry, the House follows its advice. As more committees are established, the demand for members to sit on them are sometimes not easy to meet, as the party whips can testify.

Once established, select committees in the Lords operate in a way that is almost identical to Commons committees, and they encounter many of the same logistical difficulties. Each committee or sub-committee is supported by its clerk, a secretary/administrator, a share of a committee researcher or specialist, and the assistance of an outside specialist adviser or advisers appointed for each particular inquiry in return for a daily fee. The total spending of the Lords Committee Office in the financial year 2002–03 was about £2.5 million in support of fourteen active committees and sub-committees. These costs do not include any element for accommodation, IT, security or utilities. Nor do they have regard to the cost of members, whose expenses are paid by virtue of their attendance at the House. Indeed, a committee's members are its most important resource. But the fact is that, as with Commons select committees, the monetary costs are modest (especially by comparison with Royal Commissions and non-parliamentary committees).

Lords committees have an inherent power to send for witnesses; documents are produced voluntarily. An Order of the House would be required to compel witnesses to attend or to produce papers, and none has in recent times been necessary. As with Commons committees, the prospect of embarrassment and potential adverse publicity in failing to comply has proved to be a powerful persuader. Lords committees have power to meet concurrently with Commons committees, although this rarely occurs.

As in the Commons, there are no minority reports in the Lords. Dissent – were there to be any – would have to be recorded by moving amendments and having these amendments printed in the minutes of proceedings. Lords committees usually succeed in achieving unanimity as members know that unless their conclusions can be supported by all they are unlikely to achieve the greatest impact. The chairman in the Lords has no casting vote.

The House usually finds time to debate the reports of its committees, although the timing may not always be to the liking of committee members (see page 277). Through these debates, the committee seeks to elicit a response from the government. In 2001–02, about 2 percent of the House's sitting time was spent debating select committee reports. A written response is also provided – within two months for reports of the European Communities Committee and six months for all others.

Outcomes

It is difficult to say how far government policy adapts to the findings of Lords select committees, but where those committees produce reports that accord with government thinking, rather than being deeply critical, they seem to have effect. There are several examples of this happening in the case of the Science and Technology Committee, for example, in areas as diverse as hazardous waste disposal, regulation of biotechnology and research and development in the National Health Service. Its report on Systematic Biology Research in 1991–92 helped to preserve funding for that branch of science; and a follow-up inquiry in 2002 may have had the effect of an increase in the funding of at least one of the major institutions active in this field. The Science and Technology Committee was the first select committee of either House to propose, through one of its members, an amendment to a public bill – the Forestry Bill in 1981 – but this has not become common practice.

In some cases results can be more tangible. In 1985, government support (but no government time) facilitated the passage through Parliament (under the private members' procedure) of the Charities Bill, which had been drafted by the Select Committee on Charities in 1984.

The influence of other committees lies in helping to focus debate. Thus the select committee on the Infant Life Preservation Bill undoubtedly helped to focus the debate on the appropriate maximum period of gestation after which abortion would not be lawful; and it appears that the recent report on embryonic stem cell research, which recommended the continuation of such research under strict regulation, may have a similar effect in stabilising debate in this related area of public policy. The committee on religious offences accepted that it would be unable itself to agree on any recommendations on the future of the law of blasphemy and so focused instead on setting out the arguments and options for Parliament to consider in due course.

But whatever the response of the government may be to committee activity, and despite the procedural nicety that committee reports are made to the House, the reports of Lords committees also reach a wider audience and are usually meant to. Those of the European Union Committee are frequently used by members of the European Parliament and are widely read by those engaged in scrutiny in EU national parliaments. In 2002–03, its reports on the drafts of the Convention on the Future of Europe were used by the four British members of the convention. The report of the Select Committee on Overseas Trade, although its findings were on the whole rejected by the government at the time, achieved a certain notoriety: it received the rare accolade of an unfavourable mention in the Chancellor of the Exchequer's 1986 Budget speech, received wide media attention on publication in October 1985, ran through five editions and for some years served as a university teaching aid. More recently, the report of the Select Committee on Medical Ethics received wide media coverage because it proposed no change to the law governing euthanasia; and that on stem cell research because it supported continued research.

It follows that committee members are most anxious that their reports receive the widest possible publicity. The Committee Office retains its own press and publicity officer; the publication of every report is accompanied by a press notice; and for the more significant reports press conferences are held.

Members of the House of Lords Science and Technology Committee launching their report, 'Fighting Infection' in 2003
Source: The House of Lords 2003, Terry Moore

There can be no doubt that committee work has featured conspicuously in the renaissance of the House of Lords in recent times. It suits the non-partisan temper and character of the House, and it is certain to remain a permanent – and one suspects expanding – feature of its activities.

Joint committees

We have seen elsewhere that the two Houses are able to appoint joint select committees. The best-known and most established are legislative in character, like the Joint Committee on Statutory Instruments and the Joint Committees on Consolidation Bills and Tax Law Rewrite Bills (see pages 318 and 319). Joint committees are also occasionally set up for certain kinds of opposed private business – opposed Special Procedure Orders and opposed Scottish Provisional Order Confirmation Bills. But joint select committees to consider issues of public policy, of the kind that have been the chief concern of this chapter, are rare.

Usually, they are set up to consider particular issues of concern to both houses. For example, in November 1997 a Joint Select Committee on Parliamentary Privilege was set up with a wide remit to review privilege and its application by the two Houses and to make recommendations. The committee reported in March 2000. Its report provided a definitive account of the state of parliamentary privilege at the end of the twentieth century. Its key recommendation was to restate the force of Article 9 of the Bill of Rights in respect of proceedings of Parliament (that they might not be impeached or questioned in any court of law), subject only to the possibility that either House might waive that privilege, provided that there was no risk of the member who spoke in the proceedings being exposed to legal liability as a result. Obscure, outdated and unnecessary privileges should be abandoned or redefined and the remaining privileges codified in an Act of Parliament (see also page 164). These recommendations have yet to be acted upon.

More recently, a joint select committee has met to consider Lords reform. Set up in July 2002, its first task was to report on options for the composition and powers of the House once reform had been completed. After free votes in both Houses on the options, the committee would, it was envisaged, define in greater detail the proposed composition, role and powers of the second Chamber and recommend a transition strategy for transforming the Lords into its fully reformed state. The committee's first substantive report, published in December 2002, recommended no change in powers but set out seven options for composition ranging from fully nominated to fully elected. In February 2003, both Houses voted on these options. The Lords voted for continued nomination and rejected all other options. The Commons rejected all the options.

In a further report published in May 2003, the joint committee reported again, identifying areas of consensus and inviting the government to indicate what view it now took of Lords reform. In its response published in July, the government indicated that, in the absence of consensus, its interest now would be in making the existing House work more effectively. Its chief focus would be to review the role of the Appointments Commission and the continued presence of the remaining ninety-two hereditary members of the House. In view of this response, it is difficult to see what further work remains for the joint committee to do were it to be re-appointed in the 2003–04 session. We discuss the issue of Lords reform in Chapter 13.

12   Parliament and Europe

Background

The relationship between the United Kingdom and its parliament, and the European Union has been a key theme of British politics for more than thirty years. On 1 January 1973, the UK joined what were then three 'European Communities': the *European Economic Community* (EEC) or 'Common Market', together with the European Coal and Steel Community and the European Atomic Energy Community (Euratom). The 1992 Maastricht Treaty renamed the European Economic Community simply the 'European Community' and made it part of the new *European Union*.

Membership

There were six members of the EEC established by the 1957 Treaty of Rome: Belgium, France, Germany, Italy, Luxembourg and the Netherlands. In 1972, they were joined by Denmark, Ireland and the United Kingdom; in 1979 by Greece, and in 1985 by Spain and Portugal. In 1995, these countries – now the European Union – were joined by Austria, Sweden and Finland. The biggest ever enlargement of the EU is set to take place on 1 May 2004, with the addition of Cyprus, the Czech Republic, Estonia, Hungary, Latvia, Lithuania, Malta, Poland, the Slovak Republic and Slovenia. Bulgaria and Romania are in the wings, hoping to join in 2007. Turkey has also applied to become a member.

Closer union

The preamble to the Treaty of Rome set ambitious objectives of 'ever closer union of the peoples of Europe and elimination of the barriers which divide Europe'. However, it set the EEC the less politically sensitive task of 'establishing a common market and progressively approximating the economic policies of Member States . . . harmonious development of economic activities' and so on.

For nearly thirty years, the EEC was concerned mainly with commercial and economic affairs; and during that time the Community managed with only modest amendments to the original treaty (such as those required when new member states joined). Subsequent changes were more profound and fuelled political controversy about the balance between national sovereignty and an 'ever closer union'.

In 1987, the *Single European Act* allowed legislation for the completion of the Community's internal market to be made by qualified majority voting (QMV) in the Council of Ministers. The use of QMV, which has since been applied to many other areas of European legislation, means that the Council of Ministers makes decisions by a weighted system of voting in which larger countries have more votes.[8] It also means that no single member state can exercise a veto. The Single European Act also increased the legislative role of the European Parliament and provided for political cooperation on foreign policy.

In some ways, it is surprising that the then Conservative government led by Margaret Thatcher accepted the concept of QMV, which in later years has eliminated member states' powers of veto in most areas. The completion of the internal market, which was due in 1992, was no doubt seen as a higher priority; and the introduction of QMV allowed some 280 internal market measures to be passed that would otherwise have been blocked by one state or another.

The *Treaty on European Union* of 1992 (*the Maastricht Treaty*) established three 'pillars' of the EU: the European Community, a common foreign and security policy (CFSP) and cooperation on justice and home affairs (JHA); and it instituted the machinery to bring about monetary union.

The *Treaty of Amsterdam* (1997) formalised for the first time the concept of 'flexibility' in providing for some countries to cooperate on aims that were not necessarily followed by all member states. It moved the free movement of persons from the JHA pillar to the Community pillar, making it a subject for legislation rather than simply cooperation, and it also incorporated the provisions of the social agreement.

The *Treaty of Nice* (2001) established a European Security and Defence Policy and extended the application of QMV. It also made provision for the institutional change that would be necessary on enlargement of the Union, including the size of the European Commission and a new weighting of votes for QMV.

In December 2001, the European Council set up the *Convention on the Future of Europe* to examine how the EU could be made more democratic and efficient, and to propose a constitution for the Union. The convention, which included representatives from national governments and parliaments,[9] both of current member states and the applicant countries, as well as representatives of the European Commission and the European Parliament, reported in the summer of 2003. Its draft constitutional treaty, including additional powers for the European Parliament and a new post of a more long-term President of the European Council of Ministers, led to opposition calls for it to be subject to a referendum in the UK but in the event the European Council was unable to reach agreement on the text.

The European debate

The European Communities Act 1972, which took the UK into the Common Market, was passed by the narrow majority of seventeen (and the majority on second reading after three full days of debate was only eight). The UK's relations with the EC and EU have been a matter of political controversy ever since. In 1975, the Labour government led by Harold Wilson held a national referendum on renegotiation of the terms of the UK's membership; and the subject was so divisive that collective Cabinet responsibility was suspended so that senior ministers could campaign for opposite sides of the issue.

Disagreements about Europe, both between and within parties, were never absent in the succeeding years; but it was institutional change within the European Union that brought them to centre stage. In the 1992–97 parliament, John Major's government was dogged by dissent and open rebellion on European issues, made more hazardous by the Conservatives' small majority.

Major came into office with an overall majority of twenty-one, but after the loss of eight by-elections and the defection of four MPs to other parties, the Conservatives lost their overall majority and were in a minority of three before the end of the parliament. This meant that rebels on European issues – and especially on the Maastricht Treaty – had a real prospect of bringing about the government's defeat. In July 1992, the government did indeed lose a significant vote on the Maastricht Social Protocol, by 324 votes to 316, and had to put a motion of confidence – which it won comfortably – before the House the next day. Serious 'Eurosceptic' dissent nevertheless continued, leading to the withdrawal of the whip from eight persistent rebels from November 1994 to April 1995. And in June 1995, Major resigned the leadership of the Conservative Party, standing immediately for re-election in an attempt to bring matters to a head. Although he won by 218 votes to 89, the size of the minority indicated the level of (largely Europe-fuelled) dissent.

The broadly pro-European stance of the incoming Labour government in 1997 (and also its huge overall majority of 179) meant that European issues were less prominent in the 1997 parliament; but in the 2001 parliament the Convention on the Future of Europe and the draft EU constitution have been issues between the parties, as well as within the Conservative Party.

Law making and sovereignty

It is easy to see why the EU has been a divisive issue. On the one hand, the argument runs, our interests are so similar to those of our neighbours that we should act in concert with them, giving up some freedom of action so that we can be more effective and influential as a union of states. On the other hand, this closer union is also seen as an unacceptable loss of sovereignty to a largely undemocratic and unaccountable EU in which distinct UK interests will be submerged.

It is certainly the case that the United Kingdom Parliament has lost its primacy in law making. EU directives set out what is to be the effect of the law in all the member states without specifying its detailed terms; it is up to each country to decide on the wording. However, under the European Communities Act 1972 implementation of EU directives in the UK takes place through delegated legislation (see page 227), which Parliament has no power to amend and is not particularly good at scrutinising. And EU regulations (see below) automatically become law in this country without the involvement of Parliament.

Moreover, as European law has precedence over the laws of member states, it is possible for a British court or the European Court of Justice to declare an Act passed by the Westminster Parliament to be incompatible with Community law and so of no effect, as happened, for example, with the Merchant Shipping Act 1988 in the 1991 *Factortame* case.

It would be theoretically possible for Parliament to repeal the European Communities Act 1972 and the other legislation that has incorporated successive treaty changes into UK law. To that extent it remains a sovereign parliament; but how far repeal would be a practical possibility, with the withdrawal from treaty commitments and the unscrambling of the UK's relationship with the EU that would be involved, is another matter.

If a fundamental change in the relationship between the European Union and the UK and its parliament is unlikely, then what role is there for Westminster (and for the national parliaments in each of the member states, as well as the devolved assemblies)? Before we consider this in more detail, it may be helpful to review the institutions of the EU and how European laws are made.

The Council of Ministers

The Council is the principal legislative and decision-making body in the EU. It consists of ministerial representatives from each of the member states' governments, who vary according to the business under discussion. Thus for agricultural matters the Council will consist of agriculture ministers, finance ministers will deal with economic and financial matters, and so on. The majority of Council meetings are held in private; a lot of decisions are taken by agreement, but if votes are necessary they are usually by QMV (see page 350). Most Council of Ministers meetings take place in Brussels. The presidency of the Council is held by each member state in turn for a period of six months; this can be very demanding for small states and can also lead to problems of continuity.

The Council is supported by the Committee of Permanent Representatives (member states' ambassadors to the EU), known as COREPER, which prepares

Council business and often negotiates agreement between member states so that the Council need take only a formal decision. The office of the United Kingdom's permanent representative – essentially the Brussels arm of government departments in Whitehall and elsewhere – is known as UKREP.

The European Council

This consists of the heads of state or government (prime ministers or presidents) of each of the member states and is the supervisory body of the EU, setting out strategic aims. It meets twice a year and is also attended by foreign affairs ministers and a representative of the European Commission. It is chaired by whichever country holds the presidency.

The European Commission

The Commission (based in Brussels) is the EU's executive – in some ways like a civil service, but with extensive powers of initiative, and of decision on a range of delegated matters. There are twenty Commissioners, each of whom is responsible for an area of policy. France, Germany, Italy, Spain and the UK each have two Commissioners, and the other states have one each. The work of the Commission is carried out by twenty-five Directorates-General.

The European Parliament

The European Assembly was renamed the European Parliament in the Single European Act of 1987. Since 1979, its members (MEPs) have been directly elected for fixed terms of five years; the next election will take place in 2004. The total membership is 626, eighty-seven of whom represent UK constituencies (seventy-one in England, eight in Scotland, five in Wales and three in Northern Ireland). The largest party in the parliament is the European People's Party (233 seats), to which the thirty-six British Conservative MEPs are affiliated; then comes the European Socialist Party (175 seats), to which the twenty-nine British Labour MEPs belong. The European Liberal Democratic Reform Party (fifty-three seats) includes the ten British Liberal MEPs. Other British MEPs are UK Independence (three), SNP (two), Green (two), Plaid Cymru (two), Ulster Unionist (one) and Democratic Unionist (one).

The European Parliament operates on the 'continental' model, whereby most business in plenary sessions originates from the twenty permanent committees and their sub-committees, which carry out most of the legislative scrutiny. Extraordinarily, the European Parliament continues to sit both in

Strasbourg, for a week of plenary sittings each month, and in Brussels, for a number of two-day plenaries and the majority of committee meetings.

The European Parliament employs 3,850 people (a third of whom are interpreters and translators working in the eleven languages of the EU; the next enlargement will add a further seven languages). The budget for 2002 was £625 million, which does not include MEPs' salaries. Exact comparisons are difficult, but so far as one can compare like with like, the European Parliament costs two to three times as much as the House of Commons.

Other institutions

The *Court of Auditors* (in Luxembourg) examines EU spending and makes both an annual report and reports on particular expenditure programmes. *The European Court of Justice* (also in Luxembourg) has a general duty of ensuring that in the operation of the treaties the law is observed. It decides on actions that challenge the legality of actions of the institutions of the EU, or that allege a breach of a treaty by a member state. It is assisted by the *Court of First Instance*, which hears actions brought by private individuals, companies and other bodies against EU institutions. The 222 members of the consultative *Economic and Social Committee* (in Brussels) are drawn from trade union, employer, consumer and other interests; and the 222 members of the consultative *Committee of the Regions* represent the interests of regional and local government. The *European Central Bank* in Frankfurt has become the central bank for those countries that have joined the euro zone, while the *European Investment Bank* in Luxembourg is the EU's financing institution, providing long-term loans for capital investment.

European legislation: types

There are three forms of European legislation: directives, regulations and decisions. (Strictly speaking, EU legislation is 'Community' legislation, as the European Community – within the structure of the EU – is the source of the European legal order, but for simplicity we will keep to 'European' or 'EU'.) *Directives* are binding on member states in terms of the result to be achieved by a specified date, but it is up to each country what form and method of implementation are to be used. *Regulations* have the force of law throughout the EU without member states having to take any action. Council *decisions* are binding on those to whom they are addressed; they are used for a range of matters, but especially to secure fair commercial competition throughout the EU. Regulations and directives must be published in the *Official Journal* of the EU.

European legislation: procedure

The legislative and decision-making processes of the EU are hideously complicated – much more complicated than legislative procedure at Westminster – and this book is not the place to set them out. Let us simply note the five main routes: (1) the Council of Ministers acts without the involvement of the European Parliament; (2) the Commission makes a proposal, but the parliament has a right to be consulted; (3) the *cooperation procedure*, under which the Commission makes a proposal but the parliament has the right to be consulted both on the proposal and on the 'common position' adopted by the Council on the proposal; (4) the *co-decision procedure*, which resembles the cooperation procedure, but where, if the parliament proposes amendments to the common position that the Council does not accept, a 'conciliation committee', on which both the Parliament and the Council are represented, meets to agree a joint text; and (5) the *assent procedure*, used mainly for international agreements and applications by countries to join the EU. Where the member states take decisions intergovernmentally, rather than legislatively, they do so through *common positions*, *joint actions*, *declarations*, *common strategies* or *international agreements*.

A surprising feature of the process is that the Council legislates in private; comparisons are sometimes made with North Korea as the only other place where laws are made in secret. The European Parliament is part of this process, as meetings of conciliation committees are also private. It seems likely that this will change in the next round of institutional reform, but it is hardly surprising that the EU has been criticised for a lack of openness and for being remote from its citizens.

How to influence European legislation?

We said earlier that a European regulation could become part of the law of the United Kingdom without the involvement of the British Parliament. Let us take a hypothetical example and then see whether British MPs might have been able to affect what happened.

A virus that causes severe food poisoning has been found in cockles and small clams harvested in the western Mediterranean. Several people have died. During questions to the Agriculture Commissioner at a sitting of the European Parliament he is urged to take action, and he undertakes to do so. The Commission then goes rather over the top and produces a whole new regulatory regime for shellfish, which among other things would require people catching shellfish of any kind to have their catch screened for the virus, and dealers to have similar checks carried out before selling shellfish to retailers.

The regulations go to the European Parliament and are considered in its fisheries committee. The Greens, who hold the balance of power on the committee, want the proposal strengthened to impose a ban on any catching or selling until procedures for the checks are in place EU-wide, and the Commission amends its proposed regulations. These are then discussed in the Council of Ministers. The Irish fisheries minister argues that the regulations are too sweeping, and she has the support of several others but not enough for a blocking minority; the British fisheries minister is doubtful but is unwilling to vote against for fear of unstitching an entirely separate agricultural negotiation on which the UK needs the support of countries which are in favour of the shellfish proposal.

The proposal comes into effect, and – because there is a three-month delay in manufacturing and supplying the equipment needed for the screening – effectively closes down the shellfish industry in northern Europe as well as in the Mediterranean. The proposal applies not only to the cockles and clams that were the cause of the problem but also to lobsters, crabs, prawns, scallops, mussels and oysters. Fishermen and fish merchants in Devon and Cornwall, and many other parts of the UK, face the loss of their livelihood and are outraged, as are their constituency MPs (and members of the Scottish Parliament, the National Assembly for Wales and the Northern Ireland Assembly). The only people who are delighted are the Norwegians, who are not in the EU; they are unaffected and can now sell their shellfish with very little competition.

How could the shellfish industry's case have been put more effectively? In this case, there have been three main actors: the Commission, the European Parliament and the Council of Ministers. As soon as the Fisheries Commissioner gave his undertaking to the European Parliament, industry representatives could have lobbied the Commission; and constituency MPs, alerted by fishermen's organisations, could have made the case to the Commissioner; but after giving the undertaking to the European Parliament he might well have been unwilling to change his proposal.

MPs could have contacted their European Parliament counterparts to emphasise the damage that could be done by the proposal. This might well have been effective with the MEPs (of whatever party) who had a constituency interest and were already concerned about the proposal – although with their much larger constituencies it might not have been quite such a priority as for some of our Westminster MPs. British MPs could also have approached British MEPs of their own party who did not have a direct constituency interest but who would appreciate the potential political damage. Once they had taken up the cause, the MEPs could have enlisted support from MEPs from other northern European countries that would be affected; and it might well have been that the proposal would have been toned down, or limited to the Mediterranean only, in the European Parliament's fisheries committee, rather than being toughened, as was actually the case.

But the decisive point at which to try to secure changes was in the Council of Ministers, through the stance taken by the British fisheries minister on behalf of the UK government. This is where the European scrutiny systems of both Houses would have come into play.

European scrutiny at Westminster

Two select committees – the European Scrutiny Committee in the Commons and the European Union Committee in the Lords – examine European documents on behalf of Parliament. For each one, they assess its importance (and seek any additional information or evidence they need in order to form an opinion), report upon it and, if necessary, recommend it for debate at Westminster. The Commons committee works quickly, reporting on a large number of documents it judges to be of importance (some 600 a year) and recommending some for debate; the Lords committee reports on many fewer (twenty-five or so a year) but in much greater depth, through inquiries by its sub-committees that are similar to the sort of inquiry carried out by departmental select committees in the Commons. Many other documents are scrutinised by the Lords committee by way of correspondence with the relevant minister. The two committees are doing rather different jobs, so they complement each other's work rather than duplicating it.

What is subject to scrutiny?

EU documents subject to the scrutiny process include draft regulations, directives and decisions; Commission green and white papers setting out future policy, including the Annual Work Programme; recommendations, resolutions and conclusions of the Council of Ministers; and a range of other papers including proposed actions on justice, home affairs and foreign affairs, and the reports of the Court of Auditors. Any document that is subject to scrutiny must be deposited in Parliament and provided to the committees within two working days of its arrival in the Foreign and Commonwealth Office in London.

The explanatory memorandum

Then, within ten working days of deposit, the Whitehall department primarily responsible for the subject matter must submit an *explanatory memorandum* (EM) on the document. The EM sets out who is responsible for the subject matter (both in Whitehall and the devolved administrations); the legal authority under which the proposal is made, and what EU legislative and voting procedure applies; whether there is any impact on UK law; whether the proposal meets the requirements of subsidiarity (in other words, whether action at a European level rather than at a national level is necessary); the government's view of the policy implications; a regulatory impact assessment if a proposal is likely to impose burdens on business; when required, a risk assessment and scientific justification; a note of what consultation has taken place; an estimate of the financial implications for the EU and the UK; and the likely timetable on which European decisions will be taken on the proposal. It is proposed that EMs will soon include further information on the devolution and human rights implications of proposals.

EMs are an important element of accountability; one is submitted on every document and is signed by the responsible minister as formal evidence to Parliament. EMs are also public documents and so are useful sources of information for businesses and the public. Another advantage is that the process concentrates minds, both of the civil servants who draft the EM and the minister who signs it (especially when responsibility is shared between several departments and there is a risk of a subject not being gripped early enough). An EM can be a very comprehensive document; and in our shellfish example it would have set alarm bells ringing immediately, not least on the risk assessment, the scientific justification and possible burdens on business.

Once an EM has been submitted, the two Houses have different ways of dealing with documents, so this will be a convenient place to look at the how the Commons and Lords committees operate.

The European Scrutiny Committee of the House of Commons

This is a select committee of sixteen MPs. It has a staff of fourteen (larger than any other Commons committee), which includes experts in European law and former senior civil servants with experience of negotiating in Brussels. As well as scrutinising European documents, it has produced a number of reports on EU constitutional issues, including improving democracy and accountability within the European Union. It also conducts pre- and post-Council scrutiny, in which ministers who are going to negotiate at particular meetings of the Council of Ministers come to the committee to outline their approach to the agenda (or to explain the outcome).

The committee is assisted by the National Parliament Office (NPO), which the House of Commons has established in Brussels. This small office, headed by a clerk from Westminster on a two- or three-year posting, acts as the committee's 'eyes and ears' in Brussels, gathering intelligence on likely proposals from the Commission, views in European Parliament committees, and so on. The NPO also publicises the reports of the European committees in both Houses and assists other select committees investigating EU issues.

The European Scrutiny Committee meets every Wednesday, and it may consider forty documents at each meeting. On each document the committee has an analysis, brief and recommendation from the committee staff. In an average year, the committee considers about 1,300 documents. It reports on about 600 of them and recommends thirty or so for debate (see below).

The committee must first decide whether it has enough information to make a judgement. A comprehensive EM may be enough; but the committee may ask the government for further written evidence or call a minister to give oral evidence at its next meeting. The committee then has to decide whether the document is of political or legal importance. Our shellfish proposal would definitely be of political importance because of its likely impact on a UK industry. It might also be of legal importance if the proposal went beyond the EU's legal powers, for example.

If the committee decides that the document is indeed of political or legal importance, it will cover it in detail in its report on that week's crop of documents. The committee's weekly reports, which are published and put on the parliamentary website, are in effect a critical commentary on the EU agenda and a very useful source of analysis and information for anyone monitoring developments in the EU.

Debates

A further decision for the committee is whether the document should be debated. It can choose to recommend a debate in one of the three *European standing committees*. These have thirteen permanent members, but any MP can attend and speak (although not vote). European Standing Committee A deals with matters affecting the environment, food and rural affairs, transport, local government and the regions; B deals with finance, work and pensions, foreign affairs, home and legal affairs, and international development; and C with trade, industry, education, culture, media, sport and health.

A European standing committee is a combination of questions and debate; a minister answers MPs' questions for up to an hour, and there is then an hour and a half's debate on a motion moved by the minister (to which amendments may be tabled and voted on), usually formally taking note of the documents with some words supportive of the line the government is taking. European standing committees can be a testing time for a minister; in addition to the normal debate format, he or she normally has to answer questions alone (unlike Question Time in the House, when four or five ministers will share the answering, and unlike appearing before a select committee, when the minister will have officials who can answer detailed questions). Attendances at European standing committees are not high, however, and it is surprising that

MPs do not make more use of these opportunities to question ministers on what may be hot political issues.

After the standing committee proceedings the government puts down a motion in the House, which may be the same as the motion agreed to in the standing committee (even if that was defeated) or may be an entirely new motion. That motion is taken without further debate, but it may be voted on.

On the most important documents, the European Scrutiny Committee can recommend that a debate should take place on the floor of the House; but it is up to the government to agree to such a recommendation, and it rarely does so. However, if the Scrutiny Committee recommends that there should be a debate in European standing committee, that debate has to take place. The precise timing is still up to the government, but ministers will usually want the debate to take place soon so that they can get 'scrutiny clearance'.

Scrutiny clearance and the scrutiny reserve

The 1998 'scrutiny reserve resolution' of the House of Commons constrains ministers from giving agreement in the Council of Ministers to an EU proposal that has not 'cleared scrutiny', which means *either* that the European Scrutiny Committee has reported on it but has not recommended debate, *or* that the committee has recommended debate, the debate has taken place and the House has expressed a view on the proposal. A minister may give agreement to an uncleared proposal, but only if the European Scrutiny Committee agrees, or if there is urgency, or if UK interests might otherwise be damaged (in which case the minister must provide the committee with an explanation).

For the scrutiny system to work effectively, there must be time for examination and debate in national parliaments. Over-rapid legislating is just as much of a problem at the European level at it is at the national level. This is particularly so when a proposal has been through the Westminster scrutiny process but is then changed substantially in later negotiations. For example, the final texts of such major proposals as the European Social Policy Agenda and the European Arrest Warrant were available only hours before they were agreed by the Council of Ministers in 2000 and 2001, and similar problems frequently arise.

The Commons committee had a remarkable success in getting included in the Amsterdam Treaty a protocol on the role of national parliaments that requires a six-week period of notice before the Council decides on a piece of legislation; but late changes to proposals often mean that this requirement is circumvented. In June 2003, the European Scrutiny Committee made recommendations designed to secure adequate time for scrutiny at all stages, remarking that 'the needs of national parliaments need to be built into the EU's legislative system rather than recognised only when wholly convenient'.

However, to return to our shellfish example: things might have proceeded like this. The European Scrutiny Committee recommends a debate, which takes place in European Standing Committee A. The minister is subject to some very hostile questioning from opposition MPs with fishing constituencies, and even some critical interventions from her own side. The government puts down a fairly bland motion about 'protecting public health and ensuring that all relevant factors are taken into account' but is unable to prevent the motion being amended to condemn 'an ill-thought-out proposal that will have a devastating effect on fishing communities throughout the United Kingdom'.

The same week, the Environment, Food and Rural Affairs Select Committee, which deals with fisheries, announces its intention of mounting a rapid inquiry into the possible effects of the proposal and invites the minister to be the first witness. There is now no way that the minister can support the proposal in the Council of Ministers. She votes with her Irish and other northern European colleagues; there is a blocking minority, and it is clear that the proposal cannot get through in its present state. It later reappears in a modest form that applies only to certain species of shellfish in the western Mediterranean.

How effective is the scrutiny process?

None of the institutions of the EU is answerable to any national parliament, so parliaments can exercise influence only through their own governments and ministers. No matter how strongly the shellfish proposal was criticised, the most the House of Commons could have done would have been to agree to a motion instructing the government to vote against in the Council of Ministers. The minister would have had to obey that instruction, but she could well have been outvoted in the Council.

The European scrutiny process is nevertheless valuable. It is comprehensive, and it catches a wide range of European proposals and other documents, on which ministers have to state their policy and provide evidence. It is open: EMs are public documents, and the committee's reports are published. And it also means that proposals are investigated and, if necessary, debated, before ministers vote on them in the Council – although late changes remain a problem.

But the process depends crucially on the use that is made of it. It is a little like a burglar alarm. The scrutiny process can identify an EU proposal that might damage UK interests; and a burglar alarm can tell you that someone is attempting to get into your house through the kitchen window. But just as a bit more action is required to apprehend the burglar, so the scrutiny system depends on MPs (and anyone else affected by an EU proposal or policy) making effective use of the product.

The European Union Committee of the House of Lords

The House of Lords established its Select Committee on the European Communities in 1974. Renamed the European Union Committee in 1999, its main remit has been to scrutinise the European Community and its legislation – the 'first pillar' of the European Union. It reports on draft Commission proposals and draws the attention of the House to those that raise issues of policy or principle with a recommendation as to whether or not a debate is desirable. The committee is empowered to consider the merits of proposals for European legislation, and it frequently takes advantage of the opportunity provided by the publication by the Commission of a consultative document or action programme to undertake wide-ranging investigations of EU policy in a particular area and to make recommendations. Indeed, the committee's wide terms of reference even permit it to undertake free-standing enquiries into EU issues in the absence of specific proposals. In the 2002–03 session, for example, the committee reported on various aspects of the work of the Convention on the Future of Europe.

Since ratification of the Maastricht Treaty, the committee's remit has been extended to the second and third pillars of the European Union – home affairs and justice (JHA), and the common foreign and security policy (CFSP). The government has agreed to make available to both Houses of Parliament CFSP texts once they have been agreed (on grounds of confidentiality they are not available in draft); and under the JHA pillar, the texts of any proposal that, if agreed, would require primary legislation or that are of significant importance. Most texts received fall under the JHA pillar, and inquiries are sometimes conducted into them.

The committee also monitors EU affairs in general. Thus, irrespective of the more specific policy work, regular meetings are held with Foreign and Commonwealth Office ministers, particularly following each European Council, and from the ambassadors of countries holding the EU presidency. The committee now makes a point of scrutinising the Commission's annual work programme.

The committee has nineteen members and an elaborate structure of seven sub-committees roughly covering the principal areas of competence of the European Community as well as JHA and CFSP matters. There is a total working membership (including co-opted members) of about seventy lords. The sub-committees consider whatever documents are 'sifted' to them by the chairman of the committee, as well as conducting free-standing inquiries. These sub-committees take evidence and make reports that are often of a very high quality, reflecting the distinguished membership of the committees: for example, in 2003, the Common Foreign and Security Policy Sub-Committee (Sub-Committee C) included a former Chief of the Defence

Staff, a former cabinet minister, a former senior foreign policy adviser to the government, a former Attorney-General, a former Secretary-General of the EU Commission, and a former senior member of the intelligence community.

Every year, about 1,300 EU documents are deposited by the government. Of these, about a quarter are referred by the chairman for more detailed consideration by sub-committees, but only a fraction of these will become the subject of a full-scale inquiry. Some reports of the committee are made for information only, and some for debate. In 1999–2000, nine reports were debated in the House, taking up some 2 percent of total sitting time. Whether a report is debated or not, it is replied to in writing by the government within two months of publication. However, a substantial number of other documents are considered in detail by way of correspondence with the relevant minister. This is published, and much of it is available on the Internet.

The reports are intrinsically useful as a source of both information and informed opinion. Although their target is, theoretically, the House and, through the House, the government minister and government policies, the Lords reports, like those of the Commons committee, also have a wider market in the EU institutions, including the European Parliament itself and other national parliaments of the EU engaged in the scrutiny process.

What role for national parliaments?

The European Parliament sees itself as the democratic institution representing citizens across the European Union. It is reasonable to ask: in that case, what is there for national parliaments to do? The answer is that the European Parliament is in practice remote from the citizens it seeks to represent. It also exercises few of the key powers of a parliament: it does not sustain a government in office (it can dismiss the Commission, but it has no power over the Council of Ministers); it cannot impose taxes; and, although with the agreement of the Council it may make amendments, it cannot initiate legislation.

National parliamentarians are much closer to the citizens they represent. After the next round of EU enlargement, there will be about 10,000 MPs in the national parliaments of member states, compared with 626 MEPs. Whereas a British MP represents an average of 89,000 people, a British MEP represents nearly 680,000 people. And although there is no cause for complacency about the 59 percent turnout in the 2001 British general election, total EU turnout in European Parliament elections is lower and has fallen at every election, from 63 percent at the first direct elections in 1979 to 61 percent in 1984, 58.5 percent in 1989, 56.8 percent in 1994 and below 50 percent in 1999 (49.4 percent) – despite voting being compulsory in several member states. In the UK – perhaps a country more Eurosceptic than some – turnout has never reached 40 percent, and in 1999 it was only 24 percent.

It is clear that, in most member states, voters see MPs, not MEPs, as their representatives; and in European elections they tend to vote on national issues, just as they would in a general election, and not on broader European policies. Nevertheless, the European Parliament has the important roles of considering legislation in detail and supervising the unelected Commission. The European Scrutiny Committee has said 'it is only necessary to imagine what the EU would be like without the Parliament; it would be a system totally dominated by bureaucrats and diplomats, loosely supervised by ministers flying periodically into Brussels'.

However, there is no doubt that citizens across the EU look to their national parliaments to represent them and to call their governments to account (even though EU membership constrains the freedom of action of those govern-ments). National parliaments seem certain to remain the key democratic ele-ment in the EU for at least the foreseeable future.

In recognition perhaps of the importance of promoting links between MPs and members of the House of Lords and the EU, both Houses have agreed that members should be able to claim the expenses of a limited number of visits to EU institutions each year.

Closer cooperation between national parliaments

So how can national parliaments – as institutions – be more involved at the European level? It has been suggested that the European Parliament could have a second chamber composed of national MPs representing each member state parliament; but the idea has gathered little support, and it is difficult to see how national MPs could spare the time to make such a chamber much more than a symbol.

The Conference of European Affairs Committees (usually known by the French acronym COSAC), which every six months brings together repres-entatives of the European committees in all the national parliaments of the member states and of the Constitutional Affairs Committee of the European Parliament, provides some sort of joint forum. Although hitherto COSAC has had no formal powers, the protocol on the role of national parliaments in the European Union, which forms part of the draft constitution for Europe (pro-duced by the Convention on the Future of Europe), recognises that it has a role to play with the right to transmit any submission to the Council, Commission or European Parliament.

The draft constitution (not yet agreed) also states that national parliaments shall ensure compliance of EU proposals with the principles of subsidiarity (whether action at European rather than national level is necessary) and proportionality (whether the action proposed meets the requirement, or whether it is more than necessary). So far as subsidiarity is concerned, any national parliament or any chamber of a national parliament of a member state would have to send a reasoned opinion to the Council, Commission or European Parliament stating why it considered that the proposal in question did not comply with the principle of subsidiarity. Where reasoned opinions on the same issue represented at least one-third of all the votes allocated to national parliaments (bicameral parliaments have one vote per chamber, unicameral parliaments two votes) the Commission would have to review its proposal and give a reasoned decision. If and when the draft constitution is agreed by an Inter-Governmental Conference, far more elaborate arrangements for co-operation between national parliaments, this time excluding the European Parliament, will be necessary.

Contacts also exist between policy/legislative committees of parliaments of member states that deal with similar subject areas. Arrangements for holding meetings of representatives of these committees are somewhat *ad hoc*, falling either to the initiative of the European Parliament or to the national parliament of the country holding the presidency. Many national parliaments are unhappy with current arrangements. Meanwhile, the protocol referred to above also states that 'The European Parliament and the national Parliaments shall together determine how inter-parliamentary co-operation may be effectively and regularly organised and promoted within the European Union'.

For the first time in the history of the European Union, national parliaments are coming to be recognised as forces in EU decision making. In 2003 and 2004, a programme of meetings is being held between the representatives of the national parliaments of the European Union with a view to establishing how the administrative arrangements for this heightened cooperation might best be made.

In addition, if national parliaments operate effective scrutiny systems, they can play an important part, not only in influencing their own governments but also in publicising the possible effects of European proposals. The European Scrutiny Committee has suggested that the agenda of the Council of Ministers should show whether a scrutiny reserve is still outstanding in any national parliament, and that, if the Council nevertheless proceeds, it should be required to state its reasons.

A closer relationship between MPs and MEPs?

How could MPs and MEPs be brought closer together, given that their roles are complementary? There is informal contact through party organisations, and most MPs will have a working relationship with the MEP whose constituency covers their 'patch'. MPs with dual mandates as members of the European Parliament as well as the House of Commons used to provide something of a link between the institutions; but there are now only two of these in the Commons (and three members of the Lords), although there are eleven MEPs who used to be MPs (and two spouses of MPs), and two who used to be members of the House of Lords. MEPs often give evidence to the Lords committees.

But Westminster is relatively unwelcoming to MEPs compared with, for example, the German parliament, which provides them with offices (although the pressure on space at Westminster is a powerful constraint). Nor do MEPs have any formal role in Westminster proceedings, unlike the Belgian parliament, where Belgian MEPs are full members of the European Committee in the House of Representatives.

Other suggestions have been made: that MEPs should be made temporary members of the House of Lords; or that there should be a committee in which European proposals could be debated by MPs, MEPs and peers. But the relationship has never been formalised, and it is an open question how much difference a formal relationship would really make.

There may also be a tendency to focus too much on the bilateral relationship between Westminster and the European Parliament. Just as important in many ways in the relationship between national parliaments throughout the EU, who have similar functions and many shared interests. Increased cooperation and understanding – whether through joint meetings of subject committees, the work of COSAC or contacts between individual MPs – will be factors in maintaining and strengthening national parliaments as an essential democratic element in the European Union.

Other international relations

In this context, we should note the involvement of UK MPs and lords (and staff of both Houses) in a number of international assemblies. The *Parliamentary Assembly of the Council of Europe*, based in Strasbourg, was established in 1949 as the parliamentary organ of the Council of Europe, in some ways a forerunner of the European Community. The Council of Europe has had an important role in a range of social and cultural issues, but especially in human rights matters. It consists of 626 MPs representing forty-four countries (the British delegation has thirty-six members), and in recent years it has acted as a 'waiting room' for the new democracies of Eastern Europe that have become candidates for membership of the EU.

The *Assembly of Western European Union*, based in Paris, has ten member states, which are represented by the same delegations as in the Council of Europe Assembly, and eighteen associated countries. The WEU deals primarily with defence and security issues. The *NATO Parliamentary Assembly* brings together 214 parliamentarians from the nineteen NATO countries. It is based in Brussels but holds its sessions by turn in member countries. The

Parliamentary Assembly of the Organisation for Security and Co-operation in Europe (OSCE), based in Copenhagen, was set up in 1991. It consists of 317 delegates from the fifty-five OSCE participating states. The *British–Irish Inter-Parliamentary Body* brings together parliamentarians from Westminster and Dublin.

The UK branches of the *Inter-Parliamentary Union (IPU)* and the *Commonwealth Parliamentary Association (CPA)* are based at Westminster. The IPU represents parliaments worldwide, the CPA those within the Commonwealth. Both aim to increase international cooperation and understanding, and they play a considerable diplomatic role; for example, the first formal contacts between the United Kingdom and Argentina after the Falklands War between parliamentarians of the two countries under the auspices of the IPU and the IPU-organised visit to the UK by Mikhail Gorbachev just before he became leader of the USSR proved hugely significant.

The Overseas Offices of the two Houses organise a large number of inward visits of officials and members of overseas parliaments, particularly Commonwealth parliaments, to Westminster. These contacts are greatly valued and remind us of the wider world beyond the frontiers of the European Union, whose parliaments were in many cases modelled on Westminster principles.

13 Modernisation, reform and effectiveness

Introduction

A great many people would say that Parliament needs 'modernisation' or 'reform'. But these are words to be used with some care. To the person speaking, they really mean no more than 'change of which I approve'. After all, the 'Balfour reforms' of a century ago, which entrenched the government's control over the business and time of the House of Commons, were hardly a milestone in the democratic accountability of the executive. And in the present debate over the role of Parliament, 'modernisation' and 'reform' mean different things to different people.

It is much better to focus on the concept of 'effectiveness'. The traditional roles of Parliament include representing constituents, legislating, authorising taxation and spending, calling government to account, and acting as a forum for the testing of beliefs and opinions and a focus for national feeling. What do we expect Parliament to do for us, and how could it do those tasks more effectively?

Before we look in detail at some of the issues, it is worth establishing a sense of proportion. First of all, slagging off parliaments and parliamentarians is a national sport – all over the world as well as in the UK. When the Scottish Parliament was established, it was to be the epitome of a modern parliament: accessible, flexible, getting right what Westminster had got wrong. Yet only four years later, Sir David Steel, the parliament's first Presiding Officer, was writing ruefully:

> Commentators on the Scottish Parliament spend a lot of time and energy questioning where the Scottish Parliament has 'got it wrong'. It is frustrating because we seldom read stories of the people who have benefited from the work of the Parliament, and there are many.

It is also a strange irony that, even though most democratic rights have been purchased with blood, they often seem to be little valued by those who live in democracies. 'Oh, I don't vote', you hear people say, 'I don't know anything about politics, and I'm really not interested'. Yet the stuff of politics, and the business of Parliament, affects every aspect of our everyday lives: peace and war, the education of our children, the safety of our streets, the quality of the air we breathe, our civil liberties. This lack of interest may be a symptom of the disconnection between people and Parliament, but it is also the case that, however Parliament changes, there will always be a significant number of people who 'don't want to know'.

However, the fall in turnout at general elections, from nearly 78 percent in 1992 to 71.5 percent in 1997 and to 59 percent in 2001, suggests that Parliament is seen by the public as less important than it was, with disaffection especially strong in the 18–24 age group, where only 39 percent used their vote (and only 45 percent of under-35s voted). Not only the 'usual suspects' among pressure groups and commentators but also many MPs and others close to Parliament feel that something is wrong with the way it operates. These are things to be taken seriously.

A reality check

Any proposal for changing the way Parliament – and particularly the House of Commons – works has to take into account the political and constitutional constraints. Here are six aspects of the limits within which, realistically, any change has to take place:

1. Some criticisms imply that Parliament should somehow simply stop the government doing things that are misguided or unpopular. As long as the UK has a constitutional system in which the government is *in* Parliament, the executive is always going to get its way – provided that it has a majority in the House of Commons and can persuade its back-benchers to support it issue by issue. A separation of powers – a system in which the executive and legislature are entirely separate, as in the United States – could greatly increase the independent powers of Parliament, but it would require seismic constitutional change.
2. Although many people are attracted by the more measured and less partisan approach of the House of Lords, parliamentary politics is party politics. Like it or not, free elections involve a clash of party policies and ideologies, and in any elected House – at Westminster or elsewhere – party discipline will always be a powerful factor.
3. Parliaments are by their nature reactive. They respond to events, to public opinion and constituency pressures, and to the proposals and actions of governments. There are relatively few genuinely parliamentary initiatives: at Westminster, the main ones are private members' bills (when these are indeed at the initiative of the individual MP and not government hand-out bills) and policy proposals made by select committees.
4. Parliaments are not executive. They approve principles (and in the case of legislation, detailed instructions) about what is to be done; but it is the

government of the day that is responsible for the business and administration of the state and is answerable to Parliament and the electorate.

5. Parliaments are organisms rather than organisations. They are made up of individual members, often unpredictable, who react to a range of influences but who also have their own views. This means that the law of unintended consequences is a powerful factor in parliamentary reform; it is easy to set out detailed procedural prescriptions but difficult to predict what effect they will have, or how they will be used.

6. Perhaps most important, Parliament – and especially the House of Commons – cannot change itself. It is the government of the day that has the power of initiative and the majority of votes, and that controls the business. Parliament's interests and those of the government are often at odds; change may come about because of wider political pressure, but it has usually depended on there being something in it for the government as well as for Parliament.

We now look at the issues as they affect each House.

The House of Commons

The credit side

One morning recently, the BBC Radio 4 *Today* programme ran a 'Parliament dead' story, filled with gloom about the ineffectiveness of our democratic institutions. The piece that followed was about a select committee report on the government's planned public–private partnership for the London Underground. In a detailed, compelling report, the committee had done a remarkable demolition job on the government's proposals. Not only did the committee have a government majority, but the chairman was a government MP. The programme makers evidently saw no irony in the juxtaposition of the two items.

The fact is that the Westminster Parliament does a lot of things rather well – and some things better than many other parliaments. This is not an argument for complacency; but it is as well to remember that the more hysterical rumours of Parliament's death – too often fuelled by the media – are greatly exaggerated. Westminster is well regarded by people in the same business: other parliaments, as shown by the constant stream of visiting Speakers, members, committees and senior officials from overseas – from parliaments of all types, not only those in the Commonwealth that use the 'Westminster model'. So it is worth taking stock not only of the strengths of the House of Commons but also of some of the significant changes over the last four or five years.

Present strengths

The close relationship with constituencies means that Westminster MPs put a lot of effort into an ancient function of the House of Commons: representing constituents, and getting their voices heard by ministers who are often seen as remote and inaccessible. Success in solving constituents' problems depends on the tenacity of the MP and the strength of the case, but the 'satisfaction factor' of constituency cases was rated highly by MPs in a recent survey, and this aspect of MPs' work generally gets a good rating from the public.

Select committees are a key part of the work of the Commons. The system is flexible and comprehensive; it encourages independence of view among committee members; it produces well-researched and well-written reports; as well as exposing a wide range of government activity to scrutiny, it publishes a great deal of official information that would not otherwise be in the public domain; and, perhaps most important, it provides public access to the political process.

The complementary systems of European scrutiny in the Commons and the Lords are some of the best in any EU parliament (although their product is underused).

Parliament also attracts and retains high-quality staff; and its work is supported by committed and expert people who are highly regarded by their equivalents in parliaments worldwide.

Parliamentary questions, used on a larger scale than in any other parliament, have their critics but, taken as a whole, are an important means of requiring governments to put information on the public record; and, in the hands of a determined MP, they can be remarkably effective.

The House of Commons is a natural focus of attention on historic occasions. Following the terrorist attacks on 11 September 2001, upon the death of the Queen Mother and in the lead-up to war in Iraq, the House was the forum for the expression of a national mood – and, in the last case, of profound differences in the country at large.

We should not forget the more informal role that the House of Commons fulfils. It is a place where opinions are exchanged and formed and laid open to the scrutiny of the media and the public; where pressure groups and campaigners, as well as industries, the professions and a range of other players, put their case or seek a higher profile for their cause.

However, the Commons is seen as less effective in the key tasks of examining legislation and scrutinising public spending. We return to these below.

Recent changes

There has been no shortage of drivers for change in the last five years. In 1997, the incoming Labour government had a manifesto commitment to parliamentary reform; and the Modernisation Committee, which it established, together with the Liaison, Procedure, Public Administration, and Information Committees, the House of Commons Commission, the *Parliament First* group of MPs, the Hansard Society's Commission on Parliamentary Scrutiny chaired by former Leader of the House Tony Newton (Lord Newton of Braintree), the Commission to Strengthen Parliament, set up by William Hague when Leader of the Opposition and chaired by the distinguished academic Lord Norton of Louth, and many other organisations and commentators, have become involved in the process.

There has been no shortage of changes either. Although none is in itself earth-shaking – and one or two have been controversial – as a whole they mark the most profound period of change for many decades.

The sitting hours have changed (see page 133): the House now sits at 11.30 a.m. instead of 2.30 p.m. on Tuesdays, Wednesdays and Thursdays, and the normal finishing time is 7.30 p.m. on Tuesdays and Wednesdays, and 6.30 p.m. on Thursdays, instead of 10.30 p.m. However, the Tuesday and Wednesday sitting hours – especially the former – remain controversial among MPs; and it was interesting to see that, in order to deal with the later stages of government bills in the fortnight before the 2003 summer recess, the House rose at or after its former finishing times.

The traditional summer recess from late July to early October is now broken by a two-week sitting period in the first half of September. The aim of this was to prevent the government escaping scrutiny for so long a period. The effect has yet to be assessed; the additional sittings will allow for more Question Times, the tabling and answering of more written questions, and no doubt more select committee activity; but they will also allow more time for government legislation.

For the first time, the parliamentary calendar for a year ahead was published, and this has been renewed for 2004.

A 'parallel chamber' has been established in Westminster Hall (see page 268), which has provided additional opportunities for back-benchers to initiate debates and for select committee reports to be debated, and it has been the forum for the new cross-cutting oral questions, in which ministers from several departments answer on a policy theme rather than on a single-department basis as in the Chamber. (The adaptation of the parallel chamber idea from the Main Committee in the Australian House of Representatives is a reflection of the exchange of ideas and experience between parliaments; the Lords committee to scrutinise powers to be delegated to ministers in primary legislation also traces its origins to Australia.)

Oral questions to most ministers are now tabled only three sitting days before answer, rather than ten, and can be more topical as a result. Written questions 'for a named day' are limited to five per MP per day in an attempt to reduce the number of holding replies. Questions may be tabled electronically, although so far relatively few MPs have used this method. Prime Minister's Questions is now for half an hour on Wednesdays rather than the pre-1997 quarter-hour on Tuesdays and Thursdays.

A new way of electing a Speaker has been established, differing from every other decision-making procedure in the House, with a secret ballot and the elimination of low-scoring candidates. A more comprehensible Order Paper has been introduced to assist MPs as well as those outside Parliament. In the Chamber, the Speaker has been given the power to limit the length of speeches in over-subscribed debates. The rule against quoting in a supplementary at Question Time has been abolished. The comic method of raising a point of order during a vote, in which an MP had to wear a hat in order to be recognised by the Chair, has been scrapped. The motion 'that Strangers do now withdraw' has been replaced by the motion 'that the House sit in private' (although this is purely cosmetic; the motion is used for exactly the same purposes – as a tactical waste of time, and by staging a division to test the numbers voting with the aim of getting the business postponed – as it was before).

'Deferred divisions' have been introduced for some categories of business, whereby, if after the normal finishing time a vote is forced, the vote takes place not on the spot but on the following Wednesday afternoon by MPs marking a ballot paper. This has contributed to earlier finishing times; and it is convenient for the government, which would otherwise have to keep more MPs until near the end of the sitting to make sure that the votes were not lost, but it has also attracted criticism precisely because it has made things easier for the government business managers, and because of the way in which it can separate debate and decision.

More methodical scrutiny by departmental select committees is now underpinned by 'core tasks', and the committees produce annual reports on their work, which is drawn together by the Liaison Committee in an annual assessment of select committee effectiveness. The Scrutiny Unit now supports select committees in scrutiny of financial papers and draft bills, and a further forty staff are being recruited to help committees to carry out the 'core tasks'. A new format has greatly improved the presentation and user-friendliness of select committee reports. Most investigative committees can now operate more flexibly by being able to set up a sub-committee, and two or more committees and sub-committees of both Houses can work cooperatively through joint meetings. However, the Modernisation Committee's proposal for a 'Committee of Nomination', which would have taken the selection of members of scrutiny committees out of the hands of the whips, was defeated.

On MPs' conduct issues, the independence of the Parliamentary Commissioner for Standards has been entrenched and an additional inquiry mechanism established for the more difficult cases. An MP censured by the Standards and Privileges Committee may now have his or her pay docked even if not suspended from the House.

On legislation, more bills appear in draft for select committee scrutiny (although the time available often limits the effectiveness of that scrutiny). Better explanatory material is provided on bills when they are formally introduced. Programming is now routine for government bills but has moved from its consensual origins to being a source of bitter disagreement between government and opposition, with almost every programming motion being the subject of a vote. The original expectation that more bills would be referred to special standing committees (see page 202), as recommended by the Modernisation Committee, has not been fulfilled.

A number of other recommendations on legislation made by the Modernisation Committee in the early days of the 1997 parliament have not been implemented: bills not previously published in draft to be considered by *ad hoc* first reading committees; limitation of speaking time in standing committee debates; debating the principle of a clause before considering amendments; reconvening a standing committee to consider non-controversial government amendments before report stage; considering Lords amendments in standing committee; and carrying out post-legislative scrutiny to see how Acts of Parliament have actually operated (although it is always open to any select committee to undertake this sort of scrutiny).

These changes have meant some more work for ministers and their departments, especially arising from the establishment of Westminster Hall and shorter periods of notice for oral questions. In the select committee world the changes have provided more opportunities and resources; the effectiveness of both will depend on what use committees make of them. Otherwise, although most of the changes would be seen by most people as improvements, they have not made much of a difference to the government–parliament relationship; in the Liaison Committee's phrase, they have not 'shifted the balance'. Indeed, some would claim that on legislation the routine programming of government bills has shifted the balance back the other way.

However, three other events in 2002 and 2003 are likely to work to the long-term benefit of Parliament. Despite later controversy about the reasons for going to war in Iraq, the fact remains that, unprecedentedly in modern times, the explicit approval of the House of Commons was sought for military action before troops were committed. If any future government engages in military action without seeking the view of the House of Commons, its mandate for doing so will be seen as doubtful. This may be one area of prerogative power that political circumstances have allowed the House to recapture. A related issue is the oversight of intelligence agencies. The Foreign Secretary's agreement in principle to the Foreign Affairs Committee's recommendation that this should be the task of a genuine select committee, and not a committee appointed by the Prime Minister, may foreshadow a significant change – and one that has always been resisted by governments of both parties. Finally, the twice-yearly appearance of the Prime Minister before the Liaison Committee has been a symbolic as well as a substantive change. It is difficult to see any future Prime Minister being able to withdraw from the commitment, and the establishment of the principle may lead to more frequent sessions in the future.

What next?

We now look at areas where further changes are already under way, or where further reform might be more challenging.

Reconnecting Parliament and the public: voting

In a recent debate on turnouts in elections, one MP said:

> We ask people to vote on a Thursday in one place and if they do not turn up at that place they do not get a vote. We ask them to vote on a slip of paper that seems to have been printed by the last remaining letterpress printer in the country. We then ask them to fill in their preference . . . using a carpenter's pencil attached to the wall by a piece of string. Finally, we ask them to do that in a horse box that has been set up in a school hall. That is probably one of the most bizarre activities that we ask people to do in their daily lives in expressing their opinions, preferences and thoughts.

Getting more people to vote is clearly an important way of increasing interest in, and regard for, democratic institutions (although some would say that it puts the cart before the horse: get people interested in Parliament, and more of them will vote).

We assumed earlier in this chapter that low turnouts show a lack of interest and regard, but the picture is more complicated than that. Although many people prefer more consensual politics, sharper differences between the policies of the major parties may increase turnout, possibly on the principle of voting against candidates rather than for them. It may also be that when voters see the result of an election as a foregone conclusion (as many did in 2001) they are more likely to stay at home.

The Electoral Commission set up under the Political Parties, Elections and Referendums Act 2000 has the duty of educating and informing the public about the importance of participation in the democratic process and of recommending ways in which electoral arrangements can be improved. Some changes have already been made: you do not need to have an address in order to vote; and under the 'rolling register' introduced in 2000 names can be added to the electoral register at any time during the year. Experiments in the wider availability of postal voting, electronic voting and mobile polling stations are being made, and the European Parliamentary and Local Elections (Pilots) Bill introduced in September 2003 would make further provision for this. At the local level, postal voting has already made a considerable difference: in the all-postal 2003 local elections in Herefordshire, for example, the turnout for the county council was 60 percent and for parish councils 68.5 percent; for the same elections with conventional polling in 2000, the turnouts were 37 and 48 percent, respectively. As for e-voting, the evidence on its effects is so far unconvincing, and the Electoral Commission believes that more research is necessary.

In 2004, the intention is that the European Parliament, local and Greater London Assembly elections should be on the same day, so that voters need turn out only once. The possibility of having polling on Sundays, when fewer people are working, rather than on the traditional Thursdays, is also being considered; Belgium, Finland, France, Germany, Italy, Spain and Sweden hold the majority of their elections on a Sunday. The Electoral Commission is also consulting on the possibility of votes at 16 rather than 18. Germany and Austria have reduced the voting age to 16 for regional and municipal elections, and the initial turnout has been higher among 16- to 18-year-olds than among 18- to 35-year-olds – although the novelty of the change may have something to do with that.

Some people feel that the public funding of political parties (see page 62) would have an effect on their public image that would encourage more people to vote; but the issue is contentious, and it is impossible to predict what the effect would be.

Supporters of proportional representation believe that the greater weight that PR systems could give to the votes of individual electors would increase engagement with politics and so turnout. Opponents might point to the very low turnout for the 1999 European Parliament elections, which are conducted on a proportional basis; but other factors may have contributed to that result. At the moment, however, the prospect of a change to the electoral system looks remote; as we noted in Chapter 2, the leader of the Liberal Democrats, the party most closely associated with electoral reform, said in January 2003: 'as things stand, proportional representation for Westminster is unachievable'.

Referendums

If participation in conventional voting cannot be increased, there may be pressure for direct involvement in decision making through the use of referendums – an opportunity for all electors to vote on a specific proposition. Most democracies use referendums from time to time; in some systems (Switzerland and California, for example) the result has the force of law; but elsewhere, as has so far happened in the United Kingdom, the result is advisory only (although a government may pledge itself to abide by that result).

Referendums have been used from time to time in the UK: in 1973 in Northern Ireland on the province's constitutional future; and in 1975 through-out the UK on the issue of continued membership of the EEC. They were used twice, in 1979 and 1997, on proposals for devolution to Scotland and Wales, and they have been used most recently on proposals for elected mayors. Referendums are also to be used to decide whether to set up regional assem-blies, and – should the government decide that its economic tests have been met – on the UK adopting the euro.

There are several disadvantages of referendums as a way of supplementing conventional democratic decision making in the UK. They can only be advisory; and they cannot be requisitioned by the people but are held at the government's initiative (and legislation is needed to authorise each referendum). The UK, without a written constitution, has no clear guidance about when referendums should be used; if, say, they should be used on constitutional issues, who decides what a constitutional issue is? For example, the government has refused the opposition's request for a referendum on the proposed new EU constitution.

If a referendum is held, what is a valid result? Should a minimum percent-age of the electorate vote in favour, or should the requirement be an absolute majority, regardless of turnout? And what should be the question asked? (The Political Parties, Elections and Referendums Act 2000 provides that the gov-ernment should consult the Electoral Commission on the 'intelligibility' of the question, but the final decision is still for ministers.) And however deftly the question may be phrased, what is to prevent the referendum becoming a vote of confidence on the government of the day? It may be significant that the over-whelming majority of the referendums held by the commonwealth government in Australia since 1906 have produced a 'no' vote.

We do not have a habit of referendums in this country; but as interactive technology becomes more sophisticated and widespread, they (and some of these questions and problems) may become more important.

Reconnecting Parliament and the public: improving understanding

In 2000, the House of Commons Commission (see page 54) adopted as one of its four strategic aims 'to improve public understanding and knowledge of the work of the House and to increase its accessibility'. A great deal of work is under way in this area. The parliamentary website (www.parliament.uk) has been completely redesigned to serve the needs of the general public rather than the specialist. It was launched in the summer of 2002 and was described by the British Web Design and Marketing Association as 'the best example of the adop-tion of open government technologies that we have seen'. It carries a huge amount of information about the work of the two Houses and their committees, and about current business. The new site has a news section and direct links to the Order Paper, *Hansard*, bills, select committee home pages, early day motions, the Register of Members' Interests and many other areas of parliamentary activity. In financial year 2002–03, there were 14.6 million hits on the website.

In 2002, the House's range of publications began to be produced with a common design theme, and in May 2003 select committee reports changed from their traditional blue-covered, small-print format to a less cluttered and more user-friendly design, which has been well received. The House administration and select committees draw on professional communications advice to publicise parliamentary work.

There is 'gavel-to-gavel' television coverage of proceedings in both Chambers and in Westminster Hall (representing about seventy hours of coverage each week) and increasing coverage of select committees. Webcasting of the House, Westminster Hall and Select Committees is now on a permanent basis.

The House of Commons Information Office answers questions from the public on the work, publications and history of the House, and in financial year 2002–03 it dealt with 80,000 inquiries. The office's publications include the *Weekly Information Bulletin* and about sixty factsheets on aspects of the House's work. In 2002–03, 8,500 factsheets were sent out in hard copy and a quarter of a million downloaded from the parliamentary website. The Parliamentary Bookshop now has its own website at www.bookshop.parliament.uk, which provides worldwide access and on-line buying.

While the Houses are sitting, tours of Parliament sponsored by MPs and peers are organised by the new Central Tours Office, set up in October 2002. These tours were formerly charged for but are now free. Even with the change in sitting hours, which restricts access, some 500 people a day tour the palace. A charge is made for tours during the commercial summer recess opening; in the 2002 summer recess, 82,000 people visited. Plans are under consideration for a visitor centre whose theme will be understanding the work of the two Houses.

The Parliamentary Education Unit provides support for teachers and students, including booklets and posters, visits programmes, videos and an education website at www.explore.parliament.uk. Some 8,000 students from over 200 schools and colleges participated in the Autumn Visits Programme held during the second half of the 2002 summer recess.

Reconnecting Parliament and the public: accessing the political process

If people are to feel involved in the business of Parliament, they must also feel that they can be a part of it, rather than voting for MPs every four years or so and then seeing the results on their television screens or in the newspapers.

Select committees provide one of the best ways of doing this. They draw on a wide range of evidence, not only from the 'great and the good' but also from people who know about a subject from a local or personal perspective. They operate away from Westminster, seeing things first-hand and taking evidence. Increasing select committee consideration of draft bills will bring new opportunities for people to be involved more directly in making the law. The Joint Committee on the Communications Bill ran a successful on-line consultation on the bill, and such consultations seem likely to become routine (as they already are in the Scottish Parliament). Public consultation is a key part of the regulatory reform procedure, and some of the suggestions for amendment of the law made by the Regulatory Reform Committee and its predecessor have had their origins in points put by members of the public.

In a sense, MPs' constituency work provides a link between Parliament and the public, but it has been suggested that this should be supplemented by a more formal way in which citizens can put their problems and concerns to the House of Commons. MPs can already present public petitions (see page 306) on behalf of their constituents, and this is a valued opportunity. However, although it may give a higher profile to an issue, and although the government usually publishes its observations on a petition (but is not required to do so), that is normally the end of the matter. One idea is either that a petition should be referred to the relevant departmental committee for it to decide whether to take the matter up with the government or that there should be a Select Committee on Public Petitions, which could hear the petitioners in person and could take up cases if it thought them justified.

Reconnecting Parliament and the public: the House's image

Concern is sometimes expressed about the image of Parliament as a factor in its public standing, in terms of both the sort of people who are MPs and some of its more old-fashioned or ceremonial aspects. As we saw in Chapter 2, the House of Commons is not a microcosm of the country as a whole. The average age of MPs is about 50; 18 percent of them are women, as against 51 percent in the general country as a whole; and 2 percent are from ethnic minorities, compared with 7 percent in the general population. Many people believe that the House would be held in greater regard if all sectors of the population saw it as containing 'people like us' and that that would increase interest and participation. However, a greater democratisation of the House of Commons would not *of itself* increase its effectiveness, or the effectiveness of MPs as constituency representatives.

The prisoner of history?

If one is modernising something, cosmetic change always offers some quick hits; indeed, it is sometimes said that you know when the management consultants have been in because the canteen has been painted a different colour. As will have been clear from earlier chapters, there are often good reasons for some things in the House of Commons that appear strange to outside observers. But there are also many things that are the legacy of earlier centuries. Some, like the shape and size of the Chamber, probably do have a real influence on the way the House operates; it might be a very different place if the Chamber were a 659-seat hemicycle. Others are more picturesque; and although they have their critics, it is difficult to say that they really make much of a difference. How would the perception of the House change if the Clerks at the Table wore suits rather than their court dress and wigs, for example? Or if the Mace were not carried in procession into the Chamber every day? Many people rather like the dignified framework of the House's proceedings, perhaps seeing it as a counterweight to the rough and tumble of debate or Question Time. It is part of the House's image, but it makes little or no difference to the way that the House does its job.

Information and communications technologies

ICT is intrinsic to the work of both Houses. The parliamentary network supports over 6,000 users, providing communications and information sources. E-mail traffic (internal and external) runs at about two million items a month. Users can access the network remotely, for example from constituency offices; computer equipment for MPs has been installed in 1,300 locations across the UK. Users of the network also have access to intranet sites operated by House departments; there were over three million hits on these sites in financial year 2002–03; and in early 2003 usage was running at more than seven times the level during the same period in 2002.

As well as providing communications and access to information, ICT is crucial to many of the functions of the two Houses. The 'camera-ready copy' that allows the rapid production of select committee reports, often overnight, is not produced by some specialist department but by a single person in each committee staff team. The Public Bill Offices of the two Houses use some of the world's most sophisticated text-handling software to produce lengthy bills, often incorporating hundreds of amendments, ready to print in a matter of hours. Select committees handle 98 percent of their written evidence electronically, almost eliminating the need for typesetting, and tailor-made systems have revolutionised the production of *Hansard*. The House of Commons does not yet use ICT on the scale of its Canadian counterpart, which is probably the world leader in this field, but it is not far behind. One of the limitations is likely to be the preferences of MPs themselves; for example, one select committee has experimented with a paperless meeting, but there is little enthusiasm among other committees to move in this direction. And as we saw in Chapter 6 (page 158), there are arguments on both sides about the introduction of electronic voting.

However, many MPs see new technologies as offering more effective ways of communicating with their constituents, particularly in younger age groups. A survey in June 2002 found that 89 percent of 16- to 24-year-olds had used the Internet; 74 percent of those aged from 25 to 44; 60 percent of those aged from 45 to 54; 40 percent of 55- to 64-year-olds; and 12 percent of those over 65. Some of the developing areas include MPs' websites (in June 2003, 371 MPs had their own sites), video-conferencing, on-line surgeries, better net-working between Westminster and constituency offices, and the use of mobile devices to access information wherever the MP might be.

E-mail is increasingly used to communicate with constituents, although it is slightly surprising that, in June 2003, 103 MPs were not contactable by e-mail or through their websites. However, as we saw in Chapter 5 (page 102), e-mail can bring its own problems: its speed leads many constituents to expect instant answers to what may be extremely complicated problems; and some very con-scientious constituency MPs prefer not to use e-mail for this reason.

E-mail may also not replace paper mail but add to it. The Congress Online project in the United States in 2001 found that:

> e-mail is generating a whole new source of work. With individual House offices now receiving as many as 8,000 e-mail messages per month, and Senate offices receiving as many as 55,000, the burdens on staff are viewed as unmanage-able . . . As a result, the demands of e-citizens have been wreaking havoc on most congressional offices.

Although new technologies will inevitably play an increasing part in the rela-tionship between Parliament and the citizen, there are two important caveats. First, if one creates expectations they need to be fulfilled. It is no good having an on-line consultation on a draft bill, for example, unless the process is mod-erated, and the results analysed and used. Websites need to be updated and e-mails responded to. All this needs effort and resources; otherwise the use of new technologies can actually risk a new form of disconnection with the public at large.

Second, although use of the Internet is constantly increasing, there is also what has become known as the 'digital divide'. The government intends to ensure that everyone in the UK who wants Internet access should have it by 2005, but although 40 percent of UK households have Internet access at home, household income is an important factor: in the highest income group about 70 percent of households have home access, whereas in the two lowest income groups fewer than 10 percent have access.

We have looked so far at the way in which the House is seen outside West-minster, and its relationship with those it represents. Let us now turn to the way in which it operates and some of the proposals that have been made for change.

The size of the House

As we saw in Chapter 2, the Commons is a comparatively large assembly. This has the advantage that each MP represents fewer people than he or she would in a smaller House. However, it also means that the competition for parliamentary time and opportunities is greater, and some commentators also see the size of the House as working in favour of the government of the day, diluting dissent and unfocusing opposition. The size of the government (114 ministers in the two Houses, ninety or so of whom sit in the Commons) also comes in for criticism; together with over 50 parliamentary private secretaries it represents a considerable exercise of patronage for the Prime Minister, and as 'the payroll vote' it is a rock-solid block of MPs voting the government line.

Most suggestions for reducing the size of the House focus around the 400 mark, often with the number of ministers being reduced further, to about fifty. However, although the Prime Minister could change the number of ministers in a morning, the lead time for any change in the size of the House is likely to be very long. It is certainly not an immediate prospect.

A related point is the 'West Lothian question': the ability of MPs from Scotland, Wales and Northern Ireland to vote at Westminster on matters which affect England but which in their own parts of the UK would be dealt with by the devolved administration and assemblies. This has always been an issue in devolution, but it has become more controversial; in the summer of 2003 many Scottish MPs voted for a total ban on foxhunting and were also instrumental in saving the government's proposals for foundation hospitals from defeat. In Scotland, both subjects are the responsibility of the Scottish Parliament. It is sometimes suggested that the Speaker should certify bills so that they could be voted on only by those MPs in whose constituencies they would apply. Such a procedure is theoretically possible, but it would be complicated, to say the least.

The floor of the House

Here proposed changes have centred around more topical debates – perhaps chosen on the basis of the number of MPs who requested a debate on a particular subject. Another form of this proposal is that when an early day motion (see page 271) receives more than a certain number of signatures – perhaps half of the House's membership, or half of the membership less ministers and PPSs – time should be found to debate it.

One rather surprising result of changes in recent years is that there is now no opportunity for an individual MP to put a proposition to the House for debate and decision, as used to be possible through the ballot for private members' motions. The nearest equivalent is the ten-minute rule bill procedure (see page 209), although that allows only one speech against before a vote is taken.

A business committee

There has been increasing pressure for the establishment of a committee, on the same lines as the *bureau* in many continental parliaments, and similar committees in the devolved assemblies, to plan the business of the House. Its members would include representatives of all the parties in the House, and possibly the Speaker and his deputies. Some acknowledge that such a committee would have to meet in private; others believe that it could meet in public. A business committee is seen as a way of involving all parties in the House in the planning of business and of making the process more transparent. However, it is inevitable that the government of the day would see it as a serious threat to its control of the House's business.

Parliamentary questions

Some MPs would like to see oral questions with no notice to individual departments (as are most oral questions to the Prime Minister) in order to make Question Time more topical; but this proposal was not supported by the Procedure Committee in 2002, and the reduction in the period of notice required may achieve much the same end.

The refusal of ministers to answer certain types of question, or the perceived unhelpfulness of replies, is seen by many MPs as frustrating. At the moment, the Public Administration Committee reports each session on ministerial accountability and refusals to answer. This process might bear more directly upon ministers – and their willingness to give full replies in every case – if there were some more immediate recourse, perhaps to a select committee that could in justified cases press (or, an even more daring reform, require) a minister to answer a particular question.

The Speaker's ability to grant an application for an urgent question, and summon a (perhaps reluctant) minister to come to the House at short notice to face MPs' questions, is an important part of calling the government to account. Some recent blueprints for reform have suggested that much greater use should be made of this power, and that the criteria for granting an urgent question should be relaxed.

The Royal Prerogative

As we saw in Chapter 4, many powers are exercised by ministers without reference to Parliament. These include entering into treaties, military action, public appointments and the organisation of government. Most proposals for making Parliament more effective include making the exercise of the prerogative subject to parliamentary approval. Although some changes are occurring *ad hoc*, such as the remarkable precedent of parliamentary approval for British military intervention in Iraq, and select committees are starting to examine draft treaties and major public appointments, any change to make the role of Parliament decisive rather than advisory could happen only if the government of the day were to introduce legislation.

Select committees

Select committees already have a great deal of flexibility, and they exercise considerable independence. What use they make of it is very much up to them; determined and unanimous committees can achieve a great deal. The work of select committees has developed by leaps and bounds over the last ten years, but some see them as unduly constrained.

The back-up available to select committees has been an issue in the past, but the establishment of the Scrutiny Unit, the significant expansion of committee staff to deal with the core tasks and the flexibility of the specialist adviser system mean that committees are better resourced now than they have ever been. Even so, staff resources are fairly modest. There are two aspects to this: first, a successful and influential committee inquiry does not necessarily mean asking 5,000 questions; it may mean asking five questions *but getting answers*. Second, if select committees are going to maintain their political clout they must be member-driven, not staff-driven.

Modest resources do constrain committees in one way. They may be able to support several inquiries at the same time, but it is more difficult to keep a constantly roving eye across the committee's areas of responsibility to identify where the spotlight should turn next. In this respect, the Comptroller and Auditor-General's constant monitoring of all government departments provides unique support for the Public Accounts Committee. Although some select committees have drawn upon the C&AG's reports, it is a little surprising that the PAC is supported by the work of 800 staff of the National Audit Office, while twenty-five or so other investigative committees are supported by 150 staff of the Committee Office. One way of rebalancing would be to put the resources of the NAO at the disposal of the select committee system as a whole, and for the PAC to return to its historical function of examining government accounts.

As we saw in Chapter 11, government replies to select committee reports are by convention given within two months of a report's publication. Although select committees should be well able to take action when a reply is late – such as calling a minister to give oral evidence – it would entrench the role of committees if the convention were to be made a formal requirement (perhaps with a slightly longer reply time), the breaching of which would have to be explained to the House by the responsible minister.

From time to time the powers of select committees become an issue, usually in the most high-profile and controversial inquiries. Select committees have the power to require the attendance of witnesses, but this may be difficult or counter-productive to enforce, and the power does not apply to ministers or civil servants. Although general undertakings to cooperate have been given by successive governments, select committees have often been dissatisfied with the results. Giving select committees a power of subpoena that could be directly enforced, and where non-compliance would carry an automatic penalty, is one possibility; but the legal difficulties, particularly from a human rights point of view, could be considerable. Giving select committees the power to require the attendance of ministers and civil servants, and to force them to answer questions, would require a fundamental change in the relationship between government and Parliament; but, understandably, this is an issue that is unlikely to go away.

One power that all committees have but that is almost never used is the ability to take evidence on oath. Under the Parliamentary Witnesses Oaths Act 1871, false evidence is then not something that has to be pursued through the cumbersome and largely ineffective mechanisms of privilege and contempt; the law's serious penalties for perjury come into play. In the small minority of cases where witnesses are thought to be misleading a committee, this might concentrate minds; and it might have a wider moral effect.

A number of other recommendations, mainly from the Liaison Committee and the Modernisation Committee, are still on the table. The proposal for a Committee of Nomination was defeated in the House in May 2002, but there is still some disquiet at the involvement of the whips in the appointment of those whose task it is to scrutinise government. The Liaison Committee's suggestion of a 'select committee half-hour' in prime time in the Chamber, to give immediate prominence to important select committee reports, was turned down by the government for reasons that the committee found profoundly unconvincing. The Liaison Committee also recommended that debates on select committee reports should take place on substantive motions to endorse recommendations, as a way of giving select committees a higher profile and connecting them more closely with the work of the House as a whole. This, too, was rejected by the government.

Joint committees

There has been an increase in the use of joint committees of the two Houses, most recently to examine a series of draft bills as well as human rights and the possibilities of Lords reform, and there may be scope for more cooperation. Detailed scrutiny needs considerable resources, which could be more efficiently provided on a joint basis. A suggestion made to the Royal Commission on the reform of the House of Lords was that joint committees might oversee areas of scrutiny, for example European business and delegated legislation (looking at merits, rather than the legal aspects already examined by the joint committee on statutory instruments). The 'product' of that scrutiny could then be used for investigations and recommendations by sub-committees that were specifically Commons or Lords, thus reflecting the different approaches of the two Houses.

Legislation

This is an area of the House's work that has come in for sustained criticism, and it has been made more contentious by the breakdown of consensus over the programming of bills. The huge quantity of delegated legislation made by ministers under powers given to them in Acts of Parliament is subject to relatively little scrutiny. We outlined some of the problems, both in primary and secondary legislation, in Chapter 7.

Finding better *ways* of examining legislation is in some ways a second-order question; the main problem is the sheer *volume*. It is a little like thinking of more efficient ways of mopping the floor when a better solution would be to turn the tap off. In July 2003 Robin Cook, the former Leader of the House, described the root cause of the problem, which is 'Whitehall's tendency to keep putting before us more legislation than we can properly scrutinise in any one session'.

Most would agree that the use of draft bills has allowed improved scrutiny and has contributed to better-quality legislation. However, the main complaint of committees that have examined draft bills is that they have had too little time to do a proper job.

It is possible to deploy an armoury of procedural solutions to the problems of legislative scrutiny: longer periods of notice for government amendments; prescribed intervals between different stages of bills; mandatory pre-legislative scrutiny except in certified cases of urgency; the use of Westminster Hall to increase the time available for debate on Committee of the whole House and report stages; sifting of delegated legislation for importance, combined with select committee investigation (the Procedure Committee's proposals for a sifting committee were turned down by the government, but such a committee has been established in the House of Lords); and so on.

However, the inability or unwillingness of governments of both main parties to legislate less will always be at the heart of the problem. A few years ago, an MP sought leave (only partly tongue in cheek) to bring in a ten-minute rule bill which would have required that, for every page of law put onto the statute

book, a page should be deleted. Those who grapple with the scrutiny of legislation may feel that he had a point.

Private members' bill procedure is a fruitful source of proposals for change.
As will have been clear from Chapter 6 (page 206), the tactics are complex
and the likelihood of success very limited unless proposals are uncontentious
and/or have government support. There are always back-bench MPs who have
an enthusiasm for legislating that, if unchecked, could produce a volume of
legislation rivalling that of the government. The frailty of private members'
bills has always been a counterweight to that enthusiasm. However, there
is some support for a system that would give a very few bills each session –
perhaps five – a chance of success on the basis of being voted on (under some
type of programming), rather than simply being talked out or obstructed by
lengthy debate on preceding bills. One difficulty with such a change would
be ensuring that it was used for genuinely back-bench initiatives rather than
government hand-out bills – which would simply increase the government's
legislative time.

Examining spending

Chapter 8 reviewed how Parliament, and especially the House of Commons,
deals with spending and taxation, and the lack of detailed control over how
the government spends taxpayers' money. Select committees' core tasks now
require them to examine expenditure plans, and they are equipped to explore
the detail in a way that would be impossible in a larger forum. But however
strong their criticisms, the opportunity for committees to be any more than
advisory is limited – in practice to six estimates day debates a year. And even
then the committee may well be reluctant to use the 'nuclear option' of forcing a vote on the reduction of some individual estimate. However, the formal
referral of estimates to select committees is often suggested. We consider this
in a broader context below.

Reconnecting committees and the Chamber

The Chamber is the forum in which the House takes its decisions; committees
are advisory and preparatory. In most cases – the main exception being when
bills (as opposed to draft bills) are referred to committees – the result is advice
rather than something with which the House has to agree or disagree.

One prescription for reform would allow the House to play to its acknowledged strength: select committees. Bills would invariably be referred to select
committees after second reading, for scrutiny in the light of expert testimony
and public involvement, and in a more flexible format than that provided by
special standing committees.

The same approach could be used for the estimates, with the House being able to approve only on the basis of a report from the relevant select committee, which would be able to vary individual components up and down (if necessary, provided that the overall totals remained the same).

This radical approach would have a number of implications. Committees would be taking serious decisions that the government, if it disagreed, would have to ask the House to reverse. There would be more political pressure on select committees, and it might be difficult to maintain their generally consensual way of working. The process would demand more time and resources; but it would give power to back-benchers on both sides of the House in a way that would meet many of the current criticisms of the way the Commons operates.

This 'reconnecting committees and the Chamber approach' could be taken into a number of other areas: no Statutory Instrument could be debated until the Joint Committee on Statutory Instruments had reported upon it; the European Scrutiny Committee could have the power to specify a time within which debates on EU documents should be held and the power to require a debate in the Chamber on the most important proposals; debates in standing committees on delegated legislation could take place on a substantive motion; and the motion agreed to by the committee would have to be put to the House. A similar approach could be used for European standing committees, removing the government's right to substitute a motion of its own when a document was reported from standing committee. Debates on select committee reports could routinely take place on substantive motions.

Qualified majorities

The House has adopted a novel method of decision taking when electing its Speaker. Not all decisions need be taken by a simple majority. It is sometimes suggested that the rights of the opposition parties, and of back-benchers on both sides of the House, might be protected by requiring certain decisions, such as those suspending a normal rule of the House, to be taken by a qualified majority, perhaps two-thirds.

Qualified majorities and a mandatory role for select committees in matters of legislation and expenditure are the sort of things that would cause business managers in governments of either party to have apoplexy. Most procedural change takes place if there is some balance of advantage and disadvantage to the government of the day. What is noticeable in the studies of parliamentary effectiveness over the last four or five years is growing agreement that change really is a zero-sum game: that a greater role for Parliament means a net loss of the power of governments. Whether that happens is in the hands of MPs themselves, just as it is up to MPs how effectively they use the considerable parliamentary opportunities that already exist.

The House of Lords

The background

The changes that have taken place in the Commons in recent years, and the prospects for further change, have been evolutionary in character. The House of Lords too has seen evolutionary change, as we shall see. But because of a continuing debate about the composition and powers of the House – and indeed, as to whether the House should exist at all – the Lords has lived with the prospect of fundamental reform of a rather different order for much of the last hundred years. It is useful to see this in historical context.

We saw in Chapter 7 how the powers of the House of Lords over legislation were curtailed by the Parliament Act of 1911 and again in 1949 (page 220). Although reform of the composition of the House had been promised by the preamble to the 1911 Act, nothing was to happen for a very long time. Proposals for an indirectly elected House with a continuing hereditary element were developed by the Bryce Commission in 1918, but these proposals and variations of them found little favour at the time, not least because they would not have eliminated the Conservative Party's majority in the House.

1949

Serious discussion of reform did not resume until 1949, when, in the context of the passage of the second Parliament Bill, an all-party conference discussed powers and composition. No agreement was reached on any wider issue, and the 1949 Parliament Act was confined to reducing the period of operation of the so-called 'suspensory veto' from three sessions to two. But a statement of agreed principles on the future of the House was subsequently published. This statement suggested developments like the admission of women to the House, some form of remuneration, development of a leave of absence scheme and the elimination of the then permanent majority of the Conservative Party – all of which, in time, were to come about. The most interesting idea of all was that in future the membership should be partly hereditary and partly for life. This latter concept was given effect by the Life Peerages Act in 1958, which included life peerages for women. In 1963, the Peerages Act allowed women hereditary peers to sit for the first time and any hereditary peer to disclaim his peerage for life on inheritance.

The Wilson proposals

In 1967, the Wilson government made a brave attempt to institute a two-tier House composed of 200 to 250 voting life peers, law lords and some bishops and a remainder of non-voting hereditary peers entitled to sit only for the remainder of their lives. Delaying powers over bills would be reduced to six months, and the government party would have a small majority over opposition parties. Although the proposals were approved in principle by the Lords, a curious alliance of Left and Right in the Commons opposed it, and progress in committee proved to be so slow that the bill was abandoned. The failure of this scheme had the effect of removing Lords reform from the agendas of the two main parties for a generation. The Conservative governments under Margaret Thatcher and John Major showed no interest in the question. Indeed, between 1977 and 1989 Labour Party policy was to abolish the House altogether.

The departure of the hereditary peers and a Royal Commission

Not until the election of Tony Blair's Labour government in 1997 did Lords reform reappear on the political agenda, with proposals to eliminate the hereditary members and set up a Royal Commission to consider long-term proposals. Thus the House of Lords Act of 1999 disqualified all hereditary peers from sitting, save for the ninety-two excepted by the Act (see page 33). And in January 2000 the Royal Commission chaired by Lord Wakeham produced its report *A House for the Future*. The Royal Commission confirmed most of the House's existing powers, including that of the suspensory veto under the Parliament Acts.

On composition, however, the Royal Commission made what were its only really radical recommendations. It suggested a chamber of about 550 members, a 'significant minority' of whom would be elected on a regional basis according to a list system of proportional representation and the remainder appointed. Although the commission could not agree on the number to be elected – three alternative figures of sixty-five, eighty-seven and 195 were offered – the genie of election had been let out of the bottle and was to dominate the reform debate thereafter. Both elected and appointed members would serve fifteen-year terms. Existing life peers would become members for life in the new House. Finally, an Appointments Commission established on a statutory basis would vet nominations for membership of the new second chamber and make its own nominations, chiefly of independent members.

Appointment versus election

Although a House of Lords Appointments Commission with some of the functions recommended by the Royal Commission was established on a non-statutory basis in 2000, not until November 2001 did the government produce a White Paper responding to the Royal Commission's proposals. This proposed a largely nominated second chamber with 120 elected members, regionally based, and a guaranteed independent element. The representation of the political parties would reflect the votes cast in the preceding general election. The Appointments Commission would be a statutory body, but it would have no role in selecting the appointed party members.

The government's response was not well received in all quarters. In February 2002, the Commons Public Administration committee recommended that 60 percent of the Lords be elected, 20 percent be nominated by the parties and 20 percent be independent members. The Appointments Commission would appoint the non-elected members. Then a Commons early day motion called for any reformed House to be wholly or substantially elected and received the support of over 300 MPs. And the Conservative Party called for a smaller House of 300 predominantly elected members.

Against this increasingly confused background, the Lord Chancellor and Leader of the House of Commons finally announced the appointment of the long-delayed joint committee in order to forge the broadest possible parliamentary consensus on the way forward. The joint committee was to be asked as a first step 'to report on options for the composition and powers of the House of Lords once reform has been completed'. This was to be followed by free votes in both Houses and then a subsequent report to 'define in greater detail the proposed composition, role and powers of the reformed second chamber', taking account of the opinion expressed in the votes. It would also recommend the transitional strategy for transforming the existing House of Lords into its fully reformed state.

At the end of 2002, the joint committee duly published its first report setting out options for the composition of a reformed House against a background of what the committee saw as 'broad agreement on the role, functions and powers of a reformed second chamber', which would remain largely unchanged. On membership, seven options were put forward, ranging from fully appointed to fully nominated. The House would comprise about 600 members, each of whom would serve for twelve years. Nominations of appointed members would be scrutinised by a new, statutory, Appointments Commission.

The report was debated in both Houses in January 2003, and in February each House voted on each of the seven options. The outcome was confusing. The Lords voted overwhelmingly in favour of the fully appointed option and rejected the others. The Commons on the other hand rejected all options, although the 80 percent elected, 20 percent appointed option was lost by only three votes. In view of this, the joint committee made a second report in May 2003 identifying the consensus that had been achieved – chiefly on powers – and outlining the further work that needed to be done on questions such as the future of the remaining hereditary peers, the appointments system, the size of the House and the conditions of tenure of the members. The report spelled out the five qualities required in the membership of a House that can perform the functions currently assigned to it – legitimacy, representativeness, no domination by one party, independence, and expertise – and, in effect, invited the government to indicate what view it now took of the future of Lords reform.

The future of Lords reform

The government's response, published in July 2003, accepted the joint committee's assessment that a consensus had now been reached over the role, functions and powers of the House. It also accepted the qualities required in the membership. But, in the absence of a consensus as to what the membership should be, the government's interest in further reform would be confined to making the House work as effectively as possible in the medium term.

Thus in September 2003, the government published its consultation paper 'Constitutional reform: next steps for the House of Lords', in which it announced its intention to introduce a bill 'when Parliamentary time allows' to remove all remaining hereditary peers from the House and to establish a statutory Appointments Commission. The government proposes that the commission will be accountable to Parliament and will determine the number and timing of appointments, select independent members of the House and oversee party nominations. The commission will be obliged to ensure that the balance of new nominations between the parties reflects the distribution of the vote at the previous general election. Twenty percent of new appointments will be non-party, and the target membership of the House will not, it is thought, exceed 600. The bill giving effect to these changes is likely to be introduced in 2004.

In some ways it is difficult to see what else the government could do in the light of the decisions of the two Houses. But, on the other hand, those who hoped for more radical change will no doubt have agreed with Robin Cook, former Leader of the House of Commons, who recorded in his diary as this policy was being formulated: 'Modernisation is to be limited to moving from the fifteenth century principle of heredity to the eighteenth century principle of patronage'.

Would-be reformers of the House of Lords have always faced two virtually irresolvable problems: first, how to reconcile reform of membership with the heightened sense of legitimacy *vis-à-vis* the House of Commons that would inevitably result; and, second, how to reconcile a heightened sense of legitimacy with the exercise of a range of powers that, while retaining the practical utility of the upper House, nevertheless reflected the ultimate supremacy of the House of Commons. Until answers can be found to these questions that are acceptable both across the political spectrum and within the current administration, the chances of further reform of membership will be slim. But the debate is most unlikely to go away for long.

The Lord Chancellor and the Lords of Appeal in Ordinary

The office of Lord Chancellor dismembered

On 12 June 2003, Lord Irvine of Lairg resigned as Lord Chancellor and Lord Falconer of Thoroton was appointed in his place. But at the same time the announcement was made that steps would be taken to separate the functions of the Lord Chancellor. The new Lord Chancellor would cease to sit judicially; an independent Judicial Appointments Commission set up on a statutory basis would recommend candidates for appointment as judges; and the House of Lords would be invited to consider an alternative method for appointing its own Speaker. The appellate functions of the House of Lords would be transferred to a Supreme Court. The Lord Chancellor's Department was renamed the Department of Constitutional Affairs and acquired overall responsibility for the Scotland and Wales Offices. Lord Falconer became Secretary of State of the Department. In the longer term, the post of Lord Chancellor would be abolished.

As some of these changes would require complex legislation, Lord Falconer for the moment continues to fulfil almost all aspects of the job, although he does not sit judicially. Thus it is he, rather than Lord Irvine, who will be the last Lord Chancellor. Consultation papers have been published on proposals for the Supreme Court and the Judicial Appointments Commission. And the House of Lords quickly set up a select committee to look into the question of Speakership.

Although the announcement of these changes surprised many, the role of the Lord Chancellor as Speaker of a chamber of Parliament, government minister, judge and head of the judiciary had come to be questioned by some lawyers and constitutionalists. While there is no evidence to suggest that holders of the office in recent times were unable successfully to separate their various functions and exercise them impartially, the office appeared to offend the doctrine of separation of powers. After all, the Lord Chancellor embodied in his person parliamentary, executive and judicial office. (Indeed, he illustrated only too well how the concept of separation of powers has always existed only imperfectly in the United Kingdom!)

Of these proposals, two in particular will affect the House of Lords – the change in the method of selection of Speaker, and the creation of a Supreme Court.

The Speaker

The Lord Chancellor sits as Speaker of the House of Lords by virtue of Standing Order 18, which dates from 1660. Thus, unlike some of the other changes proposed, any change in the manner of appointing a Speaker can be made by the House itself by changing the standing order. No legislation will be required.

The principal question will be how to make the appointment. Will the House make the appointment following consultation through the usual channels? Will the Crown make the appointment on the advice of the House? Or will the House elect its Speaker? And what will be the term of appointment? Will he or she be paid, and if so how much? Then there is the question of functions. At present, as we saw in Chapter 3, the Lord Chancellor plays a very limited role as Speaker. Unlike the presiding officers of other chambers of parliament, the Lord Chancellor has no powers in matters of order. Indeed, his powers of utterance as Speaker barely extend beyond putting the Question (stating the matter for decision by the House). While it seems unlikely that the House will wish to depart from the present system of self-regulation of proceedings, the question will at least have to be addressed.

Some members feel that the Speaker and his deputies should be able to give some procedural direction to the House from time to time. Currently, the House relies on the Leader of the House, or in his absence the Chief Whip or duty whip, to assist the House. And it is possible that other functions, currrently exercised by the Leader of the House, could be taken on without undermining the principle of self-regulation – like devising lists of speakers in debate, deciding on applications for Private Notice Questions and the exercise of the *sub judice* rule. If no additional functions are assumed, being Speaker of the House of Lords will be a rather strange job.

Another problem is how will the post relate to that of the Chairman of Committees, who, as we saw in Chapter 3, performs some functions that might otherwise be performed by a Speaker. At present there are large panels of Deputy Speakers and Deputy Chairmen. Should these now be reduced in size? Should there be some Principal Deputy Speakers who, with the Speaker, might do most of the presiding over proceedings? And what kind of ceremonial role will the Speaker perform?

Finally, there are a number of functions exercised by the Lord Chancellor relating to the House of Lords, although not its proceedings, that will now have to be performed by someone else – nominating Lords members of the Joint Committee on Consolidation Bills and the Ecclesiastical Committee, and holding nominal responsibility for the Lords part of the Palace of Westminster and shared responsibility for Westminster Hall.

In November 2003, the select committee recommended that the House should elect its Speaker by single transferable vote, for a five-year term. The Speaker would be salaried; would take on the current functions of the Lord Chancellor as Speaker; would play a bigger presiding and representative role; and would exercise in the Chamber the advisory role currently exercised by the Leader and whips. Self-regulation will remain. The House itself will now decide when and how to proceed.

The Supreme Court

This book does not concern itself with the role of the House of Lords as a court of final appeal, although we saw in Chapter 2 how, under the Appellate Jurisdiction Act 1876, the Lords of Appeal in Ordinary are given life peerages to hear appeals; they and retired Lords of Appeal currently number twenty-eight.

It is intended that the proposed Supreme Court will assume the current appellate functions of the House of Lords as the final court of appeal in the United Kingdom, save in Scottish criminal cases. It is also likely to acquire from the Judicial Committee of the Privy Council functions in respect of contested devolution issues. The appellate function of the House has for centuries been distinct from the parliamentary function. So vesting it in a Supreme Court, subject to appropriate legislative and administrative arrangements being put in place, will not impinge on the other work of the House at all. Indeed, parliamentary accommodation and staff will become available for other uses.

The chief effect will be the potential loss of eminent lawyers – the law lords appointed under the 1876 Act – as members of the House. At the moment, it is possible for the serving and retired Lords of Appeal to take part in proceedings of the House and to serve on its committees. Some contribute to debates on bills, especially those that relate to the administration of justice or the criminal law, and even move and vote on amendments. Others play an active part in committees – chairing the Joint Committee on Consolidation Bills, the Ecclesiastical Committee, Sub-Committee E of the European Union Committee and the Privileges Committee, for example. They provide a valuable in-house resource of legal and forensic expertise.

It remains to be seen whether, with the establishment of the Supreme Court, those members of the House who have been appointed under the Appellate Jurisdiction Act 1876 will continue to sit or not; and, if not, whether any of them will be given life peerages under the Life Peerages Act. It also remains to be seen whether any future new members of the Supreme Court are to be given membership of the House of Lords or whether the opportunity will now be taken to create a clearer distinction between the exercise of judicial and parliamentary functions. Such a distinction would, after all, be consistent with the overall thrust of the proposed reforms.

Modernisation of practice and procedure in the Lords

The House of Lords has undergone its own programme of change in working practices and procedures in recent years. Unlike the Commons, the Lords has no continuing Modernisation Committee, although the former Leader of the House's Working Group on the Working Practices of the House in 2001–02, and somewhat earlier the Select Committee on the Committee Work of the House in 1992 (the Jellicoe Committee) and the Group on Sittings of the House in 1995 (the Rippon Group) performed very similar functions. In addition, the Procedure Committee continually develops the way in which things are done. For many years, in the absence of proposals for reform of the House, it was by means such as these that the House developed – indeed reformed – itself. Developments continue in a number of areas, and while they have been recounted elsewhere in this book it is useful to pull them together here to illustrate the capacity of the House continually to renew itself.

Committee work

The expansion of the work of select committees since the establishment of the European Union (then Communities) Committee in 1974 was one of the most visible signs of renewal. The process continues, although, as we saw in Chapter 11, the Liaison Committee now arbitrates on competing claims for resources. Thus since 1997 the Economic Affairs and Constitution Committees have been established as sessional committees and the Human Rights Committee as a joint committee. Following recommendations of the Group on Working Practices in 2002, the Finance Bill Sub-Committee of the Economic Affairs Committee was established in 2003, and a Select Committee on the Merits of Statutory Instruments will be set up as a sessional committee at the beginning of the 2003–04 session. Further demands for the establishment of committees on an *ad hoc* or sessional basis are continually being made.

Grand committees

As we saw in Chapter 7, following a recommendation of the Rippon Group in 1995 some bills have been committed to unselected 'grand committees', which any lord may attend. The Group on Working Practices recommended in 2002 that more use be made of this procedure. The number of bills referred is determined by the usual channels but is now much higher than when the procedure was introduced.

In 2003, on the initiative of the then Leader of the House, the House agreed that the grand committee procedure could be used to debate some Northern

Ireland Orders. The intention was to improve scrutiny of what was, effectively, primary legislation during a period of suspension of the Northern Ireland Assembly. The Orders then returned to the floor of the House for approval. Although at present the House as a whole appears reluctant to see more business taken off the floor, grand committees could certainly do more if desired. For example, some feel that debates on committee reports could be staged in grand committees. This procedure continues to evolve.

Sitting hours

Following recommendations of the Group on Working Practices, the House agreed to make changes to its hours of sitting with effect from the 2002–03 session. An attempt has been made to establish a convention that the House will normally rise at 10.00 p.m. on Mondays to Wednesdays. On Thursdays the House now sits at 11.00 a.m., adjourns from 1.30 p.m. till 2.30 p.m. if legislative business is being taken, and business ends at 7 p.m. In addition, the House agreed to sit for two weeks in September in line with the Commons, having risen in mid-July. None of these developments proved an unqualified success. The 10.00 p.m. cut-off, combined with the relatively late start to business in the afternoons after questions and statements, has reduced the ability of the government to get its business through. The arrangement of Thursday business originally with a lunchtime adjournment followed by Question Time was not liked and has been further refined. And there are many who question the value of sitting in September, though the House has resolved to continue the practice in 2004.

Other developments, like increased pre-legislative scrutiny of bills (see page 182), carry-over of such bills if they are subsequently introduced late in a session, as recommended by the Group on Working Practices, and more Lords participation in Commons standing committees on EU matters (see page 400), may also come about in coming years. Taken alone, none of these changes amounts to a 'reform' in the traditional sense of the word, but taken collectively, incremental changes such as these have a tremendous effect both on what the House does and on the way in which it does it.

Conclusion

Blackburn and Kennon provide a timely rejoinder to some of the more apocalyptic criticisms of Parliament, reminding us that fifty years ago there was very little dissent by back-benchers: only 2.5 percent of divisions showed any dissent at all. There was no broadcasting or televising of proceedings. There was far less constituency work, and no attempt by Parliament as an institution to reach out to the public.

> Questions were more detailed, but generally less politically interesting. Governments were obliged to make few changes of importance in their bills. Select committees were much weaker and less important compared with the departmental and other select committees of today. Fifty years ago, select committees were not allowed to consider policy; they did not receive evidence from ministers; they did not engage specialist advisers; and they took all their evidence in private . . . Proceedings at that time were dull and worthy, and largely ineffective. This description must be almost incredible to those who do not remember or have little knowledge of how the House of Commons worked in practice in the 1950s and 1960s, but it was so. [Today] Parliament and its Members, for all its weaknesses and their faults, is in fact more active, more independent, more influential and therefore, for the public, more politically relevant than at any time for many years.

As we have tried to show in this chapter, there are still many ways in which Parliament might change to meet the expectations of those it represents. But although Parliament has always been imperfect, and always will be imperfect, it matters. The better people understand it, the more they will value it. We hope that this book will help.

Notes

Chapter 3

1 Full-time equivalents.

Chapter 5

2 Although it is interesting to note that up to a century ago an MP appointed to the Cabinet had to stand again in a by-election.

Chapter 6

3 Although not unusual in Victorian times: Gladstone was once elected in his 'reserve' constituency, having lost the one he had hoped to win. And he once won in both, passing the 'reserve' on to his son.

4 In the seventeenth and eighteenth centuries, Parliament would assemble in October or November for the King's Speech and then usually sat into the spring. In the nineteenth century, the House began to sit into late July or August but also abandoned pre-Christmas sittings, so that each year it sat only from February to August. Some pre-Christmas sittings crept back in after 1906, and were routine from 1928–29.

Chapter 7

5 Both Houses use the word 'chairman' in their standing orders. 'Chairwoman', 'chairperson' and 'chair' are not used formally by either House, so in this book 'chairman' is used whether the occupant of the chair is male or female.

6 Although an *instruction* from the House can widen the scope of the bill and give a committee the power to make amendments that would otherwise be out of order.

Chapter 10

7 Available on the website of the Lord Chancellor's Department: http://www.lcd.gov.uk/foi/ogcode983.htm

Chapter 12

8 Following the re-weighting of votes by the Treaty of Nice, France, Germany, Italy and the UK have twenty-nine votes each; Spain has twenty-seven; the Netherlands has thirteen; Belgium, Greece and Portugal have twelve each; Austria and Sweden have ten each; Denmark, Finland and Ireland have seven each; and Luxembourg has four. For most QMV decisions, 169 votes in favour (out of 237) are needed – with the proviso that the countries concerned represent at least 62 percent of the population of the EU. Abstention is in effect a vote against. To achieve a 'blocking minority', sixty-nine votes against or abstaining are needed.

9 A novel procedure was devised for keeping Parliament up to date on the work of the convention: a Standing Committee on the Convention was set up, to which the UK's parliamentary representatives, who were back-benchers and not ministers, could report, answer questions and have their work debated. Unusually, all members of the House of Lords and of the House of Commons could also take part along side the MPs formally appointed as members of the committee, although they did not count towards the quorum.

Glossary of parliamentary terms

In each definition, words in *italics* are further explained elsewhere in the glossary.

accounting Officer   the individual (usually the *Permanent Secretary* of a government department or the chief executive of an executive agency) who is personally responsible for the regularity and propriety of expenditure voted under a particular estimate.

Act paper   paper laid before Parliament because an Act of Parliament requires it.

additional costs allowance   an allowance to cover an MP's costs of staying away from home while at Westminster.

Address   a formal communication from either House to the sovereign. The debate on the Queen's Speech takes place on a motion of thanks for the speech (often called the 'Humble Address').

adjournment   the end of a *sitting*. An 'adjournment debate' takes place on a motion 'That this House do now adjourn'. It may be either the half-hour adjournment debate at the end of each sitting in the Commons (where MPs may 'raise a subject on the Adjournment'), or a more significant debate as part of the main business of the day. For the government, the advantage of an adjournment debate (sometimes called in the media a 'technical motion') is that any vote at the end is not on a substantive issue but only on whether the House should adjourn or not. An adjournment (for example 'the summer adjournment') is also a more formal name for a *recess*.

Administration Estimate   in the Commons, pays for the staff of the House and the services provided by the House departments.

advisory cost limit   the estimated cost of answering a parliamentary question (at present £600) above which a minister may decline to answer the question.

affirmation   a secular promise of allegiance to the Crown made by MPs or peers who do not wish to take a religious oath.

affirmative instrument   a piece of *delegated legislation* that the parent Act requires Parliament to approve explicitly before it can come into effect ('the affirmative procedure').

allocation of time order   see *guillotine*.

all-party groups   of greater or lesser formality, these bring together MPs and peers from all parties to discuss matters of common interest. They are established by MPs and peers themselves rather than being creations of either House. The total varies: in 2003 there were some 280 groups. 'Associate parliamentary groups' (about forty) also include people who are not members of one or other House. 'Country groups' (about 100) bring together MPs and peers interested in the affairs of particular countries.

ambit of an estimate   the formal description of the services to be financed from that *estimate*.

amendment   proposal to change the text of a bill, motion or draft select committee report.

amendment of the law motion   moved by the Chancellor of the Exchequer after his *Budget* statement: 'that it is expedient to amend the law with respect to the National Debt and to make further provision in respect of public finance'. It is the vehicle for the broad Budget debate that follows.

amendment in lieu   amendment proposed by one House to the other as an alternative to one that has been rejected by the former.

annulment   the act of making a *Statutory Instrument* of no effect. See also *prayer*.

annually managed expenditure (AME)   a category of government expenditure that is less predictable or controllable than that under *departmental expenditure limits*; for example, social security and Common Agricultural Policy payments.

Appellate Committee   the committee of law lords that hears appeals in the House of Lords.

back-bencher   an MP or peer who is neither a minister nor (in opposition) a spokesperson for his or her party.

back of the Chair bill   see *presentation bill*.

backsheet   the last page of a bill, which repeats the *long* and *short title* of the bill, gives the bill number and the session, and lists the MP introducing the bill ('the member in charge') and his or her supporters.

ballot bills   in the Commons, the twenty *private members' bills* introduced following the ballot on the second Thursday of each session.

bill   draft *primary legislation*.

bill of aids and supplies   old name for a bill granting *Supply* and *Ways and Means*. The principal modern example is the Finance Bill.

Black Rod ('the Gentleman Usher of the Black Rod')   an officer of the Lords responsible for accommodation, services, security and ceremonial.

Boundary Commissions   the four bodies that keep under review the size, boundaries and numbers of parliamentary *constituencies*, especially to take account of population changes.

Budget   oral statement by the Chancellor of the Exchequer, usually in March, which reviews the nation's finances and makes taxation proposals.

Business Questions (strictly, 'the Business Question')   in the Commons, a type of *urgent question* asked of the *Leader of the House* every Thursday, in response to which he announces the business for the next fortnight and answers questions.

by-election   an election in a single *constituency* when a seat becomes vacant because the MP dies or is otherwise no longer eligible to sit.

casting vote   the vote cast by the Chair to decide the issue when the numbers voting are equal. How the vote is cast is usually dictated by precedent, except in select committees.

CCLA   Commons consideration of *Lords amendments*.

Chairman of Committees (or 'Lord Chairman')   the principal Deputy Speaker of the House of Lords and Chairman of the House Committee, which oversees Lords administration. He organises the panel of deputy speakers and deputy chairmen and assigns them their duties, and he has special responsibility for *private bills*. He also chairs the Liaison Committee and the Procedure Committee.

Chairman of Ways and Means   the principal Deputy Speaker of the Commons, with special responsibilities for Committees of the whole House, *private bills* and *Westminster Hall*. In the House, he is assisted by First and Second Deputy Chairmen of

Ways and Means, who act as Deputy Speakers. He chairs the Speaker's Panel of Chairmen, which provides chairmen for *standing committees*.

Chiltern Hundreds the posts of steward or bailiff of Her Majesty's three Chiltern Hundreds of Stoke, Desborough and Burnham, or of the manor of Northstead, are symbolic 'offices of profit' used to allow an MP to resign his or her seat. If an MP is appointed to one, he or she is disqualified as holding an 'office of profit under the Crown' (an MP cannot simply resign).

clause the basic unit of a *bill*, divided into subsections, then paragraphs, then sub-paragraphs. When a bill becomes an Act, 'clauses' become 'sections' but the names of the other subdivisions stay the same.

Clerk of the House the principal officer of the Commons. Chief executive of the House Service and corporate officer as well as the House's principal adviser on the practice, law and privilege of the House.

Clerk of the Parliaments the principal officer of the Lords, with functions similar to those of the Clerk of the House of Commons, but who is also Registrar of the Court when the House acts in its judicial capacity.

closure in the Commons, a device for curtailing debate, or for securing a decision on a matter that would otherwise be *talked out*. An MP moves a *motion* 'That the Question be now put', which (if allowed by the Chair) is put to a decision immediately, without debate. If a division is forced upon it, not fewer than 100 MPs must vote in the majority for the closure, otherwise the motion is lost. If it is agreed to, the Question originally proposed from the Chair must be put immediately.

collective responsibility the doctrine under which all members of the government – that is, ministers – support the policies of the government and take responsibility for government action, even if there are elements with which they privately disagree. Open disagreement is normally followed by resignation.

Command Paper paper presented to Parliament by the government, formally 'by Command of Her Majesty'.

commencement the coming into effect of legislation. For Acts of Parliament, this is usually done by an order made by the responsible minister. If there is no commencement provision, the Act comes into force from midnight at the beginning of the day on which *Royal Assent* was given.

Committee of the whole House used for the committee stage of bills in the House itself rather than in a *standing committee*. In the Commons, Committee of the whole House is presided over by the *Chairman of Ways and Means* rather than the *Speaker*, and the *Mace* (normally on top of the *Table*) is placed on brackets below the Table to show that the House is in committee. Any MP may take part in proceedings, just as in the House itself.

Commons amendment an amendment made by the Commons to a bill passed by the Lords.

Comptroller and Auditor-General a statutorily independent officer of the Commons who heads the National Audit Office (NAO); who approves the release of money from the Consolidated Fund; who audits some 600 accounts of government departments and a range of public bodies; and who carries out 'value for money' (VFM) inquiries into the economy, efficiency and effectiveness of public spending. He has a close relationship with the Public Accounts Committee, which considers his reports.

consideration see *report stage*.

Consolidated Fund   the government's account at the Bank of England.

Consolidated Fund Bill   a bill giving legislative authority to the Commons *resolutions* approving the *estimates*.

Consolidated Fund (Appropriation) Bill   the detailed legislative authority for *Supply*. It sets out the *ambit* of each estimate and the amount to be paid ('appropriated') in respect of each, any receipts to be set against expenditure, and the numbers of personnel authorised for the armed services.

consolidation bill   one that seeks to set out the law in a particular subject area in a clearer and more up-to-date form without changing its substance.

constituency   the area of the country 'returning', or being represented by, each MP.

constituency Friday   a non-sitting Friday in a sitting week.

COSAC (known by the French acronym)   the Conference of European Affairs Committees, which every six months brings together representatives of the European Affairs Committees in all the national parliaments of the member states of the EU, and of the Constitutional Affairs Committee of the European Parliament.

Cranborne money   financial assistance to opposition parties in the Lords, named after the then Leader of the House, Viscount Cranborne. The Commons equivalent is *Short money*.

cross-benches   benches in either House facing the Chair rather than on one side or the other of the Chamber. In the Lords, cross-benchers are those peers without party allegiance.

crossing the floor   changing party allegiance (even if the MP's new party in fact sits on the same side of the House).

decision   any decision of the EU Council of Ministers is binding upon those to whom it is addressed.

deferred division   in the Commons, when on certain types of business an attempt is made to force a vote after the *moment of interruption*, that vote is held in one of the division lobbies between 12.30 p.m. and 2.00 p.m. on the next sitting Wednesday.

delegated legislation   sometimes called 'subordinate legislation' or 'secondary legislation' (or 'Statutory Instruments', which most but not all are): legislation made by a minister, or occasionally by a public body, under powers conferred by an Act of Parliament. Different types of delegated legislation are called variously orders, rules, regulations, schemes or codes, depending on what the 'parent Act' calls them.

departmental annual reports   published between March and May each year, these report on a government department's activities, spending and achievements, especially performance against objectives.

departmental expenditure limit (DEL)   total planned expenditure for a government department, but excluding *annually managed expenditure*.

deposit   sum of £500 forfeited if a candidate receives less than 5 percent of the votes cast at a parliamentary election.

de-referral   in the Commons, a motion to take business (typically, debate on a Statutory Instrument or European Union document) on the floor of the House rather than in the committee to which is has been automatically referred.

despatch boxes   boxes at the *Table* of either House, from which *front-benchers* speak.

dilatory motion   a delaying motion, for the adjournment of the debate, committee or House; or to adjourn further consideration of a bill.

directive   European legislation binding on member states in terms of the result to be achieved by a certain date.

dissolution   the ending of a parliament by royal proclamation, followed by a *general election*.

division   a vote 'to divide the House' (or committee) to force a vote. In the Commons the votes are 'Aye' or 'No'; in the Lords 'Content' or 'Not Content'.

draft bill   a bill, not yet formally introduced into either House, that is made available for pre-legislative scrutiny by a select or joint committee.

dummy bill   a sheet of paper, with the *short* and *long titles* and list of supporters, presented at the *Table* by a back-bench MP introducing a *private member's bill*.

early day motion (EDM)   motions set down for 'an early day' and so – apart from *prayers*, which first appear in this form – almost certain not to be debated. EDMs are mainly used to make political points and to test opinion.

elector   someone who has a vote in a parliamentary election.

electoral quota   the total number of electors divided by the number of constituencies.

excess Votes   these seek retrospective authorisation when a government department's spending in a financial year has exceeded what Parliament has authorised, or has been incurred for a purpose that was not authorised.

exempted   in the Commons, business that may be taken after the *moment of interruption*, either because it falls into an exempted category, or because it is covered by an order (at the initiative of the government) that specifically exempts it.

explanatory memorandum   the government's evidence on each EU document, which is subject to the European scrutiny system of each House.

Explanatory Notes   a document accompanying a government bill that sets out the bill's intention and background, explains the clauses in lay person's language and gives an assessment of the bill's effects on public service manpower and costs, and on private sector business.

estimate   a request from the government to the Commons for the resources required for each main area of public expenditure.

estimates days   in the Commons, three days in the course of a session when the *estimates* are approved; select committee reports selected by the Liaison Committee, and linked to particular estimates, provide the subjects for debate on those days.

Father of the House   in the Commons, the MP with the longest continuous service.

first past the post   the voting system in which the candidate with the most votes – a relative majority – wins regardless of how many other candidates there are or how close they come to the winning number of votes.

floor of the House   the Chamber of either House. A matter debated 'on the floor' is discussed in a plenary sitting rather than in a separate committee.

first reading   the formal first stage of a bill's passage through Parliament, taken without debate when the bill is introduced. The bill is then ordered to be printed.

front-bencher   a minister or *shadow minister*.

the gallery   collective term for the journalists primarily concerned with reporting proceedings rather than the interpretation of parliamentary and political events, which is more the province of the *lobby*.

general election   following a dissolution of Parliament, an election for every seat in the new House of Commons.

giving way   allowing another member to intervene briefly in a speech to make a point or to ask a question.

grand committee   in the Lords, for considering the committee stage of bills off the floor of the House. In the Commons, the Scottish, Welsh and Northern Ireland Grand Committees may be used for statements from ministers, oral questions, the consideration of bills and *delegated legislation*, and *adjournment debates*.

green card   available in the Central Lobby of the Palace of Westminster and filled in by a constituent seeking a meeting with his or her MP.

Green Paper   document for consultation on possible policy options.

grouping   the grouping of related *amendments* for debate.

guillotine   in the Commons; also known as an 'allocation of time order': at any stage in the passage of a bill, an order that imposes time limits on the remainder of its progress.

hand-out bill   a bill that the government wishes to see enacted and that is drafted by *parliamentary counsel*, offered to a back-bencher to take forward as a *private member's bill*, usually with the continuing support and briefing of the government department concerned.

Hansard   see *Official Report*.

hemicycle   a semicircular debating chamber, as in the French Assemblée nationale, or the European Parliament.

hereditary peer   a member of the House of Lords by virtue of inheriting a title (usually, a son inheriting from a father, although some hereditary peerages can pass to a daughter). Ninety-two hereditary peers have seats as a result of the House of Lords Act 1999 (which removed the right of other hereditary peers to sit in the Lords).

House of Lords Appointments Commission   a non-statutory commission that makes recommendations to the Queen for non-political peers and vets for propriety all nominations for peerages, including those from the political parties.

hung parliament   after a *general election*, when no one party has a majority in the House of Commons.

hybrid bill   a bill that combines the characteristics of a public bill (changing the general law) and a private bill (making provision with local or personal effect).

incidental expenses provision   an MP's allowance principally to cover the costs of constituency offices.

introduction   the formal start of a bill's passage through Parliament. The bill is formally given a first reading at the same time and ordered to be printed. Also used of the formal introduction of a new MP or peer.

joint committee   a *select committee* with a membership drawn from both Houses.

Journal   the legal record of the proceedings of both Houses (of decisions and events rather than words spoken).

LCCA   Lords consideration of *Commons amendments*.

Leader of the House   in the Commons, a cabinet minister dealing with House affairs and the organisation of business, who also chairs the Modernisation Committee. The Leader of the Lords has a similar role but plays an additional part in guiding the course of business during a sitting, and she exercises some of the functions of the Speaker of the Commons: for example, determining whether a *private notice question* is of sufficient urgency.

life peer   a member of the House of Lords for life, having been appointed under the Appellate Jurisdiction Act 1876 (law lords) or the Life Peerages Act 1958 (other peers).

lobby   (1) a room, as in division lobbies, the Central Lobby, Members' Lobby or Peers' Lobby; (2) to come to Westminster to put a case, either to an individual MP or as part of a demonstration ('mass lobbies'); (3) the group of parliamentary journalists with special access to the Palace of Westminster, reporting parliamentary and political news and opinion.

lobby terms   information given to journalists on the basis that it may be disclosed but not attributed.

locus standi   the position of someone directly affected by the provisions of a *private bill*, who therefore has the right to petition against it.

long title   the passage at the start of a bill that begins 'a Bill to . . .' and then lists its purposes. The content of the bill must be covered by the long title.

Lord Chancellor   presiding officer of the House of Lords, head of the judiciary, Secretary of State for Constitutional Affairs and a member of the Cabinet. In June 2003, the government announced its intention to separate the presiding, judicial and ministerial roles.

Lords amendment   amendment made by the Lords to a bill passed by the Commons.

LP   the Cabinet Committee on the Legislative Programme, chaired by the *Leader of the House of Commons*. Other members include the *Leader of the Lords* and the Chief Whips in both Houses.

Mace   a silver gilt ornamental mace symbolises the authority of each House. It is carried in procession before a sitting and remains on the *Table* (in the Commons, under the *Table* when the House is in *Committee of the whole House*) while the House is sitting.

main estimates   the principal request from the government to the Commons for the resources required to run the state in the following financial year. There is one for each government department (and for other bodies such as the Office of the Rail Regulator and the NHS Pension Scheme). Usually published in late March or early April.

main Question   if an *amendment* to a *motion* has been moved, the original motion is known as the main Question.

manifesto   statement of policies and intentions on which a political party fights a *general election*.

measure   legislation of the Church of England, agreed by the General Synod, then considered by the Ecclesiastical Committee (a statutory committee consisting of members of both Houses) and then presented to both Houses for approval.

Members Estimate   in the Commons, pays for members' pay and allowances.

message   formal communication between one House and the other.

minister of state   the second rank of ministers (below secretaries of state).

Ministry of Defence Votes A   published in February, these seek the annual authorisation by the Commons of the maximum numbers of personnel in the armed services.

the Minute   daily working papers of the House of Lords.

moment of interruption   the time at which the main business of the Commons day normally ends (10.00 p.m. on Mondays, 7.00 p.m. on Tuesdays and Thursdays, 6.00 p.m. on Thursdays and 2.30 p.m. on Fridays).

money bill   a bill whose only purpose is to authorise expenditure or taxation.

money resolution   a motion (when approved, a resolution) to authorise government expenditure in relation to a bill.

motion   a proposal 'moved' by a member. When approved, it becomes a *resolution* or an *order*.

named-day questions   in the Commons, written questions for answer on a stated day, with a minimum notice period of three sitting days (but including non-sitting Fridays). An individual MP may ask no more than five such questions per day.

naming (of an MP)   a power used by the Chair in the Commons, usually for more serious offences, usually including disregard for the authority of the Chair. Following naming, a motion to suspend the MP concerned (to bar him or her from the precincts and stop payment of salary for a stated period) is moved by the senior minister present and invariably agreed to.

negative instrument   a piece of *delegated legislation* that under the parent Act may be made and come into effect unless one or other House decides otherwise ('the negative procedure').

1922 Committee (sometimes called 'the 22')   body consisting of all Conservative MPs but especially important as a reflection of back-bench opinion.

National Audit Office   see *Comptroller and Auditor-General*.

new clause   a substantial *amendment* to a bill, usually introducing a separate subject or issue rather than seeking to amend the provisions already in the bill (but in order to be in order a new clause must be within the *scope* of the bill).

nod   to secure agreement to something 'on the nod' is without debate or a vote.

official Opposition   the largest opposition party, sometimes known as 'Her Majesty's Opposition'.

Official Report   the verbatim report of debates in both Houses, Westminster Hall, standing committees and grand committees. Also contains written answers to questions. Known as *Hansard*.

Ombudsman   see *Parliamentary Commissioner for Administration*.

opposition days   in the Commons, twenty days in the course of a session on which the subject of the main debate is chosen by the opposition parties.

order   a decision of either House or of a committee on a matter within the power of the body making the order for example, 'That a select committee be appointed to . . .'. See also *resolution*.

Order in Council   a type of *delegated legislation*, made in the name of the sovereign rather than that of a minister.

orders of reference   *orders* made by either House when setting up a select committee. They set out the committee's task and define its powers.

ordinary written questions   in the Commons, written questions that are put down for answer two sitting days after they are received and that by convention the government answers within a week.

Outlawries Bill   an antique bill 'for the more effectual preventing of clandestine outlawries' given a formal first reading in the Commons as a symbol of their right to deal with their own business before proceeding to debate the *Queen's Speech* after the *State Opening of Parliament*. The Lords equivalent is the Select Vestries Bill.

pairing   an arrangement between two MPs on opposite sides of the House not to vote in a particular division, so that their absences cancel each other out.

a parliament   the main division of parliamentary time: the period between one *general election* and the next.

parliamentary agent   a specialist lawyer who represents the *promoter* of a private bill.

Parliamentary Commissioner for Administration (Ombudsman)   an independent officer, reporting to Parliament, who investigates maladministration by government departments and other public bodies which has caused injustice that has not been put right. She also holds the posts of Health Service Commissioner for England and for Wales (in the latter role she reports to the National Assembly for Wales). She has a close relationship with the Public Administration Select Committee in the Commons, which considers her reports.

Parliamentary Commissioner for Standards   an independent officer of the Commons who maintains the Register of Members' Interests and other registers of interests; advises MPs and the Committee on Standards and Privileges on interests and standards issues; monitors the operation of the Code of Conduct; and investigates complaints about MPs' conduct.

parliamentary counsel   a small group of government lawyers who are expert in legislative drafting and who draft all government bills, including '*hand-out*' bills. *Delegated legislation* is usually drafted not by parliamentary counsel but by the lawyers in the government department concerned.

parliamentary private secretary (PPS)   an unpaid MP aide to a secretary of state or a minister of state.

parliamentary secretary or parliamentary under-secretary of state   the third rank of ministers, below *secretaries of state* and *ministers of state*.

Patronage Secretary   formal title for the government Chief Whip in the Commons.

payroll vote   government ministers and *parliamentary private secretaries* – the most reliable supporters of the government in any votes.

Permanent Secretary (in some departments, more formally 'Permanent Under-Secretary of State')   the senior civil servant in a government department. Usually also the *accounting officer*.

personal statement   a statement (in the Commons, made by permission of the Speaker), usually of apology, or explaining the reasons for a ministerial resignation.

petition   either a *public petition* or, in the case of a *private bill*, a case made against it by someone who would be directly affected by its provisions.

ping pong   the to and fro of bills and amendments between the two Houses towards the end of a session.

point of order   an appeal to the Chair for guidance or a ruling on a matter of order or procedure, but also a means (through 'bogus points of order') of furthering political argument.

polling day   the day on which votes are cast in a *general election* or *by-election*.

PLP   Parliamentary Labour Party, consisting of all Labour MPs and peers. Especially important as a reflection of back-bench opinion.

PMQs   Prime Minister's Questions (in the Commons, for half an hour every sitting Wednesday).

PPC   prospective parliamentary candidate: someone selected by a party organisation to contest the next election.

PPR   a *select committee's* power to send for 'persons, papers and records'.

PPS   see *parliamentary private secretary*.

prayer   a motion seeking the *annulment* of a *Statutory Instrument*.

praying time   the period (usually of forty days, excluding time when both Houses are adjourned for more than four days) during which a motion for the *annulment* of a *Statutory Instrument* must be taken.

pre-legislative scrutiny   see *draft bill*.

prerogative   sometimes 'the Royal Prerogative': power of ministers to act in the Queen's name without the approval of Parliament.

presentation bill   a bill presented at the *Table*, notice having been given on the Order Paper.

previous Question   an old-fashioned *dilatory motion* in the form 'That the Question be not now put'. If it is agreed to, the House moves to the next business; if it is not agreed to, then the matter which was interrupted must be decided immediately, as with a *closure*.

primary legislation   Acts of Parliament.

Prince of Wales's Consent   signification by the Prince of Wales that Parliament may proceed to consider legislation that would affect his interests.

private bill   a bill – a draft Act – that, if passed, will have only local or personal, rather than general, effect.

private business   proceedings on *private bills* and related matters. In the Commons, taken immediately after prayers (the religious prayers at the start of the sitting); if opposed, time for debate is found by the *Chairman of Ways and Means*.

private member's bill   a public bill introduced by a 'private member' (not a minister). Not to be confused with *a private bill*. In the Lords, 'private peer's bill'.

private notice question   in the Lords, a question of urgent importance asked orally of the government. In the Commons, the term has been replaced by *urgent question*.

privilege   parliamentary privilege (a better name would be 'public interest immunity') gives the two Houses, their committees and members, the protection from outside interference or legal action necessary to perform their roles. The two main elements are freedom of speech and the right of both Houses to regulate their own affairs. Also (as 'financial privilege') used to describe the pre-eminence of the Commons in financial matters.

privilege amendment   a polite fiction to preserve the pre-eminence of the Commons in financial matters; a subsection in a bill starting in the Lords that involves an increase in expenditure or taxation says 'Nothing in this Act shall impose any charge on the people or on public funds'. The subsection is removed when the bill is in committee in the Commons.

Privy Counsellor   a member of the Privy Council, consisting of senior politicians past and present, senior judges, some Commonwealth statesmen and certain others of distinction. Members of the Privy Council are styled 'right honourable'.

proclamation   a royal proclamation by the sovereign dissolves Parliament and sets a day for the new parliament to meet after the ensuing *general election*.

programming   in the Commons, the imposition of a timetable on the passage of a bill immediately after *second reading*. Originally designed to provide an allocation of time more in proportion to the importance or contentiousness of various parts of a bill – a compromise between informal agreement and a *guillotine* – but now the source of profound disagreement between government and opposition.

programming committee   in the Commons, when a programme order applies to proceedings in *Committee of the whole House*, *report stage* or *third reading*, the committee (chaired by the *Chairman of Ways and Means* and consisting of up to eight other MPs) that proposes how the available time should be allocated. A *programming sub-committee* (chaired by the chairman of the *standing committee*, with seven members of the committee) does the same for proceedings in a standing committee.

promoter   the body or individual outside Parliament sponsoring a *private bill*.

proposing the Question   when the Chair states the proposition on which the House or committee must decide.

prorogation   the formal end of a parliamentary *session*, which brings to an end almost all parliamentary business.

public bill   a bill – a draft Act – that, if passed, will have general effect in some or all of the constituent parts of the UK.

public business   generally, proceedings on the main business of the day (in the Commons following Question Time and statements).

public petition   an application by one or more people outside Parliament to one House or the other (usually the Commons) for some particular action or relief.

qualified majority voting (QMV)   a weighted system of voting in the EU Council of Ministers in which larger countries have more votes.

Queen's Consent   signification by the sovereign that Parliament may proceed to consider legislation that would affect her interests.

Queen's Speech   sometimes called 'the Gracious Speech'; written by the government and delivered by the Queen at the State Opening of Parliament, it recalls the events of the previous year (such as state visits) and outlines the government's plans for the new session, especially its legislative programme.

Question   (as well as the conventional meaning) a matter for decision.

Question rota   in the Commons, the order in which ministers answer oral questions.

quorum   the number of members required to be present to transact business. In the Lords the quorum is three; but on a division on a bill or on *delegated legislation* at least thirty peers must vote to constitute a quorum.

In the Commons there is no quorum except on a division, when at least forty MPs must be present (thirty-five voting, the four tellers and the occupant of the Chair). The quorum of a *standing committee* is one-third of the membership, counting the chairman (but the chairman does not count towards whether a quorum is present); in *select committees* it is three or a quarter of the membership, counting the chairman (who also counts towards the quorum). Fractions are rounded up. In *Westminster Hall* the quorum is three.

reasoned amendment   one tabled for the *second* or *third reading* of a bill that sets out why the bill should not proceed (or proceed in its current form).

reasons   given by one House to the other for rejecting *amendments* to a bill.

recall   the return of Parliament during a recess. In the Commons, it is authorised by the *Speaker* on the request of the government. In the Lords, the power is exercised by the *Lord Chancellor*.

recess   a longer time of adjournment than over a weekend, usually at Christmas, for a week in February, at Easter, the late spring bank holiday, and from late July to early October (interrupted by the two-week September sitting). Strictly speaking, the word applies to the period of *prorogation* but is rarely used in this sense.

regulation   (1) in the UK, a type of *delegated legislation*. (2) In European legislation, regulations have the force of law throughout the EU without member states having to take any action.

regulatory reform order   an order under the Regulatory Reform Act 2001 made by a minister to lift burdens on anyone carrying on any activity. An order may be made only after public consultation on a proposal, which is then scrutinised by committees of both

Houses. The committees also scrutinise the draft order that is brought forward as a result. A regulatory reform order is an unusual type of *delegated legislation* in that it may amend *primary legislation*.

remedial order   an order made by a minister that amends *primary legislation* when that has been found incompatible with the Human Rights Act 1998. Draft remedial orders are scrutinised by the Joint Committee on Human Rights and are then approved by both Houses. Urgent procedure orders may be made without advance scrutiny but must be confirmed by the approval of both Houses within 120 days.

repeal   to make the whole or part of an Act of Parliament have no further effect.

report stage   consideration of a bill in the form in which it left committee, and an opportunity for any member to propose amendments, not just those who were on the committee.

reserved matter   one not devolved to Scotland, Wales or Northern Ireland.

resolution   a decision of either House, or of a committee, that expresses an opinion (for example, 'That this House has no confidence in Her Majesty's Government'). See also *order*.

resource accounting   records the economic cost of the provision of services and the consumption of assets (including depreciation, the cost of using capital assets, and future liabilities such as those for compensation for early retirement). *Resource accounts* must be laid before Parliament by 31 January following the financial year to which they relate.

revised estimates   change the *ambit* of an *estimate* if it appears that funds already authorised may have to be spent on something outside the present ambit.

Royal Assent   the sovereign's agreement to a bill passed by both Houses.

ruling   a decision by the *Speaker* of the Commons or any other occupant of the Chair (or chairman of a *standing committee*) on a matter of order or procedure.

Salisbury convention   (dating from 1945 and named after the fifth Marquess of Salisbury) that the Lords should not reject at second reading any government legislation that has been passed by the Commons and that carries out a *manifesto* commitment.

schedule   schedules appear after the *clauses* of a bill and fill in detail.

scope   the ambit of a bill; to be in order, *amendments* must not go beyond the purposes of the bill as summarised in the *long title*.

scrutiny reserve resolutions   constrain ministers from giving agreement in the EU Council of Ministers to a proposal that has not cleared the European scrutiny systems in both Houses.

second reading   approval in principle of a bill. A second reading debate is a discussion of the principle rather than the details of individual *clauses*.

second reading committee   in the Commons, a (temporary) committee to which an uncontroversial bill may be referred for a *second reading* debate. There is then no debate when the bill is reported to the House for its second reading.

secretary of state   one of the top rank of ministers; senior minister in a government department; always a member of the Cabinet.

section   the basic unit within an Act of Parliament, divided into subsections, then paragraphs, then sub-paragraphs.

select committee   a committee of members of either House charged with investigating a matter and reporting (*ad hoc* select committees), or of monitoring a government department (Commons departmental select committees) or a subject area, or a category of legislative or other proposals) and reporting from time to time. Select committees also advise on the administration of both Houses. Select committees that are not *ad hoc* are normally permanent institutions, with their members nominated for the length of a Parliament.

selection   the decision by the *Speaker*, the *Chairman of Ways and Means* or the chairman of a *standing committee* as to which *amendments* (or, in some cases, *motions*) shall be debated or voted upon.

Senior Salaries Review Body   an independent body that, among other things, makes recommendations on parliamentary pay and allowances.

Serjeant at Arms   the officer of the Commons responsible for works, housekeeping, ICT, ceremonial and security.

session   the main subdivision of time during a parliament: the period from the *State Opening* to *prorogation* (usually from early November to late October in the following year).

sessional orders   any order of either House that has effect only for the rest of that session of Parliament; but particularly used of the traditional orders passed by the Commons on the day of the *State Opening* at the start of a *session*, providing for good order and access to the House, the protection of witnesses, and the now unknown circumstance of an MP elected for two seats deciding which one to represent.

Sewel motion   a means whereby the Scottish Parliament demonstrates its agreement to Westminster legislating on a devolved matter.

shadow minister   an MP who is the spokesperson of an opposition party on a particular subject, mirroring the responsibilities of the 'real' minister in the government.

shadow Cabinet   those opposition front-benchers who 'shadow' members of the Cabinet, presided over by the Leader of the Opposition.

Short money   financial support for opposition parties in the Commons, named after Edward Short, the Leader of the House when it was introduced. The Lords equivalent is *Cranborne money*.

short title   the title by which a bill is known during its passage through Parliament; for example, 'Criminal Justice Bill'. See also *long title*.

sitting   a meeting of either House, usually in a single day, at the end of which the House adjourns. Also a meeting of a committee.

special public bill committee   in the Lords, a committee that may take written and oral evidence on a bill within twenty-eight days of the committee's appointment, thereafter proceeding as a public bill committee.

special report   a report from a *select committee* that is not a substantive report on an inquiry but is used as a vehicle for publishing government replies or informing the House of some difficulty the committee has encountered.

special standing committee   in the Commons, a hybrid of the deliberating/evidence-taking method of a *select committee* and the debating method of a *standing committee*, to which bills may be sent for their committee stage.

Speaker   the presiding officer of the Commons and chairman of the House of Commons Commission, which oversees House administration.

spillover   the period (usually in October) preceding prorogation.

staffing allowance   an allowance for each MP to meet the cost of up to three staff.

standing committee   in the Commons, a committee to which most bills are referred for their committee stage. Standing committees are laid out like the Chamber of the House, are chaired by an impartial chairman and cease to exist when they have finished considering a bill. A number of standing committees may be in existence at the same time.

standing orders   the rules made by both Houses for the regulation of their proceedings. Standing orders remain in force until they are amended or repealed. 'Temporary standing orders' are typically made for the length of a *session* or *parliament*.

starred questions   in the Lords, four oral questions on Mondays and Thursdays (five on Tuesdays and Wednesdays) taken at the start of business. In the Commons, the term is not used, but a star on the Order Paper against a question indicates that it is for oral answer.

State Opening   the ceremonial start to a session of Parliament. The main event is the *Queen's Speech*.

statute   an Act of Parliament. 'Statute law' and 'the statute book' are collective terms for all Acts in force.

statute law repeal bill   a bill that removes parts of the law that have become redundant.

Statutory Instrument   see *delegated legislation*.

strangers   the old-fashioned and rather unfriendly description of visitors to Parliament. Now being superseded by 'visitors'.

sub judice rule   the rule against referring to a current or impending court case (more precisely, when someone has been charged in a criminal case, or, in a civil action, when a case has been set down for trial), to avoid influencing the outcome. The rule may be relaxed at the Speaker's discretion, and it need not prevent the consideration of legislation.

subordinate legislation   see *delegated legislation*.

subsidiarity   in the European context, the principle that a decision should be taken at national level unless the aim could be achieved only by action at EU level.

substantive motion   a motion expressing an opinion or taking a decision; not an *adjournment motion* (even though that involves the narrow decision of whether the House or a committee shall adjourn).

supplementary estimates   seek additional resources.

supplementary question   a follow-up oral question.

Supply   the granting of money to the Crown for the running of the country.

surgery   the time when an MP makes himself or herself available in the constituency for meetings with constituents, usually to discuss their problems.

suspend   informally interrupt the sitting of a House or committee. For suspension of an MP, see *naming*.

table   to deposit formally before the House or committee as 'to table an *amendment*' (or *motion*, question or paper). 'The Table' in both Houses is the table between the front benches, and also a collective term for the Clerks at the Table.

talking out   in the Commons, debating a *motion* or a proceedings on a bill up to the *moment of interruption*, when the business is lost or postponed.

tax law re-write bills   bills that tidy and clarify existing tax law. Similar to *consolidation bills* but with greater latitude as to the scope of amendment.

tellers   two members from each side who count the votes at a *division*.

ten-minute rule bill   in the Commons (on Tuesdays and Wednesdays), a bill introduced by leave of the House (with a vote if one is forced) following a speech of not more than ten minutes from the sponsor of the proposal. An opponent may speak for not more than ten minutes in opposition.

test roll   a bound parchment book signed by MPs when they take the oath or make *affirmation* after an election (also in the Lords).

third reading   the final stage of the passage of a bill through one House of Parliament; a final review of the contents of the bill, with debate limited to what is actually in the bill rather than, as at *second reading*, what might be included. Substantive *amendments* are allowed at this stage in the Lords but not in the Commons.

unopposed return   a motion for an unopposed return seeks the laying of a report or other paper before Parliament, thus giving it the protection of parliamentary *privilege*.

unstarred questions   in the Lords, questions that give rise to short debates of an hour and a half at the end of the day's business. In the Commons, a question that has been unstarred has been converted from one for oral answer to one for written answer.

urgent debate   in the Commons, an application is made to the Speaker under S.O. No. 24 to debate 'a specific and important matter that should have urgent consideration'. Such debates are rare.

urgent question (formerly known as a private notice question (PNQ))   in the Commons, an oral question to a minister on an urgent matter of public importance, granted by the Speaker.

urgent procedure order   see *remedial order*.

usual channels   the informal and private contacts between the *whips* and business managers on the two sides of each House.

virement   moving funds between the subheads of an *estimate* with Treasury approval but without further parliamentary authority.

the Vote bundle   the daily working papers of the Commons.

Votes and Proceedings   the legal record of the proceedings of the Commons: decisions taken, papers laid and so on. Later becomes the *Journal*.

Votes on Account   come before the Commons each November and cover some 45 percent of the estimated expenditure of each government department over the coming year; they are to tide the government over until the *main estimates* are approved in July. They must be agreed by the House by 6 February.

Ways and Means resolution   a *motion* (when approved, a *resolution*) to authorise the raising of a tax or imposition of a charge in relation to a bill. 'Ways and Means' is an old name for taxation.

West Lothian question   named after Tam Dalyell MP, then member for that constituency: why should Scottish MPs at Westminster be able to speak, question and vote on matters affecting the rest of the UK when in Scotland those matters are devolved to the Scottish Parliament and the Scottish Executive?

Westminster Hall   as well as the Great Hall on the west side of the Palace, the parallel debating chamber 'the House sitting in Westminster Hall', which takes place in the Grand Committee Room off the northern end of Westminster Hall. Used mainly for non-controversial debates on subjects put forward by back-benchers as well as by the government; for debates on select committee reports; and 'cross-cutting' oral question times (on subjects that span the responsibilities of several departments).

whips   members responsible for parliamentary party organisation and discipline. 'The Whip' is circulated weekly by the whips of each party to their own members; it lists the business for the following week, together with the party's expectations as to when its MPs will vote.

White Paper   a published statement of government policy (see also *Green Paper*).

wrecking amendment one designed to frustrate the purpose of a bill already approved at *second reading*, or of a *clause* already approved in committee.

written ministerial statements in the Commons, statements by ministers that appear in the next day's *Official Report*, before answers to oral questions. A minister's intention to make a written statement is signalled in the Order Paper at the end of the day's business.

Yeoman Usher Black Rod's deputy.

Sources of information about Parliament

Books

This is not a bibliography but a highly selective list of publications that may be of further help to readers of this book.

Companion to the Standing Orders and Guide to the Proceedings of the House of Lords, The Stationery Office, 2003.
The chief work of reference on House of Lords practice and procedure. The *Companion* describes every aspect of the House's practice and procedure as established by the standing orders, ancient practice, and decisions of the Procedure Committee and the House itself. It complements *Erskine May* (see below), which for some areas provides more detail and gives precedents.

Dod's Parliamentary Companion, Vacher Dod Publishing, 2003.
The annually published reference work with biographies of MPs and peers, detailed results of the last general election, and a great deal of contact and other information on political parties, government departments, public bodies, the devolved institutions and the European Parliament. It also has a useful website directory.

Erskine May's Treatise on the Law, Privileges, Proceedings and Usage of Parliament, twenty-second edition, edited by Sir Donald Limon and W.R. McKay, Butterworth, 1997.
Usually known simply as 'Erskine May', it is technical and comprehensive rather than highly readable, but it is the pre-eminently authoritative textbook on Parliament and the one most used by practitioners. The present edition has been overtaken by a number of changes in both Houses in the last five years, and a new edition, edited by Professor Sir William McKay, is to be published in 2004.

Griffith and Ryle on Parliament: Functions, Practice and Procedures, second edition, by Robert Blackburn and Andrew Kennon with Sir Michael Wheeler-Booth, Sweet & Maxwell, 2003.
A detailed survey of the workings of both Houses, with a huge amount of statistical information and examples of every type of event. As well as providing shrewd analysis, it also usefully sets the present operation of Parliament in the context of the institution's development over the last half-century.

Handbook of House of Commons Procedure, third edition, by Paul Evans, Vacher Dod Publishing, 2002.
An excellent practical guide to procedure, logically laid out and well cross-referenced. It is written in straightforward language and will be especially useful for those involved at first hand with proceedings in the Commons.

House of Commons Weekly Information Bulletin, The Stationery Office.
Published when the House is sitting, it provides a digest of current and forthcoming business, state of play on bills and some types of delegated legislation, forthcoming public meeting of select committees in both Houses, and forthcoming inquiries. It also lists recently published select committee and National Audit Office reports, and the titles of recently tabled early day motions. It has a useful summary of the current state of the parties in the Commons, together with a record of all by-elections in the current parliament. It is also available on-line from 4.00 p.m. each Friday at www.parliament.uk

The British Constitution in the Twentieth Century, edited by Vernon Bogdanor, 2003.
A definitive account of the development of all major British constitutional institutions in the twentieth century, with separate chapters on the House of Commons and the House of Lords. A valuable work of reference for those interested in the recent historical development of Parliament.

The Standing Orders of the House of Commons: Public Business, The Stationery Office, 2003.

The Standing Orders of the House of Lords relating to Public Business, The Stationery Office, 2002.

Parliamentary websites

The principal site is www.parliament.uk. This is a recently redesigned site providing a staggering amount of parliamentary information and text. Main features include:

▲ what's on: current and future business in both Houses and forthcoming meetings of committees;
▲ the text of Commons *Hansard* from session 1988–89 and Lords *Hansard* from session 1994–95; the *Hansard* of all standing committee debates of bills and other matters from session 1997–98. The *Hansard* for the previous day in the two Chambers is put up on the website at 8.00 the following day;
▲ the text of all bills, both public and private, that are before Parliament, and their current status;
▲ standing orders of both Houses, for both public and private business;
▲ via the Stationery Office site, the text of Acts of Parliament (public Acts from 1988 and private Acts from 1991);
▲ for the House of Lords in its judicial role, practice notes, Appellate Committee reports, judgements and cases to be heard;
▲ lists of: MPs by constituency, county, gender and party; peers; ministers and PPSs; opposition spokespeople; all-party groups and country groups; together with the state of the parties and by-election results;
▲ the Locata system, which will tell you who your MP is from your postcode (www.locata.co.uk/commons/);
▲ registers of interests;
▲ for select committees in both Houses, and joint committees: committee home pages with membership, terms of reference and contact details; press notices; text of reports, all oral and much written evidence (from session 1997–98); a guide for witnesses;
▲ explanatory notes and factsheets on many aspects of the work of Parliament;

▲ Commons library research papers on matters of current interest, together with research notes and longer papers produced by the Parliamentary Office of Science and Technology;
▲ useful links;
▲ current job opportunities in Parliament.

www.parliamentlive.tv gives access to webcast proceedings of both Houses, Westminster Hall, and select committees taking evidence in public.

www.explore.parliament.uk is the website of the Parliamentary Education Unit, which provides an education service on behalf of both Houses; provides resources and support for students and teachers; works closely with bodies such as the Hansard Society for Parliamentary Government and the Citizenship Foundation; and advises and supports MPs and peers in their work with young people. The unit produces 'Parliament explained' booklets, available on the website. The website gives details of other material, including wallcharts and videos.

www.lordswhips.org.uk (the website of the Lords Government Whips Office) gives details of forthcoming business in the Lords, speakers' lists, groupings of amendments, ministerial responsibilities, etc.

Television

BBC Parliament provides a dedicated channel, with real-time coverage of the Commons and 'time-shifted' coverage of the Lords and select committees.

Visiting Parliament

Seats in the public galleries of both Houses (unless by ticket from an MP or a peer) are free on a first-come, first-served basis. Visitors should come to St Stephen's Entrance (see plan on page 5). Visitors may also attend standing committees and any select committee that is sitting in public. Sitting dates of the Houses, and committee sittings, are published on the parliamentary website.

Tours of the visitor route during parliamentary term-time must be sponsored by an MP or peer. Further advice is available from the Central Tours Office (020 7219 3003; e-mail CTO@parliament.uk.Tours are free, and a guide is provided. During the summer recess (late July to early September) and the conference recess (mid-September to early/mid-October) free tours take place only on certain mornings, but at other times the palace is open for guided tours for paying visitors. Information on prices and dates is available, and tickets may be ordered, through www.firstcalltickets.com or by telephone on 0870 906 3773.

Other useful contact details

Palace of Westminster switchboard: 020 7219 3000.
House of Commons Information Office: House of Commons, London SW1A 2TT, telephone 020 7219 4272, fax 020 7219 5839, hcinfo@parliament.uk
House of Lords Information Office: House of Lords, London SW1A 0PW telephone 020 7219 3107, fax 020 7219 0620, hlinfo@parliament.uk

Parliamentary Education Unit: House of Commons, London SW1A 2TT, telephone 020 7219 2105, fax 020 7219 0818, edunit@parliament.uk

House of Lords Record Office: London SW1A 0PW, telephone 020 7219 3074, fax 020 7219 2570, hlro@parliament.uk

House of Commons Committee Office: general enquiry lines: 020 7219 3267/4300; recorded message service about forthcoming meetings: 020 7219 2033

Parliamentary Bookshop: 12 Bridge Street, Parliament Square, London SW1A 2JX; enquiries and telephone orders 020 7219 3890; fax orders 020 7219 3866

The Hansard Society for Parliamentary Government: St Philips Building North, LSE, Sheffield Street, London WC2A 2EX, telephone 020 7395 4000; website: www.hansardsociety.org.uk. See also www.headsup.org.uk

The Stationery Office: (mail, telephone and fax orders) PO Box 29, Norwich NR3 1GN; general enquiries 0870 600 5522; orders through the parliamentary hotline *Lo-call* 0845 7 023474; fax orders 0870 600 5533, bookorders@tso.co.uk

Devolved parliament and assemblies

Northern Ireland Assembly: Parliament Buildings, Stormont, Belfast BT4 3XX, telephone 028 90 521137, fax 028 90 521961; website www.niassembly.gov.uk

Scottish Parliament: Edinburgh EH99 1SP, telephone 0131 348 5000; website www.scottish.parliament.uk

National Assembly for Wales: Cardiff Bay, Cardiff CF99 1NA, telephone 029 20 898 200; website www.wales.gov.uk

Political parties

Conservative Party: 32 Smith Square, London SW1P 3HH, telephone 020 7222 9000; website www.conservative-party.org.uk or www.conservatives.com

Democratic Unionist Party: 91 Dundela Avenue, Belfast BT4 3BU, telephone 028 90 471155; website www.dup.org.uk

Labour Party: 16 Old Queen Street, London SW1H 9HP, telephone 08705 900200; website: www.labour.org.uk

Liberal Democrats: 4 Cowley Street, London SW1P 3NB, telephone 020 7222 7999; website www.libdems.org.uk

Plaid Cymru: 18 Park Grove, Cardiff CF1 3BN, telephone 029 20 646000; website www.plaidcymru.org.uk

Scottish National Party: 107, McDonald Road, Edinburgh EH7 4NW, telephone 0131 525 8900; website www.snp.org.uk

Sinn Fein: 147 Andersonstown Road, Belfast BT11 9BW, telephone 028 90 301719; website www.sinnfein.ie

Social Democratic and Labour Party: Cranmore House, 121 Ormeau Road, Belfast BT7 1SH, telephone 028 90 247700; website www.indigo.ie/sdlp

Ulster Unionist Party: Cunningham House, 429 Holywood Road, Belfast BT4 2LN, telephone 028 90 765500; website www.uup.org.uk

The Code of Conduct for Members of Parliament

Prepared pursuant to the Resolution of the House of 19th July 1995

I. Purpose of the Code

The purpose of the Code of Conduct is to assist Members in the discharge of their
obligations to the House, their constituents and the public at large.

*

The Code applies to Members in all aspects of their public life. It does not seek to
regulate what Members do in their purely private and personal lives.

II. Public duty

By virtue of the oath, or affirmation, of allegiance taken by all Members when
they are elected to the House, Members have a duty to be faithful and
bear true allegiance to Her Majesty the Queen, her heirs and successors,
according to law.

*

Members have a duty to uphold the law and to act on all occasions in accordance
with the public trust placed in them.

*

Members have a general duty to act in the interests of the nation as a whole; and a
special duty to their constituents.

III. Personal conduct

Members shall observe the general principles of conduct identified by the Committee on
Standards in Public Life[1] as applying to holders of public office:—

'Selflessness
*Holders of public office should take decisions solely in terms of the public interest.
They should not do so in order to gain financial or other material benefits for
themselves, their family, or their friends*

---

[1] Cm 2850, p. 14.

Integrity
Holders of public office should not place themselves under any financial or other obligation to outside individuals or organisations that might influence them in the performance of their official duties.

Objectivity
In carrying out public business, including make public appointments, awarding contracts, or recommending individuals for rewards and benefits, holders of public office should make choices on merit.

Accountability
Holders of public office are accountable for their decisions and actions to the public and must submit themselves to whatever scrutiny is appropriate to their office.

Openness
Holders of public office should be as open as possible about all the decisions and actions that they take. They should give reasons for their decisions and restrict information only when the wider public interest clearly demands.

Honesty
Holders of public office have a duty to declare any private interests relating to their public duties and to take steps to resolve any conflicts arising in a way that protects the public interest.

Leadership
Holders of public office should promote and support these principles by leadership and example.'

*

Members shall base their conduct on a consideration of the public interest, avoid conflict between personal interest and the public interest and resolve any conflict between the two, at once, and in favour of the public interest.

*

Members shall at all times conduct themselves in a manner which will tend to maintain and strengthen the public's trust and confidence in the integrity of Parliament and never undertake any action which would bring the House of Commons, or its Members generally, into disrepute.

*

The acceptance by a Member of a bribe to influence his or her conduct as a Member, including any fee, compensation or reward in connection with the promotion of, or opposition to, any Bill, Motion, or other matter submitted, or intended to be submitted to the House, or to any Committee of the House, is contrary to the law of Parliament.

*

Members shall fulfil conscientiously the requirements of the House in respect of the registration of interests in the Register of Members' Interests and shall always draw attention to any relevant interest in any proceeding of the House or

its Committees, or in any communications with Ministers,
Government Departments or Executive Agencies.

*

In any activities with, or on behalf of, an organisation with which a Member has a
financial relationship, including activities which may not be a matter of public record
such as informal meetings and functions, he or she must always bear in mind the need
to be open and frank with Ministers, Members and officials.

*

No Member shall act as a paid advocate in any proceeding of the House.

*

No improper use shall be made of any payment or allowance made to Members
for public purposes and the administrative rules which apply to such payments
and allowances must be strictly observed.

*

Members must bear in mind that information which they receive in confidence in the
course of their parliamentary duties should be used only in connection with those duties,
and that such information must never be used for the purpose of financial gain.

Index